THE
YIDDISH THEATRE
AND
JACOB P. ADLER

Jacob P. Adler as Shylock.

THE YIDDISH THEATRE AND JACOB P. ADLER

Lulla Adler Rosenfeld

Introduction by Harold Clurman

Shapolsky Publishers, Inc.
New York, NY

A Shapolsky Book
Published by Shapolsky Publishers

Copyright © 1977, 1978, 1988 by Lulla Adler Rosenfeld

First edition 1977 by Thomas Y. Crowell Company, NY under the title *Bright Star of Exile: Jacob Adler and the Yiddish Theatre*. Published simultaneously in Canada by Fitzhenry & Whiteside Limited, Toronto.

Second printing 1978 by Barrie and Jenkins Ltd., London.

Second revised edition 1988 by Shapolsky Publishers, Inc., New York.

All rights reserved under International and Pan American Copyright Conventions. Published and printed in the U.S.A. by Shapolsky Publishers, Inc. No parts of this book may be used or reproduced in any manner whatsoever without written permission of Shapolsky Publishers, Inc., except in the case of brief quotations embodied in critical articles or reviews.

For any additional information, contact:
Shapolsky Publishers, Inc., 56 East 11th Street, New York, NY 10003

10 9 8 7 6 5 4 3 2 1

Library of Congress Cataloging in Publication Data:
Rosenfeld, Lulla Adler
The Yiddish Theatre and Jacob P. Adler

Rev. ed. of: Bright Star Of Exile.
Bibliography: p.
Includes index.

1. Adler, Jacob P., 1855-1926
2. Theatre, Yiddish — History.
3. Actors, Jewish — Biography.
I. Adler, Jacob P., 1855-1926.
II. Adler Rosenfeld, Lulla. Bright Star of Exile.
III. Title.
PN3035.R6   1988   792'.028'0924 [B]   86-29677

ISBN 0-933503-26-1

To Josie and Elizabeth, to all the laughter-loving Adlers, this book of our history, our past.

Acknowledgments

———◆———

During the five years it has taken to prepare this book, I have had the constant assistance of Bernard Weller, a friend whose devotion cannot be repaid and whose excellent command of Russian, Hebrew, and Yiddish have immeasurably lightened the difficulties of my task. The contribution of the late William Mercur was also of major importance, and his death several years ago a great loss to myself as well as to the Yiddish theatrical profession.

I must mention, too, the warm encouragement and co-operation I received from Zvee Scooler, Miriam Kressyn, Seymour Rechtzeit and Jacob Jacobs, as well as the help and advice extended to me by Simon Weber, editor-in-chief of the *Jewish Daily Forward,* Chaim Suller of the *Morning Freiheit,* and Herman Yablakoff, former president of the Hebrew Actors Union.

For their wonderful living memories of Russia, I want to thank Sidney Osborne, Esther Aisenstock, Ida Walner, and Rae Sanders. Jacob ben Ami gave most generously of his time, as did Fran Corey, Abe Goldstein, brother of the beloved Jennie, and Charles Zunzer, son of the Yiddish folk poet. All of them have greatly enriched these pages.

The Jewish Division of the New York Public Library was of great importance to my research, as was the Photographic Division, where I particularly want to thank Herbert Bouscher, Carol Cronkite and James Murray for their unfailing interest and help. For the vital research relating to the London years of the Yiddish theatre I must acknowledge the generous assistance of David Carrington of the *Jewish Chronicle.* Charles Landstone and Joseph Leftwich, both formerly connected with the *Jewish Chronicle,* were also most helpful in this regard.

My material was drawn from many sources, but I should give special mention to the published memoirs of Boris Thomashefsky and Boaz Young, the monumental *Encyclopoedia of the Yiddish Theatre* compiled by the late Zalmen Zylbercweig, the autobiography of Abraham Cahan, founder and editor of the *Jewish Daily Forward,* and the uncollected memoirs of Sara Adler, published in that paper.

The uncollected memoirs of Jacob Adler himself, however, have been my most important source. It was my privilege to unearth and rediscover this document, of great value by reason of its depth of insight, its wealth of detail, and the events it brings to light, events unknown now to even the oldest of the living Yiddish actors.

Every member of the Adler family has contributed to this book, but for help beyond the ordinary I am indebted to Stella and Luther Adler, to my sister, Pearl Pearson, and to my niece Elizabeth Schretzman. My daughter Josie Oppenheim has been of invaluable help throughout these five years. Ellen Oppenheim has from the beginning done a great deal to make the book a reality. And the tireless devotion of Joanne Adler has not only sustained but inspired me.

Researches into the all-important American period were made possible through a grant from the National Endowment for the Humanities, and their assistance is most gratefully acknowledged.

An editor who approaches his task with sensitivity and feeling is a blessing for which all writers must wish. I cannot close without thanking Arnold Dolin for the intelligence and taste which have meant so much to me and to the book.

Contents

INTRODUCTION *by Harold Clurman*   xi
AUTHOR'S NOTE   xv

Part I
Russia: The Beginning

1 *Yankele*   3
2 *A Youth in Odessa*   18
3 *Curtain Rise at Jassy*   32
4 *The Rain of Gold*   43
5 *Rosenberg the Entrepreneur*   56
6 *A Real Actor*   68
7 *Love and War in a Provincial Troupe*   81
8 *The Struggle for the Marinsky*   96
9 *Last Days of Alexander II*   106
10 *The Pogram at Nyezhin*   122
11 *The Imperial Ukase*   136

Part II
London: An Actor Prepares

12 *The Jews of England*   153
13 *Adler Great Eagle*   161

14	*A London Paradise*	173
15	*Smith's Theatre on Prince's Street*	182
16	*The Sinner*	191

Part III
AMERICA: THE GOLDEN YEARS

17	*"Da Zdrastvuyet Amerika!"*	207
18	*The Magic "Professor"*	225
19	*The Revolt Against Goldfaden*	234
20	*Russian Soldier, Jewish King*	244
21	*A New Lear*	258
22	*The Great Three-Way Combination*	268
23	*The Meeting in Odessa*	282
24	*A Tragedy on the Yiddish "Theatre Street"*	293
25	*Shylock on Broadway, Tolstoy on the Bowery*	304
26	*Gordin's Theatre: The Apex*	318
27	*Shund*	332
28	*Final Appearance*	344
EPILOGUE:	*The Theatre of the Heart: A Heritage*	357
BIBLIOGRAPHY OF SOURCES		363
INDEX		365

(Photo sections follow pages 176 and 308.)

Introduction

by Harold Clurman

If it did not sound forbidding I might declare Lulla Rosenfeld's *Bright Star of Exile* a "monumental" work. For while its historical scope is extremely wide, its tone and flavor possess a quality of warm intimacy which lends its factual data a special glamor; we are *inside* the world and the personalities with which the book deals.

Its concrete material centers on the development of the Yiddish theatre from its inception in the 1870s to its decline of recent times, together with a biography of its most effulgent hero, Jacob Adler. There are many reasons why this subject matter should be of unusual interest to Americans—Jew or Gentile, with or without knowledge of Yiddish, theatre buff or only occasional playgoer. *Bright Star of Exile,* beside and beyond its immediate focus on the Yiddish theatre, is in an important way Russian history, English history, and finally New York and American history.

Most of us have a vague mental picture of Russia under Tsarist rule, or of London in the late nineteenth century. But isn't it true that we have an equally superficial or indifferent view of our own country's past? We may have some notion of the general progress of our civilization, remember signal dates or the names of leading figures in finance, politics, and the arts, but we have little personal feeling of connection with them. We cancel our native experience. What, for instance, were New York, Chicago, or Philadelphia like in the early years of this century? What were their sounds, smells, looks, pleasures, and entertainments like? In almost every one of its pages, *Bright Star of Exile* communicates vivid impressions of these aspects of social life. Lulla Rosenfeld writes the history of the Yiddish theatre from its beginnings in Eastern Europe to its culminating years in America as history should be written—with excitement and passionate personal involvement.

Through their struggle to create a theatre, we come to understand prerevolutionary Russia, nineteenth-century London, as these Yiddish actors must have known them. Through their experience in the new world of America, we grow acquainted with a broader spectrum, the land of our forbears in all its dramatic particularity.

We all suppose we know about New York's Lower East Side of yesteryear. But do we? We have heard of its squalor, its conglomeration of underprivileged minorities: Jewish, Irish, Italian, Polish. We have seen photos of its pushcarts and peddlers, its toughs and its strays, its crowded tenements and raucous streets. But we know less about its aspirations, its idealism, its boundless resources of talent. From this rich soil with its inner lyricism, amid or beneath what to the naked eye might seem only coarseness and brutality, have come some of the most popularly representative figures of American lore. Irving Berlin, George Gershwin, Paul Muni, Eddie Cantor, the Marx Brothers, Jimmy Cagney, not to speak of eminent men in politics, education, the law, did not simply "emerge" from the massive heaps of New York's ghetto, but were fructified by them.

In the evolution through which the immigrants and their native-born sons and daughters joined to become part of the red, white, and blue mainstream, the Yiddish theatre played a vital part, a part which not only influenced its own audiences but affected people in broad areas beyond its own sphere. Hutchins Hapgood, that Victorian "heir to the saints of Massachusetts Bay" and Lincoln Steffens' journalistic collaborator, once said of the Yiddish theatre in its heyday (1900–1920) that it was "about the best in New York at that time both in stuff and in acting." As I pointed out in my book *The Fervent Years,* the "stuff" was frequently Shakespeare, Tolstoy, Gorki, Andreyev, or charming folk operettas and plays modeled after original works by Sudermann, Hauptmann, and other contemporary Europeans.

In his seminal book *The Spirit of the Ghetto,* illustrated by Jacob Epstein (first published in 1902 and reissued by the

Harvard University Press in 1967), Hapgood included a long chapter about the Yiddish stage. He wrote: "In the midst of the frivolous Bowery . . . the theatres of the chosen people alone present the serious as well as the trivial interests of the entire community. Into these three buildings [the Yiddish theatres on the Bowery] crowd all the Jews of all the ghetto classes—the sweatshop woman with her baby, the day laborer, the small Hester Street shopkeeper, the Russian-Jewish anarchist and socialist, the ghetto rabbi and the scholar, the poet, the journalist."

And because it was only in the theatre that this varied populace could find a common meeting place—the more sophisticated rarely mingled with the Orthodox in synagogues—the Yiddish theatre was in every sense a *people's* or a *community* theatre, that is to say, a *true* theatre, the like of which was rarely if ever to be achieved again in our country. That is one reason why Hapgood was able to say that for him, "The Bowery and Canal Street had more significance for American life than did Broadway and Fifth Avenue."

As I have already suggested, the Yiddish theatre was based in an environment greater in ethnic composition than that of its Jewish population. It was immersed in that seething cauldron over which such Tammany bosses as the notorious William Marcy Tweed and later the wily and redoubtable Charles Murphy reigned. In this compost of raw conflict and harsh ambition, the Yiddish theatre served as a beacon light, a symbol of striving toward spirituality and human meaning.

Bright Star of Exile brings all this alive for us. We feel as if we were witnesses, as if we had been there. To some extent, I was. For though I began my career in the theatre in 1924, I ascribe my appetite for the stage to the days when my father, who practiced medicine in Manhattan's East Side, took me to see Jacob Adler act when I was seven years old. (I never saw him in private life.) From that early age I became an avid playgoer and saw many of the actors whose fantastic course Lulla Rosenfeld's book traces. She, Jacob Adler's granddaughter, was too young to have seen most of them. But I did.

Before I set down my own impression of some of them, I must cite the opinion of Jed Harris, the brilliant producer-director of the 1920s. To the question, "Whom do you consider the best actor you have ever seen?" he unhesitatingly answered, "David Kessler!"—one of the players who occupies an imposing position in the book you are about to read.

In his earthy emotionalism, David Kessler was indeed an

actor of volcanic power, just as Siegmund Mogulesko, another in the Yiddish theatre galaxy, was a character comedian whose insidious shrewdness provided deep delight. Then there was Sara Adler, Jacob Adler's third wife, who bred a bevy of versatile actors: Frances, Stella, Luther, Julia, and Jack. Indomitably female, sturdily knowing and realistic, she was in the school of what may be called romantic realism, unquestionably one of the great talents I have seen on any stage.

But there is no doubt in my mind that the brightest luminary of them all was Jacob Adler. He was extraordinary in every way. His height and bodily strength, his hair, snow white even in his youth, his large eyes and penetrating gaze, his reverberant voice and regal stance were themselves sufficient to rivet one's attention to the point of fascination, and he evoked in his audience something akin to worship. Everything about him breathed a masculine fullness which commanded the admiration of both sexes. With this there dwelled within him a sensibility which one might (even today!) call "feminine." One felt him capable of cruelty abated by an overwhelming sensual tenderness. He had the air of a prophet with a touch of humorous cynicism and not without a remainder of naivete! His skeptical smile was infectious, reflecting an understanding of the treacherous weaknesses which beset humankind. This gave rise to a forbearance due to a sense of his own sinful vulnerability.

His mode of living was lavish, and there was something larger than life in all his behavior. This gave the roles he played, for all their verisimilitude, a romantic aura that we often term "theatricality." His charm was captivating, his dignity awesome, his wrath terrifying. When he towered as the vengeful patriarch Shylock, or as Uriel Acosta raised the torch of free thought in epic loftiness, or teased as the shrewdly humorous ragpicker of *The Beggar of Odessa,* I was transported and a little frightened by him. The man's *size*—I do not refer to his physique—imposed a sense of peril. Grandeur always inspires a certain shudder at life's immeasurable might and mystery. When Jacob Adler died, two hundred thousand people came to his funeral. The image he created has never been forgotten. It has remained in the consciousness of a people, emblem of the stature of a human being, the overwhelming meaning of what it is to be a man.

Author's Note

A standard Yiddish orthography based on the Lithuanian dialect was adopted some years ago by the Yiddish Institute of Research (YIVO). Though I have tried to avoid great distortion of this orthography, I have used a transliteration conforming more to the South Russian or Volhynian dialect, spoken in the Yiddish theatre.

Readers interested in phonetic pronunciation of words and names in this book may be guided by the following:

ch or *kh* as in the Scotch *loch*
ei as in *height*
ai as in *maid*
zh as in *seizure*
ol as in *alcohol*

In the diminutive Yankele, the *a* is pronounced as in *father*, the first *e* as in *the*, but the final *e* as the *i* in *bit*. The Yiddish names Hessye, Soore, and even the proud Russian Sonya were all pronounced with this shorter, humbler final syllable.

George Moore, touching on the problems of the translator, wrote, "I do not know what a *verst* is, but when I see the word I am in Russia!" I have taken his advice, and wherever possible have left words and phrases untranslated.

Suddenly, as Raizel and Laibel watched, a very bright star passed across the heavens, flickered and went out. Another star followed it, and then another. "Look!" Raizel exclaimed in a trembling voice. "Look! The stars are falling!"

Laibel laughed gently. "Don't be frightened, Raizel," he said. "Stars don't fall. They only wander!" And like a wise, grown man he explained to her the mystery of the stars. Each star, he said, was a human soul. And those souls with a wandering star must follow it, yes, even if it led over half the earth, for only there will they find their destiny.

SHOLEM ALEICHEM, *Wandering Star*

Part I

RUSSIA: THE BEGINNING

1

Yankele

> Dear God, look down and see the poor.
> The poor man's life is hard.
> How long, how bitterly he toils,
> How little his reward!
>
> And though his soul is just as great
> As the king upon his throne,
> His pain and trouble have no end.
> Worse fate on no man come!
>
> Yet, every man may ask for better,
> And from no life is all hope fled.
> Dear God above, grant me once more
> That I be blessed with my crust of bread.
>
> BERL OF BROD

When Jews in the old days spoke of a lucky man, a man who had everything he desired and could ask for nothing more, they would say he lived "like God in Odessa." The envious phrase is occasionally heard even today. There are still living, breathing people who can imagine no spot on earth where God himself would be so content to spend eternity.

Of all the great cities of Russia, this was the most intimate, the most lighthearted. One could walk the length and breadth of the city always under the shadow of its trees. In the spring the air was scented with flowering white acacia and lilacs. There were parks and boulevards, excellent English, Italian, and French shops under gaily striped awnings. The city had tempo and movement, but it suggested leisure too, and elegance.

At night a pleasure-loving population flowed out into the

streets, drawn by the lights of restaurants, theatres, taverns, and cafes. A cosmopolitan crowd. Great Russians, Little Russians, Italians, Germans, and French jostled Serbs, Bulgarians, Armenians, Tatars, Greeks, and Jews. This was Russia's big port town, and ships flying the colors of the great powers continually moved over the Black Sea into the semicircular bay. A breath of Europe, of the great world, came with them, and with it the faint, persistent scent of danger.

But it was just this little chill in the atmosphere, just those alien flags moving into the harbor that gave the city a more bracing air than landlocked Kiev or Moscow. The Odessans have always been a special breed. They were livelier, more skeptical, more realistic than other Russians. And even the beggars were witty.

Everyone talked in Odessa, everyone had views. This was never more true than in 1855, a year of important events. In this year Nicholas I, known to his subjects as "The Flogger," unexpectedly took sick and died. He left to his son the tail end of a ruinous adventure in the Crimea, a liberal intelligentsia disgusted by Russian defeat, and a radical underground already playing with ideas of terror and armed revolution.

The newly crowned Alexander II continued the war for six more months, a gesture of devotion to his dead father that cost 40,000 Russian lives. In the end, Sevastopol fell and the Crimean War was over. The Tsar signed a humiliating peace, but promised the nation reforms on every level of government.

A remarkable era began. The thirty-seven-year-old ruler, so immovably resolved to prolong the Crimean War, was equally stubborn about his liberal reforms. Alexander II intended nothing less than the modernization of the Russian state. In the first dazzling year of his reign, steps were taken to liberate the serfs, relax the censorship, and make sweeping changes in the army, the courts, and every branch of the administration.

Among the measures passed by the new regime were certain laws affecting the Jews, most harshly oppressed of all Russian minorities. Under the old conscription laws, Russians could be enlisted only when they reached the age of eighteen, while Jews were subject to army service at twelve. When the parents hid the twelve-year-olds, boys of eight and nine were taken in their place. Few of these children survived more than the first year of their hard new life. Even those who lived rarely saw their homes again, as military service lasted twenty-five years.

The new Tsar, after reducing the term of service for all Russians, raised the conscription age for Jews to accord with that of his other subjects. All through the land Jewish children marched, singing, out of military cantons, to be delivered back to their native towns and villages. In the city of Bobruisk, a rich man donated a thousand roubles to the Jewish Town Council for the privilege of opening with his own hands the gates of the hated "Children's Barracks."

The change in the conscription laws, greatest blessing of the new regime, was followed by others. Jews were allowed into more of the professions, their sons and daughters were admitted into the Russian universities. The special Jewish tax was abolished, the restraints on residence lightened. Throughout the Pale of Settlement, tidings came each day of freedom and deliverance, and in every synagogue in Russia prayers were said for Tsar Alexander II, friend of the Jewish people.

In this year of a great new hope, on February 12, 1855, a son was born into the house of Feivel Abramovitch Adler, a small Odessa wheat merchant. The child was given the Hebrew name Yankev (Jacob), but was called also by various diminutives—Yankel, Yankele, even Yascha or Yaschenka.

Though the boy was born into a simple Orthodox home, it was a home in the great city of Odessa. His father read the Russian newspapers, had political opinions, and took an interest in the great questions of the day. Above all else, Feivel Abramovitch loved good conversation. Coming from the synagogue on a holiday or a Friday night, he would often bring with him a poor man, an ultra-Orthodox Jew, or perhaps a visiting *maggid*,* and the two men would sit at the table, talking into the late hours of the night.

There was enough to discuss and think about in those complex times. The liberal Tsar, who had stopped short of giving Russia a constitution, had also drawn the line at granting citizenship to his Jews. Without civil equality, what safety was there in even the best laws? The synagogue and the Greek church were both on the same Odessa street, and every year at

---

* An itinerant speaker, either a rabbi or a layman. Remote Jewish villages often received their only news of the outside world through the *maggid*.

Passover a mob of drunken Greeks beat up the Jews and robbed them. A lemon peddler, a very poor man, had been beaten to death in one of these "little pogroms." No legal redress existed for this atrocity. Jews had come to take official indifference to such crimes as an irremediable fact of Russian life. A few Jewish lawyers had achieved prominence in the new liberal courts, a few fortunes had been made in railroads; for the ordinary man, things remained much the same as before.

The discussions in the Adler house always came around to this question—the plight of the Jew in Russia. On this subject Feivel Abramovitch could hold a roomful of people enthralled for hours. But the genial, interesting Adler was better at talk than at business. He went from speculation in grain to grain brokerage, but both brought him very little, and the family remained poor.

For little Yankev, the light of the whole universe came from the luminous sea-blue eyes of his mother. It was often a sad light, for the shadow of a loss lay over her. When she first met Adler, the daughter of the proud Berditchev Halperins had been another man's wife.

Short of stature and not at all handsome, Feivel Abramovitch had something in his brown eyes very fascinating to women. The beautiful Hessye divorced her husband and lost the right to her child—a boy called Ephraim. Throughout his life, her second son was to know nothing of this brother but his name. Their paths on this earth were not destined to cross.

Hessye Adler read Tolstoy, Turgenev, and Dostoevsky, and delved into the new Yiddish novels, too—*The Iron Woman* by Sheikevitch, or Linetzki's *Polish Boy*—highly colored romances becoming popular at that time. She was a beautiful woman, tall and strong, with white skin of a rare perfection and magnificent eyes. The golden hair of her childhood had darkened, but lingering about her still was something golden and precious as a winter sun. She held her tall figure absolutely erect, and her character had something of the same uncompromising posture. The beautiful Hessye Adler had a way of speaking her mind. Her principal trait, however, was fastidiousness. Should one of her husband's guests exhibit an unmannerly habit, she could not remain silent. "I beg you, don't do it," she would protest. "If you must, go away! Or let me go away!"

Her husband may have felt more at ease away from this

somewhat formidable wife, for he sat more often in other houses than in his own. The young wife was often alone. She brooded at times, and more than once her son saw her brush away silent tears. In all he later wrote, one feels a note of reserve toward this father so rarely at his mother's side.

We should not assume, however, that his mother shared this coolness. Children often do not know the true relations of their parents. The house was always happier for his father's presence. If Feivel Abramovitch did not take his wife into the homes where he was popular, he may not have thought them worthy of her. The son never heard a harsh word between his parents, and from all one can gather, Feivel Abramovitch's beautiful wife was always in his eyes the great prize he had won from life.

The boy's childhood passed happily. There were joyful holidays, great Passover feasts when the family gathered thirty and forty strong at the table of the wealthy Uncle Arke, their patriarch and ruler. On these occasions the Adlers were always specially honored guests. Though Feivel Abramovitch was poor, he had intellect, which carried weight in these circles. And Hessye Adler, daughter of a wealthy Orthodox family, was looked upon by the whole community as a very great lady indeed.

Poor people moved often in those days. Little Yankev remembered best the house of Rollya the Greek because of its lively courtyard, ringing all day with the play of Russian, Greek, and Jewish children. He soon grew into an active boy, exceedingly merry and mischievous.

One day on the street outside the court, he spied an unguarded horse and wagon, the carter staring stupidly, unmindful of his cart. Instantly the child sprang into the cart, brought down the reins and tore off down the street at a breakneck speed. An uproar broke out. Looking back, he saw the driver, red in the face, shouting and running, a whole pack of people with him. This sight gave him a thrill, an emotion, he confesses, strongly laced with malice. Even more than the glorious ride, he felt an overpowering delight that because of him everyone ran, shouted, that he alone had thrown the whole street into confusion.

This streak of the perverse caused his family much worry. His tricks were never thought out in advance, but carried through by an instant rush to his object. It was too late to stop him; the trick had been played, and he was already laughing. There was something singular, troubling to the mind in this play, less like that of a child than of some merry uncontrollable element in nature. A lightning impulse accompanied by laughter remained a characteristic throughout his life.

When his father broke out in anger over his pranks, the grandfather protected him. "Let him be! Don't beat the boy!" he would say. And the mild eyes could flash fire at such moments.

With his father so often away on business and his mother occupied with household duties and private cares, it was this *zayde* who brought up the child, taught him his Hebrew letters, showed him how to pray, how to make a blessing. The *zayde* was a handsome old Jew, white-haired, tall, quiet, always in a long coat, always with a book, his whole upright figure radiating cleanliness, peace, and a belief in God. The greatest magnates of the family came on Yom Kippur eve to be blessed by Reb Avremele Fridkus Adler. The grandson always believed he must have been a descendant of those Jews who came from Galicia, bringing with them to Russia the fine old Frankish culture.

With his grandmother the boy had an excellent understanding. The old lady owned a remnant store, and the child spent whole days there, playing and rummaging about. Best of all he loved to go with his grandmother to the fair at Peresyp, a seaside resort of the Odessa poor. Every summer the old lady went to the fair to buy stockings, handkerchiefs, scarfs, all the pretty trifles that used to be called *galanteries*. The deafening babble of bargaining voices, the pushing, the crowds, the whole glorious open-air tumult was pleasure itself to the little boy, and he could imagine nothing finer.

When he reached the age of six he was sent to *cheder*.* He learned badly. He did not like the dark, filthy room, or the red-bearded, brutally ignorant *rebbe*, with his cat-o'-nine-tails always swishing threateningly through the air. At first he liked going back and forth with his schoolmates, a grown boy now, as good as the others. But soon the noise, the dirt, the strangeness repelled him. One day he came home crying and told his mother he did not want to go to this *cheder* anymore. The only son had his way. Another school was found, this time with a fine, dignified rabbi and only fifteen young *talmidim*. Here the boy learned the Five Books of Moses, some Hebrew and Russian grammar, and a little arithmetic. He

---

* Hebrew school for young children.

liked the evening hours, the guttering candle, the children around the table listening dreamily to the awesome stories of the Bible. At nightfall the kindly *meshuris* * came, put on the children's boots and led them home, each child carrying his lantern through the dark, snowy streets. Since he was poor, Yankele had only a paper lantern with a bit of candle inside. When the wind was strong the candle blew out, or the whole little contraption caught fire. But he had made his lantern himself and he loved it.

All this came to an end when his father could no longer pay for his lessons. After a time at home he was sent to study with a Reb Yokele. This violent man beat not only his pupils but also his own children and his wife. It was always the same story. The better *rebbes* asked too much money, and he learned nothing at all from the others.

When he was ten years old, a little sister was born. The whole house grew happier after this event, his mother less lonely, his father more often at the table. There must have been more money too at this time, for a tutor came who gave him lessons at home. This man, whose name was Mahler, treated his pupil as he would a younger comrade. At once the intelligent boy began to learn, to enjoy his studies, and to long for the day he would put on the uniform of a student and enter the *Gymnazia*. †

The dream came to nothing. Money ran out again, and the wonderful Mahler disappeared. Yankele was sent to learn at the Jewish county school. Here the teachers used not only the cat-o'-nine-tails but also canes, and he learned nothing but a lifelong disgust with the practice of beating children. He played truant, was caught and taken out of school, this time for good, and sent to work. His education had come to an end. The *Gymnazia,* more and more beautiful as it receded in time, became for him the great lost hope, an illusion that would haunt him for the rest of his days.

He worked at several jobs, but none for long. For a time he went out as a "custom peddler," carrying his pack of wares to out-of-the-way corners on the outskirts of the city. But his customers were mostly prostitutes and servant girls, not the best acquaintances for a boy of that age. "People very proper and respectable in society grow remarkably free and easy in such

---

* A humble assistant, used mostly for running errands.
† The *Gymnazia* gave an eight-year course, equivalent to our high school and college.

company," he later observed. "When his errands are over the delivery boy goes to The Tsar's Medal or some other tavern. Music excites his soul. Others entertain him with wine. And a longing awakes for empty pleasures, for the company of empty, idle people."

When there was nothing to do, he roamed the Odessa streets. As a child he had been strangely attracted to the slaughterhouses near the beach at Peresyp. He would watch the men take an ox, kill it with a blow on the head, and lay it on a slab. The cold act horrified him, yet he stayed and watched. Now, on the same impulse, he loitered around the bleak sections of the city near the barracks and the prison. Here the fearful sound of military drums would send him off again like a shot—*to see*. As he neared the prison a wild whistling filled the air, a signal to one and all that a criminal was to be flogged. If the offense was small, the man was laid on the ground and beaten with a *nagaika*, a leather whip dipped in water. For a greater crime, a regular scaffold was erected and the man so cruelly whipped that his horrible screams and curses drowned out the drums.

There were public executions too in those days, of nihilists, arsonists, and others who committed crimes against the state. One such event remained in his mind with a terrible distinctness. The case, widely discussed in the city, concerned a peasant who had sold himself into the army as a substitute, an accepted practice of the time. This man's trouble had started because he refused to accept the insults of his superiors. The unshakable dignity of the peasant had enraged them. They deliberately goaded him into rebellion, then threw him into the barracks prison. Here these fine officers came to taunt their victim further. When one of them went so far as to spit into his supper of grain, the prisoner flung the iron dish at his tormentor's head. He was tried for this crime and sentenced to death.

As soon as he heard the execution was to take place, the twelve-year-old boy ran off to see it. He was to remember it all his life:

"A large crowd gathered in front of the barracks, stirring restlessly as they waited for the prisoner to appear. Suddenly, an excited buzz. Here he comes now, down Scizzor Street, an escort of soldiers around him. A fine, handsome peasant, tall, robust, with a broad Russian beard. As he mounts the scaffold a fearful howling is heard, and an old woman rushes from the crowd and flings herself on the condemned man in a frantic embrace. This was his mother. A murmur of sympathy arose. For a short time she was allowed to embrace and kiss her son, then an officer gave an order. Soldiers tear her away, push her back into the crowd. Her screams die down to a continual low moaning. The condemned man mounts higher and waits. Not a quiver, not a sign of fear. His face is peaceful, full of iron resolution. His eyes are bound. A sharp command. Rifles ring out in a single report. The bandaged figure totters, sways, and falls through a trap in the scaffold into the grave already prepared and waiting. At once a group of little soldiers go to work with shovels, heaping earth on the grave until a high mound has grown over it. On this they sprang, leaping and stamping like devils, until the ground was even and no one could say which piece of earth was innocent and which had been so hideously defiled."

The boy came home from this scene in such hysterics that his parents were frightened. "A blessing on him!" they scolded angrily. "Who told him to go?"

He did not understand himself why he had gone. An overmastering necessity arose in him to be where such things happened—*to see.*

Just before his Bar Mitzva, a misfortune befell the Adler family. Reb Avremele, the good *zayde,* died. Of all that beautiful presence, of all that light, nothing remained but a terrible little figure in a black shawl laid out on the floor with candles at his head and feet.

He died on a Friday,* and the word was passed from one to another. "A saint! A saint!" people whispered. "Where such another saint as Reb Avremele Adler? He will be a good petitioner for us in heaven!"

A sorrow-stricken Bar Mitzva. His grandmother wailed all the way to the synagogue that her Avremele had not lived to see his beloved grandson come of age. His mother, too, was heavy-hearted.

As the boy mounted the altar to recite his prayer, he heard

---

* To die on a Friday, the Jewish Sabbath, confers a blessing on the dead.

his mother and grandmother weeping together in the gallery. The *shammos* * held up the Torah, prompted him in a whisper. He tried to repeat the prayer, but his voice broke, tears gushed from his eyes and he wept aloud like a little child.

In 1870 no one in Odessa talked of anything but the Franco-Prussian War. The Jews were strongly pro-French, a sympathy they would share again in 1914. Feivel Abramovitch was completely taken up with the war. He kept abreast of all military operations, and the dining table at home was piled high with newspapers and maps. His understanding of these matters was the admiration of all his friends. "Fools that you are," he would say with scorn when they came to him with their worried questions. And he would pull out his maps. "You can see for yourselves! Here stands Basin! And here McMahon! How can Von Moltke pass?"

The victories and defeats of the war faded as in 1870 cholera swept Odessa. Christian and Jew, rich and poor, young and old fell victim to the plague. People fell in their homes, at their work, on foot, and in carriages. Gravediggers fell, spade in hand, into the graves they were digging, and synagogue and church stood open twenty-four hours a day so that prayers and masses could be said for the dead.

Volunteer groups called "Rubbers" were stationed on every street. As soon as a woman or man fell, stricken, the nearest "Rubber" would blow a whistle, bringing the others at a run. All took turns massaging the victim. Apparently this sometimes prevented immediate death. Whiskey was also used as a preventative, and it was common to see well-dressed men and women stop on the street, take out a bottle, and drink.

Yankele Adler, haunted day and night by terror of death, made friends with the son of a man who kept a tavern. Between them they decided they must drink, drink as much as they could hold. The tavern keeper's son smuggled whiskey out of his father's saloon and both took turns at the bottle. "It's cholera, brother, here's health!" they shouted. It ended with the two of them dead drunk and fast asleep outside the courtyard gate, where their frightened families found them.

The cholera passed. A new epidemic raged, a passion for boxing matches. This sport originated in the Moldovanka, a

---

* A lay caretaker of the synagogue.

maze of squalid, unpaved streets in the worst quarter of the city, the haunt of derelicts, prostitutes, and thieves. In the wretched one-story hovels of this district, men and women lived in a degradation unknown to the poorest peasant. Here beggars went barefoot, drink-crazed men lurched through the streets screaming obscenities, and homeless men slept on the bare ground. But the Moldovanka was gay, as many places are where people live without hope. The sound of drunken singing and accordion music could be heard far into the night. Slummers came to "see life," to get drunk in the taverns and brothels. And as the craze for boxing spread, curiosity seekers from every part of Odessa gathered to see the gladiators contend. The excited ring of spectators, the applause of pretty women, the drama of the match itself—all this had a strong attraction. The sixteen-year-old Yankele Adler, veteran of a score of street fights, soon got a chance to show what he could do.

Turning up the sleeves of his red Russian shirt, the young boxer advanced, measuring his opponent. He had no physical fear, and enjoyed the give-and-take of blows dealt with a naked fist. The crowd liked him, and he soon became a popular fighter, his appearance greeted with applause and cries of "Yankele Adler, *molodyets!* Yankele Adler, *natchinai!*" * Because the Russian word for fist is *kulak*, he was nicknamed "Yankele Kulatchnik."

He was coming up in the world, and earning money, too, in the textile factory of the Goldstein brothers. He started there as an apprentice at five kopeks a day, but soon rose in the business. He could reckon a little, knew his Russian grammar, and wrote a fine hand, an accomplishment of some value in those days. His employers quickly put him to work on their books and correspondence, and his salary went up to ten roubles a month (about $25).

With money in his pockets and his new celebrity as a boxer, he was taken into the ranks of the well-known Odessa *voil yungen.*† These were the famous young sports and toughs who came out at night sporting their fancy vests and canes, looking for a wedding, a brawl, any chance to turn the town upside down. Sons of rich fathers, petty commission men, more sinister types, too, dabbling in prostitution and black-

---

* "Yankele Adler, good man! Yankele Adler, go to it!"
† Idle, pleasure-mad youth.

mail—whoever had money to spend and time to waste ran here with the others. Because the better streets had been paved and made smooth for light young feet by the Italian architect Boffo, the Jewish community, with their usual indifference to foreign names, dubbed these pavement roamers "Buff's Army."

The favorite haunt of the gang just then was a tavern in the dangerous Truschev district owned by a converted Jew, an ex-convict who had done time in Siberia. The magnet that drew them to this tavern was the younger daughter, Olga Petrovna, a devil of a girl on to every trick of the trade who knew how to rob her young customers of every penny they possessed. All of Buff's Army had fallen madly in love with this girl. They not only paid her shamefully padded bills, but brought her presents, too, hoping for a glance, a smile, a moment of her company.

"More than her burning beauty, it was her interesting character, her moments of unexpected compassion, that drew us to her," said Adler. "She knew to a *groschen* what each of us owed, and woe to the boy who tried to cheat! But if a boy came with empty pockets, he was just as welcome as before. And if he should be really down and out she would even give him a bit of money and put him up for the night. But he had to behave himself. If he tried anything rough he would get his bones broken by the whole crowd. There wasn't one of us who wouldn't have gone through fire and flame for her!"

It was with this Olga Petrovna that Adler had his first real love affair. Their flirtation had the added zest of danger, for it enraged Yankele Brainis, wildest of the bunch, and the jealous boy tossed a glassful of wine into his rival's face. Adler, hurt, took the insult in silence. Olga Petrovna led him into her rooms at the back of the tavern, helped him set himself to rights, and scolded him for his company. "You should not be running about with such people," she said. "You are too fine!"

After this he and Olga Petrovna drew closer. The affair cost him some pangs of jealousy, for he did not, by any means, have exclusive right to her favors. But this girl, whom he calls a "feminine Jekyll and Hyde," had an entirely different character outside her father's tavern. Walking along the boulevard on her friend's arm, she was another person, serious, well read, even idealistic. He soon discovered she had contacts with nihilists, and helped them in their work. Once she let Adler read an illegal pamphlet and he marveled that people dared write such things in Russia.

Revolutionary propaganda had been circulated for some time in Odessa, and in 1872 some of the best homes of the city were meeting places for the underground. Olga Petrovna was greatly valued in these circles for her beauty, her boldness, and her intelligence. Through his friendship with her, Adler came into contact with certain nihilist groups. It was in one of these upper-class homes that he met the attorney Alexander Oberlander and his sister, the serious young woman he later married.

At about this time he also fell in with an unlicensed lawyer called Rosenberg, a jokester and scamp, half charlatan, half genius, who was to play a tremendous role in his life. Through Rosenberg he began to get work copying petitions and documents for lawyers, notaries, and city officials, and he soon had as much of this as he could do. He gave up his job at the textile factory, became something of a dandy, and with money in his pockets began to devote himself entirely to pleasure.

Pleasure was everywhere to be found. He was never to forget these nights of his youth when all Odessa belonged to him. He became an impassioned lover of the play, going often to both the City Theatre and the Marinsky. He frequented the cafes where Russian gypsies entertained, listened to the ravishing gypsy music, and watched girls perform the dances that mounted rhythmically in excitement until a shout came from the onlookers.

Best of all he loved the wine cellars of the Jewish quarter where one heard the ballads of the Folk Nightingale, Velvel of Zbarazh, and the ballads of Eliakum Zunzer and Goldfaden.

Though the wine cellar entertainers were always called Singers of Brod, they did not necessarily come from that Galician town. They had received their name from Berl of Brod, that half-legendary vagabond who, twenty-five years earlier, had deserted wife and children to wander about with a band of penniless fools like himself, singing for his bread in the wayside inns of Russia and Galicia.

Berl of Brod was less a troubador than a wandering philosopher of the poor. His songs cry out for pity, for justice, and even the joyous ones are thoughtful. The titles alone, listed in an old book, are a kind of song: Ballad of a Shoemaker and a Tailor; Ballad of a Poor Man, of a Blind Man, of a Wanderer, of a Dead Man; Ballad of Two Stars, of a Golden Morning; Ballad of a Man Who Has Come up in the World, of an Old Father Turned Away by His Children; Ballad of a Smuggler, of a Gravedigger; Ballad of Berl Himself.

Every Jewish street in Odessa had its Singers of Brod. For the most part they were a beggarly lot who did their turn and then went around with a plate. They all had nicknames: "Azir the Redhead," "Laibele Nose," "Moishe Blind-Eye," "Mottel the Wagon-Greaser," "Schmul-with-the-Hoarse-Throat." But some of the cellar singers were famous. Old Schmul, who had in fact sung with Berl of Brod, was one of the best. He could bring tears to the eyes of his listeners, and when he snapped his fingers to a Chasidic *nigun,* old Schmul had a charm impossible to resist.

"Mayer Scabhead" was another wine cellar favorite. He would introduce himself with, "Quiet! Respect! Mayer Scabhead is here!" bringing a roar of approval from the crowd. And when he passed around the plate he would say at every table, "Give! If not—*you* sing!"

Most famous of all the folk singers was Yisrol Gradner, who had sung in Jewish communities all through Russia, Galicia, Poland, and Roumania. Gradner was a real star. He dressed in European clothes—a short coat, boots that squeaked, a hat flirtatiously tilted. He did not deign to go around with a plate like the others. He had an assistant who performed this task while he himself sat like a guest with a chosen group of friends, getting up to perform only when the spirit moved him. Gradner had a fine baritone, sang with charm and finesse, and created characters so true to life his audience gasped.

"Already there were beginnings of costume and characterization," Adler tells us. "But Gradner brought it closer to actual theatre. In Kukland's Restaurant he built a real little stage with two doors and a curtain. There he and some of the better folk singers, Moishe Finkel or Weinstein, would perfom whole scenes together."

Adler describes one of these sketches. Three *chasidim* argue, each claiming his rabbi is the best. Their claims grow more and more absurd. In the end it turns out they all have the same rabbi. They clap hands, embrace, and do a dance together. The audience went mad over it.

Adler always felt that the Yiddish theatre had started with these scenes drawn from Jewish life. His love for Gradner began in these Odessa nights when he became his follower and friend.

Avrom Goldfaden, a famous journalist and poet, was also declaiming his verses in Odessa at this time, but he performed only for a more educated audience. Goldfaden was looked upon with awe, for he was a *maskil*—a learned man—and a follower of the *Haskala* ("The Awakening"), a Jewish movement corresponding in certain ways with the French Enlightenment. A profound intellectual ferment was taking place among the Jews of Eastern Europe at this time. Writers and philosophers were clamoring for change, calling on their fellow Jews to take their eyes off heaven and fight for their place in the world.

The world in fact had already broken in. Even in the most remote villages, tales were heard of railroad tracks stretching as far north as Archangalsk, of messages flashed from Moscow to St. Petersburg along an electric wire. The *Haskala*, with its reverence for science and its struggle against superstition, was part of a larger movement coming from many directions but running one way—toward modern industrial life. The wine cellar singers with their songs of social justice, their laughter at the shy, unworldly young *chosid*, were serving the same ends as the learned *maskilim*. The very existence of these singers was evidence of a break with the past. For the first time in their history, Jews were singing not of Queen Esther and the wicked Haman, but of ordinary Jewish joys and sorrows.

Adler hung about the wine cellars as though he already knew his life would rise out of them like the genie out of the bottle. Whether the singers were crude or polished, good or bad, elegant or beggarly, he loved them and felt happiest in their company. He would have become a folk singer himself if only he had possessed a voice.

"Why are your faces so yellow?" the incurably outspoken Hessye asked when in later years he brought home these night birds. "Why are your trousers so bedraggled? And where are your moustaches? You are singers? *Komedyantchiks?* And from this do you hope to earn bread for a wife?"

These companions of her son filled her with alarm. And indeed, a *komedyantchik,* a paid buffoon, was lower in the social scale than the beggar who, after all, could claim to be the victim of some misfortune. The humblest journeyman tailor or cobbler could look down on such people and despise them.

2

A Youth in Odessa

> Nobody ever had a youth like mine! I burned up a world!
>
> JACOB ADLER

"Rosenberg's business . . . can I admit what it was? It is a shame and disgrace even to speak of it! But I am bringing back a world long dead, and so can tell the truth. Rosenberg's business was nothing more or less than swindling. He was a faker!"

With this mixture of amusement, tenderness, and shame, Adler recalls the great friend of his youth. To understand this friendship and its place in his life, one must know the class of men to whom Yisrol Rosenberg belonged.

There were at that time certain Jews in Odessa who gave themselves the title of *Advokat* (Councillor). These men had studied a little law, were allowed to plead cases in court, but had no real standing in the profession. In the main they handled pleas and petitions, and in this way were of use to the Jewish community. Rosenberg, beside being one of these "hole-and-corner" attorneys-at-law, was a well-known Odessa scamp, master of any game calling for imposture, bravado, and bluff. He immediately saw he could make use of Adler, a handsome, thoroughly unregenerate youngster, always in need of money. In spite of the fifteen-year difference in their ages, they were soon inseparable.

For a long time the gullible Adler took the older man for what he gave himself out to be, a respectable lawyer, stricter in his morals than most. He found out the truth in time, but by then it was too late. He loved Rosenberg, followed him everywhere, became his assistant, his secretary, his clerk, and for his services received an occasional bone. "A boy, a child!" Rosenberg would say. "How much does he need?"

As Adler describes him, Rosenberg was of medium height, very thin, with a small face and a long nose. His eyes were good—big, smiling eyes. He had long hands, very long fingers, always wore gloves, and never was seen without a cigarette in the corner of his lips. His upper and lower teeth did not meet properly. Because of this he spoke in a sloppy, unclear way. In his later years, Adler tells us, this grew worse.

In spite of this defect and an unpleasing appearance, his magnetism was enormous. A bachelor who lived in cafes and restaurants, he never ate alone, never shaved alone, never tried on a coat or a pair of boots alone. He was always surrounded by a crowd of hangers-on looking for some share of the money he picked up everywhere. But young people followed him simply for the lure of his company; they were drawn by the demonic energy that swept everyone around him into his plans. As soon as the man appeared, sparks began to fly. There was never a day he did not have something going, some outrageous scheme for profit, adventure, or amusement. He had a prodigious memory and could call literally thousands of people in Odessa by name. He could bluff and twist his way out of the trickiest situations, and everything he touched turned to money. Adler was convinced all his life that if only Rosenberg had channeled his talents in some useful direction the world would have rung with his name.

He defends even his friend's misdeeds: "When is a bad thing not bad? When it is done to a bad person who deserves it. When the wrongdoer cannot resist the fun of what he is doing. When he does it to show his brilliance, his ability. When done for such reasons, the bad thing is not only forgivable, it takes on ten thousand charms!"

Rosenberg, it is true, swindled mostly thieves, forgers, people who perhaps deserved no better and were not likely to lodge a complaint against him. And though he sometimes set out to fleece a fool, Adler insists it was never a poor man. He had an amazing power over those around him. Once at a private gathering Adler saw him go up to a wealthy, miserly man and reprimand him for "having so much while others have nothing." As he spoke, he unbuttoned the man's jacket, took out his wallet, pocketed several bills, and returned the rest. The rich man, nervous and resentful, was forced to put a good face on it. The thing was done so quickly and with such a show of authority that those present were not sure they had a right to interfere.

Rosenberg did sail perilously close to the edge of the law at times. Adler was afraid to be his tool, afraid to perjure himself. Rosenberg, who loved him, understood this and never brought him into court as a witness.

One day on the street, Adler saw him in conversation with a stranger. As he caught sight of Adler, a look of joy came over Rosenberg's face. "Alexei Alexeievitch!" he cried, grasping Adler by the arm. "God himself has sent you here! Just in time! I have been looking for you all day!" To his companion, in a low voice, "Money! Quick! Everything you have!" His fingers were already deftly exploring the stranger's pockets and emptying them. He handed the money over to the bewildered Adler, but somehow only the loose coins changed hands; the assignats remained in his own possession. "Remember, Alexei Alexeievitch!" Rosenberg repeated urgently. "We are relying on you! Help us! Save us!" And with this he pulled the stranger away, turning back several times to blow kisses through the air.

The stranger, a known horse thief, was hoping to get his case appealed. Rosenberg had heartlessly told him he could be saved by bribing the Secretary of the Court, who for a certain sum would remove all evidence of his guilt from the record. Adler had unwittingly played the Secretary of the Court.

Rosenberg really went too far. There were no limits to what he allowed himself. One day he fell in with a tavern keeper, a man with two unmarried daughters. He immediately promised to provide one of them with a bridegroom, and the following night asked Yankele Adler to come with him to a party, an invitation he knew Adler would never refuse. The tavern, in an out-of-the-way part of town, had been closed to regular customers that night, and the owner and his wife were eagerly awaiting the bridegroom.

Adler felt he was the center of attention, but understood nothing. Food and wine were served. The two daughters, both dressed in their best, were brought out of an inner room. A gay party began, and Rosenberg was in his element. Adler was plied with wine. Both the owner and his wife smiled encouragingly. The girls giggled. Since no one seemed to mind, Adler, who liked all women, began to play up to the older one, who was not really so bad looking. With everyone cheering him on, he finally gave her a peck on the cheek.

Soon after, Rosenberg took him home, very drunk. By morning he had forgotten the whole incident, and went about his business. When he came home at the end of the day he found his parents half dead with shame. "Good, Yankele, good!" his father cried in a heartbroken tone. "You have chosen a bride. Why should you tell your parents? You are right! Your mother and I have deserved no better!" Hessye, too, was in tears. "He is engaged, and we knew nothing!" she muttered. "The shame of it, the disgrace!" During his absence the tavern keeper and his wife, a perfectly respectable couple, had come to call on their future in-laws.

The boy cursed his friend with all his heart. His parents had been put through a mortifying experience. And the tavern owner and his wife? What must they feel? And the poor girl herself? Rosenberg's jokes were really too merciless. Yet he could not stay angry. Something in his own nature responded with laughter rather than pity. A practical joker himself, who could play a trick his victim felt under his very ribs, Adler recognized in Rosenberg his master.

The escapades with Rosenberg and the nights with Buff's Army were interruped by one episode, a thing separate and apart from other events of his youth. The incident itself was common enough at the time, and from the standpoint of the respectable community not without its sordid aspects.

In a dense network of Odessa side streets, a kind of Russian Montparnasse, a score of cafes and restaurants flourished, popular because of the Russian gypsies who performed there. Wine flowed in these places, and the revels went on into dawn.

The gypsies, rough customers distrusted alike by Gentile and Jew, were in great demand as artists. They were especially famed for an intoxicating gaiety that passed over at its height into a wildly romantic sadness. And indeed, these were simply different sides of the same emotion. The rhythm and clash of the dance over, the chorus would slowly come forward, forming a tableau. Dark heads bent over fiddles and guitars. Before the first chord was struck, a hush fell over the room.

The power of Russian music is familiar to all, but only a fragment now remains of the gypsy romances. These airs had all the magic of the Russian folk song, but another strain ran through them too, older and more tragic. Many of them were sung in parts, their chords changing like colors in stained glass. But the saddest and most beautiful were taken by a guitar and a single voice—and these girls sang gorgeously, with an untaught passion of feeling.

All Odessa soon knew that Feivel Abramovitch's son was "playing a love" with a *Tzigeinerin,* a gypsy girl. The men viewed the matter with a certain tolerance—better a gypsy singer than one of their daughters. The women seem to have sympathized. A great deal was forgiven Adler all his life; his transgressions had so much of nature about them. And while romantic love had no place in the stern code of the Diaspora, every housewife in Odessa sighed dreamily over tales of thwarted romance. The folk songs of the period are full of "hearts torn with pain," and grieving lovers who "played a love, but could not play it out."

About the girl, we know only that her name was Bronya, that she sang with all her soul, and that Adler, listening, was lost. He spent his nights at the gypsy cafe and flung his roubles about to make sure of his welcome there. He had fallen under the spell of the girl and wanted nothing more all his life than to listen to her sing.

The affair cannot have lasted long. The young man, dreaming, drifting, was being pulled by many forces. His fame as a *voil yung* was growing. He was handsome, popular in low circles. The wild nights with Buff's Army had a strong hold over him. At the same time, through Olga Petrovna, he was meeting serious young people whose passionate discussions of art, literature, and social questions were giving him glimpses of something better. The gypsy held him with her marvelous art. Yet she was of the gitanos, a queer, illiterate people with their own strange language, their incomprehensible code. While he was never to forget her, there was never any real hope for the gypsy and the Jew.

No doubt there were quarrels, jealous scenes, tears. One day she was gone. The gypsies had moved on, or some man had paid the head of the tribe to take her away. They may or may not have said good-bye. We know only that her absence came as a blow. Weighing the worth of his happiness, he had lost it.

The love that fails, the "little love," is soon forgotten, but while it aches, it aches in the deepest place. Olga Michailovna Loev, who was to marry the writer Sholem Aleichem, knew about the gypsy girl and years later told her son that the affair, which "ended badly," had a deep effect on Adler's character. As she remembered it, the destructive drives that were to work such havoc in his life began with this early unhappy love.

This may be true. Adler himself writes of a moment in his youth of "grave moral danger," a moment when the nights with Buff's Army took on a more sinister shade and he drowned out the memory of the girl he had lost in the sordid loves of the brothel. And all this did lasting harm, for he was neither a rebel nor a revolutionary, but a man who found his meaning in the laws of his people.

The Jews have a belief that man is possessed of two selves, the higher self and the lower. While the lower is accepted, even honored as a part of life, it is still indulged only at the expense of the higher. The very terms "lower" and "higher" must make a deep imprint on any sensitive mind. Adler, strongly imbued with this Jewish idea, felt he was sinking beyond all hope of salvation.

Two influences saved him. The first was his mother, for whom he felt a love all the greater for being mixed with despair. For Hessye's eyes were fading every year, and it was only a question of time before she would be totally blind. To spare her anxiety, the son put some limits on his dissipations and managed at least to sleep every night under his own roof.

The second saving influence was the Russian theatre.

In the face of sternest interdiction, the Jew, from time immemorial, has been an inveterate playgoer. It was so in Rome, it was so in Odessa, and it remains so today, when every Broadway manager knows that on Passover and Yom Kippur he will have a bad house. It happened that Aaron Trachtenberg, the great magnate of the Adler family, was an impassioned devotee of the theatre, a true "patriot" as they were then called. This family king had a sneaking affection for his unregenerate nephew. Seeing him lost and unhappy, he took him to the play. Odessa had always been noted for its superb acting companies, and young Adler caught fire the first night. He began to haunt the gallery, going almost nightly to the City Theatre or to the Marinsky.

At just that time two leading ladies, the lovely Madame Glebova and the equally celebrated Madame Kozlova, graced the stage of the City. The whole town knew that the bitterest, most implacable rivalry existed between these two actresses, and audiences at the City were divided between the *Glebovtzas* and the *Kozlovtzas*. Especially in the gallery, where there is less politeness, feeling ran high.

Finding himself in a war, the hero of the Moldovanka promptly chose sides: He became Madame Glebova's adorer and "patriot." He has been credited with choosing this actress because she represented the newer school of realism.

He himself makes no such claim: "I cannot say Kozlova was a worse actress than Glebova. I was still an undeveloped boy with a very limited understanding of such matters. What I saw clearly was that Glebova was a very beautiful woman, and I greeted her with bravos so stormy the whole theatre took fire from my enthusiasm."

Now it so happened that a certain Fraulein Aranowitz presided over the gallery buffet of the City Theatre. All the students up there were in love with this pretty girl, and whole crowds of them spent so much time buying her sugared drinks, fruits, and bonbons they often missed half the play. Because Adler came so often, this young lady grew to know him better than the others. A gentle Platonic romance sprang up, and it was through her that Glebova heard of this great admirer. The actress took an acute interest in the matter, and told Fraulein Aronowitz to bring her friend and present him.

The meeting took place in the celebrated *artiste*'s dressing room. Apparently she liked this handsome young Jew whose eyes shone with such ardent, respectful admiration. Her mind, however, was on business. She offered him a post as her *ataman*, the leader of her claque. Adler immediately accepted.

His new post was one of utmost importance. Professional jealousy in those days could be a deadly serious matter. No player, however talented, could hold his position without protection. The claque, paid to applaud their favorite, also had to deal with the plots and disturbances created by rival factions. Insults, blows, and even worse were sometimes traded, and things up in the gallery could take an ugly, and even a murderous, turn. Adler cared nothing about all this. He thought himself the luckiest man in the world. Overnight he had stepped into the innermost political workings of the profession.

"Nightly, like Hindenberg at his high observation post, I took my seat in the last row of the gallery. From there I could signal my army, strategically scattered around me. Under my generalship Glebova received such acclamations that her rival was completely crushed. It made no difference that the *Kozlovtzas* below looked upward, growling, 'Yankele Kulatchnik is at work tonight!' Though the secret of these ovations was known, enthusiasm in the theatre is catching, and Glebova's triumphs over her rival grew ever greater and more proud."

The actress was pleased with her *ataman*. Once, after an especially good reception, she made him a gift of a hundred roubles. He divided half the sum among his army and spent a good part of the remainder sending glorious bouquets over the footlights to his queen.

Such demonstrations seriously dimmed the luster of Madame Kozlova. She tried to make a secret pact with her rival's *ataman*, but Adler remained loyal to his idol.

He soon became a well-known figure, respected and even feared, for the critics took their lead from him. Happy the actor he greeted after the performance with a hearty *"Molodyets!"* Miserable the unfortunate he passed in silence, and with lowered eyes; he knew he would get bad reviews! Even the anti-Semitic Azmirov of the *Novy Telegraf*, who often baited the audience because so many Jews came, took his cue from the impassioned young critic in the gallery.

Glebova, a generous woman and fond of her *ataman*, guessed at a secret wish. What young man, handsome, fiery, steeped in theatre, did not long in his heart to be an actor? Glebova arranged for Adler to speak to Miloslavsky, the famous regisseur of the City Theatre. Adler went home in a state of intense excitement and did not shut his eyes all night. All his doubts rose up to confound him.

"Could I, Yankele Adler, rise to such heights as to be an actor, an artist? I, who had roamed the pavements with Buff's Army, who had boxed publicly in the Moldovanka? True, I had rubbed shoulders with actors by now. I knew they were big drinkers, big card players, big woman chasers. But still, they were such gentlemen! Their manners! Their clothes alone! All night I tossed, unable to quiet my hopes or my fears."

The following night, Adler met the famous regisseur on the dismantled stage of the City Theatre. After a few minutes of talk, Miloslavsky advised him to turn his attention to some other field of endeavor. Asked for his reason, he replied, "Your appearance would assure you of success, but as a Jew you could not hope to rise in the theatre."

The interview lasted less than ten minutes. The young

man left the City by the stage door. At midnight Richelevskaya Street was still alive with lights and crowded with pleasure seekers. A dozen restaurants and cafes beckoned out of the winter darkness. He walked on, a slight smile on his lips. The King of the Gallery had just been told that all this did not belong to him.

In the days that followed he put the hateful scene with Miloslavsky out of his mind. Like everything that lowered his pride, he refused to acknowledge or remember it.

Strange things spring from seeds buried so deep. From the cold "facts" on the pitiless lips of a fine Russian gentleman would come an ambition that grazed the stars in its leap.

In 1876 the Bulgarians, living under the rule of the Ottoman Empire, rose up in revolt. The Turks put down the rebellion, and all over Europe a horrified cry of atrocities went up. Pan-Slav sentiment swept Russia. A Christian people rebelling against the Turkish yoke! A Slav people! Huge sums were collected in churches throughout the land, and hundreds of Russian volunteers left daily for the fighting front. On April 12, 1877, the Tsar declared a war practically forced on him by popular enthusiasm.

In doing so he was continuing two hundred years of Russian effort to expand at the expense of the declining Ottoman Empire. While Alexander II did not dare another attempt at Constantinople, he wanted to regain command of the Black Sea and to get back some of the territory lost after the Crimean defeat twenty years earlier.

The whole country enthusiastically welcomed the "liberal" war for a subjugated people. In Odessa martial music filled the air, and crowds waited daily for bulletins on the war. The town was full of rumors. One day word spread that the Turkish fleet could be sighted on the Black Sea. Within an hour both shops selling optical equipment had not a spyglass left; everyone who was able had rushed down to the Tchornomorsky Prospekt.* Sure enough, through a glass, one could see the Turkish ironclads on the horizon! Anxiety gripped the city at news that the Russian army had crossed the Danube into Roumania. Wild jubilation followed when it was disclosed that Roumania, chafing under the Turkish Protectorate, had made a secret treaty with Russia and was, in fact, her ally!

* Black Sea Boulevard.

The Russian Commissariat was stationed in Jassy, a Roumanian town with direct rail connections to Odessa. Hundreds of people, Jews and Christians alike, left for Roumania. Everyone remembered the Crimean War, the corruption, the scandals in the Supply Department. Every flour merchant, every speculator in hay, in wood, in foodstuffs ran to Roumania to get rich. And in fact, many of these people came back with fortunes, built homes, and lived afterward like wealthy men.

Rosenberg was off, one of the first to go. Adler wanted to go with him, but instead was drafted into the army. "A wail went up all through the family that Yankele must go to war and be killed," he writes. "Yankele alone was happy. Go to war, have adventures, shoot Turks! What could be better? That the Turks might shoot me never entered my mind!"

The ever-helpful Olga Petrovna had an uncle who was an army doctor. Through this connection, Adler escaped the army and was drafted instead into the medical corps of the Red Cross. He emerged after several months as a full-fledged *Sanitar,* a sort of assistant doctor.

"Do you imagine you see a mere actor when you come to the theatre?" he would exultantly ask his audience forty years later. "You are mistaken! I am a bit of a doctor, too! I served Alexander II as a medical man in 1877, and received from him a gold medal for outstanding ability."

On a fall day in 1877, Adler marched off to war. About a thousand men went off that day, all parading from the Tsaronsky Barracks to the railroad depot, a march of several miles through the principal streets of Odessa. They went in three contingents—volunteers, recruits, and members of the medical corps. Rousing military music accompanied them all the way, women on balconies threw flowers and presents to the soldiers, and the families of the men ran alongside the line of march. The Jewish families wept. They could not forget the days when soldiers had served for twenty-five years and conscription amounted to a death sentence.

At the depot the real crying began. As the soldiers boarded the train that would take them to the front, every window full of men waving, laughing, Adler had one terrible moment. In the crowd below he saw his mother's white face, and as the train began to move, heard her low cry, "Oh, my Yankele, oh, my Yankele!" At that moment he realized he might never come back.

As events turned out, he went no further than one day's

ride. The soldiers detrained that evening at a town called Bender, where some wealthy and patriotic German colonists were building a military hospital. Men were needed to staff it, and the medical corps were lined up for the inspection of a General Meschersky. The General's wife happened to see a handsome soldier in the ranks and thought it a pity he should be killed at the front. For no better reason than this, Adler was called out and the train went on without him. He was furious at being deprived of his adventure.

All in all, he spent some six months in the military hospital at Bender. He flirted with a blond German nurse with whom he shared night duty in the typhus ward, fell in love with half a dozen girls in the town, and ended up having such a good time in Bender he forgot all about the war.

The Jews of Bender were concerned that their wounded should receive kosher food and proper rites in the event of death. In these matters they found they could work through the young *Sanitar*. Adler acquired great prestige in the eyes of these pious men. And their houses were full of beautiful Jewish girls! "What happiness in those enchanted Bender nights, God above, what happiness! May they not be reckoned against me, I will have so much less of Paradise!" he piously wrote of his army days.

His most serious Bender love was a gentle girl called Pessye, the daughter of one of the town's wealthiest men—a faithful Jewish child with dark braids, dark eyes, long brows, always silent, always soberly dressed. Adler thought seriously of marrying this girl, but was soon given to understand that this was out of the question. Though the young medical man was respected, his face, his bearing, his whole manner gave away a licentious past. The father, scenting a romance, remained friendly toward the young *Sanitar*, but stopped inviting him to his home.

Love will have its way. In the small hours of the night, Adler would go by the window and quietly whistle. The girl would spring from her bed and steal out the door to meet him. He would throw his military cloak about her shoulders and together they would walk through the first gray rainy light. It seemed to rain almost continually in this town, and these army romances always mingled in his mind with the damp back porches, the back streets, and muddy walks of Bender.

At the end of six months the draftees of 1877 were ordered home. Adler should have rejoiced; instead his heart ached. The soldiers in the typhus ward, Jew and Christian alike, had grown dear to him. He had sat beside them, read to them, written letters home for them. It gave him a pang that they should lie there, ill and suffering, while he went back with his strong body into the beautiful world.

He seems also to have broken his heart saying good-bye to both his sweethearts. The pretty German nurse turned pale, but mastered herself. A handclasp, a murmured, "*Adieu, liebe Yakob,*" "*Adieu, liebe Matilda,*" and it was over.

It went harder with the innocent Pessye. She turned white as a ghost, her hands burned as with fever. She whispered, "Take me with you to Odessa. We'll get married there!" She brushed aside his talk of money, flew to her father's safe, and opened it. Adler reeled. Pack on pack of red and blue assignats. More! Diamonds, pearls, jeweled watches, gold and silver candelabra. And this good Jewish daughter feverishly told him to take it all.

Thoughts of crime whirled in his brain. He saw himself a rich man, son-in-law of the wealthy Chasidic Jew. The dearest, truest girl in the world would be his wife. He would quiet his driving blood, tear himself away from bad company, become a citizen, a respected member of the community. Yet he could not do it.

"Stronger than all temptation," he writes, "was the thought of losing my freedom, my wild, roving bachelorhood. To give up my glorious Odessa for muddy, dull, sleepy Bender? Never again to see the beautiful cheat, Olga Petrovna? Never again to see Rosenberg!"

He swore he would come back, swore he would arrange everything. He fell on her breast and wept, mingling his tears with hers. "And I went away," he relates, "and forgot the innocent Pessye, as I had forgotten so many others, and as so many others had forgotten me."

He had come back at the right moment. War madness held the city, and it was a good time for heroes. He got a job in the distribution department of the *Odessa Messenger*, and took up his old life: the theatre, Glebova's dressing room, always open now to her old *ataman*, *cafés chantants* everywhere, and pleasure at every hand.

With all this he felt an emptiness. He was wasting his life, and found no meaning in his round of pleasures and dissipations. He had disappointed his family. Aaron Trachtenberg had wanted to make a serious merchant of him, and in the dandyish costume of his nephew the old man saw the ruin of his hopes. At times, face to face with his uncle, the boy felt as though he were "in a narrow coat." He was ashamed of his life. He longed at times to change his ways, reform, do better. He would hang uneasily about his parents when these moods came over him, or write letters to Pessye in Bender. He wished he had a friend to whom he could tell his trouble.

One day in his office at the *Odessa Messenger,* he noticed a peculiar news item: "Considerable interest," the item read, "has been aroused in Bucharest by performances of the Yiddish theatre under the direction of the poet Avrom Goldfaden." Adler, astonished at "Yiddish theatre," read on, and then sprang to his feet, his heart going fast. Listed among the actors were the names Jacob Spivakovsky and Yisrol Rosenberg.

Spivakovsky, Adler knew well. They had met at a time when Adler had performed, not very successfully, in some Russian amateur theatricals. Handsome as a prince, of an aristocratic Jewish family, Spivakovsky was the *jeune premier* and star of these productions. But it was the second name that left Adler thunderstruck.

"Yet it was there, plain for all to see. 'The Odessa attorney-at-law, Yisrol Rosenberg.' Then it was he! My Rosenberg was still among the living. He had swum back to me! And in what a new and interesting form! Rosenberg an actor? A *Yiddish* actor?"

In an instant all his melancholia, all his vague malaise fell away. New life, new energy surged through him. He had a purpose in life. He wanted the Yiddish theatre to come to Odessa. And he knew that somehow he must bring this about.

Before that day was over, he had seen to it that the news had spread throughout the Jewish quarter of Odessa. Next, he sought out Rosenberg's parents, learned from them of his whereabouts, and wrote to him. Rosenberg wrote back. A lively correspondence sprang up.

Adler had some influence on the *Odessa Messenger.* He managed to get a second item inserted about the theatre in Bucharest, and in addition, an editorial statement that these artists, so successful in Roumania, would receive a welcome in Odessa. The editorial caused a stir. The *Novy Telegraf,* despite its anti-Semitic policy, ran its own item about the Roumanian actors, suggesting that it would be a good thing to allow this troupe, "showing the negative side of Jewish life," to give performances in Odessa.

Rosenberg, encouraged by these signs of interest, sent word that he was coming. Adler counted the days. He was obsessed. Day and night he thought only of this theatre, "born under the thunder of the cannon of Plevna." He pictured it as heroic, magnificent, full of Jewish sorrow, Jewish fortitude, and sweetened with beautiful Hebrew melody and dance.

He waited for Rosenberg, on fire with excitement, joy, and loftiest expectation.

3

Curtain Rise at Jassy

> FIRST CHOSID
> If only in the lottery's grand drawing
> My great creator from his place on high
> Might grant that I should get the lucky
>   number
> Ah then, with all my riches I would buy—
>
> ALL
> What? What? What?
>
> FIRST CHOSID
> A factory of Purim bells and rattles,
> Pinwheels and tiny flags a sight to see,
> A pastry shop of tasty pies and pancakes
> And all for my dear little wife and me!
> Recruits

The Yiddish theatre, now an actuality in Roumania, had almost come into existence a number of times before. As far back as the sixteenth century, while Sephardic Jews were writing biblical dramas in Spanish, the ghetto Jews of Amsterdam were being entertained by merry comedies in Yiddish. A written manuscript in a Dutch-Yiddish dialect existed as early as 1598. This was passed from hand to hand, and though the subject was entirely profane, was performed every year at Purim. Entitled *The Busy Doings of Yeklein, His Wife Kindlein, and Their Three Little Sons So Fine*, it seems to have been a malicious lampoon on a local family.

In the first years of the eighteenth century a manuscript with the title *A Fine New Ahasuerus Play* found its way into print. The coarse jokes and low comedy, stemming from the

All Fool's Day spirit of the Middle Ages, shocked the cultured Frankfurt Jews, and all the copies were burned.

Several years later students from the *yeshivas* of Frankfurt and Hamburg took part in the production of a Yiddish play by one Berman called *The Selling of Joseph into Egypt*. The piece was apparently low in original ideas but strong on spectacle, for the audience was dazzled by fire, heard thunder, and saw the heavens open. It ran for a month, alternating with *David and Goliath*, another play by the same author. Such crowds came that two soldiers had to be posted at the door of the theatre to keep order. The authorities, alarmed at the number of Christians attending, finally stopped the performances.

Isolated attempts of the same kind were later made in Holland, Germany, Poland, and Russia. Nothing came of them. Those performances not halted by civic prohibition met with opposition from within the Jewish community itself. In Warsaw the disapproval of the Rabbinate went so far as an appeal to the city magistrate to stop the performances. The Orthodoxy tolerated such spectacles only at Purim—the Jewish Carnival, the one day of the year when, in celebration of victory over a wicked enemy, the Jew is allowed to get drunk, to frolic in the streets, and even, with the full approval of the most pious, to take part in theatricals.

With performances confined to one day of the year, the Purim play degenerated over the years into a naive charade for children. There were wandering mountebanks and clowns who performed tricks for a livelihood, but they were despised by respectable people. It was not until the nineteenth century that a professional theatre was able to take root. By that time the growth of city life, the first miracles of science, and the rationalism of a revolutionary age were making inroads on religious authority everywhere.

The groundwork for a Reform Judaism had been laid a century earlier when a hunchback from the ghetto of Dessau rose to high position, came under the influence of the Enlightenment, and fathered the *Haskala*—"The Awakening." Immensely wealthy, immensely cultivated, Moses Mendelssohn made it his life work to break the barrier that separated his people from the world. In an age when science, progress, and the brotherhood of man were not seen as separate entities, but as a single new ideal for all mankind, Mendelssohn believed that, armed with a secular education, the Jew, remaining a Jew, would take his rightful place in world culture.

Mendelssohn's children deleted from this formula only the words, "remaining a Jew." They married brilliantly, entered the Catholic or German Protestant Church, and from this safer position continued to espouse the cause of Judaism. His daughter, Dorothea Brendel, helped to found the Society for Jewish Culture and Science, that flourished in the liberal Berlin of the 1820s. For a time Heinrich Heine acted as secretary of this organization, but he soon gave up the post, complaining that the rich Jews did not need the Society and the poor ones had neverheard of it.

Too lively to give up the ghost, the *Haskala* traveled eastward. It was almost a hundred years on the journey, and it arrived in Russia with a poorer dress and a more tired face. Anti-Semitism had survived the Age of Reason, as it would later survive the triumph of the proletariat. The world had grown a century older since Moses Mendelssohn had tried to save his people from a ghetto existence. In all that time no Jewish scholar had spoken from the platform of a Russian university, no Russian Heine made his way into the literary circles of Moscow and St. Petersburg. Russia, bulwark against the rising tide of European liberalism, had not even given citizenship to its Jews.

The intellectuals of the Russian Pale had small hopes of entering the great Christian world around them. As a sort of compensation, they had remained closer to their fellow Jews. To reach these masses, it became necessary to speak their language. Yiddish, despised in the distinguished Jewish salons of Austria and Berlin, became the *cause célèbre* of the new *Haskala*.

This language of the Diaspora, born of Middle German crossed with Hebrew—this "jargon," retaining the gutturals of its passage through Holland, corrupted by Greek, further invaded by Spanish, Polish, Russian, and French—quickly took on a strong, expressive idiom of its own. Shaped by the living experience of a people, it developed a mood and feeling so original that it could not be translated without serious loss; and in its essence, it resembled German as little as Chinese. It was, moreover, the everyday speech of the East European Jew, while Hebrew, except for religious use, was known only to the scholar.

Now, while it is easy to imagine a lecture hall filled entirely by scholars, it is somehow impossible to think of them lined up at the box office of a theatre. The actors of the *commedia dell'arte* knew no Latin; they spoke their lines in the Italian of the common man. And the Yiddish theatre, like the *commedia*, came to life speaking the language of *Amcho*, the people. That the birth took place in Roumania was the result of the accidental meeting of the right man with the right circumstances.

When Avrom Goldfaden came to the town of Jassy in 1876, he hoped to make a living there as a journalist. He was at this time thirty-six years old, already a well-known poet and famous as a writer of folk songs loved by the poor.

The son of a watchmaker, Goldfaden was born in 1840 in the town of Old Constantine. At the age of eight he wrote a Hebrew poem and was given the name "Avremele Bodchen" (Little Avrom the Merrymaker). By fifteen he had already composed a score of folk songs. He knew nothing of composition, and all his life wrote in a notation of his own invention.

Because he feared his son would be conscripted, Goldfaden's father placed him in the rabbinical school at Zhitomir, a decision causing great scandal among the Orthodox Jews of the town. The rabbinical schools, established by Nicholas I in opposition to the Jewish *cheder* and *yeshiva*, were part of a ruthless "Russification" program, and great efforts were made to convert the students to the Greek Orthodox faith. Such efforts, however, met with little success, and since the Crown Schools offered students an excellent modern education as well as purely Jewish studies, progressive scholars welcomed the opportunity to teach. These *maskilim*, or followers of the *Haskala*, ran the rabbinical schools on extremely liberal lines. Dancing, masked balls, and visits to the theatre were all encouraged in a deliberate effort to bring Jewish youth into the modern world.

Goldfaden's teachers in Zhitomir took a special interest in him, encouraging his talent for light verse and his love of the "jargon," for this was the name even its defenders gave their tongue. And strange to say, this imperious youth, proud and pleasure-loving in the extreme, had a marvelous ear for the speech of his people and the warmest understanding of their most intimate feelings.

In 1862 Goldfaden appeared in the school production of the comedy melodrama *Serkele,* by Dr. Solomon Ettinger, earliest and most genial of the Russian *maskilim*. This is the first known production of any modern Yiddish play, and it is noteworthy that Goldfaden not only played the title role but also took an active part in all aspects of the production. The play created a stir in Zhitomir, and all the *maskilim* in town came to see it.

By the time he graduated, Goldfaden was already famous as a writer of poems and folk songs. Wires were pulled for him, and he got a teaching post at the Crown school in Odessa. Since the pay was poor he accepted an invitation to live with his uncle, a man called Kesselman. He came to Odessa, took up his teaching post, and began contributing regularly to several Jewish periodicals. He liked the city and soon began to feel very much at home there.

Kesselman and his wife, on the other hand, grew dissatisfied with their brilliant guest. Goldfaden was making no effort to get a better job. He spent his spare time roaming about with the writer Linetzki, went to the theatre every night, and came home at four in the morning with a coachman, rousing the whole house with his noise. Worst of all, he failed to propose to Kesselman's daughter. Uncle and nephew had a talk, and Goldfaden, who had a violent temper, flared up and left the house.

His friend the philosopher Werbel took him in, and while living there Goldfaden brought out two collections of poetry. The first produced little stir. The second included the famous *"Dus Pintale Yid,"* the first popular verses to emphasize the pride of the Jew rather than his suffering and to express his joy in his traditions. The poem awoke a tremendous enthusiasm, and the phrase *"Dus Pintale Yid,"* summing up all those traits of personality, thought, and character that make up the Jewishness of the Jew, became a permanent part of the Yiddish language.

In this collection Goldfaden also made his first attempts at the dramatic form, one of them a little rhymed dialogue called "Two Neighbors." Here two young mothers shower compliments on each other, each making extravagant predictions for the other's child. But while the neighbors embrace, their children fall out. Each mother rushes to her own child, scolds at the other woman, and reads out a long list of all her faults. This slight sketch is so fresh, so charming, and warm that these two Jewish ladies of another time seem to dance slowly before us in a circle of antique sunlight. Every line is full of authentic folk feeling and yet graceful and delicate, a combination of qualities special to this very talented writer.

The full-length play *Auntie Sosya* was Goldfaden's revenge on Kesselman and his wife. He had drawn his plot from the incidents of his stay in their home. The play was later performed many times, but never in Odessa.

Goldfaden in the meantime had married Werbel's daughter. Since the newlyweds were poor, the poet put aside his pride, borrowed some money, and opened a hat shop.

The shop did well as long as hats were delivered on credit. When it came time to pay, Goldfaden sang songs to his creditors. Extremely prolific, he composed dozens of these, some of them pornographic. Amusing as this method of payment was, it could not work indefinitely. In the end the poet-shopkeeper was forced to declare bankruptcy. He owed such a huge sum of money he had to flee Odessa entirely, and soon after left Russia for Germany.

Goldfaden took up medicine in Munich, gave it up, went to Lemberg, ran into Linetzki there and with him started a journal called *Yisrolik*. The magazine lasted three months. By that time Goldfaden had quarreled with Linetzki and gone on to Leipzig. Here, while he tried to launch another journal, he heard the operas of Verdi, Meyerbeer, and Wagner and saw Salvini in *Othello*.

In 1876 he was in Bukovina, near the Roumanian border. He had started another journal called *Die Israelitische Volks Vochen Blatt* (*The Jewish Weekly Journal*). Though the *Vochen Blatt* sold poorly, Goldfaden received a mysterious sum of money every month from Jassy. He made inquiries and learned that a man called Libresko was selling the journal there at the rate of one subscription a day.

"Dear Unknown Friend Libresko," Goldfaden wrote. "My *Blatt* would be a success, but changing the name kills the business.* To bring it out again I need three thousand gulden as security. Since there is no such regulation in Roumania, I can issue my journal there. Please let me know if this is possible. Can you advance me enough money to come to Jassy?"

The sum he requested came by the next post, and Goldfaden and his wife took the train across the Roumanian border. They were met at the Jassy station by all the *maskilim* in the town. Isaac Libresko turned out to be a learned young man who had become infected with the *Haskala* after reading

---

* Jewish periodicals were limited to a certain number of issues. After these had appeared, the journal could only be brought out under another name. A high fee apparently was demanded as security each time this was done.

Linetzki's novels. Now treasurer of the progressive society Lebanon and active in all cultural affairs, he had a practical turn of mind, limitless energy, and a capacity for infinite devotion. Goldfaden had, in fact, stumbled on just the man indispensable to the success of any artistic enterprise.

The folk singers Yisrol Gradner and Moishe Finkel were performing in Jassy every night in the vinegarden of one Shimen Marks. Since Goldfaden needed money, an "evening" was arranged by Lebanon at which he would declaim some of his verses, sing a few songs, and for this would receive 100 francs.

The evening was a fiasco. "Shimen Marks did pretty well out of it," Goldfaden comments irritably. "His place was packed, but whether with people or wild animals I can't say. Instead of the usual comedian with tattered shoes and stockings to his knees, the audience beheld an elegant gentleman in a frock coat, a man with a serious air that instilled respect. In a deep silence I begin my well-known poem *'Dus Pintale Yid.'* I recite loudly, ecstatically. They hold their breath. I end. Silence. I bow. Silence. I leave the stage. Silence. I tell myself they don't understand. Perhaps they don't care for patriotic poems. I will give them a humorous one. 'The Angel.' I recite the first part. Silence. The second part. Silence. The silence would have been all right, but when I go off I hear whistles—hisses!"

As Libresko tells the story, Goldfaden's failure was his own doing. "People had paid higher prices that night. They were used to Gradner, who sang with charm and finesse, while Goldfaden had no voice at all. Furthermore, it seemed to them Goldfaden was making fun of them—and for this some of them were so angry they wanted to beat him up. Gradner and I had to put him in a carriage and send him home."

Several people claim credit for the idea of starting a Yiddish theatre. Libresko says it was his wife who advised Goldfaden to give up journalism and become a playwright. Others assert that Gradner put on sketches and short plays long before Goldfaden arrived in Jassy. Goldfaden himself claims the idea. It is certain, at any rate, that Goldfaden, having conceived of a piece for the theatre, sent for Yisrol Gradner. Gradner heard him out, an inspired look on his face, and answered like the Israelites when Moses came from Mt. Sinai: "We have listened, and will obey!"

Gradner came to Goldfaden a day or so later with three or

four young men, all willing to take part in the new venture. Among them was a seventeen-year-old boy called Socher Goldstein, an apprentice to a saddle maker. This young man, Gradner's assistant in the wine cellars of the town, was unusually lanky and tall, but had a pleasing voice and a gentle personality. Goldfaden thought he might play girls. The rest, he decided, were fit only to be used as extras.

He was already at work on a two-act comedy with an improvised text around a slender plot line. Rehearsals took place in Libresko's home. The actors were coached as to when to kiss, when to quarrel, when to go into their musical routines. The songs and dances were the most important part of the whole thing. "Out of this, to my sorrow, came a piece—a nonsense, a hodgepodge!" Goldfaden writes. "I don't even remember the name of it!"

The comedy has survived, however, and is surprisingly like the first plays of the *commedia dell'arte*. It was based on the age-old love triangle, with Gradner, like Punchinello, receiving some well-deserved blows with a broomstick at the end. This first play of the Yiddish theatre was performed twice, on October 5 and October 8, 1876, in Shimen Marks's garden. It had only a moderate success, and Goldfaden wisely did not repeat it.

His second attempt, based on two songs of Socher Goldstein's, met with an obstacle. With the fall holidays over, performances in Shimen Marks's garden had come to an end. The owner of another hall, an Orthodox Jew, told Libresko he would not dirty his premises with anything so profane as Yiddish theatre.

Goldfaden, together with Gradner, Socher Goldstein, a bookbinder called Schwartz, and one or two others, set off for the town of Batushan. Money for the trip was supplied by Lebanon. On this modest scale, the Yiddish theatre began.

Batushan had a large population of Galician Jews who knew Gradner and loved him. Goldfaden, counting on this, took the biggest theatre in town. He ran into immediate trouble because of a recruiting drive. Six months before the outbreak of the Russo-Turkish War the alert had sounded, and orders went out to round up men for the army. The Roumanians did their recruiting in rough style. Officers simply went into all schools, cafes, and theatres, dragging every likely prospect off to the barracks. Questions were asked later.

Overnight the young men of Batushan vanished. Some went into hiding, others fled across the border to Bukavina. An innkeeper was kind enough to let the actors hide in his garret. Here, with time on their hands, they prepared their repertoire.

Goldfaden, with a sure theatrical instinct, realized that with only one reliable performer, he needed a foolproof idea. He chose as his theme the tribulations of a raw recruit in the army, a subject still successful in our own times.

Gradner had a song about a soldier called *"Klugt Sich"* ("Bewail Your Fate"). Goldfaden took this ballad, strung it together with some songs of his own, composed a few new ones, wrote a monologue in the second act for his hero, and *told* the rest to the actors. He called the play *Recruits*.

In the meantime, the recruiting drive came to an end. The young men returned, and the whole town took on a livelier aspect. Goldfaden and his actors came down out of the attic, took their theatre, and put on their play.

Goldfaden was in a terrible state during the first performance. Several members of his cast had deserted because of the recruiting scare, and Gradner and Socher Goldstein had to double in several parts. The extras were townspeople, men who had never been on a stage in their lives. Goldfaden passed continually from the audience to the actors backstage, and shouted frantic directions from the wings.

The play included one stunning theatrical effect. The close of the second act called for a military march across the stage with fife and drum. For this scene, Goldfaden engaged real soldiers, a touch of "production value" that produced a roar of enthusiasm. And indeed, it is hard to think of a better effect during a popular war.

Recruits drew good audiences in Batushan, but once expenses were paid, hardly any money remained for the actors. They moved on.

The tiny troupe toured the Roumanian provinces all that fall and winter. Their appearances aroused unparalleled curiosity and excitement, but they rarely cleared a profit. One by one the men who had started with them dropped out. Finally only Gradner, Socher Goldstein, and Goldfaden remained. If not for the help of the always-generous Lebanon, the three of them might not have survived the hardships of that winter.

In February, just before Purim, the troupe arrived in Galatz. There was a branch of Lebanon in this town, and the actors got a heartening welcome. A temporary stage was erected for them in the Hotel Sager; they were housed in comfortable quarters and assured of a well-filled hall.

It was in Galatz that a woman first appeared on the Yiddish stage. Goldfaden, always on the lookout, saw possibilities in a sixteen-year-old seamstress called Soore (Sarah) Siegel. This pretty, dark-eyed girl had a charming, buxom figure, and a voice so remarkably sweet that all Galatz called her *pasarica*—the bird.

Goldfaden had tried in several other towns to bring an actress into the troupe, but had always failed. No respectable Jewish girl was willing to show herself on a stage, and to bring a woman of loose character before the Jewish public would be risking a terrible scandal. Soore Siegel herself was burning to appear, but her mother held out against it. Goldfaden put forth all his charm. Either this succeeded or the prestige of Lebanon told in his favor, for the girl was allowed to play.

Goldfaden was presenting his first "dramatic" operetta, a piece called *The Intrigue, or Dvosye the Gossip*. It was his most ambitious effort so far, and he wanted to put it on in Galatz. The original manuscript, written out carefully in Goldfaden's hand, was cast as follows:

> JOSEPH, a young man about thirty-two years old ...... Gradner
> ROUCHEL, his wife, twenty-two years old . the girl, Soore Siegel
> HERSCHALE, their son, eight years old ....
> ....we will see. A child will be found.
> JOSEPH KURTMAN .... a street boy
> CHAIM, Rouchel's brother, a Jew about forty ...... a street boy
> DVOSYE, their neighbor, a woman of forty ... Socher Goldstein

Goldfaden put in two easy numbers for the new actress, a duet with Gradner called "A Kiss" and another song, stolen from the popular operetta *The Daughter of Hell.*

The Intrigue was Goldfaden's first success. The Galatz newspapers praised it, and Roumanian actors came backstage after the first performance with compliments for the whole cast.

Soore Siegel, however, was not permitted to appear after the first performance. Furious domestic scenes and quarrels ended with her mother's immovable dictum: When the daughter married, she could do as she liked; while she lived in the home of her parents she would not set foot on the stage.

These actors had built a world so frail and unsubstantial that the least adverse wind could blow it down. Yet no one has ever entered that world without an extraordinary sensation of freedom and happiness. Soore Siegel, unable to get her way by tears and domestic scenes, risked a secret meeting with Goldfaden.

Desperate cases call for desperate measures. Goldfaden needed this child. He could see only one way to get her. Both he and Gradner were married men, but Socher Goldstein at eighteen was still single. He was prevailed on, for the good of the troupe, to marry Soore Siegel.

The girl herself seems not even to have hesitated. This sixteen-year-old seamstress, destined to become one of the Yiddish theatre's most beloved stars, was ready to give up honor, comfort, and happiness itself for the life of the theatre. A passion for the stage was to rage within her all her life, and in the end it killed her.

Though the wedding ceremony was performed, the company had to leave Galatz without the new prima donna. An outraged brother had found some loophole, some legal formality that prevented the bride from leaving Galatz. The facts grow hazy here, and something about this incident seems to have been concealed.

The company went on without her to Braila. Here a heated debate broke out. The Braila intellectuals complained that *Recruits* made fun of Jewish soldiers and demanded that Goldfaden withdraw it. He hastily wrote a new piece, a two-act operetta titled *Granny and Her Granddaughter*. Since they were again without an actress, Gradner played the grandmother and Socher Goldstein played the girl.

The piece went over well, and Goldfaden, fired by ambition, left for Bucharest. There he was able to arrange only one performance at the Jignitza Theatre, but got an offer from a man by the name of Lazare who had a hall in the Jewish quarter.

It was this Lazare who went out to Braila and put up the money to bring the actors to the capital.

4

The Rain of Gold

> Farewell, the worn-out lectern where
>   I studied,
> The benches, tables, dusty window, too.
> Tzulik is called and must defend his
>   country,
> Tzulik must bid these friends a last
>   adieu.
>
> Peace, all the holy books the student
>   pondered!
> Rest once again, rest in a happy hour!
> He comes no more to turn your ancient
>   pages,
> He goes to fight for Fatherland and
>   Tsar!
>
> Recruits

The troupe gave one performance of *Recruits* at the Jignitza, then went on to Lazare's Hall in the Jewish quarter. Here they played their longest engagement so far, twelve performances over a period of a month.

To keep his small audience coming back, Goldfaden had to continually turn out plays, curtain-raisers, and couplets for the divertissements between the acts. He also had to take care of business problems, bribe officials, rehearse the actors, and often as not, jump in and play a part himself. The man was single-handedly creating a theatre out of little more than his own energy and talent. He may perhaps be forgiven if, along with so much that was original, he borrowed too, with the recklessness of his desperate necessity. It must be admitted that one early operetta opens with a chorus from *The Flying Dutchman.* On the other hand, he was also turning out classics like *The Witch,* a play in which we find characters so real, dialogue so fresh and authentic that reading it a century later we are breathless to know what will happen next. *The Witch* was performed for some fifty years in the Yiddish theatre, the songs are remembered to this day, and the character of Hotzmach, the peddler, has passed into Jewish folklore.

Throughout all the early pieces, even those that are imitative or entirely trivial, we find the running thread of the *Haskala:* whether it be comedy or melodrama, the Jew is seen as standing between twin dangers—the temptation to assimilate into the immoral non-Jewish world around him and on the other hand, the peril of sinking into bigotry, darkness, and superstition. Goldfaden's hero always represents progress and enlightenment; his antagonist, usually of the older generation, is capable of any absurdity or villainy in the service of his bigoted faith.

For a short time the company at Lazare's Hall included a woman who had taken up with one of the actors in Jassy. Goldfaden allowed her a tryout in his two-act operetta *The Dumb Bride.* Since she played the bride, she had no lines at all.

Rosa Friedman had some years before sung and danced in the coffee houses of Constantinople. Her first youth was gone, and she had lost her looks as well as her voice. Her past in Constantinople told against her, too. After *The Dumb Bride,* Goldfaden let her come on only as an extra, and she soon gave up and went back to Jassy.

The lack of actors continued to be a serious problem. Goldfaden had been hampered by this in the provinces, and here in Bucharest, where he wanted to put on something worth seeing, the need was growing urgent. Until now he had searched among the folk singers for potential actors. Now he turned to the choirs of the *chazzonim*—the cantors.

This was an excellent field for his purposes. The cantor, revered by Jews for his evocation of the divine spirit, was in many cases a virtuoso indifferent to everything but his art. In selecting his choir, neither piety nor learning were of any use to him; what he wanted was musical talent. As a result, his young *meshurers*—choir members—were usually blessed with a healthy appetite for the pleasures of this world and a total absence of interest in the next. They sang prayers in the synagogue, but they sang very differently at weddings, where they were in universal demand for their liveliness and their dancing. B. Gorin, in his classic *History of the Yiddish Theatre,* writes: "In every Jewish town, the *meshurers* were the gayest, the least reverent part of the population. No one was so holy as to be safe from their laughter, nothing so solemn it escaped their jests. They were the troubadors of the people, bringing song, dance and gaiety wherever they went."

The choir of the famous Bucharest *chazzen* Israel Kupfer was made up of just such lively, happy-go-lucky young men, all greatly interested in picking up a little extra money. Zelig Mogulesko, leader of the choir, was known to all Bucharest. He entertained at Kupfer's home every Saturday night, and the wealthiest Jews of the city came to see his extraordinary imitations of the famous Roumanian comedians. Goldfaden, immediately interested, asked a friend to bring him together with this Mogulesko.

Kupfer's choir leader turned out to be a frail, slight boy of seventeen, rather sad, but friendly, open to all ideas, and quick to understand what was wanted of him.

Zelig Mogulesko, born in the Bessarabian town of Koloraush, came of an unusual family. His father had been a shopkeeper, but his mother, daughter of the famous Judge Laizer Schagall, was so learned and wise she sat with the rabbi of Koloraush, consulting with him on all the town problems.

This remarkable mother had died when her son was eight years old. The following year the greatest *chazzen* of all South Russia, Nissim of Belz, came to visit Koloraush. Urged by his schoolmates, the child went to the cantor's house and sang for him. The great Nissim opened his eyes very wide and said, "My dear little boy, go home at once and fetch your parents!"

A three-year agreement was signed the same day, and Nissim took the boy back to South Russia as an apprentice. Here little Mogulesko became the pet and mascot of the choir. He hung about the older singers, ran their errands, and in return asked them to teach him to read music, an art he mastered so rapidly they nicknamed him "Little Zelig the Note-Eater."

He had served only one year of this apprenticeship when Chazzen Kupfer of Bucharest heard of the marvelous child and made a trip to South Russia to get him. To avoid the penalty for breaking his contract with Nissim, Kupfer stole the boy off at night and did not break his journey until he had crossed the Roumanian border.

At sixteen Mogulesko and several other members of Kupfer's choir were admitted to the Bucharest Conservatory. French operettas were all the rage in Roumania at that time, and these boys earned some extra money singing in the chorus. They sang in church choirs, too, though this had to be done very quietly, as it would have been a great scandal if discovered. All these young men were in demand at weddings, circumcisions, and other joyous occasions, where they led the traditional dances, sang couplets, and "made the whole world happy."

Mogulesko had seen theatre in Bucharest, and had "burned to be an actor," but short of conversion this was not possible in Roumania. The idea of Yiddish theatre struck him as extraordinary, and his meeting with Goldfaden opened up undreamed-of possibilities.

Soon afterward, he came back to Goldfaden, bringing with him four singers, all on fire to have a go at Yiddish theatre. Laizer Zuckerman sang an aria from *Lucia* and was engaged on the spot. Two others, Moishe Silberman and Simche Dinman, also passed with honors. The fourth singer, a blond giant of seventeen called Abba Schoengold, failed to get an offer. Schoengold, handsomest of the five and with by far the most beautiful voice, desperately wanted to be an actor, but hid his longing under an air of indifference and disdain. Goldfaden took a dislike to him, and he lost his chance. He was left behind to envy the luck of his friends and feel all the ache of his missed opportunity.

Goldfaden at one stroke had acquired four new members for his cast, all of them, with the exception of Simche Dinman, destined to play an important part in Yiddish theatre history. Dinman suffered from stage fright, could not overcome it, and was forced to leave the company.

Of the remaining three, Mogulesko showed the greatest promise. Zuckerman had an excellent bass voice, danced with talent and fire, but lacked a sense of measure and nuance. Mogulesko had inborn comedy genius and was also musical to his fingertips. He had already composed a great many songs, and Goldfaden was to find him extremely valuable in this respect.

The greatest success in Bucharest just then was the farce comedy *Vladutzul Mamei—Mama's Youngest*. Mogulesko advised Goldfaden to write a Yiddish adaptation of this play. Goldfaden took the basic plot line of the comedy, turned the hero into a petulant little *chosid*, made some other adaptations to Jewish life and emerged with *Shmendrick*, his first smash hit.

So great was Mogulesko's success as the foolish young Shmendrick that Gradner became sick with jealousy. Violent quarrels began to erupt. Gradner insisted that Goldfaden must write a play for him too—a serious play, a drama, for Gradner wanted to show he was not limited to comedy.

To pacify him, Goldfaden wrote a three-act tragedy called *The Desolate Isle*. The dramatic role of the "European" was played by Gradner; Socher Goldstein played the feminine character, Regina; and Mogulesko brought in a bit of comedy relief as "A Little Black Boy."

Mogulesko ran away with the show.

This worked on Gradner so badly that he left the company and went back to Jassy. There he got together some amateurs, made Rosa Friedman a character actress, took in the Odessa folk singer Moishe Finkel, and with the backing of an innkeeper called Maurice Roth started out on his own.

Goldfaden was shocked. He had never reckoned on competition at all; moreover, the loss of Gradner, an important star, worried him. But his fears were soon forgotten. Overnight, Mogulesko had become such a drawing card that Gradner was not even missed. As for the new troupe in Jassy, it still depended entirely on Goldfaden's plays, and Goldfaden never let a manuscript out of his hands.

Word soon came out, however, that Gradner had pieced several of the operettas together from memory. With the dialogue still largely improvisational, this was hardly difficult. Though Goldfaden raged, no copyright laws existed in Roumania and he could do nothing. He consoled himself with the thought that the Jassy troupe must soon collapse; once Gradner ran through his stolen repertoire, he would have nothing more to show his audience.

The new company, however, continued to be a bone in his throat. And they soon had plays of their own. A certain Joseph Lateiner, one of the *maskilim* who had met Goldfaden at the Jassy railroad station, was inspired by his example to write a play of his own. A humorous German story, "Nathan Schlemiehl," provided the basis for this first effort. Lateiner dramatized the story, utilized a current political issue among the Jassy Jews, and put in one or two speeches decrying fanaticism. Called *The Two Schmil Schmelkes*, the play was performed in Jassy and the outlying towns, and did well. Encouraged by his success, Lateiner was soon turning out plays with all the commendable zeal of a day laborer.

Goldfaden could not permit such a state of affairs to continue. He sent Libresko to Jassy with orders to win over the new playwright. After a secret meeting with Libresko, Lateiner left for Bucharest in the middle of the night. As a sign that he was dead to the troupe, he left a candle burning on the trunk that had held his plays. Deserted by its playwright, the Jassy company collapsed.

Goldfaden put Lateiner on salary and then forgot his existence. It was not *The Two Schmil Schmelkes* Bucharest audiences saw, but Goldfaden's vastly superior comedy *The Two Kuni Lemmels,* adapted from the same "Nathan Schlemiehl." Lateiner, seeing he had made a mistake, went back to Gradner.

It was now open war. Inspired by both ambition and revenge, Gradner wrote in turn to each of the actors in Bucharest, offering them more money and more recognition of their talents than they were ever likely to receive from Avrom Goldfaden. Socher Goldstein was the first to desert. Silberman followed. Finally, Mogulesko himself left for Jassy. He and Gradner had a talk. They agreed that Goldfaden was the real enemy, and Mogulesko came into the troupe as Gradner's partner. Only Laizer Zuckerman, cynically dubbed "Eleazer, Slave of Abraham" by the others, remained with Goldfaden.

In a panic, Goldfaden sent Zuckerman to the provinces to fetch Simche Dinman. This proved useless. Dinman grew rigid with fear at the mere thought of the stage. Goldfaden persuaded him to appear in the second act of an operetta and to speak the one line "Who are you?" The unhappy man was unable to utter even these three words. He left the theatre forever, went back to the provinces, and became a cantor.

In spite of these blows, Goldfaden survived. He found an actress called Golditza, a wild kid who had grown up on the Bucharest streets and was afraid of nothing. She replaced Mogulesko as Shmendrick and imitated him, it is said, very well. Yiddish theatre had caught on in Bucharest, and a small but steady audience continued to support it.

With the re-forming of Gradner's troupe, however, Goldfaden's supremacy had come to an end. His actors had taken abuse, insult, and starvation wages, all out of a deadly fear that without him they would have no livelihood. Now they saw the beginnings of an open field. Goldfaden's prestige did not weigh heavily against the prospect of better wages and a more generous recognition of their talents. Finding they had some bargaining power, the actors began going back and forth between the two companies. Open competition soon began, and

Gradner, hearing about the actress Golditza, could not rest until he too had a prima donna. He sent Socher Goldstein to Galatz with orders to bring back his wife.

A year had passed, but the little seamstress, Soore Siegel, had never forgotten her one night on the stage. She was seventeen now and a married woman. This time she had her way and in the face of pleas and tears, left her parents' home. The same night she arrived in Jassy she replaced her husband as the heroine of *Granny and Her Granddaughter*. Since the name Soore had too prosaic a ring, she was billed as Sophia Goldstein.

The coming of the woman, as everyone knows, means trouble in Eden. In this case, two women had come onto the scene. While waiting for Socher Goldstein to return from Galatz, Gradner had written to his own wife—a girl he had married during his days as a folk singer. Annetta Gradner, daughter of a Kremantchuk bootmaker, had a willowy, graceful figure, a lovely voice and, it is said, the seventh degree of charm. Gradner had wanted her to sing concerts with him, but the young wife was afraid to sing in public. She could not take the hardships of her husband's gypsy existence and went back to her parents. Now Gradner wrote her to say he was a full-fledged entrepreneur, that it was time they took up their life together, and that she was to come to Jassy and be his leading lady.

Mrs. Gradner arrived to find Sophia Goldstein already installed as the company prima donna. Gradner fought for his wife. Mogulesko protected Sophia Goldstein. And Mogulesko's position was stronger.

It was just here, in fact, that the root of the trouble lay. Mogulesko was fast becoming a legend in the Jewish world of Roumania. People who had never set eyes on him spoke of him as though he was part of their lives. "If someone sang with charm, everyone said, 'Just like Mogulesko!' " writes the actor Leon Blank. "If someone danced with fire and grace, it was again, 'like Mogulesko!' At every good joke, people wiped tears of laughter from their eyes, saying, 'Ech, Mogulesko, Mogulesko, may God give him health!' Everything that tickled, pleased, charmed, convulsed had to come from Mogulesko!"

Nowhere is the difference between success and failure more grimly marked than in a theatre. The actor who loses his place feels himself both laughable and pitiable. The best and the worst of his own nature combine to torture him, for he is insulted alike in his vanity and in his talent. His loss deprives him at once of his position among his colleagues, of the love of his public, and of his very means of subsistence. And thrust down, cast out, annihilated, he always sees, high on the glittering ladder, bathed in the light of a thousand adoring eyes, the beautiful, the fortunate, the detested rival who has replaced him there.

If these deadly passions raged in the stately theatres of London, Paris, and St. Petersburg, if they continue to rage even today, how much more terribly they must have ruled these desperate beginners, struggling to hold their small, poverty-stricken audience.

Mogulesko's fame, the adoration of the public, the screams of laughter that greeted his entrance, the crashes of applause after every song, every dance were death itself to Yisrol Gradner. He left the company, which immediately became the Mogulesko Troupe. Annetta, Rosa Friedman, Finkel, and one or two others joined him, and the shaky little troupe went out on their own into the Roumanian provinces.

On April 14, 1877, the Russian army crossed the Danube. The countryside was overrun by Bulgarians fleeing from the Turks, and hostilities began. The Russians, expecting an easy victory, met with an unexpected setback. The Ottoman Empire, in the process of "declining" for some two hundred years, seemed still to possess a quite ferocious vigor. It took the combined Russian and Roumanian armies three months to get through the Turkish fortifications at Plevna.*

As Europe rang with news of the brilliant defense of Plevna, Russia celebrated her glorious victory. After Plevna, Russian advance through the country went practically unimpeded.

The war brought prosperity to Roumania, and as already noted, Jassy and Bucharest filled up with *podradchikes* from Russia—contractors, agents, salesmen, middlemen, all intent on doing business with the Russian Commissariat.

At this time a second recruiting drive had sent the actors into hiding again, and Goldfaden was a ruined man. One day, walking through Bucharest he ran into a friend from Odessa. This man informed Goldfaden it was "raining gold" and said he could bring fifty people if Goldfaden would put on a Yid-

---

* A town on the southern shore of the Danube in a Turkish-owned territory which, after the war, became the independent Kingdom of Bulgaria.

dish play that night. Goldfaden managed to round up his actors and put on the performance. His friend had promised to bring fifty people; he came with almost two hundred. All Odessa was in Bucharest, everyone bored to death, making piles of money, and looking for ways to spend it.

The actors forgot their hungry days. No longer were the seats filled by the poor, the *déclassé*, the ignorant. Wealthy Jews came. Intellectuals came. The great Jewish aristocrats came. Even Russian and Roumanian officers came. They too liked the songs, the dances, the divertissements after the play. And it gave them a hearty laugh to see the long coats and beards of the Jews onstage. "If all this did not elevate the theatre," the historian B. Gorin dryly comments, "at least it swelled the cash receipts."

Admission rose overnight from eight francs to twenty, and the actors began to live like kings. They did not even have to spend the money they made. After each performance newly rich agents and contractors took them off to the best restaurants of Bucharest where they ate, drank, laughed, and caroused until dawn. A story of this period relates that a sick actor, told by the doctor that he had "water on the lung," swore, laughing, that he had drunk nothing but champagne for a month.

No need to write new plays; new audiences came nightly to see the old ones. Actors, too, more than were needed. The folk singer Finkel deserted Gradner and joined up with Goldfaden. The Roumanian-born journalist Spivakovsky, handsome as a prince, resigned his post as a war correspondent for the *Odessa Messenger* and became a leading man. And Rosenberg, in Bucharest to make a fortune, forgot his schemes and deals with the Russian Commissariat, and became a comedian. Within a short time, Goldfaden had not one prima donna, but two—the sisters, Annetta and Margaretta Schwartz, both beauties, both with excellently trained voices and both absolutely respectable.

On top of all this, Goldfaden came through with another success. Rosa Friedman had left Gradner's troupe and come to Bucharest to try her luck again. She had played small parts with both Mogulesko and Gradner and could be considered a seasoned actress now. Goldfaden had a serious talk with her. He asked her frankly about her life in Constantinople. She answered with equal frankness. He became fascinated. Goldfaden liked to create his plays around the personality of an actor. He had created *Recruits* for Gradner, Shmendrick for Mogulesko. For Rosa Friedman he wrote *Breindele Cossack—A Dream Picture in Six Acts*. The play was an adaptation of Offenbach's *Bluebeard*, but with the sexes reversed. It was Breindele who was the Bluebeard of the play, and instead of seven wives, seven husbands went to their doom.

With *Breindele Cossack* Goldfaden had cast the perfect actress in the perfect role. Rosa Friedman's fiery temperament, so wrong for innocent heroines, crossed the footlights with sensational impact as the sinister Breindele. She grew young again on the stage, and even took on a dark, sultry beauty. Her hoarse, rasping, broken voice, a drawback in every other play, became inseparably associated with the character she portrayed. She became so identified with the part that her own name was forgotten and people pointed her out on the street, whispering, "There goes Breindele Cossack!"

Goldfaden put on his new success at the Jignitza Theatre, and when the Jignitza had to close down for repairs, took it to the Pomul Verde (The Green Garden). The Russian journalist Shigorin reported that the Yiddish company gave four performances a week there. "The garden was always packed," he wrote, "and hundreds turned away, many not Jews."

With affluence came an inevitable slackening of effort. Goldfaden sarcastically notes that his actors had begun to drink the good Roumanian wine, passionately, and to think less about their art than the perpetual round of pleasures that awaited them. He himself was immersed in business affairs, and felt these distracted from his creative efforts.

"There was no help for it," he writes defensively. "When I lost myself in my art, I would wake up to discover my actors had plundered me, and my business managers had dealt with me as a father!" By which he meant they had robbed him.

On top of his other duties, Goldfaden was also expected to recite and sing couplets between the acts. He did not like this duty and tried to avoid it, feeling he was not talented enough. "I stood on the stage, spoke casually in a friendly voice, jested with the public. But business problems were overwhelming me. Backstage there was quarreling and disorder because things did not go as they should. At that moment the audience would call me out, and I would come before them with an angry face, in a bad mood."

In truth, his appearances had a bad effect. It is a curious

fact that this poet, whose every line is flooded with sunlight, had a manner that acted on his audience like a dash of cold water. The actors felt the sting of an imperious nature that allowed no light to shine but its own, and though they revered him, they did not love him. He knew how to deliver an insult that rankled a lifetime, when he died thirty years later, Isaac Libresko did not come to his funeral. His wife once warned him in Libresko's presence that the actors would throw him out of the troupe someday. The lady spoke prophetically. Goldfaden, an object of almost religious awe in the theatre he had created, was one day to be driven out of it entirely.

With the success of Goldfaden's theatre it was only a question of time before he was once again threatened with competition. One day placards in the Jewish quarter announced that an "Israelite Dramatic Society" would present a three-act musical drama by one Professor Moishe Isaac Halevy Hurvitz at the Israelite National Garden, with each ticket holder entitled to one free glass of beer.

Goldfaden had met this Hurvitz immediately after the first rehearsal of *Recruits*. Gradner had brought him around because the man claimed to have an original play for sale. His appearance did not inspire confidence and Goldfaden made some inquiries. This Professor Hurvitz, he soon learned, was a remarkably queer fish. Though he claimed to be a professor of geography in a Bucharest academy, he had actually been the director of a Hebrew school. Dismissed from his post, Hurvitz had converted to Christianity, and in fact the man was now a well-known Bucharest missionary.

He had come around with his manuscript the following day. "I thought he had an original play," Goldfaden writes. "It was simply Linetzki's *Polish Boy*."

When Goldfaden asked what had induced him to convert, Hurvitz replied, "Hard times. My family and I ate potato peels. I didn't earn much with the old God. The new one brought me 90 francs a month." Goldfaden, somewhat taken aback, said he could not present a play written by a convert before a Jewish audience. Hurvitz flew into a rage and left the theatre, swearing vengeance.

When the "rain of gold" began, this Hurvitz gathered together ten wagon drivers and laborers, ordered five measures of wine, and declared himself a Jew again. "As our grandfather Terach served strange gods, yet his son Abraham was Jewish, so my sons may also be called Jewish," Hurvitz proclaimed to these witnesses. By his "sons," he evidently meant his plays.

The Israelite National Garden, where Hurvitz put on his operetta, was the back yard of a restaurant. Hurvitz promised the owner he would give him the whole of the box-office receipts, keeping only enough money to pay "the musicians, the tinsmith who made the scenery, and the boy who painted it." The actors performed without pay.

The Polish Boy was a dramatization of Linetzki's heartrending novel of a child enticed into bearing false witness and thereby dooming a whole Jewish town. Into this story Hurvitz had inserted some songs and dances of his own creation. A small audience came, attracted mostly by the promise of free beer. Hurvitz followed *The Polish Boy* with a play of his own called *Banker Tyrant,* and then with *The Clockmaker's Hat,* a comedy which could not have been his own since Goldfaden also produced it.

Disturbed by this continuing activity, Goldfaden sent spies to see what was going on. They told him the proceedings were a meaningless jumble, adding that the leading man, though he knew nothing about acting, looked well and had a good voice.

This leading man was Abba Schoengold, the young singer dropped by Goldfaden after his audition. Goldfaden immediately sent him a message holding out a possibility of a place in his own troupe.

The stakes had risen since Mogulesko had brought around his four young friends. Yiddish theatre then had been little more than an interesting speculation. It had since become a reality bathed in glory and gold. Schoengold came to the meeting keyed up to the highest tension point, all his ambition flaming. Without his mask of disdain and self-importance, the young man had far more appeal. He was undeniably handsome. He wore his shabby cloak with pride. He had, in fact, an air about him. Goldfaden began to talk business.

Hurvitz's company, losing its one strong player, fell apart. Gathering whomever was left, Hurvitz went out into the provinces.

Having destroyed the opposition, Goldfaden repeated his old mistake. Once he had secured the best actor of Hurvitz's troupe, he promptly forgot about him. Shoengold saw parts he might have played going to others. He hung about, longing for the chance that never came, and gradually realized he had made a mistake. In Goldfaden's troupe he was one among many. With Hurvitz he had been a star. He left the company and went out to join his old troupe in the provinces.

On March 4, 1878, the Russo-Turkish War came to an end with a resounding Russian victory. The affair of the Russian Commissariat was over. One by one the *podradchikes* packed up and went home. As the actors had come overnight into prosperity, so overnight it vanished. Only a very small part of the Jewish population of Roumania had ever supported the Yiddish theatre. The great audiences had been made up of those who poured into Bucharest and Jassy from Russia. The actors now were once more thrown back on their first public, poor, unworldly people and small in number.

These wretched conditions were bitterly felt after the luxury of the war.

Though everyone had known the war must end, nobody had planned for it. Some of the actors gave up and went into other professions. Rosenberg and Spivakovsky went out together to try their luck in the provinces. Rosa Friedman went back to Jassy.

Conditions on the road, never the best, were now miserable indeed. Gradner hung on awhile, then lost heart and took ship with his wife for Constantinople. Hurvitz barnstormed with Schoengold. Mogulesko and three other actors formed a quartet and went about giving concerts. Since the others felt it was beneath them to go around with a plate, it was Mogulesko who collected the honorarium.

The "rain of gold" had dried up at the source. Bad days lay ahead for the actors.

5

Rosenberg the Entrepreneur

> Oh, how I hear them, the voices of those still living and those long dead! As I watched that night a prophetic spirit seized me, a thought, a fleeting dream. I glimpsed the future. Some day the true history of the Yiddish theatre will be written, and in festive flaming words it will be told how from that poor hall, from the smeared, frightened faces of those first actors, there arose a new and wonderful epoch.
> JACOB ADLER

In Odessa, Yankele Adler and the folk singers got together nightly to discuss the subject that now consumed them, the Yiddish theatre in Roumania. Adler was determined to bring that theatre to Odessa. His energies were bent to this one end, and he did his work so well that the matter was talked about in houses he himself could not have entered.

While he and Rosenberg corresponded, there was an important change in his life: He became an official of the City Department of Weights and Measures—the first Jew in Odessa ever to occupy that post. He owed this piece of luck to the good offices of General Meschersky of the military hospital at Bender and the recommendation of Abram Markovitch Brodsky, a Jew of great wealth and influence.

He accordingly went about his new duties with the government cockade on his hat and a respectful policeman as his assistant. The new inspector was strict in his demands, but noticed that the Russian policeman waved off the worst violations with a smile. Finding the Jew was a "young lord who took no bribes," the Jewish shopkeepers, who habitually cheated on weight, had come to an understanding with his companion. When this failed, they would appeal to the new inspector's mother, and a messenger would run up with a note from Hessye saying, "Yankele, such and such a person you must not report. They are good people. Your father and I know them." The inspector soon learned to take his duties less seriously.

Adler's real life went on at night in Akiva's restaurant in Rivnoya Street, where he and his friends received all reports from Roumania. One night Rosenberg's sisters brought news. The next it was some boon companion who brought the latest. Rosenberg was on his way. Spivakovsky was coming with him. Each new piece of information produced more speculation and excitement.

It was a strangely assorted crowd that assembled at the railway station when the great day finally arrived. Half of Buff's Army had trailed after Adler, and their "ladies" after them. Rosenberg's soberly clad mother and sisters hardly dared glance at these gaily plumaged birds of the town. Spivakovsky's aristocratic family had come in their carriage. They kept a distance between themselves and the folk singers, bearded Jews all and so nondescript they could be taken for small-town fiddlers, hangers-on of some poor synagogue, or beggars altogether.

The train pulled in, and everyone waved and shouted as Rosenberg and Spivakovsky were sighted on the platform. Rosenberg's parents ran to meet him, fell on his neck, and wept for joy. Spivakovsky's family, too, gave him a hero's welcome. The others watched, grinning with pleasure and quite moved.

"At the same time, we felt rather queer," Adler confesses. "We looked at each other uneasily. Our eyes even held a hint of mockery. Rosenberg and Spivakovsky—what can I say? They were the same, yet not the same. Rosenberg, who had always worn side whiskers like any Odessa lawyer, had not a hair on his face. No moustache, no beard—a regular priest! Spivakovsky, too, had shaved off the elegant little moustache that had been his pride. Both men were dressed alike in winged capes with high hats, pince-nez, suede gloves, lacquered shoes, spats. In a word—a couple of barons!"

The returning heroes were taken off by their families, but the following noon everyone came together at the Palais Royal for lunch. From there they went on to Falconi's pastry shop. Rosenberg ordered coffee and *pirozhene,* talking all the time about the Yiddish theatre in Roumania.

"Tens of thousands in Bucharest! Right, Spivakovsky?"

"*Da, da!*" Spivakovsky nodded his assent.

"Millionaires came! The king and queen of Roumania came! Right, Spivakovsky?"

"*Da, da!*" Spivakovsky did not lie as well as Rosenberg. He got red at times.

Rosenberg used Roumanian phrases, showed his Roumanian coins, and told such stories about the Yiddish theatre in Roumania that everyone laughed until their sides ached and strangers gathered around their table, also laughing.

"Let's only get a permit from the government," Rosenberg said, frowning. "But Adler is a big shot now, an official! He will arrange everything!"

In the midst of all this, he took Adler aside. "Yankele, we must have money," he said urgently. "Things are going well with you, so share with a brother, eh?" Rosenberg's eyes confessed everything. "You think we did well there, in Roumania? We hungered, Spivakovsky and I! We hungered, brother!"

Adler had the whole story in a moment. Goldfaden had seen that Rosenberg and Spivakovsky had talent and ability. He hounded them, insulted them. They left him. For a time they did well. They had Goldfaden's plays, and they made money. "The plays I still have," Rosenberg said, "but money goes fast."

He was already exploring Adler's pockets as he spoke, his fingers, as always, very nimble in these operations. Half of what he found he put back. He divided the other half with Spivakovsky, with the terse comment, "Partners are partners."

With money, Rosenberg became gay again. They finally parted, Rosenberg speaking Roumanian, Adler and the others Russian.

Adler was already imagining himself as Hamlet, as Chlestakov in Gogol's *Revizor,* as the great Uriel Acosta. In Russian all this was so magnificent, but how would it sound in Yiddish? And he, who had only finished the second class of school, he who had been a boxer in the Moldovanka. . . . He sighed, finding no answer to his own questions.

Rosenberg rounded up the *podradchikes* he had known in

Roumania. These middlemen, agents, and distributors had come home rich from the war. They had supported Goldfaden in Roumania, and Rosenberg wanted to win them over in Odessa. He threw a party, a gay affair; the guests did not go home until dawn. Rosenberg, too excited to sleep, took the others off to a tavern. There he addressed himself to the folk singers.

"Listen to me, miserable slaves that you are!" said Rosenberg. "How long will you rot in the wine cellars and go around afterward like beggars with a plate? Don't you feel, don't you see how your sun is rising? Look at Moishe Finkel, who once sang in the cellars like you. See what the Yiddish theatre did for him. A high hat! A cane! He is a king! An artist! You will be artists, too, all of you. I tell you people will bring you armfuls of money. They will give it to you before they even see you! Never mind! There is enough in you, enough talent!"

He turned to Adler. "And you, Yankele, you, too, will be an actor! You will be with me! I feel it!"

They parted in broad daylight. The folk singers were in heaven at the thought of being rescued out of the cellar cafes.

Rosenberg decided on his first program—two Goldfaden vaudevilles followed by *Recruits*. He began casting the folk singers, but the coarse appearance of the new players, their beards, their bedraggled clothing interfered with his inspiration. "It's no good!" he finally broke out. "Damnation take it, you look like chimney sweeps, not actors! I need human beings, do you understand? Go and make yourselves into human beings!"

Beards, moustaches fell to the ground in snips. Off came the short coats, the low hats, the deep boots. With his last money, Rosenberg worked a transformation. In frock coats and narrow trousers, high silk hats, white shirts with flowing black cravats they looked like Englishmen, Frenchmen, or the upper-class Roumanians who were now Rosenberg's ideal.

"Woe to a Jew without a beard!" Adler recalls. "It was painful to see them come together again. Shaven Jews! Chins, beards, cheeks, and mouths never before seen! They laughed, but their laughter was hollow and hysterical, more like the squealing of a slaughtered chicken. Each of them joked bitterly at the others, looking miserably at his own reflection in the restaurant mirror, feeling unhappily for the beard that no longer existed."

Adler laughed at them. His small moustache was a recent

addition to his face, and he rather liked the way he looked without it.

The performance was to take place at Akiva's restaurant. One morning the actors, in a happy, holiday mood, gathered there for their first rehearsal. Rosenberg's friends and backers had also come. They couldn't wait; they remembered Roumania and wanted to see a little Yiddish theatre. This was Rosenberg's great moment. His joy affected everyone, and for Adler, he grew in stature that day.

It was a warm, summery June morning, and a whole crowd of girls, women, and children gathered outside the open window, laughing and applauding. Everyone asked for a song, a dance.

"*Domnele, gospoda!*" Rosenberg exclaimed. "We are no folk singers, no wine cellar clowns! You will have to pay if you want to see us. We are actors! Artists!"

He launched into an excited speech about the triumphs of the Yiddish theatre in Roumania. Great names reeled off his lips: Goldfaden, Annetta Gradner, Madame Sophia Goldstein, the famous Laizer Zuckerman. Last of all, Rosenberg spoke of Mogulesko, whom he described as handsome, young, a great singer, a marvelous dancer and a genius. "Yes, the actors in Roumania were great," he ended. "But they will never be as great as we! And therefore, we now will create a Yiddish theatre for the Jews of Russia—and right here in Odessa!"

A storm of applause at the window. The *podradchikes*, beside themselves with pleasure, bought tickets on the spot at five and ten roubles apiece. Rosenberg stuffed the money into his pockets, and relenting from sheer joy, told the singers to give everyone the song from *Breindele Cossack*. Rosenberg himself did his scene as Yankev the Drunk, and Spivakovsky recited the dramatic monologue from *Recruits*. Joyous cries of bravo from the open window. The *podradchikes*, carried away by enthusiasm, ordered food and wine. Waiters set up tables and everyone ate, drank, sang, danced, embraced. The enthusiasm, in fact, reached such a height that a policeman came around and asked what was going on. At this a sudden silence fell. Adler explained that a play was to be given on these premises and those present had gathered for a rehearsal. The policeman took down every word in a notebook.

This looked bad. "Something had to be done," Adler remarks, "so that the Yiddish theatre should not die in the belly of its mother before it was born!"

The officer left, but, fortunately, Akiva went with him. The restaurateur came back with a broad smile. Money had changed hands. All was well again.

At the sight of police, the crowd at the window had disappeared like a flock of frightened birds. The guests also took their departure. Left with his actors, Rosenberg showed himself in a new light, that of the good, benevolent boss. Holding high his new roubles, he asked the folk singers who among them needed money to "make Sabbath." Everyone needed, and to each was given according to his need.

"What did I tell you?" Rosenberg exclaimed, radiant with happiness. "They gave us the money before they even saw us! That's theatre!"

When things go well, they go well from every side. Two well-known folk singers, Weinstein and Yankele Katzman, both favorites, came in on the venture. With actresses, too, Rosenberg had luck. The lawyer Alexander Oberlander brought great news one day. His sister, a personage in Odessa circles, had consented to be their prima donna. Rosenberg also had something to show. He passed around a photograph of a rare beauty, young and slender with marvelous red-gold hair. "The real thing!" Rosenberg remarked with satisfaction. This young lady, Fraulein Masha Moskovitch, had also agreed to join the troupe.

They gave their first performance on June 23, 1879. Akiva hammered together some tables, laid down boards over them, and hung a calico curtain that did not roll up, but came together in the center. Rosenberg reckoned on 150 seats, with some room at the back for standees. He charged one rouble for a place in the first bench, 50 kopeks for all the others, and 25 kopeks for standing room.

Lamps in the hall were lit as evening fell. The audience began filing in. Behind the scenes fear and tension showed on every face. Rosenberg was trembling with emotion. He told Adler that the first time he had played in Roumania he had gone to a synagogue and prayed. "Nobody saw my tears!" he said. "Only my God!"

A terrible doubt seized Adler. Rosenberg, the cynic? Was this one of his jokes? But no! Great tears shone in his eyes. "No, Yankele," he said, answering his thoughts. "This is no longer the old Rosenberg, that scoundrel and swindler! When I go on the stage, no matter how foolish the play, I remember that Goldfaden wrote it, and every word is holy to me. I will go hungry, I will lose all, but never will I stain the name of my theatre!"

The actors were dressing, one as a *chosid*, another as a drunk. Adler felt something strange, a quicksilver sensation in his bones, a desire to be part of this, to *act*.

Music, followed by a sharp, nervous bell. The curtain went up.

Three short vaudevilles, then the operetta *Recruits*—all by Goldfaden. Rosenberg played three comedy parts, each one in a different wig and costume. He impersonated characters well known in the Odessa Jewish quarter, but though his imitations were skillful, he brought to them nothing of his own. A clever performance, Adler decided, but not art.

Rosenberg was warmly received, but more as the entrepreneur than for his acting. In *Recruits* he played the comedy soldier created by Gradner, while Spivakovsky took the dramatic lead. Spivakovsky acted with feeling, wept real tears, sang charmingly, and had a great success. Between the acts the folk singers sang couplets.

The audience, mostly relatives of the folk singers or neighbors from nearby streets, laughed at the jokes, the nonsense, and enjoyed everything. At the end of the program the audience moved out into the street, and friends came backstage with compliments and encouragement. Even the sternest critic admitted that it had been worth seeing and that it had "looked like theatre."

Waiters brought tables back into the hall, and a celebration took place. Rosenberg and Spivakovsky made speeches. Everyone felt a start had been made, and a good one.

Two lovely ladies were present at this party, the Frauleins Masha Moskovitch and Sophia Oberlander. Both had consented to join Rosenberg's company, but only if they performed in a proper theatre or hall. Rosenberg, anxious that both ladies should be pleased, asked Adler to entertain them. Adler felt especially drawn to Sophia Oberlander, whom he had already met through Olga Petrovna. This serious young woman, an intellectual, a *coursiste* at the university, had made a deep impression on him.

At their previous meetings Adler had said little, painfully aware of his own lack of education. Only when the talk touched on theatre had he ventured to speak at all. Fraulein Oberlander had acted in dramatic productions in *Gymnazia*, and the drama was the burning interest of her life. Adler felt more secure on this ground because of his experience in the City Theatre. He was familiar with Shakespeare's popular tragedies, with Ostrovsky and Schiller, and because of this would sometimes venture an opinion.

Now, as they met again, they drew closer. When Adler left Akiva's that night, he had fallen in love. He thought only of the present he would send on the night of Fraulein Oberlander's debut.

For his second program Rosenberg rented the Remesleny Club. This hall, where German organizations often put on theatricals, had everything needed for a theatre, even loges.

Two full-length operettas were announced: *Granny and Her Granddaughter* to be followed a week later by *Breindele Cossack*, with Sonya Michelson. The last announcement caused a stir. Everyone knew Sonya Michelson was Sophia Oberlander, a person who really counted for something.

According to the actor Weinstein, people "stood on their heads to buy tickets." The crowd gathered hours in advance at the Remesleny Club, and the arrival of each actor produced more excitement. When Rosenberg appeared, many cried out that they knew him, that he was an Odessa lawyer.

At nine o'clock, with the hall packed to the doors, the curtain rose, revealing Weinstein as the Granny. In his days as a folk singer Weinstein had often mimed an old wife, a *Yidane*. Now, on a real stage and in costume and makeup, he looked as though he had been an old Yiddish *buba* from the day he was born. Though Weinstein's acting was somewhat exaggerated, he made a good impression and prepared the audience for the masterstroke: the entrance of the granddaughter.

"All honor to the first actress of the Yiddish stage in Russia!" Adler writes. "On the stage appeared the slender figure, the milk-white arms, the noble face of Masha Moskovitch. What was it that stirred the hearts of these Jewish men and women? Perhaps simply the freshness and charm of a young girl, perhaps a prophetic feeling that with the appearance of a woman on the stage the Yiddish theatre had become a reality. The stormy welcome rose to a height seldom equaled in the theatre. The hall rang with bravos. Many in the audience rose."

According to Adler the young actress played like a child. She was frightened. It was clear, however, that she would be a favorite, and that this warm reception would not be her last.

Her duet with Spivakovsky was warmly applauded, and the audience brought them back again and again.

The following week Rosenberg followed up this success with *Breindele Cossack*. He gave this production a great deal of attention and surprised the audience at the curtain rise with a rich and tasteful set. As Breindele, Sonya Michelson wore a ball gown, spoke in a commanding tone, and showed surprising dramatic power and control. Every flicker of her sensitive face showed her emotions. The audience gave her tumultuous approval, and at the final curtain the stage was covered with flowers.

Sonya, tactful and discreet in her success, thanked the audience with blown kisses and had a special smile for her great admirer in the first row. Adler had made sure that the prettiest roses came from him, and that his name and hers were written large on the streamers.

Rosenberg now played his strongest card. Russian-language posters appeared all over Odessa announcing Goldfaden's smash success *Shmendrick*. Rosenberg was so sure of this play that he planned not one but three performances, to be given on Friday, Saturday, and Sunday night. A new star, the folk singer Yankele Katzman, was cast as the lead.

Adler had hardly noticed when the role opposite Masha Moskovitch, promised to him, had gone to Spivakovsky. Now Rosenberg had broken his word a second time and cast Spivakovsky in *Breindele Cossack*. It was clear the two directors meant to keep things to themselves, with Rosenberg as the first comedian, Spivakovsky as the dramatic lead. But anger gave way to Adler's irresistible need to see *Shmendrick*.

"Shmendrick! The very name called up whole mountains of fun and laughter. Just the sound of it suggested a small-town booby, a spoiled, naive, ridiculous child. And what they do to him! They lead him around by the nose, fool him, change his bride! The very title was a guarantee of success, the word was already so well known. Odessa housewives called each other Shmendrick, cursed each other as Shmendrick. 'Have you seen my Shmendrick?' one wife asked another, continuing with, 'And where is your Shmendrick?' The expression was so broad, so elastic it could mean a dozen different things. People swore by Shmendrick, blessed each other with Shmendrick. A sickness was called a Shmendrick. A rouble was also a Shmendrick. 'The goods are here,' one merchant said to the other, 'Where are the Shmendricks?' "

Adler wanted no favors from Rosenberg. He put down his six Shmendricks and bought his own six tickets. He was taking his parents, his little sister, and his uncle and aunt to the first performance. He bought a high silk hat for the occasion, the first he ever possessed. Hessye and Feivel Abramovitch were lost in admiration, but the little sister laughed at him and said he looked like Shmendrick.

They found the hall crowded and many people in evening dress. Adler was nervous. His family knew now that he wanted to be an actor, and a great deal depended on how they liked this performance.

The curtain went up on Weinstein and Rosenberg. Jokes and some foolery led up to the entrance of the young folk singer Yankele Katzman as Shmendrick. Laughter in the audience. More jokes. Songs and dances. Everyone applauded madly as the curtain fell.

Adler's parents had not uttered a sound. They had not even smiled. The curtain rose on the second act. More foolery, more songs and dances. His uncle lost patience. The wedding scene seemed to him a mockery of the Jewish marriage service. The coarse jokes offended him. He shrugged as the final curtain fell. He was ashamed, he said, for the Germans. This was not theatre, but a circus. "Where is your taste?" he asked his nephew. "It is supposed to be taking place in Roumania! Was there one drop of Roumanian atmosphere?"

Feivel Abramovitch shook his head sadly. Hessye, sighing, said, "And the boy was doing so well, dear Uncle! Now he wants to throw himself away in this dark hole!" Only the aunt and the little sister clapped, laughed, and did not want to go home.

The coarseness did not bother Adler; he had a strong stomach and had mingled in low circles. But at the verdict of his family the scales fell from his eyes. He saw the falseness, the crudity of it all. The disapproval of his uncle really crushed him, for Aaron Trachtenberg was in truth something of a connoisseur. Adler went home with bowed head. "Fallen was I in my own eyes," he writes, "for fallen was that which had been great in my eyes!"

His disillusionment brought about one of the greatest events of his life, his engagement to Sonya Oberlander. It was to her that Adler confided his disappointment and his decision to give up the Yiddish theatre.

Sonya's white face turned whiter at this news, and her eyes

filled with confusion and fear. In a small voice she admitted it was only because of him that she had ever come anywhere near Rosenberg or his troupe.

The young man passed in a moment from a state of dejection to highest happiness. This girl, so far above him in every way, had wished to unite her destiny with his! The thought transported him. And it must be noted that this surge of joy came from the rebirth of all that was best in his nature, reaffirming for him that life itself was meaningful, was *worthy*.

All that spring the lovers walked together through the city, pausing dreamily at the house where Pushkin had passed his exile or wandering down the Tsar's Steps to the sea. Jacob was accustomed to girls of quite a different sort. But it was just the restraints Sonya put on him that gave him his joy, proving to him continually that he had found a higher love.

They talked, this curious pair, less of their love than of the Yiddish theatre. Adler confessed all his doubts, certain Sonya would share them. To his surprise, she came to the defense of the Yiddish theatre. She defended even Rosenberg's troupe. Bad and weak as it was, she said, hesitant as she had been to enter it, it was still Yiddish theatre, still a beginning, a start.

"How was it she saw it all so early and so clearly, this girl of an assimilated family from Courland?" Adler writes. "At a time when our young people were mad for everything European, everything Russian, Sonya took the poor Yiddish theatre under her wing. She spoke of the Greeks, how they smeared their mouths with grape juice, rode about in wagons, and yet from this beginning made their great art. She spoke of Shakespeare's day. No scenery, nothing but a shield with a word written on it. Juliet, Ophelia, Lady Macbeth, all played by boys because no woman would demean herself by standing on a stage. She spoke of the noble Rachel, of the divine Sarah Bernhardt, of Sonnenthal in Germany, of the American giant, Booth. A heaven opened for me at her words. Long after my doubts were overcome I returned to this theme, only to hear her speak again!"

Sonya's family was not pleased with her choice, but had to accept it, for she was not to be swayed. When Alexander Oberlander one day spoke slightingly of her lover, his well-bred sister threw a book at him!

Sonya had a strong position in Rosenberg's company as the only actress. She pressed Rosenberg to give Adler his chance, and he was finally promised the role of Guberman in *Breindele Cossack.*

A thunderbolt fell on these plans. News came by telegraph one day that Goldfaden was on his way to Odessa. His debts had been forgiven, he was bringing a cast of forty-two actors, and he had already engaged the Remesleni Club.

Rosenberg's actors held an emergency meeting. Some of them felt they should stay in Odessa and compete for the field. Rosenberg was more realistic. Once the Goldfaden Dramatic Society arrived, who would care for the Bucharest Troupe? He knew he must run, but did not want to run far. Suddenly he struck himself on the forehead and said excitedly, "Wait! They have a Goldfaden? We also have a Goldfaden!" The playwright's brother, Naphtali, a watchmaker, lived in a nearby town. With him as their manager, they could also call themselves the Goldfaden Company.

A tour was quickly planned, taking in the towns of Cherson, Ackerman, and Chandrikova. Alexander Oberlander went out as their advance agent. He took money and posters with him, and three days later sent back a triumphant telegram: "Cherson is ours!"

The troupe set out, bag and baggage, on the steamboat *Jason.* Adler took a leave of absence from the Department of Weights and Measures and left with the others. He was to make his debut in the town of Cherson.

They sailed on a fall day of strong wind. The *Jason* rocked, and the new actor's heart pounded. Everyone was laughing, joking, all were in highest spirits. Only Adler was sick with fear. Sonya told him this was the best possible sign. "It shows you are not a light-minded person, but serious, responsible, an artist!" she said.

The *Jason* steamed on. Cherson. The Dniester grows very narrow at this point. Flowers. Trees. On the shore a crowd of Jews, all beautifully dressed, the women in flowered summer hats, the men in frock coats. The *Jason* drew near. A hurrah went up from the pier, and a band struck up in honor of the Yiddish actors.

6

A Real Actor!

> A moment to measure the audience like an opponent in a duel, and then I heard it—my lullaby, my Kaddish, my dirge—the first, the eternal, the sound of applause!
>
> JACOB ADLER

Cherson seemed to be populated entirely by ex-soldiers of Nicholas I. The whole town lived on municipal money, and every second person held an official post. In spite of this, the Jewish streets were shabby, poor, with small, rundown houses and stores.

Oberlander had not been able to get the theatre, and they were to play in a warehouse. The owner, Lipitz Beygun, had cleared it of grain, oats, and flour, built a stage for the actors, and imported scenery for them from Spain. He did all this from love of art, asking nothing in return. A tall, stern, red-faced, red-haired man who looked more a Russian than a Jew, he had served his Tsar as a soldier for twenty-five years.

"Tulya" (Naphtali) Goldfaden joined them two days later. This Goldfaden looked very like his brother, but unlike him rarely spoke or laughed.

At their first rehearsal a young tailor's assistant showed up. Avrom Fishkind had once longed to be a folk singer. Now he yearned to be an actor. Rosenberg gave him a tryout. The nineteen-year-old boy recited a poem and performed a little dance of his own devising. Rosenberg saw he had talent and gave him the role of Hotzmach in *The Witch*. Fishkind and

Adler made their debuts on the same night. Though neither of them could know it, they were to gypsy it together for some fifty years to come.

As his opening drew near, Adler began to suffer from sinking spells and sensations of heat and cold. He asked himself a thousand times why a man with his desire for success should have chosen such a horribly uncertain profession.

On the night of his debut, Sonya and Rosenberg stayed with him in his dressing room, trying to put some heart in him. He could see nothing ahead but humiliation and ruin.

A rap at the door, and the sharp call "Adler! Adler!" told him his moment had come.

Rosenberg had once seen a Russian director make the sign of the cross over an actor making his first appearance. He gave Adler his own version of this blessing, a hand stretched over his head in the sign of the *Kohanim,* and a whispered, "May God be gracious unto you! May God give you his light!"

Adler took his place in the wings. Onstage a party scene, the birthday of Mirale, his beloved. The guests are calling him through the garden. "Marcus! Marcus!" He heard the cue through the roaring in his ears.

"Once on a stormy day I saw a peasant on a raft out in the river. He hesitated, braced himself, and making the sign of the cross, plunged into the unknown. I am no peasant, I did not make the sign of the cross, but like him, I braced myself and plunged. Onto the stage—and into my life!"

From the first he had luck. The audience, sensing his fire and strong determination, broke instinctively into applause. He shot out his first speech as though from a gun and went through the whole act without understanding his own lines. Thinking he had surely failed, he heard applause and, as the curtain fell, Sonya's enthusiastic, "Bravo, Adler! *Prevoskhodno!*" * He had gotten through. The actors were clapping him on the back and Rosenberg, all smiles, exclaimed, "Well, you were a marvel! A real beauty!"

He passed a more serious test a few nights later as Guberman, the sixth husband, in *Breindele Cossack.* Determined to conquer the terrible Breindele, Guberman ends up, like the others, as her victim. It was an interesting role, calling on the actor to portray not only love, hate, jealousy but also fatal character weakness. Best of all were Adler's scenes with Sonya.

---

* "Excellent!"

A real love affair can always be sensed by the audience, and theirs was flaming.

With the success of *Breindele,* the company gave itself over to pleasure. They idled, had good times every night, and spent their days strolling about in Potemkin's Gardens, a famous feature of Cherson.

In those years a statue of Catherine the Great adorned the center of this park. Stories of the Empress and her many lovers had often been heard, but Adler declares that never were there such stories as Rosenberg's, and never were they so masterfully told. Such shouts of laughter came from the actors that strangers drew near, also laughing, and Adler marvelled at his friend anew.

Everywhere they went they were pointed out with a whispered, *"Evraiski aktiory!"*—"Jewish actors!" People stared, some with wonder, some with mockery, one or two even with fear. One day a frightened peasant spat at the sight of them; when one sees the devil, one does what one can to protect oneself.

The streets of the town were drowned in sunflower seeds. Couples walked in Potemkin's Gardens, flirted, courted each other, and spat seeds. For years afterward any mention of the great Empress reminded Adler of the streets, the alleys, the people of Cherson.

Days of unclouded pleasure could not last forever. One morning Rosenberg received a telegram. Goldfaden had made a triumphal entrance into Odessa, had gone on to St. Petersburg, and had obtained there a permit good for all of Russia. His troupe was soon to open at the Remesleny Club. At this news a treacherous emotion awoke in Adler's breast:

"How ungrateful is the human heart! We played, we had success, money—what more did we need? Now I heard Goldfaden was in Odessa. *My* Odessa. And a voice whispered, 'If it must be Yiddish theatre, let it be the real thing! To him, to him, to Goldfaden'!"

His own guilty longing showed in every face, even Sonya's. Rosenberg saw it all and turned pale. With a forced laugh, he remarked that an actor had to be a lunatic, a fool, to have anything to do with Goldfaden. The man kept everything for himself—for the actor not a *groschen*. Honor, recognition, not a taste of it! Only Goldfaden existed! "Go to him!" Rosenberg advised them, laughing. "You'll soon come back to me for life!"

Nobody answered. Rosenberg broke out again, this time more sincerely. What magic did they think Goldfaden possessed with this great Roumanian troupe of his? "We can show all of Russia our *Shmendrick!*" Rosenberg flung out passionately. "We are ten times, a hundred times better than all of them!"

He spoke with a heart full of insulted pride, and at that moment Adler respected him. But the moment passed. Once again Rosenberg was the mountebank, the clown. He began to caper about madly, to predict they would all go to China, play *Shmendrick* in pigtails. . . . The spark in his soul had gone out.

One fine day the troupe boarded ship and steamed back to Odessa on the same *Jason* that had taken them to Cherson.

Adler had brought home a pocketful of press notices and could not wait to show them to his mother. He burst in, joyfully shouting that he had passed his examination, that he was an artist, an actor! Hessye met him with tear-reddened eyes, and handed him a letter from the Department of Weights and Measures. Adler had overstayed his leave of absence and lost his job.

Great ladies are so clamorous and full of complaint as any other where their sons are concerned, and Hessye at this point sounds like any mother in Odessa. Her son had thrown away a golden, an honored position! And for what? For a career as a clown, a buffoon! He had done nothing less than kill himself with his own hands.

At this moment a rift might easily have opened between mother and son. Another man might have allowed himself bitter reflections, reached at best a cold, intellectual tolerance of a mother so out of touch with his own views of life. But the emotional impulse that united these two was too powerful and too simple to allow such a division. Neither of them would have survived it.

Of all the arrows the son possessed, he reached for the one that could not fail to find its target: the inmost truth of his feelings. He described his passion for the stage, a passion that could take health and even life. He confessed his terrible need for success, recognition. He swore to his mother he would one day stand with the greatest. He described what it meant to hold an audience, lift it to the heights. Ablaze with his vision, he cried, "Mama! There is nothing greater in the world than to stand, a true artist, on the stage!"

Hessye felt grief and bewilderment, but felt most of all, that her son still belonged to her. She dried her tears, tried to grasp these ideas of a time so different from her own, and found refuge from her fears in the dreams of her son.

That evening, dressed in his best, and at peace with the world, Jacob met his fellow actors at Falconi's pastry shop. He found them with one name on their lips—Goldfaden. They talked of the sensation his arrival had made, his performances at the Remensleny, his plans. The actors were dying to meet him, and were badgering Rosenberg to arrange it.

Rosenberg himself seemed to be sitting on hot coals. He looked at once downcast, helpless, and resentful. Besieged on every side, he still refused. Adler, who knew him best, felt there was more here than anger at their ingratitude, more even than fear of competition. Rosenberg, always open-hearted as a child, broke down finally and came out with the truth.

He had tried to make up his quarrel with Goldfaden in Roumania. He had come onto the stage of the Jignitza Theatre, held out his hand in friendship. Goldfaden greeted him with, "So you are back, the Odessa dog who stole my plays!" And instead of taking Rosenberg's outstretched hand, he had struck him a blow in the face. Rosenberg almost fell to the ground with shame. He made his way out into the corridor and wept there for two hours.

"Now he is in Odessa," Rosenberg told the actors. "This is my city. Here I could pay him back. But he is greater than I! I will not lift a finger against him, but go to him—never!"

After such an insult the actors could hardly blame him. Yet they could not give up their own hopes.

The following day a group of them went to the Remesleny and the two acting companies met for the first time. The Roumanians, busy with their rehearsal, took little interest in the Odessa actors. The two leading ladies, Annetta and Margaretta Schwartz, wore dresses made in Paris, and not even the richest ladies in Odessa had such dresses. Both sisters carried parasols set with false stones that glittered when they walked, drawing all eyes to them. They hardly deigned a glance at Sonya Michelson in her modest costume.

Maurice (Moishe) Finkel, the folk singer, had also become exceedingly grand. Now Goldfaden's *regisseur,* he hardly had a word to say to the Russians. The only one who talked and jested with them like an actor and a colleague was Laizer Zuckerman. Adler had been curious to meet this famous young comedian now captivating Odessa audiences. Slender as an eel, mercurial in his moods, Zuckerman liked a drink, was far too lively to put on airs, and was often to be found in low company. Adler found him much more to his taste than the icy Finkel:

"Finkel was all importance, Zuckerman was all gaiety," he writes. "Finkel's eyes said, 'Careful, rabble, remember who I am!' Zuckerman's eyes said, 'Brother, let's drink and have a time together.' Finkel looked down at the world from the top of a high mountain. Zuckerman played at the foot of the mountain with puppies, kittens, and children. Naturally, I preferred Zuckerman."

Goldfaden was never seen at the Remesleny these days. The details of productions were all in the hands of Finkel, while Goldfaden devoted himself only to his business affairs. He had opened offices in Richelevskaya Street, and even the actors were announced by the uniformed porter at the door. Sonya and Adler sought out a rich friend, a manufacturer called Fischandler, who knew Goldfaden well and promised to introduce them.

They met the following day in the anteroom of the Richelevskaya Street office, an imposing room, richly furnished and already filled with those who had come before them. A low hum of voices filled the air. It was rather like a small court, with everyone waiting for the king to appear. After a long wait, the inner door opened, and everyone sprang to their feet. All hats came off as Goldfaden entered.

Adler saw a handsome man, tall, stalwart, charming, with a tiny beard, a smart little moustache, and a serious look that struck a false note—it did not go with his laughing eyes. Goldfaden wore a blue Hungarian uniform with Brandenberg epaulettes. A typically Roumanian costume. Adler was conscious of a certain disappointment. This was neither a great man nor a great Jew, but a worldling, a *bon vivant*.

The millionaire Fischandler presented his friends, and after some compliments, Goldfaden turned and called a familiar name. To their astonishment, Rosenberg trotted out of the inner room. He had somehow gotten back in Goldfaden's good graces, and they were again on good terms.

Rosenberg made some nervous jokes, admitted that Adler and Michelson had talent, adding with a laugh, "But they are mine! Don't take them away from me!" Realizing he could not prevent them from coming, he had come ahead of them to bar the way.

After some pleasantries Goldfaden introduced Adler and Sonya to the character comedian Moishe Teich, not without making some jokes at his expense. Teich, who was stone deaf, read the actors' lips onstage. "Catches his cues as a dog catches fleas," Goldfaden said with an unpleasant laugh. Since Teich heard nothing, he continued to smile. He was a small, middle-aged man, ugly, bald, but with fine eyes. He was wearing a suit too big for him, shoes too big for him, a broad tie with a cheap clasp and a handkerchief none too clean. As he withdrew Sonya asked pityingly if he had not a wife to look after him.

"He is married, but stingy," Goldfaden replied.

Sonya, disregarding this, went up to the deaf comedian, drew up a chair near his, talked with him a long time, and when it came time to leave, pressed his hand with unaffected warmth and respect.

Her lover did not think less of her for it.

With Rosenberg and Goldfaden friends again, the two companies began to mingle. Not far from Odessa were the fashionable Baths of Liman, noted for their curative effect on rheumatism, gout, and other infections. Goldfaden took a *datcha* for the summer, and both troupes gathered at the table of their father and rabbi.

The actors took up almost all the rooms in the town, and hired a little tram that took them around the salt coastal lakes to a German establishment they christened the *Liebenthal*.*

Adler and Sonya, a sedate engaged couple, came every day by train. They could not afford the expense, but Liman drew them like a magnet.

Life that summer centered on the beach. Rosenberg, chief clown and fun maker, specialized in practical jokes on the Roumanians, which Goldfaden repaid in kind. As the summer wore on, the jokes got rougher. Goldfaden capsized a rowboat one day with six of the Odessa actors in it.

With the coming of fall, the directors put on their winged capes and went back to the city. The season had begun and all Odessa was alive with theatre news. Goldfaden, indulgent Papa,

---

* The Valley of Love.

gave his blessing to the new company, put his brother at the head of it, and sent them out to the provinces again.

Adler was in the doldrums. He had set his heart on an engagement with Goldfaden, but only Spivakovsky had been taken into the Roumanian company. Rosenberg laughed and told him to buck up, better times would come. His troupe had been given over to Tulya Goldfaden, yet he did not lose heart. Adler plucked up some courage. Here Rosenberg had lost everything, and still he was gay!

They left the city almost unnoticed. They were only the "Provincial Troupe." The others were the great "Roumanian Academic Dramatic Society." The Remesleny could no longer hold their audiences; they were soon to play at the Marinsky! The Russians were glad to leave Odessa, where they felt like shadows.

Low spirits lifted on the way to Kishinev, first leg of their tour. They arrived at nightfall. A big lively town, with the streets lit by gas. Officers swaggered along the boulevards, showing off their uniforms. *Coursistes* with short hair strolled arm in arm, and everywhere one saw dark, charming, laughing Moldavians. Their posters were up all over the Jewish quarter, and everywhere Jews crowded around them. The troupe explored the town and went into a restaurant to try the rare Bessarabian wine.

They were quartered in Grossman's hotel, and were to play in a little theatre on the same premises. It was a real theatre, the only one in the city, and complete with red velvet seats, scenery, and even loges. They were to open Sunday night, which gave them three days to rehearse.

Sunday morning Adler woke to find Rosenberg, very pale, bending over him. "Adler! Adler! Look!" Rosenberg said in a low tense voice. "Look into the court!"

Adler sprang to the window. The ground below was covered with hundreds of sleeping men, women, and children. The word "pogrom" flashed through his mind. But no. These people had not been driven from their homes by a Cossack raid. They had spent the night on the bare ground of the court so as to be sure of tickets that night to the Yiddish theatre.

One by one the actors stole in, some in coats, some wrapped in blankets. Many of them were brushing tears from their eyes. "You see, Yankele!" Rosenberg murmured. "You see a love, a gratitude! And all for Yiddish theatre! Did you and I ever dream of Yiddish theatre, brother?"

"I see that picture," Adler wrote forty years later, "with all its thousands of details as though they were before me yet. A thousand times in my moments of doubt I have called it to mind, and a thousand times it has given me strength. Great God! When my end draws near, grant that with my last breath, before my eyes close forever, I see that picture one last time!"

In Kishinev a traveling Russian troupe performed at Grossman's on the nights they did not play. Adler and Sonya went to see them and agreed they had not seen a better troupe even in Odessa. But they did not invite the Russians to their own performances. Adler hoped, indeed, that they would not come. He felt shame for the foolishness of their plays, the makeshift carelessness of their staging.

The Yiddish troupe was enjoying a great success in Kishinev, and the Russian company, friendly at first, could not keep back sarcastic remarks that gave away their true feelings.

With ease and money came idleness. No new plays, no rehearsals. Nobody cared. The best Jewish homes of the city were open to the actors. Card parties were organized. Adler learned to play Oke, a game of four cards with the high card taking the other three. An indifferent player, he wanted only to win—and always lost.

The cellar singers did not take part in these evenings. Slaves of the troupe, they did not mingle, or want to mingle, with the others.

The most popular actor was Rosenberg. Adler, however, got better press notices. On the field of love, too, he easily beat his friend. In no city was Adler so honored by the feminine sex as Kishinev. The fancy women of the town were particularly enamored of him and fought each other for his attentions. Relations between Sonya and Adler were growing cool. Sonya took little interest in his doings these days, and did not protest even when he lost at the card tables. One day they met by appointment on the boulevard, and Adler asked, with some apprehension, about their future. Sonya answered coolly, "We will see." After a moment she added, with a look of repressed pain, "You are too much the Don Juan, Yakob. I am not sure I can trust your character."

One evening, when Adler had indulged too liberally in wine, Sonya took Tulya Goldfaden's arm on the street in preference to his own. Instantly he was wild with jealousy. He made a scene as soon as they got to the hotel, and spent the rest of the night in a brothel.

He had known these rages before, often when the woman herself meant nothing to him. In houses just off Odessa's Deribosovskaya Street, there were enchanted princesses in silk dresses who spoke in accents of sugared refinement. He had felt an insane rage when the princess of his choice happened to show her favors to another. He had even experienced jealousy when the girl was far from the most beautiful in the place. At such moments it was right and proper for a young gentleman to smash mirrors, rip down hangings, overturn furniture. As long as he paid, these excesses were not held against him.

Now the darkness of those nights closed in on him again. He was losing Sonya and would not see that it was his own doing. At times he wanted to pack up, go home, forget everything. This was not the life he had dreamed of. Under the management of Tulya Goldfaden, the theatre had been reorganized on a crass business basis. No more idealistic comradeship, no more communistic "shares." Managers and stars spent their time in low places, with people of low character.

"The police and militia had become our boon companions," Adler writes. "And every night, before the performance ended, the snorting of their horses could be heard outside. As soon as the curtain fell, a wild masquerade began. The officers flung their brass-buttoned uniforms to the actors while they themselves put on the costumes of rabbis, *chasidim*, village fools. All the officers fought for Katzman's Shmendrick costume. Katzman himself was thrown into a general's coat and set up on a horse. His head fuddled with wine, the eighteen-year-old boy rode in this fashion over the streets of Kishinev, for the first time truly looking like a Shmendrick! And these wild doings went on every night. Together with the petty police officials and the night patrol of Cossacks, we rioted and caroused until the small hours, stopping everywhere to drink and make merry. Others joined our revels, women became our followers. . . .

"I looked for the earlier 'I,'" Adler continues, "but could not find it. I will not pretend I was a saint until now, but my follies had been those of a young man, a boy who might still hope to do better. Now I was drawn every night into the lowest company. I learned to come home at daybreak with an unsteady step, to sleep away half the day, to receive love letters.... In the new career to which I had so long aspired I had as yet shown no great marvels, but I was already 'a real actor'!"

One incident before they left Kishinev must be noted. A friend approached Adler one day and told him that a young man called Kessler who had once put on some kind of show in the town was hoping to be taken into the company. Adler agreed to look him over.

This David Kessler was the son of a Kishinev innkeeper, a dour, pious man with a houseful of children and no money to feed them. Since the innkeeper's son had no turn for books, he was sent out as a peddler on the Kishinev streets. There he was called "Dovidl-with-the-Kobze" because he sang his wares, accompanying himself on a kobze, a kind of beggar's guitar.

At night young Kessler would come home and describe the people he had seen, some of them guileless and innocent, others cruel and false. The bad sort enraged him. He would mimic their false smiles, their brutality, finishing the performance with a deep growl and a curse on their heads.

Yiddish theatre was much talked about in the town restaurants and wine shops, and Kessler was a frequenter of such places. One day he saw a poster announcing the coming of a Yiddish troupe. The star, Abba Schoengold, was praised in terms so absurd that the sixteen-year-old boy turned away with a shout of sardonic laughter.

Years later, when Kessler told the journalist Abe Cahan how he had laughed at the poster, he added seriously, "But when I saw him on the stage I went along with every word of it!" He had left the theatre in a daze. He could think of nothing but Abba Schoengold, his appearance, his cloak, the spell of his voice. And the thought came into his head that he too would be an actor.

Kessler went home, cleaned out an empty stable, hammered together a stage with his own hands, dragged in some benches and, gathering some boys and girls of the neighborhood, began to put on "plays." He had no idea a play was performed from a text; he simply strung together what he remembered of Abba Schoengold's scenes and speeches. A few people came out of curiosity and went away laughing. His father, enraged at his craziness, shut him out of the house, but his soft-hearted mother sneaked him in again.

An educated man called Geller looked in on one of these stable performances, and it seemed to him there were flashes of talent in the posturing of this young Kessler. Geller had once tried his hand at a comedy he called *Mechtze the Matchmaker*. Since he was leaving for Paris, where he later became a physician, he made Kessler a present of the manuscript. Kessler gave the comedy lead to a boy called Leon Nadolsky, took the dramatic lead himself, and put the play on in Moser's Hall, a public room where weddings and other celebrations took place. A man who owned a hall in the nearby town of Dubasori invited him to come and give his show there, and the troupe put on two performances of Geller's comedy in this town.

Two years later, when Rosenberg's troupe came, Kessler began hanging about the theatre. The actors did not even notice the angry surly boy. Kessler finally asked a friend who knew Jacob Adler to speak for him. Their meeting took place soon after at the gate of the New Market.

Adler, coming to the appointed place, saw a powerful-looking boy, about eighteen years old, with the neck and shoulders of a bull and a lowering, angry brow. He was wearing heavy boots, a rough cloak. His entire demeanor was not promising.

The conversation was brief.

"You would like to be an actor?"

"I have thought of it."

"You've had some experience?"

"Here in Moser's Hall. Also in the town of Dubasori."

"Good. Come to the theatre tomorrow and let us see what you can do." Adler turned away, unaware he had just met his appointed rival and adversary.

Kessler appeared the following morning and went through the dramatic scene of his "success." The actors could not restrain roars of laughter, and one of them, a wag, kept stealing up behind the tragic hero and giving him a blow on the top of his head. The second time this occurred, Kessler caught the jokester by his collar and said in an even tone, "Listen to me, my friend. One more such trick, and you will have cause to remember me." He got through the rest of his tryout without interruption.

Adler has tactfully omitted all reference to this incident from his memoirs; it is from Kessler himself we learn of it.

Rosenberg would have taken him on as an extra, but as things turned out, he did not leave with the troupe. Such a storm broke in his family, there was such an outcry from his father that his son should go off to be an organ grinder, a *katarintchik,* that he was forced to submit. Two years later a wandering troupe came through Kishinev. When they left the town Kessler and Leon Nadolsky went with them. They remained three years with this little company, playing in the backs of grocery stores and suffering great hunger and want.

When Kessler left his home to be an actor, his father and mother sat *shivve* as for the dead.

Rosenberg and his actors left Kishinev at the end of November. A great crowd came to the station to see them off, and handkerchiefs were waved and tears shed, for they had been much loved in this city. They had a fine journey back to Odessa, and at every stop along the way Adler ran out to the station buffet to fetch fruit, candy, and tea for his Sonya. Throughout the trip he hovered about her; no trouble too great if it would bring her a momentary pleasure. Without words, without explanations, the rift between them was healing. Their eyes, their smiles spoke of a growing happiness. They could not bear to be a moment apart.

A beautiful journey, and with a beautiful ending. A great crowd of friends had gathered at the station, among them Adler's mother and little sister, come to welcome him home. Hessye had come with arms full of flowers and eyes full of tears. News of her son's triumphs had come home before him. She embraced him with a heart bursting with pride.

"Hardest of all, to win the recognition of those nearest and dearest," Adler observes. "Have you, my readers, ever tasted this particular satisfaction? Take my word for it—it is not at all bad!"

A man who has truly experienced a pain or a pleasure does not exaggerate, but describes it precisely. "Not at all bad" is hardly the phrase a man would use to describe his greatest moments. But it is precisely in its lesser moments that life sometimes offers us a joy unmixed with pain or disappointment, a joy, moreover, that cannot be snatched away again. Adler's modest "Not at all bad" sums up very well all the savor of this perfect little victory.

7

Love and War in a Provincial Troupe

> The profits of a Yiddish troupe were divided into one hundred even parts, or, as we called them, *marks*. Each player received so many marks according to his value in the troupe. It was supposed to be a communal system, but it did not work out that way. The managers took more than half for expenses, the big stars took their big bear's share. What was left for the rest of us? *Sechka!* A mash of straw, hay, and oats that left the belly swollen and the mouth dry!
>
> JACOB ADLER

They had to remain in Odessa for a number of weeks. Tulya Goldfaden was awaiting tour directives from his brother; Rosenberg wanted the new Goldfaden operettas. Zuckerman advised them both to apply to Maurice Finkel. Goldfaden, he said, had now grown so great one needed a ladder to look at him!

Everyone spoke of Adler as an actor now. Even his father, once so pessimistic, kept the Kishinev reviews in his pocket and with the slightest encouragement, read them out to everyone. Adler, however, was passed over again for an Odessa engagement. He was gnawed by jealousy of Spivokovsky, now treading the boards of the great Marinsky in roles he himself had played only in Kishinev and Cherson.

Finkel finally came through with some plays and the company went on to Elisavetgrad. They were excited at the prospect, for this was a really big city, and they wanted to succeed.

It was their first long journey. Sonya and Adler read the Russian papers, and the rest of the actors played cards to pass the time. Pullmans were as yet unknown. They slept on their luggage, with a fist for a pillow, and awoke at dawn to see snow-covered villages and fields gliding past the train windows.

They got off the train at seven in the morning with unwashed faces and unsaid prayers. In those early years these actors, good Chasidic Jews, still recited a morning prayer and felt guilty if they left out or hurried through any part of it. The sight of Elisavetgrad, stately and beautiful in the morning sun, sent their spirits up again. "We will take her!" they shouted, laughing. "We will conquer! We will rule!"

People turned to stare as they went laughing down the street. Their high silk hats, a type of headgear unknown in this city, produced a particular sensation.

Since an opera company occupied the City Theatre, they played at the Voronsky Hall, an officers' club with a small but adequate stage. They opened, as usual, with *Shmendrick*.

A newspaper critic called Lehrman, a little man with a red beard and small, fierce red eyes, took an interest in the Yiddish players, came to all their rehearsals and went out with them each night after the play. Adler was hoping for a word of praise from this critic, but found himself ignored in every review. He waited impatiently for *Breindele Cossack*, for he felt that his Guberman would surely make the journalist sit up and take notice. Instead, no review of the play appeared at all. The whole company felt this was bad. Never before had they been completely ignored, and in such an important play, too. They told each other the review would probably appear the following day, but Adler's heart was filled with misgivings.

At noon the actors gathered for rehearsal, and the usual jokes and horseplay began. Suddenly Lehrman himself appeared. He made a deep bow, did not offer to shake hands with anyone, and addressing them all in the severe, dry tone of the pedagogue, said, "*Gospoda*, the performance of *Breindele Cossack* convinced me first that the writer himself should be sternly rebuked for having written such a piece, and second that the whole company, with the exception of Fraulein Michelson, deserve to be castigated for such playing as I saw last night."

Adler's heart began to pound. Lehrman went on to characterize them all as mountebanks and clowns, not actors. He came down hardest of all on Rosenberg, whom he accused of resorting to every cheap trick to wring a laugh from the most ignorant part of his audience. He ended by declaring he would not come to the theatre again until he was told they deserved to be reviewed. And in a deathly silence, he left the hall.

"Well, Adler, I am sorry for you," Rosenberg remarked. "Your good looks, and your success with the *M'amzelles* turned your head. Now you have heard the truth. The applause has fooled you. The bravos are empty. Study, observe life, learn—and someday you may deserve to call yourself an actor."

Adler broke out in a sweat. Seeing this, Rosenberg began to prance madly about the stage. "To hell!" he cried recklessly. "The public wants to laugh! Let them laugh!"

Bad days followed. Adler's success lost all meaning for him. He grew thin and pale, and slid through the streets like a shadow. "Nobody sadder than a sad clown," he recalls. "Who wants to be his friend?"

He added up his achievements. Except for one or two character bits, he had postured, posed, and shown his fine face and figure to the public. Nothing more. It was a sorry reckoning. He spared himself none of it. One day on the street he exclaimed aloud, "Enough of the fake! Let's be an actor!"

That same day he took himself to the barber, emerging with no more hair on his head than other ordinary mortals. He threw away his white cravat, his cane, and with them, all his youthful gaiety. His thoughts continually returned to Lehrman. Study, learn, the critic had said. But study where? Learn from whom?

After pondering for some days he decided Lehrman himself must be his help. Since he could tear down, destroy, he must know also how to build. On a sudden impulse he made his way to the critic's doorstep. Lehrman opened the door and was silent with surprise. Adler, raising great melancholy eyes, said, "You told me to learn. Here I am. Teach me."

Lehrman, touched, drew the whole company into his inner circle after this. Some fine things came of it, evenings the actors never forgot. The critic brought them together with all the serious intellectuals of the city. These people came regularly to his home to talk, to listen to readings of Rabinovitch

(Sholem Aleichem), Bogrof, and other writers of the day. The actors came away from these evenings with a sense of renewed purpose, for Lehrman and his friends all felt they had a great mission to perform.

The troupe got mixed reviews in Elisavetgrad, but the audience liked them. Things in fact were going well when, one morning, Spivakovsky walked in. A "black cat" had run between him and Goldfaden. He had come back to Rosenberg.

The actors hailed him with joy, but Adler's heart sank. He knew this boded no good. He and Spivakovsky were rivals, for both of them played romantic leads. Sure enough, posters soon went up, announcing *Breindele Cossack* with Spivakovsky in the role of Guberman.

For Adler it was as though someone had taken a great whip, and in the middle of the marketplace, struck him full in the face. For the first time he begged Sonya to intercede for him, begged her to refuse to play with Spivakovsky. But the cool-headed Sonya declared this would be a mistake; it would look to everyone as though Spivakovsky was the better actor and Adler played only through her protection. Sonya was certain that although Lehrman had reservations about Adler's Guberman, he would like Spivakovsky's even less. And there it ended, for Sonya would not be swayed.

Adler could neither stay away on the night Spivakovsky played, nor watch the performance. He remained outside in the corridor, pacing restlessly up and down. When Spivakovsky's entrance was greeted with a round of applause, Adler had an attack of hysterics. Oberlander had to take him out of the hall, get him home, and put him to bed. He lay there in a raging fever.

At one in the morning Sonya, Rosenberg, and Spivakovsky, all very worried, came from the theatre. They brought good news for the sick man. Spivakovsky had fallen through as Guberman, failed completely. Spivakovsky himself assured Adler of this, swearing he would never have taken the role had he known it would cause his friend a moment's pain.

Adler sat up in bed. His fever went down. He wanted to hear everything, every last detail. His friends did not leave him all that night, and when daylight came, Rosenberg ran down to get the papers. With joy and relief, Adler saw stretched half across the page the blessed headline: SPIVAKOVSKY'S FAILURE.

It had fallen out just as the clever Sonya had predicted.

The critic wrote that while Adler still suffered from certain faults in the role, his interpretation was superior to that of Spivakovsky. What a difference from the first time, when he had waited in vain for the review of *Breindele!* And the good Spivakovsky shared his happiness. He gave the role back to Adler with his whole heart, and these good friends all rejoiced together.

Only once again did Adler live through such a night followed by such a morning. This was in 1903, after the Broadway opening of *The Merchant of Venice:* "What would American critics say of a Shylock performing in Yiddish in a cast all speaking Shakespeare's immortal English? How would they accept an actor from New York's East Side ghetto in the role played by Booth, Novelli, and Sir Henry Irving? My family and friends stayed with me through the time of my ordeal. My agents, my managers, my American director, all of us waited out the hours. And with the daylight came our triumph. Every review an acclamation, extolling with highest praise my creation of Shylock. Great God, it had happened! Never did lover greet his love as I greeted that day—with joy, with champagne, with the congratulations and embraces of those I loved. Sleep? Who needed such a thing? I was alive in every nerve, alive as though I had been born again! Wonderful mornings, and both so different! The first in the morning of my life. The second only a little before its night."

With a frankness remarkable for that day, the aging actor confesses that the greatest triumph of his career did not exceed in joy what he felt in his youth at the downfall of a rival!

November went by, and December. Elisavetgrad lay deep in snow. Adler's great moment had come and gone; he was a fallen giant. Rosenberg and Tulya Goldfaden had valued him when he was their only *jeune premier*. Now, with Spivakovsky back, he felt the bitter difference. Then he had been consulted, advised with, the directors had treated him almost as one of themselves. Now he was shut out of their conferences. He had grown cheap in their eyes, and to become cheap meant less money. His clothes grew shabby and he could not afford new ones. He, who had thrown his roubles about, had to tremble over kopeks. He pawned his watch, fell into debt, learned the soul-shrinking shifts and evasions of poverty.

He was not the only one to suffer. Katzman, Oberlander, and others, too, felt the pinch. Sonya did somewhat better. Either because she had to support her parents or because of her power as their only actress, she was paid more regularly. Everyone else was living on diplomacy, delays, and promises. Tempers grow short on a diet of this kind. Rebellion was in the air.

At this worst possible moment, Yisrol Gradner suddenly turned up. He had returned from Constantinople to Odessa, patched up his quarrel with Goldfaden, and created a furor in the role of the Buba Yachne, the "Witch" herself. But the truce had not lasted. Goldfaden disliked Gradner's success and intrigued to push him down. Gradner, furious, stole his best actors and took them off with him to Nikolayev. Goldfaden wired the Nikolayev police master who stopped the performances, and Gradner went off, leaving the actors stranded. The troupe got back to Odessa only through the generosity of the Nikolayev Jews. Luckily, Goldfaden forgave them and took them back. Gradner, out of the troupe, went to Roumania, but was unable to make a living there, and had now come in desperation to Rosenberg.

It could not have been easy for this famous actor to come, hat in hand, to a wandering provincial company, but Gradner was no longer the great figure of former years. Reversals and failures had taken their toll. His wife had left him, and he had not recovered from this blow. His temperament had always worked against him. He had begun as the greatest star and never could accept any lesser place. His decisions were emotional and often did him harm. Word had gotten around that he was unreliable, a dangerous reputation in the theatre. Worse yet, he was said to bring bad luck!

Spivakovsky knew Gradner from Roumania and revered him as the first actor of the Yiddish theatre. Adler's memories went back still further, to the Odessa nights when they had been companions. Forgetting their rivalries, Spivakovsky and Adler joined forces to get Gradner into the company.

They met with strong opposition from Rosenberg. Although Gradner was an all-around character actor, he had won his chief fame as a comedian. Rosenberg could boast of only a limited talent in either genre. Gradner sang with charm and had a fine baritone voice. Rosenberg had no voice at all and relied on comedy antics to put over his songs. To these excellent reasons for dislike, Rosenberg added another: Gradner came from the north, from the Lithuanian provinces; the

Lithuanian speaks another dialect from the southern, or Volhynian, Jew. The "Litvish" dialect sounds harsh and ugly to the south Russian; the speech of the south has a lower-class ring to the Jew of the cultivated north. So as not to clash with the other actors, Gradner had to assume a "Deitchmerish" diction on the stage, a Germanized affectation that was to plague this theatre for many years to come.

To Rosenberg, a Lithuanian was a creature of another species, hardly a Jew at all. He threatened to quit the company if Gradner came into it, and swore that only bad luck would come of taking in "the Litvak." Adler and Spivakovsky, however, found an ally in Sonya, and another in Tulya Goldfaden. Rosenberg, outvoted, had to give way. Gradner came into the troupe.

Though still far from the mere shadow of himself that he became in later years, there was little trace now of the gay folk singer of Odessa days. Gradner was at this time in his mid-thirties, a man of medium height with gray eyes, long hair to his shoulders, and something of the poet about his brow. He dressed gallantly, careful of any speck on his black coat, his black hat. And though in his heart he probably did not think much of the provincial actors, he was merry with them and behaved like a colleague. One day Gradner went off without warning. He had gotten an offer elsewhere. Rosenberg was left in the lurch with his name already advertised and tickets sold to his performances.

All of Rosenberg's predictions had come true. Business had not improved while Gradner was in the troupe. On the contrary, it had fallen off. Now he was gone, leaving the company to meet its losses. And business got worse and worse. Rosenberg kept the troupe together by promising them better times as soon as they got to Kremantchuk. The Jews of that town had never seen theatre, and Rosenberg assured everyone they would make their fortunes there.

Things did pick up in Kremantchuk, an ugly but lively town; but still the actors got barely enough to keep body and soul together. They began to murmur, to complain they were starving while Rosenberg, Spivakovsky, and Tulya Goldfaden grew rich. Adler, seething over his own wrongs, organized a strike.

Sonya, Alexander Oberlander, Katzman, and one or two others met in Adler's hotel room. They swore they would stick together and make no separate terms with the management, and Adler drew up their demands: full salary or no performance that night.

Oberlander took the ultimatum to the three directors. He returned, very pale, with their answer: The performance would go on without them. This seemed mere bravado. *Shmendrick* had been announced. Katzman played the title role, and Katzman was with them. They waited, confident the directors would back down.

Time wore on, however, and no counteroffer was made. At seven o'clock, together with the loyal members of the cast, the three directors left the hotel for the theatre.

Adler and the others racked their brains. Katzman *was* Shmendrick! Unless they had gotten an actor from Odessa, how could they play? At nine o'clock, no longer able to bear the suspense, they sent Oberlander to the theatre. Oberlander returned after midnight, looking like a dead man. Rosenberg had played Shmendrick. The audience had gone mad for him.

Soon after this the three managers came through the hotel corridor. Their flushed faces, their triumphant air, all spoke of victory. They did not glance at the strikers, but went straight into Tulya Goldfaden's room across the corridor. Their talk came clearly through the closed door: *"Who needs them? Let them go!"* Words full of hatred and contempt.

Oberlander went back and forth from the directors to the group outside, coming back each time more pale. He finally brought a message for Sonya. The directors wanted a word with her. Adler guessed instantly that Oberlander had gone over. Flaming out, he declared that there would be no secrets! If the directors had anything to say, it must be to the whole group!

A wrangle began. Sonya, torn, felt she should go, listen at least to what they had to say. Adler argued against it. As she began to waver, her brother cried in a terrible voice, "Sonya! Our parents must have bread! Go to them!"

Adler lunged toward Oberlander, fists clenched; Sonya clung to him and held him back. She reasoned with him, swore she would make everything right if only he would let her go. "You can see they have beaten us!" she pleaded.

Full of rage, he denied it. How long could Rosenberg keep it up? How long would the audience accept him, an old man in the role of a boy, a child? Sonya was no longer listening. A set look had come into her face. She tore away, crossed the hall, and disappeared through that terrible door. Two of the strikers followed her. Only Katzman and Adler were left. The seventeen-year-old boy assured Adler in a trembling voice of his own loyalty.

The two of them sat together like people already buried. Snatches of song and laughter came from the room across the corridor. Waiters passed in and out carrying trays. Champagne corks popped. People of the town heard of the festivities, and newcomers arrived. Laughter was heard, singing.

Rosenberg came out at one point, laughed, and went back again. Something in his face told Adler the worst had happened. He jumped up like a lion, ran across the hall, and banged at the door, his blood boiling. He did not care if he caused a scandal, and banged like a madman. Spivakovsky finally opened the door, looked at him with bloodshot eyes, and closed it again, too drunk to speak. Adler began to pound again. "Let me in!" he shouted. "I want to see Sonya. I am going away. I want to say good-bye."

Oberlander opened the door. "You are going? With God's blessing! Mother, father, brother mean more to her than *love!*" He pronounced the word with a sneer, and slammed the door shut.

Adler went back to his corner, beaten and dazed. An hour later, Sonya came out. Surrounded by the three directors, she mounted the stairs to her room. She had not enough courage even to look at the man she had betrayed.

The company played a week without either Adler or Katzman. Adler would have gone back to Odessa, but lacked the money to get there. Katzman pawned his rings and then, with heartache, parted with a medallion that held his mother's picture. Adler had already let his watch go. Other trifles followed.

The days went by. The actors made merry, had parties. Adler lay in his corner and felt a snake drinking his blood. He grew thin and gaunt, pinched his cheeks to give them color before he left his room. Often he wept.

Deep winter came on. The actors organized gay sleighing parties on the lake, and Adler watched them from behind a bush. "My Sonya amuses herself, mingles with my enemies. One tucks her in, one covers her feet. Spivakovsky hovers about her. How charmingly she accepts his attentions! The bells jingle, the whips crack, the sleighs fly here and there over the frozen lake. I see Sonya's rosy face, hear her laughter, and wild plans of revenge seethe within me. I will make a scandal, do them all some terrible harm. Then, with inner weeping, no—better to harm myself! A hole in the ice. A note. Ended. No more Adler. Let them see what they have done to me!"

The stormy wind wailed, the frozen reeds at the edge of the water seemed to weep. He ran wildly along the lake. The snow drove into his face, the icy wind blew through his thin, worn fur. He ran until he was exhausted, then went to his room, put himself to rights and went to call on a friend named Zemlinsky. There he learned the company was leaving next day for Ekaterinoslav—a two-day journey by sleigh.

Sure enough, the following morning great covered troikas were brought around to the hotel door. Servants carried out boxes and baggage. Adler looked on with sick eyes. They were going on, leaving him.

The actors crowded around the sleds, Sonya among them in a red scarf, heavy furs. Spivakovsky danced about her. She smiled, looked happy. Adler noticed Katzman, too, among the others, his face full of a timid joy. He, too, wore a red scarf. His eyes fell away from those of his friend with a weak, guilty look. Adler understood. "A lonely Odessa kid had become a favorite, a star. Give it up? For what? For friendship? Could I ask him to put out his own sun? And would it help me if Katzman lost everything?"

Adler forgave him, but the sense of his own misfortune was not lighter. He searched among these old friends for one face, one pair of eyes that would look into his with sympathy, even with pity. "Bad when a person wants pity," he comments tersely, "but to be alone is worse."

Suddenly he noticed that Rosenberg was behaving strangely. He stood far from the others, and gazed at Adler with frightened eyes. Adler turned into the hotel and went into his room. Rosenberg followed, but at a distance. In a few minutes the company prompter, a man called Avrom Zetzer, knocked at Adler's door to say that the managers wished to speak to him.

"No!" Adler answered—but waited for the request to be made again. The prompter repeated it, and Adler replied quickly and drily, "Very well."

Zetzer left, and a moment later came back followed by Rosenberg. A silence ensued.

"You are going away?" Rosenberg asked timidly. "You are leaving?"

Adler answered him with a profound volley of curses. "Where should I go, sickness rot your soul? And with what?"

Rosenberg leaned against the wall, covered his face, and began to weep. Adler looked at him with the unutterable contempt of a good actor for a bad one. Zetzer, overcome with pity, murmured, "Adler, how can you have such a heart?"

After a moment, Rosenberg raised his head, took Adler's hand and said, with pathos, "Yankele, let us part friends. Go in good health. If you should see my wife, my parents, give them my greetings."

Adler cursed him again for a charlatan and a faker. The whole of his anger came out in a torrent, and he flung it at Rosenberg's head. They had stolen Sonya from him, stolen his friends, cheated him of his wages. Now, robbed, naked, he was to go?

"I don't tell you to go!" Rosenberg protested with a pathetic look. "For my part you can stay!"

But Sonya's name had given Rosenberg the opening he needed. He began pouring fire and brimstone on her, painting in darkest colors the story of her treachery. "Two hundred roubles!" he exclaimed. "Two Katarinas meant more to her than all your love!" Never once in all these days, Rosenberg continued, had Sonya said one good word for him. His heart had ached to see such coldness, such indifference. He urged Adler to send her and all women to the devil, and to come along to Ekaterinoslav. They were traveling in covered sleighs, taking along the Kremantchuk musicians. In every inn along the road they would stop and have a time of it. "Hey! Off the road!" Rosenberg cried in Russian, cracking an imaginary whip. "Odessans are on their way! Yankele Pavlovitch Adler is on his way!"

Adler, plunged in thought, was forming his own pictures. In Ekaterinoslav, a gay town, he would find another bride, prettier than Sonya, richer, and even better educated. He would marry, establish himself as a great actor. And he pictured, with gloomy exultation, how Sonya would then regret her mistake.

On this dark thought, he said he would go.

Rosenberg's face lit up with joy, and Zetzer began to dance around the room. Rosenberg ran off to get Adler some money. "A hundred roubles, Yankele," he promised. "And let it be in a good hour!" He came back with a hundred-rouble note and a red scarf, which he himself knotted around his friend's neck.

Everyone in the courtyard cheered when they came out together; only Sonya remained discreetly invisible in her sledge. Adler would go with none of the others; he sulked haughtily in his own troika. At the last minute Rosenberg sent him company in the person of little Bettye Vinyavitch, the seventeen-year-old daughter of their orchestra leader. This child, as everyone knew, was hopelessly in love with Adler. He stroked her hair gently, but his thoughts were with the other, the false one.

Guests and servants came out of the hotel to shout Godspeed, and the actors began their journey. Whips cracked, troika bells rang out, the sledges glided merrily over the snow. All along the Jewish streets people came running out of stores and houses to wave farewell to the actors. "Good-bye, Shmendrick!" they called, laughing. "Sweet Shmendrick, ours, come back soon!"

From Kremantchuk to Ekaterinoslav was a two-day journey, ample time for the advance and retreat familiar to all quarreling lovers. Sonya courted him; he turned away in contempt. Sonya laughed with the others, forgot his existence; the ground fell away under him and he felt death approaching.

Throughout the journey Bettye Vinyavitch did not fail to give him a thousand instances of Sonya's faithlessness with Spivakovsky. Adler would have loved her better if she had told him less. Seething with jealousy, he determined that as soon as they got to their destination, he would take revenge on Sonya in a brothel.

They arrived far too late for any such expedition. It was well after midnight when they rolled into Ekaterinoslav, waking all the dogs in the town as they passed. In all the city only Lutzki's hotel was still lit up. The actors crept in, shivering. Servants were stuffing great bundles of straw into two big stoves. A table had been set with steaming dishes and a samovar. Rosenberg introduced Lutzki, owner of the hotel and greatest theatre lover in the town.

Adler in an evil mood went into another room, lay down on a couch, and fell asleep. He was awakened by a kiss. Sonya was bending over him. "Listen to me, Yakob," she whispered tenderly, "and I will explain everything."

"Away from me!" cried the enraged lover. Starting up, he pushed her off, threw her faithlessness at her head, and at last called her a vile name.

Sonya turned scarlet. Her eyes grew suffused, bloodshot,

and Adler, stunned, felt a stinging slap. Having avenged herself, Sonya promptly fell into a chair and went into convulsions. So violent was the outbreak of the restrained woman that half the hotel was roused. She was carried, alternately weeping and laughing, up the stairs to her room.

Adler remained below, feeling he had killed her. He had succeeded in putting himself completely in the wrong. Spivakovsky told him bitterly that he did not deserve the love of such a woman. Oberlander, too, heaped reproaches on his head, telling a story quite different from that of Rosenberg. According to the brother, Sonya had all along played a double game. Knowing Rosenberg and Tulya Goldfaden wanted to break up a love affair that gave Adler too much power in the troupe, Sonya had pretended to go along with them. Only after she had won their confidence had she brought her influence to bear. Adler had been taken back into the company, Oberlander assured him, only through Sonya's ceaseless work and persuasions.

Adler wavered. Could Sonya not have found some way to see him during his terrible isolation, his ordeal? Her smiles, her gaiety—could all this have been a mask? Yet he could not doubt her long. To lose faith in Sonya was to lose faith in heaven itself.

His heart full of questions, he left the hotel. Ekaterinoslav was deserted except for a heavily coated constable going his rounds. He walked through dark, unfamiliar streets, passed the Conservatory of Music, came to Lutzki's theatre, saw his name large on the posters, and in the midst of his great sorrow, rejoiced.

It was near dawn. Big wagons began rolling toward the market with produce from the country. Dogs lay on top of the wagons, guarding them. As it grew lighter church bells broke out on every side calling good Christians to mass.

He went back to the hotel. The night porter woke at the sound of his footsteps and, kind man, got him a cup of tea and a bagel. He ate, drank tea, read the Russian papers, fell into a doze, and woke to see Tulya Goldfaden and Rosenberg watching him.

"So it's peace, eh?" Rosenberg remarked with a poisoned smile. "I wanted to save you from the woman."

Adler turned away with something close to loathing. He was certain now that Oberlander had told the truth and that Rosenberg had lied. He went to his room and poured out all his doubts and his love in a letter. Broad daylight had come. He forgot the letter, went to Sonya's room, and in the classic manner of that more open-hearted time, fell at her feet and was forgiven.

They played together that night, and their love scenes "went with fire." Spivakovsky sent a bouquet with one word: "Forgive!" Adler forgave Spivakovsky, forgave Rosenberg, forgave the whole world. He was too happy to hate anyone.

He and Sonya were lovers now. They went about arm in arm, and everyone teased them. "Love!" Rosenberg would say, laughing, as soon as they appeared.

One night they came back to the hotel to find the main hall covered with flowers, a rabbi and a *shammos* both waiting. Zorach Vinyavitch and his orchestra, hidden behind a bank of flowers, struck up, and everyone came out of hiding and surrounded them, laughing.

They signed the wedding agreement that night. Telegrams came from Odessa. Rosenberg improvised couplets and Spivakovsky danced with Charlotta Spinner, a pretty cabaret singer who was now their ingenue. Happiest of all were Oberlander and Rosenberg.

Some weeks later, the actors gave another great party to celebrate their engagement. This was just before they left Ekaterinoslav.

They were married late that summer on the stage of Vassilievski's Hall in Poltava. A gala performance of *The Two Kuni Lemmels* was planned right after the ceremony, with the whole proceeds of the evening going to the newly wedded pair. Tulya Goldfaden wanted them to be married before the audience, but Sonya put her foot down. In the end, so many townspeople came as "witnesses" that it amounted to almost the same thing.

Adler walked about like an automaton, seeing and hearing nothing. He did not want to be married without his parents, but was afraid the actors would laugh at him. Doubts tortured him. He felt he had no right to marry Sonya, that his life had made him unworthy of her.

The night before the wedding he came to her door, white as a ghost. She had laid out her wedding dress on the bed, and at the sight of it he groaned aloud. He told her everything. All the sorry exploits of Buff's Army, all the sordid episodes of Odessa and Kishinev. He warned her that he had a bad heart, told her he would not live long. He had developed a morbid obsession that he would soon die, and believed what he said.

Sonya made light of everything. His weak heart, she assured him, she would soon cure. As for his character, his confession itself would be her guarantee. "Never mind, Yaschenka," she said rather sadly. "You will lift yourself out of all that. We will have a good life. You will become a fine man, and you will be a great artist." With a swift change of mood she suddenly pushed him backward onto the bed and with a hysterical laugh, wrapped him in the dress.

Everything went wrong at the wedding. Adler was told to come in with his right foot; he came in with his left foot. He stumbled as he was led to the marriage canopy. As the rabbi began his prayer, he thought of his *zayde* and broke into a loud sob. But these mishaps were soon forgotten. The rabbi completed the seven prayers. The symbolic goblet was shattered. Shouts of *"Mazel tov!"* came from every side. A crash of Chasidic music came from the orchestra. Over everything was heard the wild, medieval trumpet call of the wedding celebration. On that evocation of the lower world in all its untrammeled power, Jacob and Sonya Adler embraced as man and wife.

8

The Struggle for the Marinsky

> Holy Sabbath and night of the new moon.
> My chamber lonely, sad my Sabbath prayer.
> The holy Ark before me all my own,
> Vision no other eyes than mine may share
> My sad, forsaken heart my only altar,
> And hidden safe within my sorrow lies.
> There when I seek, I find my love again—
> Oh, burning pain! Oh, fire that never dies!
> *Shulamith*

When Spivakovsky had reappeared in Elisavetgrad, neither Adler nor anyone else had an idea of the far-reaching changes he had just brought about in Odessa. Spivakovsky had, in fact, set in motion a chain of events that were to affect the entire course of the Yiddish theatre.

When Goldfaden and an actor parted company, it was always on the worst of terms. A "black cat" had indeed run between him and Spivakovsky. We do not know their quarrel, but when Goldfaden left Odessa for a tour of the nearby provinces, Spivakovsky was out of the troupe. He remained in Odessa, raging over his wrongs, his mind bent on revenge.

The owner of the Marinsky, a Greek called Omer, had brought over the Goldfaden company under the impression they were the only Yiddish actors in existence. Spivakovsky sought out this Omer and sang him a song about Mogulesko, greatest of all Yiddish stars, and surrounded, moreover, with a company of players better than any Odessa had yet seen.

The theatre owner listened with interest and eventually gave Spivakovsky money for a trip to Jassy. Here the actor found Isaac Libresko. This devoted man had been dismissed by Goldfaden and sent home. He was never to forgive the insult, and willingly took a hand in Spivakovsky's plot. The two of them went out to the provincial town where Mogulesko and his actors were living a hand-to-mouth existence. They snatched at Spivakovsky's offer, and in November 1879 Spivakovsky, Libresko, Mogulesko, and the playwright Joseph Lateiner came very quietly to Odessa. Knowledge of their arrival had to be kept secret from Goldfaden. Mogulesko also wanted time to look around; he was not sure Yiddish actors could make a living under the Russian tsar, even were he the liberal Alexander II.

The four conspirators remained more or less in hiding while Omer took Lateiner's plays to St. Petersburg. As soon as they had been passed by the censor, Mogulesko sent for his cast. They arrived, bringing with them Abba Schoengold. Rehearsals began, and Omer announced the first appearance of the "Famous Mogulesko Troupe of Roumania."

Spivakovsky played with the new Roumanian troupe for several weeks before he returned to Rosenberg in Elisavetgrad. He probably did not like the roles he received in Odessa, and in any case he had accomplished his purpose. Goldfaden came back from his tour to find the doors of the Marinsky closed against him, and the rival company in possession. He had no alternative but to turn back to the provinces.

Mogulesko opened in Lateiner's *Yente Piepernoter,* sang couplets between the acts and was an overnight sensation. The Russian critics compared him to Coquelin, and even Azmirov of the *Novy Telegraf* expressed a regret that such a great artist should be a Jew. Everyone came to the Marinsky to see the little Yiddish comedian, and there was a night when Odessa students unhitched the horses of Mogulesko's carriage and drew him home in triumph through the streets.

All this had its effect. Goldfaden, in danger of being outshone, promptly sat down in the town of Nikolayev and turned out his masterpiece.

The opera *Shulamith* is based on an ancient legend which Goldfaden's father-in-law, Werbel, had written up in story form. Werbel called this tale, the study of a false love and a true, "The Wildcat and the Well." Goldfaden had tried to fashion a play out of Werbel's story as far back as his time in the garret of Batushan. Not having enough actors then to fill out the cast, he had laid it aside and written *Recruits* instead. Now he learned that Lateiner had used Werbel's tale as the basis for an operetta called *The Lovers of Zion*. With a family right to the material, Goldfaden could not let this pass. He got out the old Batushan notes and went to work.

Once again, as with *Two Kuni Lemmels,* Goldfaden seems to be following Lateiner. And once again it is clear which of the two is the man of talent. Lateiner's opera was played for a season and passed into oblivion. Goldfaden, working from the same material, drew from it the great folk classic of the Yiddish theatre. *Shulamith* lived on as long as Yiddish theatre itself, and has been performed successfully in Russian, Ukrainian, Polish, Hungarian, and German translations.

The story is as naive as it is poetic. Shulamith, an Israelite girl, loses her way in the desert. Dying of thirst, she descends into the depths of a well and is trapped. Her melodious cry, beseeching God to help her, is heard by Avesholem (Absalom), a young man journeying toward Jerusalem. Avesholem rescues Shulamith, and at first sight of each other both are smitten with love.

Avesholem must go on to Jerusalem, but swears he will come back and make Shulamith his wife. She in turn vows she will marry no one else while he is gone. Spying a wildcat in the desert, both lovers swear an oath, "by the wildcat and the well," that they will be true. "For it is God Himself," they sing, "who brought us together."

In Jerusalem Avesholem comes upon the courting games of a group of youths and maidens. Joining the chase, he captures the gay, beautiful Avigail. He forgets his vow and marries Avigail.

The sad Shulamith waits, keeping faith with the lover who has forgotten her. So as not to be wed to the suitors asking for her hand, she feigns insanity. In this way she can talk incessantly of her love, for her pretended madness circles always around the "wildcat and the well" of the desert vow.

The happiness of Avigail and Avesholem comes to a dreadful end. One of their children is devoured by a wildcat, the other drowns in a well. Now Avesholem remembers the oath in the desert. He tells Avigail of the earlier love, forgotten and betrayed. Avigail feels in her heart that the first love was the true, the predestined one. Fainting, she bids Avesholem farewell.

Shulamith's madness is cured by the sound of Avesholem's voice. The lovers whom God once brought together are reunited.

The opera, performed for the first time in the town of Nikolayev, created such excitement that audiences, breaking an age-old taboo, flocked to the theatre even on Friday night. For the first time Russian Jews saw before their eyes the great days when they had lived romantically, heroically, and in freedom. Avesholem, more than a hero, stood for the glorious youth of their lost nation, and youth, as we know, is forgiven even when it strays from perfect righteousness. Avigail, so charmingly vain of her riches and her beauty, gave them the delight parents feel in a spoiled, happy daughter. But it was Shulamith herself, the beautiful forsaken girl, whom the Yiddish public took to its heart. The simple sadness of her "Sabbath Eve" song, the touch of terror and tragedy in her "mad" aria, touched something deeper than sympathy. Shulamith, symbol of unswerving love, shone out for these oppressed people as the living vessel of their own Jewish faith.

The songs of the opera were soon familiar in homes throughout Eastern Europe. Indeed, folk singers carried them to villages so remote they had never even heard of theatre. The lullaby "Raisins and Almonds," with its blend of hope and heartache, is perhaps the most famous, but the whole opera is full of wonderful folk melodies.

Unhappily, Goldfaden had never gotten over his habit of filling out his scores with the all-too-familiar themes of other men. The first act, opening with the gorgeous "Flicker, Fire, Flicker" of the caravan scene and closing with the repeat of the "Song of the Oath," breaks from time to time into choral and orchestral passages strangely reminiscent of Beethoven's Pastorale Symphony and Handel's "Hallelujah Chorus." The rest of the opera, luckily, is pure Goldfaden, and lyrics and music both have his special authenticity and charm.

Goldfaden lost no time in bringing *Shulamith* to Odessa. He put it on at the Remesleni Club, and the public, given something really fine, went mad over it. Mogulesko did his best with a production of Linetzki's *Polish Boy*, a play on a serious dramatic theme. But what could equal the noble line of Goldfaden's masterpiece? Odessa had fallen in love with *Shulamith*.

100 Russia: The Beginning

Mogulesko had from the first longed to show himself in Goldfaden's plays. And actually, most of Lateiner's operettas were simply imitations of Goldfaden's with the names changed. With the new triumph at the Remesleny Club, it was harder than ever to go on with this poor, thin stuff.

In a time of flowering, a new growth will thrust its way over and around every obstacle. At this point in our history the curious figure of Osip Michailovitch Lerner enters.

Lerner is not easy to understand, for at every turn our image of him shifts and changes. A recognized critic writing for Russian newspapers, Lerner had the courage to publish articles and essays in Yiddish. And he did this when even scholars thought of that language as a vehicle unworthy of Jewish thought. In this act we see the "great" Lerner, the critic fighting selflessly for the "jargon" that had produced a Sholem Aleichem and a Peretz. Even his enemies do not deny it was Lerner who brought to the Russian public the work of these two men, and of other important Yiddish writers of that day.

Yet a shadow already lies over this fine career. In 1873 this greatly respected journalist had fled Russia to avoid a criminal charge involving forgery. Lerner's guilt was never proved, and the charge against him seems to have been dropped, for he returned to Russia and retrieved his prestige. His character, however, had suffered a certain damage. And later, when the years of reaction came, we see a Lerner terrified for his own safety, betraying everything and everyone in a desperate fight to keep his position. The scholar, the burning "Yiddishist," is giving way to the darker figure of the renegade. The thinker, teacher, and idealist begins his career under a cloud; he ends it in the murderous ranks of the Cossack Black Hundreds.

The road of betrayal goes only one way. Hated by the friends he had sold, Lerner paid them back with an always darker hatred. We find him at the last in the service of the pogromist *Novy Telegraf*, a convert, a missionary, the author of a book calumniating and denouncing his people.

Not one word of mention appeared in the Yiddish press when this once-respected man died. Even in his best days, it seems, he was not loved. We are concerned with him, however, for only a short period, that portion of his career when he stepped into the Yiddish theatre and gave it a new, important direction.

Along with other journalists, Lerner had gone to Bucharest at the time of the Russo-Turkish War. The wild comedy antics, the clapped-together plots of Goldfaden's theatre, offended this man of taste. He did not go along with the dictum of his day, that the *maskil* must go to all lengths to reach the masses. While austere Jewish scholars wrote childish jingles and even stooped to coarseness to bring home their message of enlightenment, Lerner, with a finer instinct, aimed at an art that would elevate and inspire.

Watching the early Goldfaden operettas of 1877, Lerner had felt that something better than this could be done with a Yiddish theatre. In Odessa in the spring of 1880, Mogulesko asked him to step in as artistic director at the Marinsky, and he got a chance to put his ideas to the test.

Finding no serious play by a contemporary Yiddish dramatist, Lerner turned in a new direction. From the French theatre he selected Scribe's *La Juive,* from the German, Karl Guzkopf's *Uriel Acosta*. Every important European theatre of the time included both plays in its repertoire. Both were on Jewish themes.

If Shulamith and Avesholem may be described as the great romantic pair, the folk Romeo and Juliet of the Yiddish theatre, Uriel Acosta from the actors' viewpoint may be called its Hamlet. No dramatic actor could reckon himself of the first rank until he had shown what he could do as Acosta, the great Rationalist, the martyr who faced excommunication to bring light to his people.

As Acosta, who dies for truth, Abba Schoengold took Odessa by storm. He played with great dramatic fire, and held audiences spellbound by the romantic grace of his love scenes with Sophia Goldstein.

Schoengold followed this triumph with another ringing success in *La Juive* (called *Zhidovka* in Lerner's adaptation). Again he showed outstanding dramatic talent, this time in a character role.

Violent competition soon broke out between the Remesleny Club and the Marinsky. Cutthroat tactics were used on either side, and actors continually left one troupe for the other. In the fall of 1880 both Mogulesko and Schoengold deserted Lerner for Goldfaden. Without his two great stars Lerner was ousted, and Goldfaden made a triumphant reentry into the Marinsky. The following season Lerner got his stars back and with them, his theatre. Goldfaden took his company on tour, this time going as far north as Moscow, where his great success was *Shmendrick*.

In the fall of 1882 he was back in Odessa with *Bar Kochba (Son of the Star)*, a new opera celebrating Simon ben Cozeba, the "Messiah on horseback," hero of the third uprising against Rome. In spite of a success second only to *Shulamith*, he found it hard to tolerate the continued prestige of his rival. Odessa audiences soon had their choice of two *Acostas* and two *Zhadovkas*. While Lerner had adapted the Scribe play in its original dramatic form, Goldfaden, determined to outdo him, included the famous Halevy aria "Rachel." We are told he even inserted songs and dubious jokes into the austere text of *Uriel Acosta*.

In the winter of 1882, Jacob Adler was to spend several months in Odessa. Adler had resolved to give up the stage but found it hard work keeping to his resolution, for at this time, with new and tragic events casting a shadow over Jewish life in Russia, Odessa had become the hub and center of all Yiddish theatre. The novelist Sheikevitch had turned playwright and formed a troupe of his own. Three Yiddish companies were playing nightly to large and excited audiences, and Adler found the whole city boiling over with excitement about two men, Mogulesko and Abba Schoengold. Catching his first glimpse of Schoengold, then at the height of his career, Adler was dazzled:

"Standing at the door of the Marinsky I beheld a blond giant with the blue eyes of some Viking hero. It was Abba Schoengold, and I can say without exaggerating that never before or since have I seen a man so handsome! He was wearing a coat of sable, and over this had thrown a black cloak. To this day I remember the color of that cloak and against it, his white and exquisite hand. I stopped dead at the sight of him, and not only I, but everyone on the street stopped, asking each other who this man could be."

Schoengold and his young wife, Clara, were the real-life stars of a much-talked-of romance. These two had met in the Roumanian town of Berlad, when the troupe stopped at the hotel of a man named Granovsky. The brown-eyed Chaya Soore, the hotelkeeper's stepdaughter, was in a state of wild excitement about the actors, and as she was a born mimic and very pretty, Schoengold offered to take her into the company. When the choleric hotelkeeper learned about this, his wrath had no bounds. He followed the actors through the streets shouting insults after them, tried to have Schoengold put out of the town, locked his stepdaughter in her room, and threatened to drive her out of his house forever if she went near the actors or the theatre again.

On the night of the last performance in Berlad, Abba Schoengold came to the hotel after midnight in a carriage and Chaya Soora Granovsky left her stepfather's house by way of the bedroom window. They were married in the next town and three days later the new actress, now Clara Schoengold, sang a first timid duet with her husband. With her lilting voice, her auburn curls, and a certain natural theatricality of speech and gesture, she very soon became a popular soubrette. For some years husband and wife played together throughout the towns and cities of Roumania, king and queen of the Yiddish public there.

Adler admits he envied this actor, whom Odessa connoisseurs were comparing to the great German Sonnenthal. But he came to know Schoengold in time and grew fond of him, for the great star was of a charming, playful temperament and had no real conceit.

Of Mogulesko, whom he saw for the first time in Odessa during that winter, Adler wrote: "While he had not yet reached the full genius he would show in America, he was already adored. In *The Bigamist,* by Moishe Laib Lilienblum, he had a role with many serious, even tragic moments. He played it marvelously, and the public idolized him anew."

Mogulesko, however, worshiped by his audiences, was an endless tribulation to the dramatists and writers now gathering around the Marinsky. Lilienblum, the journalist and freethinker who later founded the Russian Zionist movement, came to the theatre one night to find the comedian had written songs, dances, and comedy routines into his serious play. Mogulesko had learned his trade in the early theatre of Goldfaden. At his best when he improvised, he saw no reason to stick to a text when he could liven it up with a joke, a song, or a brilliant comic effect. Others in the cast also sinned in this respect. The playwright Bezelinsky leaned over in his seat one night to whisper despairingly, "Tell the truth, Adler! Do you hear one word up there of my play?"

With Lilienblum, Adler felt an important chance had been missed. Except for Mogulesko's performance in the tragic lead, his play had no real success. Indeed, the playwright was criticized for dramatizing a subject his fellow writers preferred to ignore. Very poor and angelically beautiful, Lilienblum did not complain. In *The Bigamist* he had exposed a sore spot, the practice of criminal elements among the Odessa *voil yungen* who lured Jewish girls into their nets and sold them to the brothels of Constantinople. Lilienblum had written the play as a warning to his people.

"And good it would have been if the intelligentsia of that time had appreciated his work and helped him!" Adler warmly declared. "After this first drama drawn from life, would have come a second, a third, and the Yiddish theatre would have begun to have a face! Lilienblum had the courage to bring the shameful thing into the light, to pioneer as a dramatist. But he was not encouraged, and the Yiddish theatre had to wait twelve long years before Jacob Gordin made it into a stage of the living day, equal to any other."

Another opportunity lost was Katzenellenbogen's *Rashi*, a play about Solomon ben Isaac, the twelfth-century rabbi of Troyes. "This, too," Adler comments, "might have begun a new epoch. If Katzenellenbogen's example had been followed by others, Orthodox Jews might have been drawn in as friends of our theatre. But the Yiddish theatre, sad to say, has always been a theatre of youth."

Of the three Odessa companies, Adler was most powerfully drawn toward that of Osip Lerner. Here he saw his own dream realized. In one bold move, Lerner had raised the Yiddish stage to a world platform. From *Uriel Acosta* and *La Juive*, it was only a step to Gorki's *Lower Depths*, a play without a Jewish theme and with humanity itself as the hero.

In the space of a few brilliant years, from 1880 to 1883, a sort of dress rehearsal took place for the great American decades ahead. Goldfaden had tapped the historical past. Lerner had opened a door on world literature. Serious Jewish writers began turning their attention to the stage. A dozen new companies, professional and semiprofessional, sprang up throughout the cities and provinces. The tone of the Russian press was changing to one of interest and respect. Left to itself, the Yiddish theatre might well have become a recognized feature of Russia's cultural life.

It was reaching this peak, however, when its existence in Russia was drawing to a close. The signal had already sounded, clear and unmistakable. It went unheard. Men are often deaf to warnings that their way of life must come to an end. The events had already occurred that were to alter the whole course of Yiddish theatre, drive all these actors into exile, and profoundly affect the history of Russia itself.

9

Last Days of Alexander II

> The sun comes up, sinks down again,
> But in my prison all is dark.
> Day and night the sentry watches,
> Passing by my prison window.
>
> Why do you guard me, sentry?
> I will not run away.
> I no longer yearn for freedom,
> Nor can I break my chains.
>
> Oh, my chains, my chains!
> Sentry of iron!
> I can neither tear nor break you.
> Bitter is the prisoner's lot.
>
> The sun sinks down and all is night,
> Dark as night my prison cell.
> And yet the sun will rise again.
> Yes, tomorrow the sun will surely rise again.
> *Song of the Russian prisoners*

In the fall of 1880 the splendid rivalry of Goldfaden and Lerner in Odessa reached Rosenberg's troupe only as faraway rumors, and the events that were to alter everything had as yet cast no shadow on their lives. They were still in Poltava, and doing well. The newly married Sonya had a fine fur coat, and Jacob was even able to give her a few small diamonds as a wedding present.

The troupe was playing nightly to good audiences when trouble suddenly came up over their permit. Tulya Goldfaden and Spivakovsky went to Odessa to see what help could be found, and the worried company waited for news. They could not stay in Poltava where the police had turned hostile, nor play in any of the nearby cities for fear of more trouble.

Rather than let the company break up, Rosenberg decided to try the provinces, little rural communes that had sprung up over the years throughout the Russian Pale. Though these remote Jewish settlements were known as *shtetlach* (small towns), many of them were no more than tiny, self-contained villages, far from the central authorities and relatively safe.

The troupe stopped first in the town of Kabalyak. A dark rainy spot, the Jewish streets steeped in mud, the faces sad, a call to prayers at six every morning. They lost money there and moved on.

On the eve of Rosh Hashona they arrived in Smila, in the Province of Kiev. Here they could not find so much as a hall or a clubroom, and had to put on their play in the garden of a tavern.

"As luck would have it, it rained all through the first performance," Adler tells us. "The rain blew onto the stage. Yellow leaves flew in our faces. But the Jews loved it! All Smila came to see *Shmendrick*. They came under umbrellas and in their long coats. They stamped, yelled bravos, roared with laughter, and to the actors, Smila was a big town!"

They had decided to stay over until the festival of Succoth, when a telegram came from Odessa. Avrom Goldfaden was ordering the whole provincial troupe back to play at the Marinsky.

The actors rejoiced; Rosenberg saw his world collapsing. He had built up a reputation on the road as a comedian. In Goldfaden's troupe he would be nothing at all; he would be murdered by Zuckerman and Mogulesko.

He hammered away at the actors, begging them to face facts. They would have the honor of playing at the Marinsky and there it would end. Goldfaden would pay them a pittance, and they would break their hearts waiting for the chance that would never come. "Your parts, Adler, he will give to Spivakovsky or his new stars. Sonya's will go to his Odessa favorites," he said. And seeing he had made an impression, Rosenberg pressed further. They needed neither Goldfaden nor his brother. They had coined money in Poltava, and would do so again. He sketched the possibilities: Rostov-on-Don, Taganrog, Kiev, Kharkov, why not Moscow, even St. Petersburg? Adler's imagination caught fire, as he saw a great prospect stretching before him.

By the time Tulya Goldfaden arrived in Smila, Rosenberg had won over five members of the company. He counted them off on his fingers: Adler, Sonya Michelson, Katzman, Fishkind, and the new ingenue Charlotta Spinner. All these were remaining; the rest could go to Odessa.

"All must go," Tulya Goldfaden said with a wooden face.

"This is not Roumania," Rosenberg reminded him. "Here we are not paid with fish scales. Here we are accustomed to taking in thousands of roubles."

"How much money does he offer?" Adler asked.

"All must go," Tulya Goldfaden repeated.

Sonya flared up. "What is this? Slavery? Managers in Russia come to artists with contracts, money. This is an insult! No one is going!"

In the end only Fishkind and the Adlers held out. Everyone else left for Odessa and the Marinsky. Rosenberg kept Fishkind with the role of Hotzmach in *The Witch*. He also hid his coat.

The rebels remained in Smila, but their hearts sank when the others left them. They were the mere skeleton of a company. Oberlander, their advance agent, manager, and wardrobe master could only be reckoned half an actor. They had taken in Krastoshevsky, an ex-cantor with an operatic baritone, but the man had no crumb of acting talent.

With such a small cast only *Kuni Lemmels* could be attempted. Even for that, two actresses were needed and Charlotta Spinner, their ingenue, had deserted for Odessa and the Marinsky. Rosenberg, so the story goes, went through the streets of Smila, praying to heaven to send him a prima donna.

Heaven immediately obliged. Through an open window came a plaintive song of the Ukraine, the words half Russian, half Yiddish. A woman singing at her work, her voice strong, fresh, fiery. Rosenberg stood a moment lost in thought, then turned in at the door.

The woman at the window worked for a dressmaker. Her mistress had gone out, and she fell readily into talk with her amusing visitor. As they bantered, Rosenberg studied her: A working girl in her late twenties, with the fierce pride and independence typical of her class. A stubborn face, full of bitter knowledge. A small, pliant body that spoke of latent nervous strength. With all this, a gay, brave creature, with something about her odd, distinct, and original.

Kraindl Sacher had come from a village near Zhitomir in South Russia, where her father drove a *fiacre*. She had lost her mother at an early age, and her father had remarried. The stepmother disliked the dead woman's child, treated her harshly, and sent her out at the age of twelve to earn her own living. At eighteen the girl was married off to a cabman in her father's employ. In less than a year she ran away.

Since then she had worked in a number of towns, moving about with a somewhat remarkable freedom. She had come to Smila looking for a place as a seamstress, and had worked there only a short time when Rosenberg came in with his troupe. Caught up in the general curiosity and excitement, she had paid her admission to the tavern garden, where she saw *The Witch*. Adler's performance brought her to her feet shouting bravo with an enthusiasm that infected the entire audience. The young seamstress had, in fact, led what amounted to a demonstration for Adler that night.

She must have recognized Rosenberg as soon as he entered the house since he was known by sight to everyone in Smila. No doubt she received his proposal with some astonishment. We know only that after an hour Rosenberg went back to the actors and told them he had a prima donna.

Next morning as they all sat over their breakfast, the young woman appeared. The actors liked her on sight. She was gay, spirited. The idea of theatre had begun to act strongly on her imagination, yet she did not bend, she had pride. The actors joked with her, teased her about wanting to join them, advised her against it. She gave back jest for jest, held her ground, and by the time she got up to sing, they were amused, interested, and very much on her side.

In the half-deserted dining room of a country inn, the girl took up a position and in a strong *mezzo* voice, sang:

> Let me love you,
> Let me give my heart,
> Take all my kisses, take my fond embrace—

No audience is more generous, more easily carried away than an audience of actors. She finished her song to excited laughter and cries of approval from the whole company. The girl had something better than beauty, something theatre people refer to as "high visibility." Even when she went wrong, her gestures, her miming, everything about her "carried."

More than this, the song "took" her. She gave herself to it with passion, and that is the quality needed above every other.

"A girl like the devil's own sister!" Adler said, summing up his first impression. "Ready for anything! Full of fire and temperament. A strong voice. A clear diction. As she stood, you could put her on the stage!"

Rosenberg, excited over his find, decided to put on *The Two Kuni Lemmels* without delay. They rehearsed the play that afternoon, the whole company joining to help and coach the new actress.

She went on that night as Carlina, sang a little, acted a little, and so went through her ordeal by fire. Rosenberg had cut her part to almost nothing. According to the actors, she had to wait weary weeks and months before she got anything worth doing. If not for Sonya, who befriended her, the nervous, easily discouraged girl might have drifted away again. It should be noted, however, that during those first days she leaned heavily on the marked interest and belief of the prompter, handsome Volodya Liptzin.

Since she was afraid to use her own name, she was billed as Keni Sonyes. It is, however, as Keni Liptzin, the name she took years later, that she is remembered by those who know the great days of Yiddish theatre.

With two actresses, Rosenberg felt he had a troupe again. They moved on through the immense distances of the Russian countryside. No railroad lines passed through these remote regions, and the actors traveled from town to town in wagons.

"When it rained," Adler writes, "great puddles formed in the roads, and the jolting numbed the very soul. But we had marvelous days. Fall days in the Ukraine. A landscape of changing colors. On one side, dark forests, on the other, endless fields. Golden wheat fields against deep blue skies, white clouds. Cornfields. Tobacco fields with their saffron leaves. Vegetable gardens, orchards—everywhere the perfumed orchards of the South, rich with golden apples, brown pears, blue plums, deep red grapes, blue and white watermelons. The actors would get out of the wagons just to drink it all in."

Somewhere along the road they lost Alexander Oberlander. He had gone ahead to Brest Litovsk, but could not get a theatre because it was Lent. On the way back, Oberlander stopped at the town of Brisk. There he remained. He had met the Masha he was to marry, and the company saw him no more. He settled down to the practice of law and the raising of a family.

Heaven again sent help in the form of one Cheikel Bain. This little Odessa businessman, with a stammer and an asthmatic cough, came into the troupe as its manager, advance man, and all-round good angel. Where he had acquired his peculiar last name is now unknown, for this was none other than one of the two Goldstein brothers who had given Adler his first leg up in the world. Cheikel, like his brother, had given up the textile business in Odessa to throw in his lot with the new Yiddish theatre.

With a new entrepreneur, the tour went on. Spolya, Zlatapolya, Novomirgorod, Bogoslav, Pereyaslav—lost little hamlets where Jews sometimes lived out entire lives knowing nothing of the outside world but what they heard from some traveling *maggid*. In many of these villages the coming of the actors was the greatest event anyone could remember.

In Zlatapolya, the troupe could not find so much as a tavern. They put on their play in a stable on a stage built for them by a peasant carpenter. Crowds of Jews climbed up onto the chicken roosts. Here, by removing a slat or two, they could look down and see the play. Adler, playing the lover in *Two Kuni Lemmels*, had a song in the second act:

> Birds in the heavens,
> Tell me, I pray,
> Where is my Mirale?

Raising his head to the heavens, he saw faces, beards. Instead of the song, he called out wrathfully, "You, up there! Can't you buy tickets?" This overhead audience was scared off, like birds, by the applause at the end of the act.

In Pereyaslav the older Jews did not believe that there were such things as railroad trains. When the actors told them the locomotives could pull not only one but a whole string of cars, these old people listened awestruck, murmuring, "God's wonders!"

The actors did best of all in Pereyaslav, but in the end fell into great danger there through the overfriendliness of the local *ispravnik*. This police master stood at the back of the hall talking loudly with his friends and from time to time called out in a booming voice, "You like it, eh Jews? It's good, eh?"

When a song or a piece of comedy business pleased him he would boom out again, "Excellent! I like it! Bring the posters tomorrow, Adler. I will sign them, never fear!" Because the official had taken a special fancy to him, Adler was always assigned this task.

One night, as they sat over a card game, a petty officer entered the hotel. An uneasy silence fell. The man reeked of liquor and looked insolently at the women. He had come with a message: his master, the *ispravnik*, was entertaining friends that night. He requested that Rosenberg send two actresses, the youngest and prettiest he had.

Rosenberg went white to the lips. Adler staggered, and almost fell. In a voice he did not recognize, the voice of a man coming out of a nightmare, he shouted, "Tell your master he is an ignoramus and a lout!" The policeman, astonished, fell back a step and left the hotel.

Rosenberg stammered, "So here is a man of Alexander's who thinks we are a bunch of white slavers, and our theatre a traveling bordello!"

"We forgot we were living in Russia!" one of the actors remarked quietly.

Next morning Adler had to take the new posters to the police station. He found the *ispravnik* talking to his messenger of the night before. After giving Adler a glance of contempt, the officer said carelessly to his man, "Why didn't you kill him?"

Addressing Adler directly, he said, "Do you think we are fools here? We know very well that your theatre is a blind and that your real business is with Jewish prostitutes." Leaning back in his chair, he added deliberately that he had seen Sonya in a Kiev brothel.

All the blood rushed to Adler's head. Pictures of the Moldovanka flashed before his eyes. He saw floggings, executions. Hardly knowing what he was doing, he lunged toward the *ispravnik* with a strangled cry and a fist raised to kill.

The officer, startled, ran into his cabinet and locked the door. The scared clerks advised Adler in whispers to get help from the postmaster of the town, a wealthy Jew called Aaronson. Adler ran back through the streets like a madman. The postmaster's influence was all that saved them. This man had very great power in the town because of the regard felt for him by the liberal governor of the province. He came to the hotel immediately and turned red with anger when he heard the story. "To the Governor!" he exclaimed. "I will take him to court! He will remember me!"

Within a half hour the *ispravnik* himself, in a pitiable state, appeared at the hotel. The postmaster took him into another room where the frightened actors heard Aaronson exclaiming angrily that he had insulted artists and would pay for it. A little later the officer, white and shaken, emerged, asked forgiveness of the whole assembled company, bowed before them all, and with an especially low bow before Adler and Sonya, departed.

Rosenberg broke down completely. Cheikel Bain stammered out, "To l-l-live through such a thing!"

They left Pereyaslav soon afterward. Cheikel Bain had finally settled the matter of their permit, and got them to Tchernigov. They were out of the provinces at last.

In Tchernigov they shared the theatre with a Russian company, and the actors, unlike those in Kishinev, remained friendly even when the Jewish troupe took some of their audience away. The Russian *regisseur* Cherkassov came to all their plays and became particularly friendly with Sonya and Adler. "My theatre is supported mainly by Jews," he remarked on one occasion. "Yiddish theatre is a phenomenon."

Cherkassov wanted to get the Adlers away from Rosenberg. He invited them to guest star in a production of *Boris Godunov*. As soon as they agreed to make this appearance, posters went up all over the city announcing in giant letters: "For the First Time, the Famous Adlers in Russian!"

The twenty-two scenes of Pushkin's dramatic poem have never been attempted on any stage. Cherkassov was giving his public the Moussorgsky opera, first heard at the St. Petersburg Marinsky in 1873. Sonya sang the proud Polish-born Marina, a part calling for a commanding presence and a strong *mezzo* soprano. It is a comment on Adler's growing powers that Cherkassov cast him as Godunov. A Russian Macbeth, haunted by the child he murdered for his throne, this role had yet to receive the supreme interpretation of Fyodor Chaliapin. Adler had always *acted* his songs, taking a line or so of the melody in a voice not unpleasing to the ear. He was apparently required to carry off the vocally demanding role of Boris on his dramatic talents alone.

Cherkassov had counted on a packed house for the opening and was not disappointed. The Yiddish actors, present in force, loyally joined in the applause for the two friends now lifted to heights so far beyond them. But when Cherkassov brought them out after the third act, pointedly presenting them to his audience as *Russian* artists, a well-known voice shouted above all the applause, "Over my d-d-dead body!" Cheikel Bain, in the last row, could no longer restrain his feelings.

An extraordinary vista had opened before these two wandering, homeless players. From early youth they had both adored the Russian theatre, and indeed it was acknowledged by all Europe as among the greatest. No barrier had been set in their path, no renunciation of their faith demanded of them. They would enter those portals as Jews. True, by law they could play only in the cities of the Pale, but laws were known to change. Goldfaden had gotten a permit good for all of Russia. What might not happen in these changing times?

They were free, too. Nothing held them. Cherkassov's offer had silenced even Rosenberg. Their fellow actors were happy, proud of them. They would go their way, wishing Adler and Sonya the best with all their hearts. Yet the thought of that parting, that generous adieu, tore at their hearts. After all, it was of a great *Yiddish* theatre they had both dreamed. They talked it over. Sonya said they were pioneers and must not give up the fight. And in the end these foolish idealists went back to their own poor stage.

They were taken back with such faces, such unspoken pride in shining happy eyes, such laughing imprecations from Rosenberg, such embraces from everyone else that they knew ten times over they had chosen aright.

A whole round of parties and dinners celebrated the return of the friends. Every trifle—a new joke, a new hat, an odd piece of profanity—everything served as an excuse for laughter and new festivities. A wonderful closeness and joy united the company.

It was fated, just the same, that Tchernigov should be the scene of great changes for Adler and his wife. One evening as the troupe sat over dinner, Avrom Goldfaden suddenly fell in on them. The actors sprang to their feet with a glad "hurrah" at the sight of their rabbi, their father. Their joy soon died in an uneasy silence. Goldfaden had brought a face like a thundercloud. He had come to collect his royalties and turned red with anger as Cheikel Bain faltered out excuses and explanations.

"Don't talk to me of business!" he cried, jumping up as

though a snake had bitten him. "You will have no business!" He launched into accusations, called the actors parasites, vultures, living high on his work, his talent. "And the creator?" he demanded. "What does he get? Nothing but your ingratitude?"

Adler, stricken, murmured that out of a month the company ate fifteen days; the rest of the time they lived on credit. Goldfaden would not listen. Only when Cheikel Bain promised to pay the full sum over a certain time did the angry man calm down.

But he had taken a dislike to the little manager, and in the days that followed never lost a chance to make jokes at his expense. Cheikel's thick frame, his spectacles, in particular his ears were an unfailing occasion for Goldfaden's wit. Though the actors swore to him that aside from his ears, Cheikel was the best of men, the fairest, the most honest, that he had put much money of his own into the troupe, nothing helped. The unfortunate Cheikel had only to appear for Goldfaden to remark, *sotto voce*, "But tell me honestly, how does a Jew allow himself to wear such ears? Did he bring them with him into the Yiddish theatre? Could he have come by them here?"

He amused himself in this fashion until one day the tormented little man had an emotional outbreak, waved his fist in the air, and ran out of the room, sobbing. The actors, who had often enough grumbled at Cheikel over their weekly "shares," sat silent, an ache in their hearts. Goldfaden laughed.

The playwright had come to Tchernigov in the worst possible temper. After losing Mogulesko and Schoengold, he had taken his company to Moscow, where *Shmendrick* became, for a time, the rage of the town. But the frivolity of Goldfaden's theatre had shocked the elite Moscow Jews, and the Yiddish press abroad finally came out in a strong concerted attack, charging that with his portrayal of Jews as drunkards, thieves, and fools, the playwright was doing disservice to his people. Goldfaden at last became disquieted. He could take little pleasure in his box-office receipts when Russian officers pointed to every Jew on the street, gleefully exclaiming, "Shmendrick!"

After five years of extraordinary activity, this playwright, composer, actor, director, and impresario had finally grown weary. He sent his troupe to Minsk with Laizer Zuckerman and himself went off with a court of relatives, friends, and admirers for a well-earned rest in Kiev.

Bad news followed him. By sending the company to Minsk

with Laizer Zuckerman, he had mortally offended Maurice Finkel. Out of sheer spite, Finkel married Annetta Schwartz and went off with her to form his own company. Goldfaden had at one crack lost Finkel, his *regisseur* and best character actor, and his star prima donna. He had come to Tchernigov in urgent need of new stars. He dropped a strong hint about this to Adler and Sonya, remarking that his troupe was soon going on to St. Petersburg and that, if they were good children, they could go with him.

The Adlers could not take advantage of this opening. With the loss of Spivakovsky they had become Rosenberg's greatest attractions. The troupe would go under without them. Goldfaden, noticeably colder, changed the subject and with sinking hearts they saw their opportunity vanish.

On his last night in Tchernigov Goldfaden played out a singular comedy. With the whole cast at table he began to speak of his St. Petersburg plans. Something in his tone set pulses fluttering. Rosenberg already looked green; Goldfaden had never thought much of him and he foresaw that he would be robbed of his troupe and ruined. Goldfaden, however, took everyone by surprise. He declared that he must above all have Rosenberg, and would not go to St. Petersburg without him.

Rosenberg's surprise and joy were painful to see. His face flushed a deep red. A foolish smile twisted his lips even before the offer was fairly out. Goldfaden pressed him sharply: "You will go at once? You will leave the others?"

Rosenberg answered impudently, "A fish swims for deeper water, a man runs to better money!"

"False serpent!" Cheikel Bain shrieked, and left the table.

Deliberately, Goldfaden proceeded. Bypassing Sonya and Adler, the two actors he really wanted, he asked each actor to join him in St. Petersburg. Not one of them refused.

The cast could not conceal their joy. Rosenberg, in particular, could scarcely contain himself. He went about for the rest of the evening with a broad smile, continually transferring his hands from one set of pockets to the other. Yet he was not altogether lost to shame. His eyes dropped when they met those of his friends. The actors, too, knew in their hearts that they had done something not right, not fine. And with the victims still there before them!

Sonya and Adler went to their rooms early, unable to bear the heartless gaiety of the others. They were crushed. At midnight they were still talking in low, disheartened tones when they heard a furtive tapping at a side door. Goldfaden entered with a conspiratorial air. He had brought with him a large sheet of foolscap, which he held out for Adler's inspection. "See for yourself!" he said, with a significant look. "All have signed it! All!" The paper was covered with the signatures of the actors. Only Cheikel Bain had refused to sign it.

Adler could not control his anger. Twice this man had broken up the life of the troupe, once in Smila and now again. He remarked with some bitterness that *Herr* Goldfaden seemed to take pleasure in destroying what he and the others had built.

But Goldfaden was slowly shaking his head from side to side.

"Adler, it was a *chantage,* a hoax," he said. "It was perhaps not altogether fine. It may perhaps be criticized—but I had no other way!"

With this he laid bare his strategy. Adler had refused his offer, refused out of loyalty to Rosenberg. Well and good! Goldfaden had now shown him how little Rosenberg or the others deserved such loyalty. "You may take Cheikel Bain with you, if you wish," he said in conclusion. "I need no one but you and Madame Adler."

Adler took this with a strange mixture of emotions. Restored pride, anger at those others who would have so lightheartedly abandoned them, pity, too, for the trick that had been played on them. More than all, a flood of joy and a sense that life was at last opening its doors.

Late as it was, he sent for a samovar, and the three theatre people sat around the table to talk, a scene Adler later remembered like something in a dream. By the time they had thrashed out the last detail, day was breaking. All had been settled, and the moment had come to decide one way or the other. He turned to Sonya, always his guide in any question of right and wrong. After some reflection, Sonya threw her weight to Goldfaden. "We are betraying no one," she said firmly. "Rosenberg and the others have betrayed themselves. No remorse, Yakob! No regrets! We leave! Sign!"

Goldfaden, looking like a general who has won a great battle, rose and shook their hands.

At seven that morning, while the others slept, a covered sledge with two white horses drew up at the door of the hotel. A porter carried out their boxes and trunks. Adler wrote two letters, one to Cheikel Bain asking his forgiveness, but congratulating him that he still "kept shop." The second letter, written in more blistering terms, he sent to the traitor Rosenberg.

He and Sonya entered the covered sledge, where Goldfaden awaited them. "A last wrench at the heart for the small, poor actors who would wake to their miserable surprise. A last pang at the thought of how much we had all lived through together. A last glimpse of Tchernigov—and away. Pity, regret, all was lost in a wave of exultation. Further! Further! Life calls! Our sledge flew over the snow, and before it, on the swifter wings of the telegraph, Goldfaden's message: "Adler and Michelson make their debut in *Capricious Daughter!* Make arrangements."

In Kiev they boarded a train for Dannenburg, where a whole crowd of actors, friends, flatterers, and hangers-on met them at the station. The Adlers felt some disappointment that their debut was to take place in Dannenburg rather than St. Petersburg, but consoled themselves with the fact that the capital was only days away.

Goldfaden had chosen *The Capricious Daughter,* a melodrama from the German, as a test of his new star's powers. Adler played the strong role of the father to such effect that the audience gave him ovations, and Goldfaden began to have dreams of gold and glory in St. Petersburg.

These hopes were not to be realized. Tragic forces were at work, and events gathering momentum.

Alexander II, torn by the two conflicting ideas of his age, had ended by satisfying no party at all. The liberated peasants rioted against a new economic servitude. The Poles continued to want autonomy. The liberals still demanded elected representatives. Every concession seemed to release only a more dangerous discontent. Russia was too vast, communications too uncertain. Some of the outlying provinces had never heard of the new laws. In others they were modified at the whim of local officials.

Liberal hopes had long since died. At Bezdna, thousands of unarmed peasants were massacred by government troops. The Polish insurrection was put down with a ferocity that horrified the world. At home, underground groups multiplied, and scuffles of students with police were followed by expulsions, arrests, executions. Hundreds of intellectuals went out into Siberian exile. The familiar features of Russian life were all emerging again through the thin shell of liberal change. The flare-up of patriotic feeling that had accompanied the

Russo-Turkish conflict soon subsided. England and France, alarmed at Russia's greed, had sharply reduced her territorial gains. And on top of diplomatic defeat came the old, sickening revelations of corruption and bribery in the Army Commissariat. Public sympathy was veering once more to the left.

By 1879 the revolutionary forces, reduced by arrests and executions, had split into two main groups: Plekhanov's peaceful party of propaganda and the terrorist *Narodnaya Volya,* "Party of the People's Will," a formidable organization that had as its aim social revolution through a program of sabotage, prison raids, and assassinations.

On September 7, 1879, Alexander Mikhailov, leader of the terrorists, formally condemned Alexander Romanov to death. Several days later Mikhailov rescinded this "sentence" on condition the Tsar set up a Constituent Assembly. Forty-three police searches were made for the illegal press that had issued these pronouncements. It was never discovered.

The terrorists received no reply to their ultimatum, and from that time on concentrated on one objective: the death of the Tsar.

A first attempt was made to blow up his train as he returned from a visit to the Crimea. The attempt failed. Two of the mines along the route did not go off, a third exploded minutes after his train had passed. A second plan also failed. A baggage train was blown to bits outside the Moscow station; the royal train, as it happened, was still en route.

The Tsar was forced for his own safety to take up permanent residence in the Winter Palace. Elaborate precautions surrounded his every movement. He was an embittered man, served by an inefficient police and bewildered by the forces arrayed against him.

In February 1880, a master carpenter called Khalturin, who belonged to *Narodnaya Volya,* secured employment in the Winter Palace. For weeks Khalturin smuggled sticks of dynamite into the palace and at last succeeded in setting off a bomb in the dining room. The blast demolished the room and killed or wounded some forty Finnish guards in the hall below. The Tsar, detained in the corridor by the new king of Bulgaria, escaped unhurt.

Clearly something had to be done. Government policy swung wildly from frightened concession to equally frightened reaction, and with each of these violent movements back and forth, the whole weakening structure shook.

For the terrorists, too, the sands were running out. Arrests had cut their numbers to a handful. A last grand plan was staged. Mines were laid in the Malaya Sadovaya, one of the principal streets of St. Petersburg, and a shaft filled with enough explosive to blow the nearby buildings sky-high was run through another street often used by the Tsar. This plan, however, was abandoned because it would have killed innocent people. Four of the terrorists volunteered instead to throw individual bombs.

On March 1, 1881, the Tsar left the palace for his weekly inspection of the guards. As a routine precaution, he always took one route on leaving the palace and another on his return. In some way the conspirators learned that the Tsar's return that day would take him through Catherine Street along the Catherine canal. Sophia Perovskaya, leader of the conspiracy, walked up and down this quiet thoroughfare. As the royal sledge entered, she gave the prearranged signal.

The first bomb was flung by the student Rysakov. The explosion wounded two of the royal Cossack escort and spattered the horses with blood. The Tsar, against his driver's advice, came out of the sledge to speak to the wounded Cossacks. To a bystander who asked if he had been hurt, he replied, "No, thank God!"

"Thank God?" cried the Polish student Hrinwiecki. He hurled a second bomb which exploded at the feet of the Tsar, shattering both his legs. As his brother Michael came galloping up on horseback, he could only whisper, "Home to the Palace—to die."

He was carried back to the Winter Palace in his brother's arms. That very morning, resigned to the inevitable, he had signed a paper allowing elected representatives a voice in the drafting of new laws, a step that might well have paved the way to a constitutional government. It was this paper that gave rise to the persistent rumor that Russia's first constitution had been found in the pocket of the murdered Tsar.

Chaos prevailed for many hours following the assassination, and the news reached Dannenburg only at nightfall. Adler and Sonya, who had gone to a gala performance of *Shulamith*, heard it in the theatre.

"After the overture there was a very long wait," Adler writes. "The curtain finally rose, but immediately came down again. There was a murmur of laughter as the audience guessed at some mishap backstage. But the curtain did not go up again. Instead, a Russian officer came out. With an ashen face and a voice choked with tears he announced that dark tragedy had descended over the land, and that the beloved Tsar, Alexander II, had been assassinated by criminals.

"In one instant the scene changed to one of horror and dismay. A fearful wailing broke out. Women fainted. Some screamed. Others wept. Every face had gone deathly white and fear looked out of all eyes.

"Outside the theatre church bells continually tolled as though for a funeral, and Cossacks rode about driving everyone off the streets. It was only with great trouble that we got back to our hotel, where the porters, in frightened whispers, told us what had happened."

At dawn next morning the Dannenburg police distributed a circular ordering everyone in the city to swear allegiance to the new Tsar.

All that day and the next, great crowds massed in church and synagogue, taking the oath of allegiance.

10

The Pogrom at Nyezhin

> Fly, feathers! Fly up to heaven itself!
> GOLDFADEN POEM, 1881

Alexander II had long been criticized in official circles for his weak, drifting policies, and the news of his assassination, we are told, was received with remarkable apathy and indifference.

The feelings of ordinary people, of course, are not always recorded. Most Russians, neither aristocrats nor revolutionaries, had simply gone on with their lives through the storms of his reign. These people must have grieved over the death of their Tzar. The great mass of Jews, especially those old enough to remember the preceding reign, mourned him sincerely. Though they had murmured against him in life, in death Alexander II became once more the great protector, the father who had saved them.

Twice Adler had seen the Tsar, once at Yalta and again at a midnight mass in Odessa. On this last occasion he had been close enough to see the iron rings he wore on his fingers. Both times, by his own admission, he had felt love for his emperor, the friend of his people.

This did not prevent him from sharing in the almost universal sympathy felt for the six arrested terrorists. The tragic love of Sophia Perovskaya and the Odessa worker Andrey Zheliabov was arousing a particlar interest and pity.

Zheliabov, head of the Southern wing of *Narodnaya Volya*, had been arrested several days before the assassination. He

The Pogrom at Nyezhin 123

therefore had no part in it. His place was taken by Sophia Perovskaya, daughter of the former governor-general of St. Petersburg.

Zheliabov learned in prison that the police had caught two of the terrorists and that Rysakov, who had flung the first bomb, had turned informer. Zheliabov immediately announced that he himself had organized the assassination plot and been its leader. In this way he told the world it was not traitors like Rysakov who had killed the Russian Tsar, but revolutionaries like himself, ready to die for their beliefs.

Sophia Perovskaya collapsed after the assassination, and for a time her mind wandered. In spite of the entreaties of her friends, she stayed on in St. Petersburg where she spent her days devising wild schemes to get Zheliabov out of prison. One of the conspirators stayed with her and, torn by pity, pretended to go along with her mad plans. The two of them were caught and sentenced to be hanged with the others.

The period of mourning for Alexander II lasted from March 1 until after Easter. Six weeks of mourning with no theatre of any kind, and certainly not Yiddish theatre. The actors pawned their watches, but to keep up appearances kept the watch chains. Heartrending comedies were played out when some person happened to ask one of them the time.

Sonya's possessions soon found their way to the pawnshop. A little gold medallion, a watch, and two bracelets prepared a path for her winter coat. Adler also pawned his coat. Passover was drawing near and the weather getting warmer, but they both shivered a bit when the wind blew.

The actors met the holidays with heavy hearts, uncertain of the future. Strangers took some of them in. Sonya and Adler, less fortunate, had a Passover dinner of *matzoh* and potatoes.

Some days after this, they called on Goldfaden at his hotel. They found his rooms full of actors, and everyone talking about the six arrested terrorists. On all sides the names of Perovskaya and Zheliabov were heard in tones of peculiar sympathy and respect. There was some astonishment that Hessye Helfmann, a Jewish girl, should have taken part in the conspiracy. In fact, this girl had merely allowed the conspirators to meet in her home. She had been arrested as part of the government campaign to connect the Jews with the assassination.

After an hour of talk, Goldfaden invited everyone to take

tea with him. At this Sonya sprang to her feet. "Tea!" she exclaimed, indignantly. "We have had nothing else all through the holidays!" Relapsing into excitable French, she exclaimed, "Three days we have not eaten!" And she turned away, dashing angry tears out of her eyes.

Adler, seeing her cry, began to blubber himself, and the whole room of hungry actors followed his example. "From Passover," Adler comments wryly, "it became Tisha Bov!" *
Goldfaden looked sharply at the whole crew, turned pale, and calling in a waiter, told him to bring everyone whatever they wished.

"Why didn't you tell me?" he asked defensively. "Am I a prophet? I am penniless myself, but still I am an impresario, they give me credit. If you had come earlier we would have all dined together."

He walked up and down, greatly agitated. "To go hungry? Fools that you are! The world has everything! One must take!" And lowering his voice, a look of pain on his face, he went on. "Yes, when people are hungry, they take! That is why the nihilists have brought down the Tsar, showing the world with this act that the present regime cannot continue!"

Two waiters entered with a large table, and began pouring wine and passing around hot dishes of food. "We fell on everything!" Adler relates, "swallowing food and drink like hungry animals, or, better still, hungry actors."

"St. Petersburg is finished, my friends," Goldfaden informed them all in a melancholy tone. "We must look for bread where we can find it." And taking out a telegram, he outlined a tour of White Russia—Minsk, Bobruisk, Regensburg, Dinabourg, and Vitebsk.

"Never mind! We're not beaten yet!" Goldfaden said. He held his head high as ever, and the unbreakable strength of the man sent new courage into all of them. "Don't lose heart, children!" Goldfaden said strongly and with warmth. "We will still see better days!"

Immediately after Easter the troupe left Dannenburg for Minsk.

A whole pack of creditors came with them. Every actor had some innkeeper or restaurateur who had fed and housed him during the lean weeks. Each of these creditors thought himself

---

* A day of fasting and penitence.

the only one, and wild comedies were played out when they saw each other at the station.

Since the only hope of these unhappy men lay in the actors themselves, they had to buy them railroad tickets to Minsk and feed them, too, on the train. They looked upon the troupe as a kind of living collateral and since they were paying for everything, kept a sharp watch on every morsel they put in their mouths. When the actors begged Goldfaden for a small advance so they could eat in peace, he replied angrily, "These people are strangers! They must be paid first!"

"I don't say he was wrong," Adler writes, "but if we were speaking of debts, we ourselves had something to say. We owed, true enough, but we too were owed, and by Goldfaden himself! None of us had received a penny for the Dannenburg performances. I don't say Goldfaden was to blame for it. The assassination of Alexander II had transferred all debts to the great Book of Death. All the same. . . ."

He and Sonya had more luck than the others. They had taken their innkeeper's sister along as an actress, and in this way paid off their own board and lodging.

In Minsk the company fell into the hotel of one Shmaye the Minsker. This famous restaurateur took in not only the actors but their creditors, too. Since Shmaye had agreed to underwrite all the expenses of opening the theatre, the poor man's pocket grew emptier every day. The actors and their creditors took up all his tables, and Shmaye's steady customers had to take their meals standing. Worse, word got around that you could eat at Shmaye's for nothing, and such crowds came that the restaurateur began to see black ruin staring him in the face.

As money began trickling into the box office, a murmur arose among the actors. It was time they stopped being in Shmaye's debt and had a corner they could call their own. But every request met with the same angry reply: The creditors must be paid first.

Though Adler grumbled with the others, he didn't really care. It was May. Minsk was beautiful. And on the great St. Francis Boulevard everything shone as in a polished mirror. The town was gay, the people not too depressed by the assassination. He himself was a young man in love, his star rising. What need had he for money? It was enough for him that he and Sonya got more than the others.

From Minsk they went on to Bobruisk. Here an unexpected blow fell. Yiddish theatre was suddenly forbidden by government decree, and every Yiddish troupe in Russia was paralyzed. However, the restriction did not last long. It was quickly lifted, and the actors forgot their scare.

They would have done better to have heeded this warning.

The troupe had a success in Bobruisk and went on to Regensburg, Dinabourg (later called Dwinsk), and then Vitebsk, site of an ancient fort. Here Goldfaden announced a new policy. No more eating at one table, no more communal "shares." Everyone must shift for himself, and those who did not like it were free to go.

No matter how hard things had been before this the actors had felt they were together. Now a wall came up, dividing them from the directors of the troupe.

The whole company drove from the station to the splendid hotel in the center of the city, but only Goldfaden and his managers passed through its doors. The actors remained outside, "feeling," as one of them tellingly describes it, "like immigrants for whom nobody has sent."

A group of passersby formed a ring around them, sensing their outcast condition. The actors looked at one another, the whole book of Job in every face. Slowly they separated, one to a relative, another to a friend, another to find an inn, a boardinghouse.

A man in the crowd gave Adler an address in the German quarter. He had to hire a *drozhky* to get there, a worrisome expense. As they rattled over the cobblestone streets, his spirits sank lower and lower. His heart ached for his delicately bred Sonya. He had taken her into this terrible life, and it seemed to him she must regret it. Drowsing over his sad thoughts, he fell into a doze. Sonya woke him as they drew up at their boardinghouse.

In Vitebsk they played in a park called Birch Gardens. Poor gardens, the actors thought. No flowers, no fountains. Nothing but a few trees, a bit of grass, a broken picket fence, and in the center of a fenced-off enclosure, an open-air stage lit by gas lamps.

In spite of these conditions, Yiddish theatre became the talk of Vitebsk. One by one, as the creditors were paid off, they packed up and went back to Dannenburg. The innkeeper's sister tearfully departed, never to forget her time in the Yiddish theatre. But though the creditors had now been paid and the garden was packed every night, Goldfaden still gave his old excuse. Debts.

"Sonya and I had long grown accustomed to the whistling of poverty," Adler says. "Now it came to our door and began whistling on notes!"

The German innkeeper did not press them, but with every meal served them their growing bill. They both agreed to eat as little as possible. Sonya grew pale and thin and Adler's choler rose. What kind of life was this? Feasts on the stage and at home a belly swollen with hunger! He began to agitate among the actors. "No work without bread!" was the cry of this hot young socialist.

Goldfaden flew into a rage and put Adler out of the company. Since in any case he was not paid, he hardly cared. He came every night to the open-air theatre, talked to everyone there, told them his story, and asked them for justice.

All his life Adler brought his wrongs to his audience. They never failed to side with him, and it never failed to infuriate his managers. Goldfaden, in a rage, gave orders. Since the Adlers paid no admission, and were no longer part of the company, they would not be allowed into the theatre.

"Air and wind!" Adler remarks scornfully. "Sons and daughters of Israel paid for our tickets with the greatest pleasure. And when they saw us in the garden, the public gave us ovations!"

The actors drew up their demands. First, the Adlers must be taken back. Second, the company respected Goldfaden's debts but from now on half the weekly intake must be paid out to the cast.

The strike soon collapsed. Goldfaden got some of his actors back with a few roubles, some with a promise, the least important with one or two smart fatherly blows about the ears.

Adler had gotten his second taste of defeat. He dragged himself about the German quarter, isolated from the others and penniless. Sonya was pregnant with her first child. Rosenberg sent letters from Nyezhin in South Russia, begging them to come, but he sent no money. Their situation was getting desperate. Adler decided to go to court.

The German innkeeper gave his approval to the idea, and Adler took himself to the Vitebsk justice of the peace. This man suggested, not without a slight smile, that a quarrel among serious people, artists, should be conducted in a dignified way without public scandal. A hearing was arranged.

Goldfaden appeared with a fire-breathing attorney, and a stormy scene was soon enacted. Adler claimed that his lawful wages had been withheld, that he had been falsely lured away from his own troupe who were now like sheep without a shepherd. He showed letters from Rosenberg saying that as soon as Adler arrived, the Jews of Nyezhin would cover him with gold, and that with Adler at the head of their company, they would immediately go on to St. Petersburg.

The attorney countered by describing the actor as an agitator, a dangerous nihilist, adding a hint that the government would do better to march such a character out of the city with a police escort. He denied that Goldfaden owed him anything whatever.

Adler sprang up, hotly demanding that the books be brought to court. The attorney declared no books had been kept. This made a bad impression. The judge observed that the smallest shopkeeper had books. The denial in itself seemed to him a suspicious circumstance.

A more formal hearing was set for the following morning. Goldfaden came without his books, and lost the case. The court ruled that Adler and his wife must be paid 600 roubles in back wages.

After the hearing, the justice detained Adler and quietly pressed twenty-five roubles into his hand. Adler was so overcome by this piece of human kindness, he almost broke down. He ran home on wings and found Sonya talking with the German innkeeper. They gave him twenty of their roubles, and decided to spend the remaining five on pleasure, for they could not remember their last happy day.

The two of them ran out to the hill over Birch Gardens, played there like children, lay on the grass, watched the ants at work, and then went to take tea at an open-air restaurant near the theatre. Here they found Goldfaden. A parley took place.

Goldfaden, somewhat shamed-faced, apologized for the threats of his attorney, declaring they were not meant to be carried out, but only to frighten. Adler answered that he wanted only what he had asked, money to leave the city and find work elsewhere.

At this Goldfaden spread both arms wide and said simply, "Adler—from where?"

Adler paused thoughtfully. A sum of that size, as he knew, would be enough to ruin the company. After a moment he came up with a plan of two "benefit" evenings, one for himself, the other for Sonya. On this an agreement was reached. An end to war.

By sundown of that day every Jew in Vitebsk knew that

Goldfaden and Adler had made friends. A capacity crowd packed the garden that night. The two men came onstage together and shook hands to stamping feet, applause, and joyous shouts of "Sholem!" from the audience.

The two benefits were played in the same holiday mood, and in a spirit of renewed friendship, all feuds forgotten, Adler and Sonya left Vitebsk.

They traveled first class, for Rosenberg had written that the wealthy Jews of Nyezhin were coming to meet them at the station. Adler had on a new silk hat and a coat with a winged cape, his shoes were lacquered until they shone, and he carried a beautiful new cane with an ivory handle. Sonya, too, had given care to her attire. Her jewelry had been redeemed, she had bought a fine velvet cloak, and carried a many-colored umbrella in the latest Paris style. Even after this outlay Adler still had, folded away in a fine leather wallet, crackling new bills in high denominations.

At Nyezhin they grabbed their luggage and sprang down from the train. Adler looked around the dark station and delivered himself of a heartfelt string of curses. Rosenberg had written that the rich Jews of the town were coming to greet them with a military band. Not even a dog from the troupe was there. A *gendarme* with a feather in his hat, a sleepy stationmaster, one or two strangers. Aside from these, not a soul.

Having relieved himself by wishing fervently that the devil might enter Rosenberg and also his father's father, Adler hired an ordinary *drozhky* and directed it to Shimen Kaplan's hotel on Commercial Street.

Here they found nothing but a small sleeping chamber had been prepared. With this they had the privilege of warming themselves in the parlor, where through four front windows they could see a small park on one side and on the other the city prison.

After a long, dreary wait, Rosenberg finally appeared with Cheikel Bain.

"So, Yisrolik!" Adler said, greeting him quietly, "I have come to organize you and take you to St. Petersburg."

"Yankele, I lied to you," Rosenberg admitted with a lowered head and shame in his eyes. "I cheated you, got you by a trick."

"As long as you are here," Adler said, sighing.

They agreed to have a glass of wine, a bite to eat, and then to take a look at the theatre.

Rosenberg walked behind them along the Jewish street,

and with such an air of respect that shopkeepers all along the way came out to stare. "What did I tell you?" Rosenberg whispered loudly to everyone. "Did you ever see such great people?" Adler and Sonya did not know where to look for embarrassment.

A long walk. Small houses. Small stores. Yards. Soon they had reached the outskirts of the town. Adler stopped. "Where is the theatre?" he asked in bewilderment.

"Yankele, the last swindle is out," Rosenberg said heavily. "There is no theatre."

After a pause Adler said quietly, "Then where will we play?"

Rosenberg pointed across an open field. "Behind those trees, Yankele," he said with shame. "We have put up a tent like the gypsies. That is our theatre." Seeing how his friends' faces fell, he went on passionately, "And even here the greatest millionaires will come! Yes, they will come if they die for it! To see you, and not the theatre!"

"Yeh, yeh, Yankele," Cheikel Bain chimed in. "As true as I am a Jew, they will c-c-come."

Touched by such faith, neither Adler nor Sonya could remain angry. That night they came to see the performance. The tent was pitched in a yard and lit inside by lanterns. A few people scattered here and there. Mostly empty benches. In the center, a makeshift stage clapped together with boards. On this the ingenue, a young woman in the last stages of pregnancy, sang from *Bar Kochba:*

> Young is the grass
> As long as it grows.

"As she sang," Adler remarks, "she bent down, plucked straw from the stage. And each time she bent, she came closer to her confinement. Thirty-seven years have gone by, never again have I seen such a play—or such an ingenue!"

Week after week went by, and still there was no getting out of this accursed Nyezhin. Rosenberg had staked everything on Adler's growing reputation. He had miscalculated. Summer was coming on, people of means going off to *datchas* in the country. Those who remained were not hurrying out to Rosenberg's tent.

"A bad world," Adler grumbled, "does not care for poor

people! Are wood and bricks the theatre? Does scenery alone give the aesthetic thrill?" Thus Adler, unconsciously echoing Lope de Vega, who turned scornfully from the elaborate court spectacles, saying, "Give me some boards, a trestle, two actors, and a passion!"

The actors were all in pawn to the Commercial Hotel. They had nothing to fear from Shimen Kaplan, an easygoing old fellow, but his wife wanted to call in the police and attach their belongings. Only the four daughters, madly in love with the actors, prevented her from carrying out this threat. Adler and Sonya trembled for the four hundred roubles they had hidden in their trunk. Rosenberg would not care if they lost everything. He would shrug and say, "Why should you have, if I have nothing?"

Spivakovsky had gone to Berditchev to close a deal with a watchmaker. This man, Schneiderman by name, was willing to bring the company to Lodz, but insisted he must sit in the box office until he had recouped his investment. Ordinarily the actors would have disliked this condition. Now they agreed at once, feeling God had taken pity on their misery. Everyone wrote out their debts, their expenses, calculating and figuring how much to ask of the watchmaker. "A thousander this Schneiderman will have to schneider in!" Cheikel muttered, bending over his figures.

"Only a thousander?" Adler objected. "For a mere thousander are we so many tragedians, comedians, prima donnas, singers, and even an entrepreneur?"

He joked, but had a bad conscience. Day after day was going by, and still Spivakovsky's deal hung fire. The four hundred roubles in his trunk would have gotten the whole company to Lodz, yet Adler said nothing, fearing to lose the last he had in the world.

His hesitation all but cost them their lives.

After the Tsar's assassination, a wave of pogroms had swept South Russia. In Kiev a raging mob destroyed the synagogue, raped women, murdered and maimed hundreds of innocent people. Full-scale massacres followed in Elizavetgrad, in Odessa, and other cities of the south.

The scum of St. Petersburg would come into a town by train, inflame the most ignorant part of the population with stories of Jewish wealth, get the pogrom started, and disappear again. Jews referred to this lumpen army as the "Great Russian Brigade." It was well known that these criminal mobs had secret contacts with the St. Petersburg police and acted with their connivance. In Berditchev the Jews surrounded the railroad station and prevented them from getting off the train. In Odessa, Jewish and Russian university students fought them together through the streets, and the police themselves dispersed them. Actually, many high officials opposed these riots, for the anger of the mob, once released, could easily turn against the nobility and the regime. The government, aware of this danger, would allow the pogroms to rage for a day or two, then send in troops to stop them before they got out of hand.

The May riots died down, but broke out again that summer with renewed ferocity. A massacre took place in Pereyaslav, and harsh, restrictive laws followed. Jews were deprived of all official posts, closed out of all professions. Jewish women were forbidden to wear silk, velvet, or golden ornaments. Homes, shops, and land were all confiscated.

Other towns went the same way. First the pogroms, then the wholesale confiscations. Day by day the contagion spread, and the terror was coming always closer to Nyezhin.

One morning as the actors sat at breakfast, they heard a shrill, continual whistling, followed by the sound of running footsteps, the crash of glass, the thud of doors being torn open and the wild, inhuman cry, "Kill the Jews!" The Nyezhin pogrom had begun.

The four daughters of the innkeeper began to wail, terrified for their father, old Shimen Kaplan. The family hastily carried their valuables to the ice house, and finally hid themselves, too, under the straw.

Adler could not tear himself away from the window. He was in the grip of the old compulsion—to see, to see everything. And he saw:

"Every house on the street was surrounded by murderers. Some of them broke down windows, walls, even roofs; others, inside, threw furniture and household gear out into the street. From a high window across the way a piano crashed to the ground and lay there, all its strings humming. A whole featherbed was pitched out of another window. The mob ripped this open, jeering as feathers drifted through the air, a strange summer snow. This was a sport hugely enjoyed in every pogrom. While the men wrecked homes and stores, their wives, armed with great sacks, hunted through the destruction, thrusting everything of value inside them. And so it went in Nyezhin, all through the morning and the afternoon."

Toward evening the rioters, after working havoc through the town, circled back again. The actors had no time to make a plan before the drunken mob burst into the hotel, the leader demanding who and what were this bunch of Jewish faces. Behind him the cry went up, *"Baie Zhidov!"*—"Kill the Jews!"

Rosenberg burst into gay laughter. *"Oui, oui!"* he cried. Pointing to himself and the others, he repeated several times, *"Francuski aktiory!"*—"French actors." But he added in quick Yiddish, "Jews! Speak French!"

The actors all began gabbling some sort of gibberish. Rosenberg laughed and bowed continually. *"Je vous prie!"* he cried. *"Au revoir! Bon jour!"* As the mob still eyed him suspiciously, he pointed to Sonya, who began rattling madly away in real French.

Their fine actors' clothes and Rosenberg's quick wits saved them. The mob hesitated, and at last went off. Minutes later Spivakovsky drove up in a carriage. He had chosen this day to return to Nyezhin. "Fools!" he cried. "Save yourselves! To the station!"

The four hundred roubles came out of their hiding place, and the actors piled into carriages. As they drove through the town they saw fearful scenes enacted. Jews ran through the streets hatless, their faces bloody, and were beaten anew as they ran. Soldiers and police stood by watching, and those who ran to them for help were beaten back into the carnage with the flat of their rifles.

The mob had done its worst in the synagogues and Houses of Study, where they took a special pleasure in defiling the Sacred Scrolls that hold the Torah. They tore out whole pages, threw them in the gutter, stepped on them, danced on them. Jews running for their lives stopped at this sight, their faces filled with pain. Many tried to save what was left. As the mob rushed on, these Jews crept out of hiding places, picked the pages out of the gutter, kissed them, wept over them.

The tree-lined road to the station was crowded with people fleeing for their lives, crazy-looking people with torn coats, torn-out beards, many with bundles, many with children in their arms. Other children hid behind trees, wailing for their parents.

When they were halfway to the station Sonya suddenly

cried out in horror. They had forgotten Vinyavitch, their orchestra leader, and his young daughter, Bettye. For one terrible moment everyone hesitated. To go back into that butchery? "Back! Back!" Sonya screamed hysterically. The pregnant woman was ready to fling herself out of the carriage.

They found the Vinyavitches, father and daughter, in the cellar of the house. The young girl rushed into Sonya's arms, sobbing for joy. She thought they had all been killed.

As they drove back through the marketplace their blood ran cold. Every door and window had been broken, wine ran through the gutters, and a drunken mob was carrying away laces, satins, silks. At one crossing a Russian officer with a small group of soldiers was trying to bring this mob to their senses. Shouts, jeers, curses answered him. The officer threatened to fire unless they dispersed. At this, a howl went up. Bottles flew through the air. The soldiers fell back, guns at the ready. The officer shouted a command. Rifles rang out. Dead and wounded fell to the ground. Not far from the actors' carriage a well-known notary lay dead, an innocent bystander.

Months later the actors read in the *Gazette* of a Russian officer sentenced to eight years of hard labor for "actions during the riots at Nyezhin."

At the station panic had broken out. A rumor had spread among the crowd that the killer mob was headed that way. The stationmaster and some of the younger men were attaching a rubber pipe to a locomotive engine. "Let them come!" they said grimly. "We'll burn their eyes out!" These men were also trying to organize a collection for those without money. An effort was made to quiet the crowd, but they were milling about now in great confusion. A woman with a baby in her arms fell at Spivakovsky's knees and begged him to take her child. Another woman caught at Adler's sleeve, imploring him to save her. Others, too, thought such finely dressed people must surely be Christians.

"Shame rose in all of us for our shaven faces, our fine clothes," Adler writes. "Why had we denied our people, denied our language? What right had we to save ourselves? The tears in our eyes were our answer. The handsome, elegant Spivakovsky sobbed aloud, turned out his pockets. We all did the same. The women kissed the children, fell on the other women's necks, and we all wept together."

A shout went up as the train was sighted coming down the

track. Everyone pressed forward on the platform to board it. A frightful moment. Fortunately, no one was trampled.

It was not a journey but a flight, a rout. Children wept. Sick and wounded moaned. Sighs filled the air. An hour later through the train windows the actors saw cavalry galloping toward Nyezhin. The pogrom had gone far enough. The government was sending in troops.

11

The Imperial Ukase

ACOSTA
Close your eyes, all of you! And you too, blind mother, close your eyes! Enough! Let me go! (*rushes out*)

JUDITH
(*crosses to window*) To the synagogue, the synagogue! (*sinks to her knees*) And it is I who have done this!
Uriel Acosta

Their savior, the watchmaker, was waiting at the Berditchev station, and the actors met him there with tears of gratitude. Herr Schneiderman had brought with him both money and contracts, asking only that he be allowed to sit in the box office of the Victoria Theatre in Lodz until he got back his investment. Rosenberg got 100 roubles out of him, which he sent to his family in Odessa. He praised Adler as their "hidden millionaire," but gave him back no part of his four hundred roubles.

They spent an idle week in Berditchev. Adler looked up his mother's people, somber Orthodox Jews, masters of far-flung factories and mills. Hessye's other son had either left the city or had died at a youthful age, for there is no record of a meeting between the brothers.

Adler did not dare tell his grand Berditchev relatives that he was an actor, a dancer, and trickster. The truth was known to only one uncle, the humblest of the tribe. When Adler and Sonya left, this old uncle, who owned a shop, loaded them with shawls, warm winter underwear, and good Breslau socks.

The trip to meet the watchmaker had taken the company

south. Now, on the way from Berditchev to Lodz, their train made a stop at Nyezhin. As the conductor called that place name the talk and laughter of the actors died and they sat in silence.

There was a two-hour wait at the station, and the actors got off the train. Nyezhin looked like a town after a bombardment. Broken walls, wrecked, looted stores, hardly a soul on the streets. Soldiers with rifles were posted at every corner, and mounted hussars rode about the town, driving away those who loitered. The actors looked up the few friends that remained and exchanged a few low words with them. What was there to say? They went back in silence to board their train.

Hearts lifted in the great Polish-German-Yiddish city of Lodz. A gay, elegant town, this Lodz, with many open squares, many sidewalk cafes, many trees. The people were well dressed, clean, prosperous looking. Many merchants and bookkeepers lived in Lodz, as well as a number of writers and actors.

The Jews here spoke still a third dialect, the Polish-Galician, most poetic of the three. But the official class of Lodz, Jew and Gentile alike, spoke German. Even the posters were in German. The actors cut their German names out of the posters and pasted them on their doors. Rosenberg clowned in German, everyone bought German coats, German high hats; they forgot their recent troubles, and acted like millionaires. Just as Adler and his wife had gone without question into a pogrom area that offered them a livelihood, so now they accepted without question the safety and prosperity of Lodz.

The White Russian and Lithuanian governments had always seen the danger of the pogrom policy. Their police had dispersed the anti-Jewish mobs, and the courts dealt firmly with any attempt to riot or loot. The Jews, like any reprieved people, gave themselves to pleasure and amusement, spent money freely and, above all, flocked to the theatre. Much cash ran through the fingers of Herr Schneiderman the watchmaker, and Cheikel Bain, in the best of spirits, went off to conquer other towns.

At just this time, in the fall of 1881, the Odessa newspapers carried news of the two rival productions of *Uriel Acosta,* Lerner's and Goldfaden's. Excited by the news, Rosenberg declared that he, too, would have an *Acosta,* and one that would put both the others to shame.

Adler threw himself heart and soul into the project. He went through the manuscript twenty times, comparing it carefully with the Russian text. All his ambition flared up. To do Acosta, a historical figure, and in a classical play, one he had loved on the Russian stage! His heart did not stop fluttering between hope and self-doubt.

"My *yaitzer horre* * from the bad Odessa time whispered, 'Yankele, not for you! Greater men than you will play Uriel. Who are you to dream of such a thing?' My *yaitzer hatov* told me, 'The world is a battlefield! Fight for your place, or remain forgotten in your corner!'"

This conflict of the soul belonged to the world of dreams. Rosenberg gave the part to Spivakovsky. Adler hid his feelings under a smile, and told Rosenberg he had done well. He could not bear to show his humiliated hopes to anyone, not even Sonya.

He listened with bitter scorn as Rosenberg and Spivakovsky conferred on the role. The great Ivan Kozelsky had played Uriel in this fashion and that, Sonnenthal had interpreted the part so, read the monologue so . . . "I saw there would be a little Kozelsky, a little Sonnenthal, but very little Spivakovsky!" Adler remarks dryly. From the beginning, he had felt scorn for those actors who imitated others, playing their roles like beggars grinding out an old tune on an organ. "Wait!" he told himself darkly. "If ever I play it, it will be *my* Acosta!"

All his life Adler had luck. Three days before the opening, Rosenberg came to his door with a nose three times longer than usual and a letter in his hand. Spivakovsky sent greetings to his colleagues. Their wandering life had wearied him, and he had gone away.

Once or twice before Spivakovsky had gone off in this fashion. He always returned. This time, however, it was serious. They had to put on *Uriel* in three days.

Sonya sprang to her feet, her face flushing. "No great harm!" she declared with energy, "Yakob will play it! As well as Spivakovsky, and perhaps better!"

Yakob refused with violence. His ambition had melted away at the first onset of a terrifying reality.

Rosenberg begged him to be reasonable. "Consider, Yankele!" he pleaded. "We are far from home. We do not hear

---

* *Yaitzer horre* and *yaitzer hatov* represent the "lower" and "higher" natures of man.

from Cheikel. There is no permit yet from Warsaw. If the play is a success, all is well. If it fails, we will at least make enough to get back to Odessa." He added with bitterness, "Why don't you want to play it? If I had your face, your voice, your figure, I would play it!"

Sonya declared with flashing eyes that Spivakovsky lied in his letter. He had not wearied of their wandering life, but feared to stand on the stage with an actor greater than himself. She added with force, "My Yakob, my Uriel, take heart! We have three days. We will work, we will study, and you will be victorious!"

Rosenberg murmured a grateful, "*Spasibo*, Sonitchka," blew her a kiss, and ran off gaily to change the posters.

Adler was already begging God not to desert him.

At the first rehearsal he silenced the prompter. He wanted nothing to destroy his illusion that he was, in truth, Uriel.

The whole cast understood his fear, and respected it. Keni Sonyes, who had thrown herself passionately into the project, had devised a surprise in her desire to help him. At this first rehearsal she appeared in a grey wig, with a shawl on her head, and in full makeup as Uriel's blind mother. Seeing her grope toward him as with sightless eyes, Adler blurted out, "Mama! Mama!" and burst into a torrent of tears.

The actress did not know how deep a spot she had touched.

So many carriages lined the street on opening night one might have thought the Victoria Theatre the opera house. Women in décolleté and men in frock coats and white vests took up the orchestra and box seats, but the gallery was packed with students, tense young rebels to whom this play about a heretic brought a message of liberation.

Rosenberg, who was playing one of the rabbis, came into Adler's dressing room just before the curtain. He had put a great clanking sword at his side, and brought another with him. "Wear it!" he urged. "It will give you equality with your fanatic oppressors!" He began to demonstrate the advantages of a sword on the stage, how you could lean on it, take poses with it. "Remember, Yankele, how you led the charge at Plevna!" he exclaimed excitedly. "Yes, I saw you there, and knew you were riding to victory!"

In spite of himself, Adler felt a shiver go through him. "To this day," he admits, "I don't know whether that unforgettable scoundrel was making fun of me, or meant it!"

He did not wear the sword, and for that reason or another, the first curtain was a fiasco. The act closed on Acosta's line,

"Justice will fall from the heavens, truth come even from under the earth." Adler delivered it quietly, musingly, as he thought fitting for a great philosopher, Spinoza's teacher. But the curtain fell on a dead silence, and going offstage, he heard Rosenberg's angry sigh.

"If I had bawled it out like a wagon driver, they would have cheered me to the rafters!" he comments irritably. All the same, he felt badly, for he had deprived everyone of their applause, and in those days applause was often the actors' only reward.

Sonya, a strong favorite with the Lodz public, picked up the second act, playing their scenes with tempo and fire. She closed the act with a speech to Uriel on all that united them, and finally, revealing her own Judaism, came toward him, with the words, "We both love one God!" The curtain fell on their embrace, and the applause overwhelmed them. Bouquets came over the footlights for Sonya, and backstage the joy mounted to a celebration. Rosenberg vowed they would play all winter in Lodz. Give them the third act," he told Adler jubilantly. "There you can shake Spivakovsky out of your elbow!"

In this act Uriel must choose between his passion for scientific truth and the Judaism that is his soul. Humbled and broken, he confesses his heresy and falls from the altar to the ground, there to be trampled by the fanatical, cruel congregation. Adler had rehearsed the fall, but in the excitement of the opening, miscalculated. He struck his head against the stage, and fainted in a pool of blood, one last thought spinning through his head: *"If I live, I must learn to fall better!"*

He came to with a doctor taking his pulse, and heard Sonya asking with anguish if he would ever play again. "Even tonight!" came the cheerful reply. "A little courage, a glass of cognac, and he is as good as ever!"

Adler opened his eyes. Rosenberg, white as a ghost, bent over him, waiting for instructions. Was he to call off the performance? Adler asked for a mirror and a little alcohol, sprang to his feet, washed his wounds, put on a fresh beard, set his costume to rights and called, "Curtain up!"

Bravos greeted his entrance. He spoke his first line, and was surprised by a second ovation. A rumor had spread in the theatre that the fall had knocked out all his teeth!

The play came to a triumphant close, and as the curtain fell Rosenberg, half laughing, half sobbing, threw kisses from the wings. "Yankele, I blessed you the first time I sent you onstage, and now I bless you again!" he cried through his tears. Twenty curtain calls followed. Adler, stepping forward for his bow, heard through the applause out front the one music sweeter still to every actor's ears—the bravos of his colleagues onstage.

Adler's Acosta became a legend among the theatre-going public of Lodz. One night in the recantation scene, he was startled by a noise backstage like thunder. One of the Polish actors rehearsing in a room above the stage had come down to have a laugh at the Yiddish performance. He was so excited by what he saw that he called out, "Quick, everyone! You must see this!" The thunderous noise was made by the feet of the Polish actors rushing down the iron staircase. Adler marked off the event as a red-letter day in his life.

These triumphs were short-lived. The Lodz audience was limited, and even with *Acosta*, the troupe could not play there forever.

When things went well, these children spent everything. Bad times found them always unprepared and penniless. Debts began, hunger began. The landlord of the hotel refused to give them wood for their stoves. They shivered, took sick in the freezing Polish winter.

Worse than poverty and cold, a falseness crept into the atmosphere. Envy and intrigue were at work. Spivakovsky returned with a new backer called Hartenstein, a handsome, brainless boy, born in Galicia. This youth with a classic effeminate face, hair to his shoulders, and diamonds in his watch had acting ambitions. Taking command, Hartenstein put Adler and his wife out of the troupe, together with their friend Rosenberg and their protégé Keni Sonyes. The dismissal left all four stunned. After the triumph of *Acosta*, they could hardly believe it. Hartenstein was taking the company south to the Ukraine without them.

Rosenberg found a way, but only for himself. Somewhere or other he found the money to get him back to Odessa.

"How is this?" Adler asked him reproachfully. "You and I have been brothers. Now you desert us, leave us here?"

"Forgive me!" came the hasty, shamefaced reply. "I must go to my family. I will send help if I can."

Adler, who understood all human weakness, did not blame him too much. Rosenberg had an extraordinary devotion to his mother and sisters, and would have committed crimes to protect them.

The three ousted actors took counsel with each other. The company still owed them, all told, some 150 roubles. Adler went to see Hartenstein at his hotel. The young entrepreneur, surrounded by his flatterers and hangers-on, received him at a desk covered with cigars, bank notes, and photographs of girls. He admitted casually that Adler had a grievance, but made the mistake of using the intimate form of speech, an insulting familiarity. Adler flamed up in anger and surged forward, ready for blows. Happily, others were present, among them a certain Herr Manyevitch, a play agent for Goldfaden and Sonya's good friend. This man managed to quiet both parties, and Hartenstein agreed to give the three stranded actors fare back to Odessa.

They traveled on the train with the troupe, but in a third-class carriage. All three felt as though they were going to their own burial. Keni Sonyes looked out the window the whole way and wept. The troupe was going to Zhitomir, the town of her birth. It was ten years since she had seen her mother's grave.

Manyevitch did what he could to keep their spirits up. The kind man continually came into their carriage, and at every stop brought them tea and food from the station buffet. Toward evening he came in with a beaming face and good news. He had persuaded Hartenstein to take them back into the troupe. They were going on, with the others, to Zhitomir.

Keni Sonyes promptly fainted. Manyevitch thought joy had overcome her, but as soon as she recovered she began banging her head against the wall. "To Odessa! Odessa!" she screamed. "Not Zhitomir! Better suicide!" She was afraid to meet the father she had disgraced by her youthful indiscretions.

Sonya and Adler tried to calm her. They promised they would hide her for a while in some quiet hotel, that they would speak to her father, prepare him, soften him. She finally became a little less hysterical.

The Adlers could not carry out their plan. Zhitomir had no railroad station; travelers going there had to de-train at Berditchev and go the rest of the way by coach. As fate would have it, no sooner had they alighted at Berditchev when the actress came face to face with the very person she feared most. Her father, a burly, black-bearded giant, whip in hand, had come to pick up the actors and their baggage. He was the driver of their coach.

The actors went off to a side, frightened at how the matter would end.

"Of all the scenes this artist was to play," says Adler, "this was the bitterest and most painful. She stood before him, her body swaying back and forth like a weak branch. The coachman said nothing. He sighed, his honest face worked, the big hands trembled. Suddenly a terrible outburst. Tears spurted from his eyes. 'Daughter!' he cried hoarsely. 'Little orphan!' Enough! The great heart of the ordinary man of the people had broken. She fell on his breast, wailing, 'Father, forgive me! I was young! I didn't understand!'

"We had to help her, weeping bitterly, into the coach. The cabman climbed onto his high seat and started his horses. We sat in silence as the coach rattled over the endless road. A gray autumn night. A gray moon. Sad little stars. 'Zhitomir!' the cabman called. A sob came from the coach."

In Zhitomir the troupe went bankrupt, largely because Hartenstein insisted on playing all the leading roles. His old father came from Galicia, examined the books, and tore his hair, screaming, "Ruined! Ruined!"

Luckily, a wealthy townsman took matters in hand, and a series of benefits was organized. A Russian troupe in the city took an interest in these better performances, but the enthusiasm of an actress almost brought them to an end.

This talented girl, a Mademoiselle Kislova, made a speech from the stage one night, praising the dedication of the troupe, and berating the Jewish public for not supporting them. "Why are you so cold, why are you such mathematicians?" she scolded. "Art cannot exist without a childlike belief, a childlike spirit of trust!" Bankers and financiers in the audience stirred restlessly, but students in the gallery broke into hot applause. The situation was getting out of hand. Instead of the Jewish public, Kislova was beginning to blame Russian society. A roar of applause broke out in the gallery. It was turning into a political demonstration, and the police master came up on the stage and shouted for the curtain to come down.

There was a hearing next day in the office of the Governor. All the Russian artists came. Borisov and Philipovsky, stars beloved of all Zhitomir, testified to the worth of the Jewish company. Kislova brought her parents to the hearing. There were introductions, compliments—the actors began to breathe again. Since they were playing in Zhitomir without a permit, the matter might have ended badly. But luck was with them. The Governor, in love with a beautiful Jewish girl, was not badly disposed toward the actors. He relaxed and asked them for a song.

Resigned glances were exchanged. It was not the first time the great lord had to be entertained. They gave him an irresistible Goldfaden tune: *The Rabbi Bids Us Be Merry.* The Governor applauded unrestrainedly, and in a transport of enthusiasm, exclaimed, "Play as much as you like. On my responsibility!"

"I hear you, your Highness!" the police master cried. With a low bow to Kislova, he withdrew.

With a permit from the Governor, Adler played *Acosta* to a packed house. He repeated the triumph of Lodz, but after this the troupe fell apart. Sonya, about to be confined, went back to Odessa to have her child. Adler, left to himself, did some serious thinking.

All was not well between himself and Sonya. There had been an incident in Zhitomir with a girl called Itta, a *gymnazistka* with beautiful eyes and a charming enthusiasm for the theatre. Adler had dallied a little with this child, perhaps not altogether harmlessly.

A handsome actor finds many opportunities. In the provincial *shtetlach,* the bolder girls had sent Adler notes and had even thrown themselves in his path on the deserted country lanes. He had gone to Sonya once in great agitation, and confessed that he found some of these girls terribly attractive. Sonya had received the confession with her usual tact, betraying neither jealousy nor alarm. The episode in Zhitomir found her less patient. Her leavetaking, cold and without an embrace, frightened him.

After worried reflection, he decided that he must make a drastic revision not only in his relations with Sonya but in his whole way of life. "For three years I had wandered about the cave of *The Witch* wearing the motley of *Shmendrick*. I was nearing thirty, about to become a father, and still had no sign of a home. It was time to forget the applause, to bow low before Uncle Arke, and look about me for some better way of supporting my wife and family." With this decision, he left for Odessa.

"So you have come home," was his father's sad greeting. "And what have you achieved in these three years?"

The little sister was his great surprise. She had grown tall as her mother, but her eyes, of the same sapphire blue, were more roguish and laughing. This young queen already had a slave. She was soon to marry handsome young Isaac Levovsky, owner of the famous Lilliputian Bazaar on Richelevskaya Street.

There were other changes, too. Hessye's hair had turned white, and she was grown strangely silent. She had to be led about the house these days, for she was almost totally blind. Some inner pride held her erect and tall as ever. And if the son guessed at the wish for death that lay behind that stony gaze, he never dared show his own despair.

Sonya greeted him weakly. A Sonya in white clothes with a tiny, wonderfully human creature at her side. The barrier between husband and wife dissolved in a wave of tenderness for this little fellow mortal. To the Hebrew Rivke (Rebecca) and the Russian Vera, they added another name, Nunia, and for some reason the last one suited her best.

"Enough, Yankele!" his Uncle Arke adjured him. "You are a father now, so become a human being!"

He went to see the merchant friends of his uncle, went to see the notaries with whom he had once worked so closely. But nobody wanted to talk dull business with Adler. They asked him instead for a song, a dance.

"Hard for an actor to give up the theatre," he admits. "The way back is barred. I missed the excitement, the applause, the hurrying to the theatre at night. Sonya, too, longed for our old life. She, the clever, the strong said nothing, but it was as though a light had gone out in her soul. At night, when she thought me asleep, I heard her restless sighs."

In spite of his resolutions, Adler could not stay away from the Yiddish theatre. All Odessa throbbed with it. He saw the two *Zhidovkas*, the two rival *Acostas*, and the new Goldfaden opera, *Bar Kochba*. He fell under the spell of the "God-gifted Mogulesko," and it was at this time, too, that he met Abba Schoengold.

In the end sheer necessity forced him back to the stage; he could find no other way to make his livelihood. He joined neither Lerner nor Goldfaden, but went into the troupe of Sheikevitch, the popular Yiddish novelist now turned playwright and manager. Madame Sheikevitch liked his looks and cast him as the lover in her husband's melodrama *The Bloody Adieu.*

He did not stay long in Odessa, but formed a troupe of his own. With Fishkind, Keni Sonyes, his wife, his baby daughter, and a wet nurse, Adler went out again on the road. After traveling for a year or more, he fell in with Rosenberg again. The troupes joined forces and went on to play in Kharkov, Rostov-on-Don, and other cities of the White Russian and Lithuanian governments.

In Dinabourg Rosenberg took fire again with the old dream of St. Petersburg. "What do you say, Yankele?" he urged. "Shall we play the capital? See the spot where Alexander II fell?"

Cheikel Bain put in a few hundred roubles and they were off, traveling first class by special express. They drew packed houses in Riga and were every day expecting the St. Petersburg permit when the final blow fell.

Alexander II once asked Metternich in his perplexity, "How much liberty can you give the people before you begin to undermine authority?" That question, still unanswered, contains the enigma of his life and his death.

The terrorists had believed the assassination of the Tsar would be followed by the revolution. It was followed instead by the reign of his son.

Alexander III was torn by none of the conflicts that beset his father. He had from earliest youth hated his liberal reforms, and he mounted the throne proclaiming the divine origin of his rule. In a short time he succeeded in bringing back the days of Nicholas I. The press was gagged, the shadow of the church fell over the universities, spies and informers multiplied. The "Eighties" had begun, that era of despair when every liberal hope of the past quarter-century seemed doomed. Poles, Finns, Armenians, every Russian minority suffered, but the hand of the regime came down hardest of all on the Jews.

Legal methods of repression were soon added to the dangerous two-edged pogroms. Jews were forced out of all government posts, driven off the land, excluded from the professions. Their schools were shut down, their press outlawed, their societies banned.

The worst fate was suffered by those who had infiltrated the central cities of Russia proper. They were ruthlessly expelled, and when they fled to the rural communes, were driven out again. Within a year ten thousand of these people were wandering over the land, destitute and homeless. Masses of them went over into Galicia, drawn there by a false rumor that the French government would take them in. Sickness and famine broke out in their camps. Public collections for these victims were forbidden, and in St. Petersburg the governor general would not allow sums already donated to be distributed among them.

In May 1883, by imperial ukase, a High Commission for the Revision of Current Laws Concerning the Jews was created. This body met for the next six years without uncovering the slightest evidence that the Jews had worked harm either to the people or the state. Two rabbis were permitted to sit on the Commission, but without a vote. After one of the sessions in which Jews were deprived of due process, the rabbi of Mohilev went home, got into his bed, and died.

On August 7, 1883, by special order of this High Commission, Yiddish theatre was forbidden throughout the length and breadth of Russia.

One may search the histories of this period without finding any mention of this law. Even Jewish historians have passed over it, so great was the prejudice of the intellectual class against Yiddish theatre. There can be no doubt, however, that the law existed. It is mentioned without exception by every writer, journalist, and actor who wrote of these events. By Adler's account, the Russian newspapers were full of the news, and the Russian and German theatres glad to be rid of a galling competition.

For the little group in Riga it was as though the thread of their lives had snapped. They were stunned, paralyzed, and only after days had passed could they take counsel with each other and try to find some plan.

Adler writes: "Our first thought was to send someone to St. Petersburg, but we soon gave up the idea. Our first frightened inquiries in Riga brought the inescapable truth. No way existed around the ukase. It was steel and iron—the law. Nothing remained, then, but to leave Russia entirely. But where to go? Roumania? If the great Goldfaden had fled there as from a plague, what chance had we, little atoms that we were? The reports from Galicia were such that not even a lunatic would go there in his dreams. As for America, we could form not even a picture of a place so distant, so vast. And how to get money for such a journey? Only one ray of light could we see in the darkness around us, one piece of land still visible above the flood. London. At that time Jews spoke of London as a little later they did of America. But could we survive there? Would Yiddish theatre be possible? Could we play, earn our bread? Questions there were in plenty, but where to go for answers?"

Actually, had the company known it, possibilities in Russia still existed. Goldfaden was able to hold on for several more years at the El Dorado Theatre in Warsaw. Finkel, with effort and labor, got a permit allowing his troupe to give "musical entertainments." Spivakovsky, Zuckerman, and Schoengold banded together and survived for several years with "German concerts."

The group in Riga knew nothing of this. They had gone too far. They had lost connection with the others.

In the midst of their misfortunes, a greater blow befell them. Cheikel Bain, who had always found money for them even from under the earth, fell sick. In the three years Cheikel had been with the troupe, his cough and his stammer had both gotten worse. Now he was weaker every day, and soon could hardly leave his bed. To spare him the exertion of climbing a stair, the actors found rooms for him on the ground floor of a poultry dealer's house. Like everything they tried these days, it worked out badly, for the court outside the sick man's window echoed from morning to night with the cackle and noise of chickens, turkeys, and geese.

Cheikel remained cheerful in spite of everything. He took

part in all plans about the coming trip to England, and to the last day believed that the voyage on the sea would cure him.

Emigration had become the great question of the day. A few rich men in Moscow and St. Petersburg opposed the idea, fearing a mass departure from Russia would be seen as disloyalty. A handful of revolutionaries were also against it, holding that Jews should stay in Russia and fight. The great masses, unconcerned with theories, saved themselves as they could. Numbers of them left every week for Palestine, England, South America, North America. But the actors hung back, undecided, frightened of a step that meant the end of everything they knew and understood.

It was the dread word "conscription" that finally made them act. For Jews the army of Alexander III would be worse than a death sentence. Yet they feared a London remote to them as another planet, wondering fearfully whether Yiddish actors could survive there.

Rosenberg hit on a plan. Every week boats from London sailed into Riga harbor. On one of these boats there was sure to be a Jew. They would question him, ask him about conditions in England. He would tell them what kind of Jews lived there and, above all, whether they were the kind who would take to Yiddish theatre.

The plan succeeded at the first try. They sighted their man getting off a London boat, surrounded him, plied him with questions, and carried him off to be questioned by Cheikel. But they got little help from this stranger. The man spoke a Yiddish so villainously mixed with English words they hardly could make out what he said.

"Reb Jew, are you a Jew?" Cheikel demanded impatiently. "Speak so we can understand you!"

The stranger, more and more suspicious, had begun to roll his eyes in fear. He finally said in hollow tones that England was a country with very strict laws, and that all thieves there were sure to be hanged.

"Reb Jew!" Cheikel broke out wrathfully, "we are not going to England to steal! Out of my house! Out!" And rising from his bed, Cheikel drove the stranger out the door.

The outbreak took his last strength. He died two days later. It was the first death in the troupe, a bitter loss to all of them. His wife and brother came from Odessa. The wife wailed over her lost husband. The actors gathered at his bedside, and each time the door opened to admit new mourners, chickens, geese, and turkeys entered with them. Rosenberg, reciting the prayer for the dead, continually broke off to whisper, "Yankele, chase away the rooster before it lights on the body!"

"In spite of our sorrow we could not help it, we laughed hysterically," Adler writes. He adds bitterly, "It is always a comedy when actors die."

Through the help of a clever man in Riga, the troupe finally got passage to London on a cattle boat. They were required to provide their own food during the voyage, a hard condition, but they were in no position to bargain.

A last complication arose just before they sailed. Yisrol Gradner came in on them one day out of the blue, crying, "Children! I am guilty before you. I sinned against you in the past. But this is no time to bring up old debts when our actors' bread is being snatched from our mouths! You are leaving, going to foreign parts. I am here in Riga with my wife. You know what we both can do! Take us with you!"

Adler was overjoyed. Gradner, the great actor! A marvelous prima donna! Good friends, beside, from the old Odessa days! Without hesitation he came forward, clasped Gradner's hand, and said with warmth, "You are with us!"

But Rosenberg flew into a violent passion as soon as he heard the news. "Again Gradner?" Rosenberg cried. "Again the Litvak who never brings anything but misfortune?" And he swore that if Gradner came with them to London the others could count him out. Though the whole company argued and reasoned with him, Rosenberg would not change his mind. He could not abide the Lithuanian. He insisted that Gradner was unlucky. He knew that with such a star in the company he would be overshadowed, and he would not be budged. It was Gradner or himself. Adler had to choose.

One day while he and Adler were arguing the question near the Riga harbor, Rosenberg suddenly said, "Do you see that Jew over there, the one with the sack on his shoulder? He will decide!"

Going up to the Jew, Rosenberg took him familiarly by the arm, saying, "Come along, Uncle, we need you to judge a case!"

The stranger, wary, not knowing what he was getting into, allowed himself nevertheless to be led.

"Look at this man!" Rosenberg said, pointing to Adler. "He and I grew up in the same town, learned our prayers at the knee of the same rabbi, danced together at strange weddings, and dragged ourselves side by side through all of Russia. We are actors, theatre folk. Now we are forbidden to play, and are leaving. Suddenly between us there comes a stranger, a Litvak, a bird of ill omen who never brought us anything but misfortune. I refuse to go if he comes with us." Rosenberg finished by saying, "And now I am going to buy myself a cigar. While I am gone, consider the case. You are the judge! With whom should my friend go? With me, his brother, or with the Litvak?"

Leaving the Jew in deep thought, Rosenberg darted across the street, bought himself a cigar at a kiosk, and as quickly came back again.

The stranger, freed from his grasp, studied first his back as he crossed the street, then his face as he returned. Next he carefully perused Adler's face. "Young man," he said, coming to a decision, "go with this man!" pointing to Rosenberg. "With this man here!" And shouldering his sack, he went on his way.

Rosenberg fell into Adler's arms, sobbing for joy.

"For all that," Adler goes on to relate, "it was with Gradner that I sailed, and not with Rosenberg. My mind, my practical brain, told me I did well. In my heart I knew better. The deed must stand, a blot and a stain on my youth. And yet, what could I do? Rosenberg would not give in. In that great, cold, unknown world of London I already guessed how bitter would be the fight to survive. With Gradner there was a chance. With Rosenberg I knew I would go under. And beyond London there rose that other image bathed in an unimaginable light — the land beyond the sea, the land where there was no king, no Tsar, and where men lived as equals. I made my decision, and I held to it. Rosenberg went back with a broken heart to South Russia. I sailed with the Gradners for London."

Before they left the actors pooled what money they had to buy a stone for Cheikel Bain, and came together one last time at his grave. "Farewell, Cheikel," Rosenberg cried in a broken voice. "We will see each other in a better, a truer world!"

On a windy day in November the little company took ship for England. One or two friends came to the dock to give what help or advice they could, to call a last farewell, show a last brave flutter of a handkerchief from the shore.

The group huddled at the ship's rail as they cast off anchor. They had little reason to love their country, yet hearts swelled and tears burned and fell as they saw its shores recede.

Good-bye, mother, father, and little sister. Good-bye, Rosenberg, dearer to me than any friend I will know again. Good-bye, a long, long, last good-bye, my Russia, my Odessa, my home.

Part II

LONDON: AN ACTOR PREPARES

12

The Jews of England

> In London there is an East End and a West End. In the West End are those fortunate ones who are sent into the world with a kiss. In the East End are the others. Here live the poor, the shamed, those whom Fate, seeing how shrunken and bent they are as they creep through the gates of life, spat in their face for good measure. In this East End a corner has been set aside where, not content with the spittle, Fate sends the poor on their way with a blow, a kick, and their hats shoved over their eyes. In this spot, with the holy name Whitechapel, a piece of Israel existed. There we would have to sink or swim, survive or go under, find bread, or if we could not, find death.
>
> JACOB ADLER

As far back as the eighth century, there were travelers of the Jewish faith who found their way across the Channel seas to England. But these early visitors were few in number, their very existence lost in legend; it is only with the Norman Conquest that we find an actual Jewish community in that land.

These first true settlers bear little resemblance to the Jews of a later date. They came from France or the Rhineland, where some of their ancestors had lived since the days of Charlemagne. Rich and poor spoke Norman French, the language of the court, and their dress, too, was that of the Christians. They aroused no ill will among the population, but from the first they are set aside from others by their strange ancient faith.

With the preparations for the First Crusade, anti-Jewish

riots broke out in Rouen, followed by similar occurrences in the Rhineland and Germany. Some years later we hear a first accusation of child murder. A boy in the town of Norwich vanished mysteriously, and the Jews were accused of having killed him for ritual purposes. A wave of horror swept the land. Although the Norwich boy was soon found, alive and unharmed, the damage was done. The incident remained in the popular mind and could not be eradicated. Jews everywhere were mistreated, and many of them fled back to the continent.

Migration revived during the reign of Henry II, and it is under that masterful ruler that the Jews come into prominence. Nine great abbeys were built by Henry with money raised in large part by the Jewish community. They were also heavily taxed for his various crusades. In return they were permitted to own land, to levy taxes for the upkeep of their community, and to settle their internal disputes by rabbinic law. They took part, too, in the great fairs where most of the kingdom's trade was carried on. At St. Giles near Winchester the fair went on for eighteen days, and was like a temporary city with whole streets of tents. Prelates, barons, even ruling princes, sent agents who bought of Jewish merchants dealing in plate, jewels, horses, cattle, arms, armor, cloths, spices, rare drugs and wine.

These are their great days in England. In spite of the growing medieval fear, we find instances of friendship with those around them. Even the clergy was not altogether unfriendly. A bishop or abbott, strange to say, would occasionally employ a Jew as his steward. Literacy in the Jewish community was high, with girls as well as boys receiving an education. Jewish women, in contrast to their English sisters, had important proprietary rights, and some of them engaged in sweeping financial operations. Christians came as guests to Jewish weddings. Royal proclamations were posted in their synagogues. Their family life was admired, their learning respected.

By the end of the reign, however, Henry's extravagance had brought the community to the brink of ruin. Their usefulness began to wane, and this was dangerous. All the "merchant strangers" were hated, and the Jews were so incautious as to be strangers without a country of their own. The priests detested them for their beliefs, the barons for their allegiance to the king. And their great and powerful friend was growing old.

In 1189 Henry died. The coronation of Richard I, known to the people as *Coeur de Lion,* was the signal for a mass onslaught on the Jews—an attack carefully organized by certain barons who were heavily in their debt.

The riot began in the great open square outside the church. Mingling in the vast throng assembled here were Jewish deputations from all over the kingdom who had come with costly gifts to the Coronation.

A tussle in the crowd was the pretext for a sudden murderous assault on these men. As the riot grew Jews throughout the city were beaten, maimed and hounded through the streets. Jewish homes were torn down, or set afire with everyone in them. In the joy of rapine and plunder, two or three Christian homes were also looted and burned.

Angered that his coronation was marred by this hideous disturbance, Richard stopped the looting and hanged three of the rioters. All three, it must be said, had also broken into and robbed Christian homes.

Richard protected the Jews as long as he remained in England, but when he rode off on his Third Crusade, violence erupted in almost every city. In the town of York, the entire Jewish population was hunted down and put to death. Large numbers of them took refuge in an old watchtower and committed suicide there rather than fall into the hands of the mob. There may have been fifty who died in the tower; there may have been a thousand. Records of the event are old and unclear.

When their remains had been burned, a group of local barons forced their way into the Royal Palace, where they destroyed the records of their debts to the Jews. The names of these men have been carefully preserved. They are Richard de Malebisse and his squires, Walter de Carton and Richard de Cuckney, Sir William de Percy, Picot de Percy, Roger de Ripun, Philip of Fauconbridge, and Robert de Turnham. Richard hanged two of them on his return from Jerusalem. Since Jewish estates reverted after death to the Crown, the barons had destroyed evidence of their debts to the king himself.

Richard's death in 1199 deprived the Jews of their last protector. The demands of his father had strained their resources to the limit. The greed of King John reduced them to beggary. Their persecutions at the hands of this king are in fact so barbarous as to be recorded even in non-Jewish history.

John began his reign at the dawn of a century that saw religious hysteria mounting to madness. In 1215, the year Magna Carta gave mankind a new conception of freedom, the

Fourth Lateran Council decreed excommunication, the yellow badge, and the ghetto for all Jews throughout Europe. In France and Rome, the Talmud was burned. Massacres took place in Germany. Blood accusations multiplied. In England, all debts to Jews were annulled and their synagogue in London was twice destroyed. They were forbidden to lend money, forbidden the professions, forbidden to own land, forbidden to join in guilds and fraternities. Christian evidence stood higher in all courts than Jewish evidence. Several municipalities expelled them.

A privileged few kept a remnant of their position. A few still traded in wool or corn. Most were destitute. They were of no further use to anyone as paupers, and in 1290 they were ordered, "for their extortion, their diminishing the coin, and other crimes to leave in peace." They were allowed to take with them their movable belongings and unredeemed pledges, and were given thirteen weeks in which to depart. About sixteen thousand went out into exile in this first great expulsion of medieval history.

In the next four hundred years the same formula of taxation, ruination, expulsion was to be repeated in France, in Germany, and in the papal states. By the middle of the sixteenth century, only a handful of wanderers, a few licensed and unlicensed physicians, and some dealers in contraband remained in all Western Europe. The whole Jewish population had fled eastward to Poland and Lithuania.

Yet even as they fled, they were reappearing. Disguised as the neo-Christians of Spain, we find them in Flanders, Holland, France, England, and the Levant. We see them in these countries as early as 1391, for it was a full hundred years before the Inquisition that the flames of the first *auto-da-fe* lit the skies above Seville. Thousands of Jews perished for their heresies in those flames. Thousands of others, however, were baptized to escape burning. Of these survivors, a certain number clung secretly to their own faith.

A good many of these Marranos* made outstanding careers in commerce, politics, and the arts. Some of them married their daughters into the Spanish nobility, and they were particularly successful in the clergy, rising to be bishops and even archbishops. Yet, though they looked upon themselves as a proud, integral part of Spanish culture, these Marranos continued, at the risk of torture and death, to hold secretly to their Judaism.

*A Spanish word meaning pig. A term of derision and insult aimed at all Jews, but particularly at secret Jews, who were especially hated.

As the Inquisition drew near, many of these "hidden Jews" found it wisest to emigrate. Of these a certain number came to England, some directly, others roundabout from Holland, Italy, and the Levant. They were drawn to England by the quarrel of Henry VIII and the Church, a schism that gave them hope that some day they might drop their disguise.

It was in fact the quarrel of the king and the pope that led to the realization of this hope. The Reformation brought the Bible to the people, and this image of a God present as a spirit among mankind was a religious revelation of such power that, as we know, it finally overturned the throne itself. The language of the Puritans continually refers to the Old Testament. They rode into battle with the Lion of Judah inscribed on their flag. The Marrano colony in London, many of them men of wealth and prominence, gave their full support to Cromwell.

Puritan rule brought sweeping political and ecclesiastical changes, and with these came a great stirring of conscience. An interest in the Jews had been awakened, and a feeling that an injustice had been done these "People of the Book." Roger Williams wanted to give them citizenship, and the American colonies, founded on the embattled love of religious freedom, had a far-reaching influence in England.

In 1647 a book by Edward Nicols appeared entitled *An Apology for the Honorable Nation of the Jews and All the Sons of Israel.* This work, which made a deep impression, declared that England's troubles had been sent by God as a punishment for their treatment of his Chosen People. The same year, Johanna Cartwright, a Dutch Puritan, petitioned Lord Fairfax and the Council of War to revoke the Edict of Banishment and permit resettlement of the Jews in England. Cromwell reacted favorably to the petition. The matter was set in motion when John Thurloe, his representative in Holland, sought out one of the most famous Jews of that day.

The sensual face of Manasseh ben Israel, the rich magnificence of his apparel, his enigmatic worldly eyes have all been immortalized in the etching made by his friend Rembrandt van Rijn. Manasseh's scholarly works had from his early youth aroused interest among academicians of the Christian faith. A correspondence with Puritan scholars made his name known in important English circles.

John Thurloe advised Manasseh to write Cromwell, petitioning for readmittance. Instead of a petition, he wrote a book. *The Hope of Israel,* a visionary work, leans on the biblical prophecy that once the Jews are dispersed among all nations the millennium will come about. The Latin edition was dedicated "To the High Court of England, the Parliament and the Councell of State."

The Puritans were pleased, and two passes to England were sent to Manasseh in Amsterdam. Because of hostilities between the two countries, the great rabbi did not arrive until 1655. He came accompanied by his son and three rabbis, and with his second book, the famous *Humble Addresses to the Lord Protector,* in his pocket. The *Humble Addresses* wasted no time on Messianic visions or Lost Tribes. Manasseh wanted refuge not only for those who had fled the Inquisition but also for the victims of the murderous Cossack hordes in the Ukraine. The book requested resettlement, asked for freedom of worship for Jews in England, defended them from charges of ritual murder, and pressed hard on the advantages to England of allowing them to return, to trade, and thereby to increase the commerce and prosperity of the nation.

It was perhaps this last point that most interested Cromwell. In an atmosphere of fierce public controversy, the question was submitted to the Whitehall Conference. That body could find no valid law excluding the Jews from England, but failed to pass an Act of Readmittance. Cromwell was disappointed. Manasseh returned to Holland despondent, and died two years later feeling the great mission of his life had failed.

The door, however, had been opened. Directly after the Whitehall Conference, twenty-five Marrano families petitioned for the right to live openly in their own faith and to bury their dead in Jewish consecrated ground. Cromwell had long suspected the true nature of the Sephardic colony, and was not averse to letting them drop their disguise. The petition was granted. In 1655 they leased a house in Creechurch Lane for use as a synagogue and shortly after, purchased some land at Mile End as the first Jewish cemetery in England.

A year later the *Ashkenazim* came. There was no formal law recalling them. They simply came, a steady flow of destitute Jews from Poland and Germany. Their presence stirred angry debate, and when Cromwell died in 1658, an attempt was made to nullify the Act of Readmittance. Since no such act had been passed, however, there was no way to revoke it. No one knew how to proceed, and the lines of the poor continued to flow into England.

Now the Spanish *Sephardim* were in the main cultivated men and women, quite at home in the best English society.

This procession of ghetto dwellers were a breed entirely new to them. The German and Polish Jews read from a different prayer book. They spoke a jargon that fell harshly on ears accustomed to the musical *Ladino*. They had a different way of pronouncing Hebrew. The great world culture, the pride of the *Sephardim,* had never penetrated their ghetto walls. They were looked upon as strangers and inferiors. The poorest were given five shillings and sent back to the continent as mendicants.

Denied posts in the Sephardic synagogue, the *Ashkenazim* rented a house in Duke's Place and made this into a small synagogue of their own. Twenty years after Resettlement they had established only two small elementary classes for boys and girls. Scholastic standards were low. The language was Yiddish.

With the *Hahamate* of the Venetian-born David Nieto, the two congregations moved even further apart. Nieto, a graduate of the University of Padua, wrote in Spanish, and his treatise denouncing the Inquisition was dedicated to Cardinal Francesco de Medici. During the twenty-six years he was *Haham,* a great part of his congregation had become increasingly Anglicized. They were country squires now, patrons of the arfts, friends of the great, and the wealthiest had homes in Bishopsgate and Tooting. They regarded themselves as Englishmen, and actually many were now native-born.

But if the eighteenth century belongs to the Spanish Jews, the nineteenth shows the rise of the *Ashkenazim.* Great rabbis began to appear among them. Moses Hart of Hamburg tore down the synagogue in Duke's Place and built a stately *schul* in its place. Ashkenazic families intermarried and founded dynasties. The wall around the proud Sephardic families began slowly to yield. Meir Barent Cohen married one daughter to Sir Moses Montefiore, another to a Manchester cotton exporter called Nathan Meyer Rothschild. The Goldsmid brothers were financiers to the king and Julian Goldsmid entertained the royal family at Morden, his country estate.

The close of the eighteenth century saw hostility against all Jews declining. The atmosphere was changing. Great liberal figures sympathetic with the American Revolution were becoming prominent. In Richard Cumberland's play *The Jew,* a plea for more acceptance was greeted by prolonged cordial applause. A century earlier, a bill to end the civil disabilities of Jews had been defeated and its supporters insulted on the London streets. By 1843 Lord Lyndhurst, Disraeli's friend, supported a bill that opened to Jews all municipal offices under the Crown.

But the numbers of the poor were also growing. Cheap steamboat travel, the upheavals of 1848, persecutions and wars on the continent brought them. From 1850 to 1880 one-third of the Great Synagogue income had to be spent on relief for the poor. There were funds for poor brides, for poor widows, for the sick, for hospitals, for old-age homes, for orphanages. In those three decades ten thousand Jewish immigrants had entered London.

This, however, was a mere rivulet compared with the avalanche that began with the Russian "May Laws" of 1882. In a single year the number of immigrants multiplied by ten, and Rabbi Adler of London sent up a cry: "Do not come! Woe! We cannot support so many!"

His plea was lost in the human flood. It was impossible to feed and house them all, and frightful conditions soon developed in the East End. Highly placed people were horrified by the condition of these refugees, and a move got underway to send an official protest to the Tsar. Tennyson feared this might do more harm than good, and there were Jewish members of Parliament who shared his fears.

In 1882 a public protest meeting led by Sir Whittaker Ellis, Lord Mayor of London, was held at the Mansion House. Present were Campbell Tait, the Archbishop of Canterbury, Cardinal Manning, Charles Darwin, and Matthew Arnold. Lord Shaftesbury moved the principal resolution, to raise a Mansion House Fund of 100,000 pounds by public subscription for the oppressed.

Even had the sum been raised, it would not have covered the need. Too many were coming.

The winter of 1883 was one of the hardest in memory, a time of widespread unrest, anxiety, and fear. The first great colliery strikes broke out in the north, and in London whole families of homeless people roamed the streets all night like ghosts. The shadow of unemployment and hunger fell on every home, and in the East End uneaten bread was left outside the windowsills for the poor.

In December of that year a boat from Hamburg came into London Harbor bringing, together with hundreds of other refugees, a small band of Yiddish actors — first of the troupes to be driven into exile by the Tsar's edict against their theatre.

13

Adler Great Eagle

OLD JACQUES
(*sorts through his basket*) Let's see, now. What have we today? A pair of suspenders. They'll do for the old man. A torn petticoat. That's for the old woman. Now, if I could find a pair of trousers the whole family would be dressed. What in the world can this be? (*fishes up a corset cover*)

The Ragpicker of Paris

The cattle boat from Riga had carried the troupe only as far as Hamburg. Here after some delay they shipped out again for England. Sailing with Adler were his wife and child, Volodya and Keni Liptzin, now listed as man and wife, Yisrol and Annetta Gradner, two young comedians by the name of Kempner and Baum, and Frau Tchizhik, a character actress.

They had bad weather on the North Sea, and at times all of them thought their last hour had come. Annetta Gradner was very weak. She had a bad heart, and Gradner was in mortal fear she would not survive the crossing. Adler and Sonya, too, were continually frightened for the safety of their little girl.

They docked on a cold December day. No one knew they had arrived, no one expected them or greeted them. They had come without money, without a word of the language or a friend in all of England. Their whole fate rested on a letter from Jacob Adler's father to the Chief Rabbi of London.

Aside from this letter they had only an address scribbled out for them by a friend in Riga. Every one of the actors knew this address by heart. The street was Mansion Street, and there a Jew called Sonnenschein owned a restaurant. Sonnenschein was a Roumanian who had seen Yiddish theatre in Bucharest. On a thread slender as this, their welcome in London depended.

Kind fate gave them a day without fog and a London policeman in a cape who was a gentleman. This sympathetic man, used to the wreckage off these boats, found them a fellow Jew who, for a shilling, agreed to take them to Mansion Street. Following this guide, the actors took themselves out onto the cobblestoned London streets, and gray and grimy they must have looked to eyes used to the colors of Russia.

After walking a way, each with his baggage, Adler also carrying his excited little girl, they boarded a tram. This took them through the East End into the Jewish quarter, where their journey continued on foot. After traversing several crowded streets, they came out onto an avenue loud with noise and packed from end to end with men and women calling out their wares.

"Petticoat Lane, a long, narrow thoroughfare once lined with trees, now with barrows and beggars, was the marketplace and stronghold of London's Jews," says Israel Zangwill, poet of the London ghetto. "No missionary dared set foot there, and every street and alley abutting on it was covered with commerce."

The "Lane" was, in fact, neither a lane nor a street, but a whole little district taking in Sandyrows, Frying Pan Alley, Catherine Wheel Alley, Tripe Yard, Hebrew Place, Little Lovecourt, Little Middlesex Street, Hairbrine Court, and a score of other nameless lanes, rows, passages, alleys, and yards, all ringing with the cries of street vendors. The farther the actors penetrated into these narrow, crooked ways, the grimmer and more dreadful they seemed. Dark little shops full of crazy, worthless goods, ancient houses with crooked walls and lopsided roofs, women in ragged shawls shivering at the corners, and men waxen-faced and old before their time, pushing their barrows. Never in the poorest streets of Russia, never later in the worst slums of New York were the actors to see such poverty as in the Whitechapel of the 1880s.

They stopped at last at a small lodging house with a tavern on the ground floor. Outside this establishment an enormous man in an apron was stirring a kettle from which came the aroma of frying fish. This person, round as a barrel and with pale, runny, fishy eyes, was none other than Sonnenschein himself, the very man whose name they had pored over a thousand times on the ocean.

Sonnenschein, known to Whitechapel Jews as Velvel Fish, had a partner as thin as he was fat, and called, for some reason, Chaim-the-Devil. From these two men the actors got their first meal and lodging in London. Grateful as they were for food and rest, their hearts ached. The rooms above Sonnenschein's restaurant were miserably cold and poor, a tallow candle on the table all their dim, sad light. Sonya, the strong one, broke down, sick for the Russia she would never see again. Adler almost wept with her. The child, mercifully, was soon asleep.

They ventured out the following day, but their spirits sank before the cold pride of this gray, alien city. Great London with its distant shadowy towers, its historic bridges rose before them, indestructible as time and as remote from their pitiful concerns. These actors who had only to walk along the Richelevskaya to feel they were millionaires, hardly dared set foot on the glorious streets of the London rich.

Nor was the East End much better. The tough, young British Jews frightened them, and the older ones seemed to go about their work without joy, without grace. Best of all they liked the old Sephardic synagogue on Church Lane, feeling there some connection, some echo of their own life, their own story.

They could give no more than a day to the sights of London. Next morning Adler put on his high hat and best coat and, armed with his father's letter, went to present himself at the residence of the Chief Rabbi. He went on this errand alone, and reasonably certain of success, for he had never yet gone in person to ask for help and not received it.

Adler had often been told by his father that his family came originally from Germany, and that Rabbi Adler of London was a distant family connection. Learning that his son was about to leave for England, Feivel Abramovitch had sent on to Riga a Hebrew letter presenting his son to this illustrious relative.

The Very Reverend Dr. Nissim Hillel Adler, now in his eightieth year, was spiritual leader not only of the London Jews but also of Orthodox Jews throughout the British Isles and the Empire. Among his many accomplishments, he had helped found the nonsectarian National Society for the Prevention of Cruelty and Better Protection of Children, laboring in this gigantic task with Dr. Benjamin Waugh, Herbert Spencer, and the Cardinal Archbishop of Westminster. The Chief Rabbi has a place, in fact, among the great reformers of the Victorian era, and visitors to the Jewish Institute will find it today on the East End thoroughfare called Adler Street.

The Chief Rabbi's duties were so arduous that his congregation had given him as an assistant his son, Dr. Hermann Marcus Adler. Though the younger man had his own congregation in fashionable Bayswater, he was usually to be found in his father's company. Jacob Adler made the acquaintance of both men on his first visit to Crosby Square.

The old rabbi received him with the official manner typical of those occupied with serious community problems. His greeting, however, was not entirely without friendliness and even a certain sweetness. And when he learned it was a member of his family who stood before him, and with a letter of introduction in Hebrew, he became truly warm. He presented the visitor to his son, begged him to be seated, and ordered that refreshments be brought.

The conversation was carried on in German, which the two rabbis, both from Hanover, spoke very well. Adler ate a few morsels out of politeness and exchanged some remarks with the son while the father looked deeply into his letter. The more the old man read, the more relaxed and pleasant he became. From time to time he raised his eyes with a smile, as if to assure himself that before him was indeed a lost little branch of the great Adler tree. At last, seemingly satisfied, he folded the letter, made some inquiries about Adler's parents, and expressed regrets for the passing of his grandfather. Coming down to brass tacks, he asked his young relative what he wanted in London and in what way he could be of use.

At just this crucial point, however, the warmth of his manner vanished. When he learned that his guest was an actor, his purpose in London Yiddish theatre, the pleasure on his face faded. Adler, stammering on, sensed he had in some way lost his advantage.

Often in Russia, when his troupe was stranded or in trouble, Adler had sought out the rabbi of some small town. He had always been received with tolerance and a willingness to help. He saw none of this kindly forebearance in the eyes of his illustrious grand-uncle.

"His head no longer moved up and down in smiling approval, but forbiddingly, from side to side. His smile, too, now expressed mistrust and even mockery, as one smiles at the impudent lie of a child one does not mean at that moment to punish and correct. The very twist of his mouth as he pronounced the word 'Yiddish' told me our beloved language held no honored place in his heart. And I had come to spread this 'jargon' further, popularize it still more? Worst of all, to do so in a theatre where, God forbid, strangers might come and jeer? In the eyes of both rabbis there was fear and anxiety."

Adler, without knowing it, had touched an extremely sensitive nerve. The wealthy Jews of the West End, English-born for generations, were galled by the Yiddish of their poorer brothers, feeling it separated them from the rest of the nation. But though Lord Rothschild inveighed against it as "socially degrading," the Jews of the East End laughingly refused to give it up. Yiddish is, above all, the language of courage and survival; no other tongue could express their experience.

It was particularly important that Dr. Nissim Hillel Adler, a vigorous fighter against reform, do nothing to further alienate the Jews of the West End. He had, over the years, succeeded in welding together a score of quarreling secessionist congregations into one United Synagogue. Unity was his great contribution. Dr. Adler was in hopes that the East End in time could be weaned away from this divisive language. He was the last man in the world who would sponsor a Yiddish theatre in London.

Yet the great rabbi remained polite. He suggested the matter might perhaps be discussed at some other time, assured his grand-nephew that he would be welcome should he call again, sent greetings to his worthy young wife.

Adler left the house stunned by his defeat. Money, help, even a theatre—the powerful rabbi could have arranged all this with a mere wave of the hand. Who could open the hearts of the London Jews so easily as this influential man? Instead, he had turned his back, leaving the actors to their fate. Adler had to go back with empty hands.

As often happens with bad news, the actors imagined matters could still be righted. Only Yisrol Gradner grasped the finality of what had happened in Crosby Square. "Adler! Adler! How are we going to play?" Gradner cried. At that panic broke out. Starvation, beggary, deportation—all of these rose up, grim and real.

There is no telling how far the despair of the troupe might have gone if some of them had not kept their heads. Adler, frantic himself, tried to control the rising hysteria. Annetta Gradner, strongest of all, insisted they had come through worse than this, and with tears in her eyes, declared they were among their own people and would not fall.

Little by little the actors calmed down, and began casting about for some way out of their trouble. Someone threw out the idea that the rich Jews of the West End might support them. For a time everyone caught at this as a hope, a possibility.

In the end help came from humbler circles. It came, as it had in Russia, from small Jewish businessmen, from impoverished young intellectuals. Above all, it came from the "folk masses," poor working men and women who supported the theatre because they loved it.

It was in Sonnenschein's restaurant they made their first friend, a young journalist called Rabinovitch who wrote for a little anarchist weekly. Rabinovitch turned out articles and stories for this sheet, wrote potboilers, labored at translations, and was still so poor it was heartbreaking to see. But he was young and handsome, of an easygoing, genial nature, and did not take his poverty greatly to heart. He introduced the actors to everyone he knew, never failed to put in a word for them in his anarchist paper, and comforted them when they fell into despair. "Never mind, dear ones," he would say tenderly at their worst moments. "Your sun, too, will rise! You will see that the Jewish people will yet honor and accept you."

But it was from Sonnenschein himself that the troupe got the most important intelligence. For, as it turned out, Yiddish theatre had already been seen in London. Sonnenschein and his partner, in fact, had both been actors themselves, and Chaim-the-Devil had received his peculiar nickname playing the devil in a one-acter performed in a London club. "I don't know who brought it, or how it got there," the surprised Adler remarks, "but when we arrived in London, we found the Yiddish theatre already there before us!"

The mysterious Yiddish players of Whitechapel were simply amateurs who had played in little groups in the towns of Russia, Poland, and Roumania. They had found each other in

London and, still fired by a longing for the stage, began putting on plays, rehearsing evenings after a day's work in a factory or shop.

Having no money for a theatre or even a hall, the amateurs performed in little so-called club rooms. Such performances were permitted by city ordinance as long as they were given privately, that is, for the entertainment of the club members and with no admission fee. These were not easy conditions, for the young actors had to pay for the room and their own expenses. Needless to say, all who came were admitted, and money also changed hands. If the pence could not pass over the table, they could still pass under it, and the coin not taken on one side of the door could always be collected on the other.

Soon after their conversation with Sonnenschein, Adler and the troupe met two of these amateurs. Annie Eisenberg, daughter of a Russian epaulet maker, and Solomon Manne, son of a Cracow merchant, had met in a London "dramatic club," fallen in love, and married. The young couple were at that time performing on Prescott Street. The actors lost no time and looked the situation over that same night.

As it chanced, it was in this very room that they were to give their own first London performances. The hall itself, rather long and lit with gas, was drab and poor. There was a platform, covered with a dingy cotton curtain, at the back of the room, and several rows of benches along the walls, placed lengthwise to show that this was a club, not a theatre. A large wooden table with chairs occupied the center of the floor. This was reserved for the president and his committee.

About twenty people were drifting about the room, finding seats, laughing, arguing, relating some incident at work that day, or criticizing the actors who were to perform. A thick haze of smoke from cigars and pipes rose to the ceiling, and the noise was such that no one could he beard without shouting. After some time the president and committeemen came out from behind the wings and, with some pomp, took their seats at the table. The president rapped his gavel, silencing the racket, which immediately broke out again. At last he gave three loud raps, signal to both audience and actors that the play was to begin. Two or three musicians struck up a bit of a tune and the curtain was drawn to one side.

Actors appeared, recited lines, sang, danced, all without

stopping the chatter of the audience. Clearly, these people had come more for warmth and company than for the play, which was, in truth, very weak.

Prescott Street looked good enough to Adler and his actors, but willing as they were, they could see no way. They could not play without scenery, musicians, and costumes; they themselves had to live. In the days that followed, even the Whitechapel clubs seemed a dream out of their reach.

Even as they despaired, however, forces were acting in their favor. Their very presence in Whitechapel was awakening curiosity. A certain sympathy and respect grew up around them. People began to take an interest, and after a while, to help.

It was not only idealists like Rabinovitch who came to their aid. Hard-hearted usurers found a buried spark in their hearts for the actors. And even those who took interest on their loans did so on more lenient terms than for others. When the problem of costumes arose Adler looked up a certain Posover, a man he had known in Odessa who now loaned money on percentage. Posover did not refuse, though his only guarantee was Adler's word, and the profit for him light as a feather. "I don't know how he was with others," Adler writes, "but we remembered him as a good man." A small agent called Gutman also advanced them certain sums. Neither a pleasant nor a friendly man, he loaned the money, caring little about his interest, simply out of friendship to people playing Yiddish theatre.

Their greatest help in London came from one Herman Fiedler, who turned out to be related to Sonya. Fiedler, a musician and also a playwright, was to lead the orchestra, rehearse the chorus, and eventually to provide the troupe with plays, of which he had an inexhaustible supply.

"It was friends like these that started the mill of our theatre," Adler wrote. "Because of them we felt we were no longer alone, that in cold, gray London were hearts that beat for us, eyes that looked on us with warmth. We threw off our fears, became brave as lions, and began to rehearse."

They opened with *The Penitent* by Sheikevitch, a melodrama with good parts for everyone in the cast. Adler played the handsome Dr. Weinglass, who forsakes Judaism for love of a beautiful but heartless woman. The cruel enchantress was played by Sonya Michelson. Annetta Gradner played the good Jewish sweetheart whom the doctor throws over in his mad infatuation, and Gradner, the true friend who marries the jilted sweetheart and stands by the doctor when his trouble comes.

As the rejected sweetheart, Annetta Gradner had the perfect setting for her special pathos and appeal. Her success was shared by Gradner, who performed a lesser role with a power that drew applause in every scene and whose songs were encored over and over in a tumult of bravos. The actors had never expected such a success. The immigrants of Whitechapel were like children in their joy. They fought for tickets, talked of nothing but the play for days before they went, and lived for days after in the spell of what they had seen. The actors caught their excitement, and played as they had never played before. Never had they been so loved as by this audience of exiles to whom they brought the scenes and pictures, the very essence and perfume of the life they had lost.

Adler as Dr. Weinglass had failed to score as heavily as the singing stars, and Gradner in a small role had overshadowed him in the lead. He took this as part of the fortunes of war, rejoiced with the cast, but gave some careful thought to his second appearance.

Instead of selecting something from the old repertoire, he decided on a piece Herman Fiedler had given him, a play called *The Beggar of Odessa*. "A play about a ragpicker," Adler relates. "I don't know where Fiedler got it. It was done on the French stage, I believe. On the Russian stage they also had a play on the subject. Maybe Fiedler put them together. To tell the truth, I never bothered to ask. What does an actor want? Give him a play, a role, he is satisfied. Perhaps that is how it should be. The actor is not a literary historian or a keeper of archives. A play about rich and poor, nobility in rags, and crime in silks. A work perhaps of no great literary value, but the scenes offered so much room for variation, the role had so wide a range, and called so greatly on the art of mime—in short, I decided this was an excellent, a truly theatrical play."

As Adler had guessed, the comedy did not originate with his friend Herman Fiedler. It was, in fact, performed for the first time in Paris on the eve of the 1848 revolution, a moment when economic chaos was reaching a crisis and Paris was the scene of gigantic demonstrations of the poor. The theatre of the Paris boulevard was a huge, rowdy arena where dangerous popular sentiments could be expressed. And the overwhelming success in 1847, the year of the gathering storm, was Felix Pyat's *The Ragpicker of Paris*.

The play itself has that delicious theatricality that was later to characterize the silent-movie era. The Ragpicker is a tragicomic figure who can remember neither father nor mother, and whose first recollections are of the Paris streets. Old, witty with the ironic wit of the poor, he goes about collecting in an ancient basket the crazy odds and ends he finds on the city streets.

But this figure, ridiculous in its poverty and rags, is radiant with honor. He cares nothing for wealth, and loves only one creature, the daughter he has raised as his own and with whom he shares his all. When, grown to charming womanhood, this daughter is threatened with imprisonment, the Ragpicker shows his true face. No longer the victim of society, he is brilliant, fearless, omniscient. The comic mask is thrown off, and we glimpse instead the more formidable figure who will soon be manning the barricades of the revolution. The thrones of the mighty shake at the Ragpicker's cry for justice. Great magistrates and judges follow at his bidding. He saves an innocent girl, exposes foul murder, rights all wrongs. Yet he scorns the corrupt temptations of the world. Asked to name his reward, he advances to the footlights and lifting high his arms, makes one exultant last request: a new basket—for the Ragpicker of Paris!

The play had been pirated a dozen times before it fell into Herman Fiedler's hands. Versions of it had been seen in Russia, in America, and as early as 1864 at the Surrey Theatre in London. Fiedler had simple given the characters Russian names, turned the Ragpicker into a Jew, and transported the action from Paris to Odessa.

In the days with Rosenberg, Adler had once played a ninety-year-old itinerant preacher, a pathetic old man who had spent his life wandering from town to town and now went about repeating words whose meaning he had forgotten. Adler had felt a peculiar excitement as he worked out this "bit." Now, as the figure of the Odessa streets took shape in his imagination, the same excitement gripped him again. What figure on earth so tremendous in its meaning as the figure of the Beggar! What role greater for any actor!

He spent days wandering about London, hearing in these streets the echo of Garrick's mighty Lear, haunted by the memory of Kean, thrilling in every nerve as his creation came to life in his mind. The *jeune premier*, capitalizing all these years on a handsome face and figure, had discovered he was a character actor.

In the city of Zhitomir two famous Russian actors, Borisov and Philipovsky, had initiated Adler into the mysteries of *grim*—the art of creating with greasepaint and putty a character mask. Adler had felt shame for his own theatre. The Jewish actors wore the same wig, the same costume in a dozen different roles; they worked with a few sticks of colored chalk, used black pencil for character lines. The Russian actors could rebuild their faces like sculptors; they could make themselves shorter, taller, fatter, thinner. They wore real silks and velvets on the stage, paid their scenic artists as much as their greatest stars, imported French landscape painters for their outdoor scenes, chose every detail, every prop so that the whole stage lived, a thing wonderful to the eye.

Adler had spent six weeks in Zhitomir, absorbing the superb stagecraft of the Russian theatre. And all this art he put into the outward aspects of his Beggar. Out of rags he designed a costume that hung about him, hiding his powerful chest and shoulders but revealing his thin legs, and thus creating the scarecrow effect he wanted. With this cadaverous body he devised a face at once ancient, shrewd, witty, and pathetic. The portrait that emerged was so hilarious, yet so authentic, that it brought shouts of laughter followed by a roar of applause. As the Beggar, Adler sat on the ground drawing from his basket his crazy odds and ends, and his perplexity as he examined these objects was unforgettable. He had a drunken scene that he turned into an actor's tour de force. Looking for a place to hide, he crawled into his own basket, a contortionist feat that brought a roar of appreciation. Best of all was the courtroom scene, in which the Beggar told his tragic story and pleaded for the daughter he loved as his own. And at the final curtain, when he proclaimed that he stood forever with his own, with the poor, the audience stamped, thundered, shook the walls with their tribute.

In that drab Whitechapel room, on a stage so small he could hardly turn about, Jacob Adler had become a great actor.

Two months later, when he played *Uriel Acosta,* the company took a theatre in Holborn and invited the great Jews of London. Such was Adler's fame by then that Rabbi Adler himself came to see the play and brought a member of the Rothschild family with him.

"I was nervous, restless before *Acosta,*" Adler writes, "but I felt in myself the energy of demons and knew I would play as never before, knew that my spirit was opening and my soul itself would play. And it was so. I spoke the monologue with power, confidence, believed what I said, lived it, felt and suffered the tragic situation of my Uriel. With him I loved, hated, with him suffered insult and wrong, with him was martyred, went through shame, broke, bent, became a slave—and only in the secret depths of the soul, the inward tears and hidden wounds. I turned, flamed, and the audience felt my fire. I suffered, and they were shattered with me. And the same with my Sonya as Judith. If she received less acclaim than I, it was only because her part was smaller. A storm of applause at every sharp speech, every strong movement, every passionate clash of will. And I fell beautifully, not as I had fallen in Lodz, but gracefully, lightly, receiving not even a scratch! And just as easily and lightly I sprang to my feet again. At the end of the play we were overwhelmed by the applause. Many in the audience stayed, could not leave until they had gripped my hand, expressed their gratitude!"

The Whitechapel Jews, awestruck by his Acosta, whispered that this was no actor they had seen, but indeed an *adler*—an eagle. And they gave him the name that would remain his throughout the history of Yiddish theatre: *Adler Nesher haGadol,* Adler Great Eagle.

What king more adored by his people than Jacob Adler as he walked, a great actor, through the streets of *his* London! For it was his now. London had given him his art. He had felt its eternal pulse beat. All his life he would love it as his own.

And with his triumph another joy, too, that came with a stab like fear. A meeting on a stairway. An uncertain greeting. Dark eyes full of wonder. At this moment when his art had flowered, the foundations of his life were beginning to crumble.

14

A London Paradise

> If in Russia the Yiddish theatre was destined to go through its infant years and in America grow to manhood and success, then we may say that London was its *cheder,* its school.
>
> JACOB ADLER

In their effort to halt the incoming flood, the Great Synagogue withheld all assistance to newly arrived immigrants for six months. This harsh policy had a certain success, for numbers of these people, starving in London, found their way back to the continent. There were, however, members of the Jewish community who could not watch their sufferings, and in 1884 one Simche Becker opened a Jews' Charity Shelter in Church Lane.

Becker's enterprise found powerful friends. Among them was the Member of Parliament for Whitechapel, Sir Samuel Montagu, a native-born gentleman noted for his warm sympathy with the Russian and Polish immigrants of his constituency. With the support of Montagu and several others, the Shelter existed for some years, providing newcomers with useful advice, a room, all necessaries, and two meals a day for fourteen days at a nominal fee.

On a certain day in the fall of 1884, a group of newly arrived Yiddish actors made their way to this establishment. The head of this company and its leading comedian was one Moishe Heine Chaimovitch. Moishe Silberman, of Goldfaden's pioneer troupe in Bucharest, was company manager and the troupe's romantic lead. In the cast were Chaimovitch's wife, the former Sara Levitzkaya; Max Karp, a handsome bass baritone; the playwright Joseph Lateiner; and the assorted singers, character players, and comedians making up the usual provincial Yiddish troupe.

At the Shelter the actors were served a Ukrainian meal of grits, potatoes, bread, and tea which they drank Russian style, biting on a piece of sugar. After resting a bit, they made their way to Sonnenschein's hotel, where they were told they would find the Jewish actors.

They were not encouraged by their first walk through Whitechapel. Madame Chaimovitch found these streets and alleys so grim and dreadful, she wondered how they were to live in such a place. The other actors were as despondent, and the sight of Sonnenschein's hotel hardly improved their spirits.

"What was your outlook in coming here?" Sonnenschein asked these new arrivals. "Didn't they tell you in Odessa that Adler himself is hardly keeping body and soul together in London? Not that people here don't want Jewish theatre. They do want it! But times are bad. One hardly comes out. Folks are glad if they can keep a roof over their heads."

The observations of his partner were even gloomier. "Russian actors are very fine people," Chaim-the-Devil observed politely as he showed Chaimovitch and his wife to their room. "I myself was once an actor, and as you see me here, I once shook hands with Goldfaden himself. God knows they made money there in Roumania," he went on with increasing excitement, "but as soon as they get to London they become *schnorrers*. Go keep them in a hotel. And if you dare ask for your rent, they are insulted!"

The newcomers soon discovered that the whole life of these partners was bound up with the Yiddish theatre. They cursed the actors, calling them murderers, pogromists, thieves, but even as they cursed, they bragged of their closeness, their intimate connection with these same actors. Both partners adored Adler, gladly took tickets to the theatre instead of their rent, and were never so happy as when their idol kibitzed with them about their hotel or their fish business.

The London troupe had come to love their two eccentric little landlords and thought of them as the dearest of men. Young Madame Chaimovitch, nursing one infant and pregnant with another, viewed them with less affection. She had expected a very different arrival in London, and she never forgave her husband for taking her first to the Charity Shelter and then to Sonnenschein's miserable hotel.

Gifted with a lovely warm soprano, Sara Levitzkaya had been accepted at seventeen into the Odessa Music Conservatory, where she was much admired for her solo renditions of the sacred Russian hymns. Charmed by her beauty and vivacity, some wealthy Russians took her up, and her girlhood in Odessa was very gay.

Most of her wealthy friends did not suspect the origins of "the beautiful Levitzkaya," and it may have been at this time that she formed certain habits of dissimulation. The gay laughter of the dazzling young actress often had a nervous ring; the triumphant assurance she wore before the world was, often as not, a mask hiding different, darker moods.

Above everything, Madame Chaimovitch loved splendid surroundings, gorgeous attire, the freedom and pleasures of wealth. The poverty of Whitechapel was a terrible shock, and she begged her husband to take her back to Odessa. Her distress was the greater because Chaimovitch, usually a strong character, seemed to be lost in London. In Russia and later in America he was a man capable of finding a way out of every difficulty. But for some reason London overwhelmed him. He walked about as though he were in another world, lost weight, and spent whole nights without closing his eyes. He had brought enough money to keep his troupe going until they began to play, but he did not know how to go about things, and every day saw his capital shrinking.

His best hope, clearly, was to make an arrangement with Jacob Adler. The two men talked several times. Chaimovitch had already introduced his actors to the London star. Only Sara Chaimovitch hung back, hoping perhaps, with the pride of a beautiful woman, that Adler would express a wish to see her. But several days passed, Adler made no such request, and Chaimovitch warned his wife that her absence was giving offense. After some thought she decided to deal with the situation as a neighbor, and to simply come in, unannounced, with her husband.

Accordingly, at about five that afternoon, she and some of the others climbed to the top floor of the hotel, where a hubbub of talk and laughter came through an open door. Adler was at cards with some friends, and for some moments he continued to play, as though unaware anyone had entered. Madame Chaimovitch, mortified, was tugging at her husband's sleeve and asking him to come away, when a pale, thin woman came up. Introducing herself as Madame Adler, she turned to her husband and said, "Yankev, it will soon be time to go to the theatre, and here we have guests from home."

Adler rose and bowed. He had in fact heard of Madame Chaimovitch in letters from Sheikevitch and had been curious to meet her. He paid her some gallant compliments, congratulated Chaimovitch on the beauty of his wife, and turning to the others, said, "But how could it be otherwise? She is from Odessa!" As it happened, Spivakovsky had once courted the young Sara. Adler brought his name in slyly, and Chaimovitch turned yellow with anger. Madame Chaimovitch felt that the great star was spoiled and imagined no one would criticize him no matter how he behaved.

Adler invited them all to come to his performance that night. "We are in exile here," he remarked with a sigh. "You will have to see and hear such theatre to believe it!"

Though the two troupes decided to join forces, the merger did not last. Sara Chaimovitch was so horrified by the club rooms of London that she wanted to give up the theatre altogether. Faced with her tears and hysteria, Chaimovitch decided to go on to New York.

He was racking his brains about passage money when help came from an unexpected quarter. Rabbi Adler, pleased that these Yiddish actors wanted to leave London, extended a friendly hand. Introductions were made, doors opened, and within a week a benefit was organized at the Holborn theatre where Adler had played *Acosta*. The actors, bitter and envious, saw a troupe far inferior to their own playing in a good London house while they struggled on in the miserable Whitechapel clubs.

The Holborn benefit was a success, and Chaimovitch and his troupe soon left for America, first of the professional Yiddish actors ever to sail for those distant shores.

In the year that had gone by since Riga, Adler and the others had come to terms with their new life. They were familiar now with London, with the damp and cold of its winters. They had even grown accustomed to its fogs, which did not hang in the air as in Russia, but spread over the ground like a giant carpet, darkening every moment until lights went on in windows and torches appeared in the streets. They continued

Siegmund Mogulesko
(earliest known photograph)

Avrom Goldfaden

(*Left to right*) Max Karb,
Abba and Clara Schoengold.

Annetta Gradner

Jacob P. Adler
(earliest known photograph)

Sonya Michelson Adler

Sophia and Socher Goldstein

Keni Liptzin
(earliest known photograph)

Zalmen Zylbercweig Collection

(*Left to right*) David Kessler, Max Abramovitch, Rudolph Marks, Siegmund Moguleski, Siegmund Fienman, Jacob P. Adler.

Boris Thomashefsky

Maurice Heine

Maurice Finkel

Dinah Feinman

Zalmen Zylbercweig Collection

Yiddish Theatre in London—1880's

Anna Held

Jacob P. Adler
in unknown melodrama.

Jennya Kaiser

Max Rosenthal

Jacob Gordin

Sara Adler

Famous Stars in Gordin Plays

David Kessler
in *God, Man and Devil*.

Siegmund Mogulesko
in *The Outsider*.

Morris Moskovitch
in *The Oath*.

Keni Liptzin
in *Mirale Efros*.

Jacob P. Adler's Grand Theatre on Grand Street in the Bowery (circa 1908).

Jacob P. Adler (right) with six of his children. (*Left to right*) Luther, Stella, Julia, Jay, Frances, and Abe Adler.

Jacob P. Adler in Four of His Great Roles

Uriel Acosta

With Sara Adler in *A Sailor in Distress*.

Zelig Itzik the Fiddler

In *The Wild Man*.

to play illegally in club rooms, and had grown careless, too, of the stick held over their heads by the Orthodox Jews.

London was not so gray, nor were its people so dour and forbidding as they had at first appeared. The Whitechapel poor were not bitter about their more fortunate brothers in the West End, and said, laughing, that they were the ladder on which the rich man climbed to Paradise. The center of their social life was Petticoat Lane, and at Purim Wentworth and Goulston streets overflowed with men, women, and children jostling each other in a deafening carnival crowd. Delicious Purim confections were sold at carts and stands, there were *bolas,* "stuffed monkeys," peaked hats, cardboard noses, masks. At holiday time the young British-born Jews packed the galleries of the East End theatres. But the immigrants thronged to the clubs, and the actors did well.

The year had made changes, too, some of them, inevitably, not for the best. Adler and Gradner had quarreled and parted, and two troupes now played where there had been only one before.

"In Paradise, Adam and Eve knew not of sin," Adler writes. "They lived in peace with the beasts, ate roots and flowers, and were refreshed by the sight of their own beautiful forms in the mirror of the lakes. They lived under God's protection. Could anything be better? But man is bad from the time he is born, corrupted even in the belly of his mother! Came greed, curiosity, came slyness, envy, hatred, ambition—came, in short, the Serpent! This, as we know, led to the parting, the separation from Paradise and death.

"A small Paradise," Adler continues, "existed for us actors in the London theatre clubs of the 1880s. Though we were divided into peasants and aristocrats, great stars who lived by art alone and humble players who performed after a hard day in a workshop or factory, our life together had still the heartwarming spirit of the commune. We lived together in one corner, this one a flight above, this one a flight below, we met after the play at Moishe Kibin's restaurant or Sonnenschein's, we laughed together, ate, drank, jested together. True, we played for a tiny audience on a stage no bigger than a cadaver, but we played and played well, with a drunkenness of happiness. Though we got our pittance with pain and trouble, woes paid for in the end by frail women and little children, in time these material problems might have been overcome. The Yiddish theatre might well have reached heights in London had it not been for the Serpent, for our jealousy over parts, plays, *genre*. And between whom should the Serpent have come if not between the two most popular stars, between Gradner and myself?"

It was a young, relatively harmless serpent that had glided between these two, not yet the deadly Adversary that would later wreak havoc with great talents and careers. But at the time it worked harm enough.

The problem that arose was perhaps inevitable. Gradner had come out of Goldfaden's theatre of comic characters, song, dance, and jest. Though *Shulamith* and *Bar Kochba* began a finer, more serious phase, it was still, in its essence, the light, musical theatre of Avrom Goldfaden. Gradner had his greatest success in this type of repertoire, while Adler, even if he had possessed a voice, would sooner or later have found his way to purely dramatic roles.

They were thus divided from the beginning by a difference in the way they saw their art. Along with this basic disagreement, a wrangle began over parts. In *Shulamith,* the Gradners were at the top of the poster, while Adler had to come on in the uninteresting role of the father, Menuach. In *The Beggar of Odessa,* on the other hand, Adler was cock of the walk, the Gradners unimportant, almost invisible. With a larger troupe the difficulty might have been avoided. As things stood, each star smarted under the necessity of playing second to the other.

Once, in the duel scene of *Esther of Engeden,* Adler accidentally touched Gradner under his arm and drew a few drops of blood. A mishap. They joked about it. "Later," Adler relates, "we wounded each other worse. With words, with dry, biting sarcasms. And these hidden insults were exchanged on the stage itself. In such cases the actor with the most skill at improvisation wins. I was an old hand at such tricks. I would put in a word or two that Gradner understood all too well. Beside himself, he would answer. And between us such a curtain scene developed as the playwright had never dreamed.

"For Gradner," Adler goes on, "there was no escape but the grave or America. America was too far, the grave too cold. Gradner went to Paris. But not so fast. First he broke away, made a troupe of his own. He stole my actors. I stole his. So we practiced on each other, and neither of us licked honey or drew health from it."

With the original company divided in two, both had to go

on with only half their audience. Both troupes desperately needed actors. And out of this need, important new forces were drawn into the Yiddish theatre.

In the back room of a Whitechapel tailor shop, a young seamstress heard about the Yiddish theatre, and felt a desire to see it. The sixteen-year-old Dinah Shtettin had come from the Polish village of Lipna, a spot so remote no hint of progress had ever reached it. She had been raised by her father and a kind stepmother in a pious Orthodox home, knowing nothing of the world but the simple Jewish traditions of her village. Until her parents brought her to London, she had never so much as heard of theatre. Now, in the back room of the shop, the chatter of the girls, their excited talk about the Gradners, the snatches of Yiddish song aroused her curiosity. She agreed to go with her friends and see the marvels they described. The expedition had to be carried out in secret, for the pious Joseph Chaim Shtettin, *shammos* of a Whitechapel synagogue, would have died of shame if he knew his daughter had set foot in a place so sinful and worldly as a theatre.

The girl had no sooner walked into the club on Mansfield Street than she wanted to run out again. The room was dark, dirty, with a sawdust-covered floor. A deafening racket filled it. Smoke stung her eyes and choked her. People sat at long tables, drinking beer, *kvas,* or tea, eating out of paper parcels, calling to each other, quarreling, laughing, screaming. She felt she had come to a low place, a kind of saloon. But her friends told her the stage was behind the curtain, and curiosity kept her there.

After a while a light went on, and a short time later the curtains parted. From that moment the girl was carried into another world.

As a child Dinah Shtettin had put on her mother's shawl and made the little girls laugh by pretending to be a toothless old lady. She had been roundly scolded for her "foolish tricks." Now she watched, hypnotized. Actors sang, wept, tore their hair. And though she had never seen theatre before, it was all somehow not new to her.

For days afterward she walked about in a dream. And when the Gradners advertised in a newspaper for extras, this obedient Jewish daughter had the strength and daring to go back to Mansfield Street, to stand in a line with girls of quite another sort, and to admit, half dead with fear, that she wished to be an actress. The Gradners were overjoyed to have her, for respectable girls were few in the Whitechapel chorus. She was taken in at once and even got a salary of two shillings a week, an unusual thing for an extra.

In some way or other Dinah Shtettin managed to elude a watchful family, and to play every Saturday and Sunday night on the Yiddish stage. Annetta Gradner was her greatest friend. She protected the young girl from gossip and slander, encouraged her in her ambitions, and once, when an actress in the company fell sick, gave her a small part in *Shulamith*.

Business, however, grew steadily worse, and the club finally closed down. Gradner and Annetta, adored as they were, could not keep afloat in London. They packed up, said farewell to their public, and with heavy hearts set out for Paris. Two weeks later Adler and his troupe came into the Mansfield Street club. Most of Gradner's actors were taken on again, but Dinah Shtettin, loyal to the Gradners, refused even to see their rival.

She remained stubborn in her decision until one day two of her friends from the chorus pointed out Jacob Adler as he sat with some actors in a Whitechapel restaurant. As she gazed through the window the whole party rose. A moment later they came out onto the street. "But who are these beauties standing here?" Adler asked, laughing. Dinah's friends pushed her forward, and Adler, who already had a marked fancy for very young girls, chucked her under the chin and told her she was a pretty darling.

Apparently her feelings changed after this. She went to the Mansfield Street club the same night and got into an argument when the man at the door would not admit her without a ticket. In the midst of the commotion, Adler appeared in the corridor and asked sternly why she was giving the doorman trouble. She answered angrily, "I am not giving him trouble. I have more right to be here than he has. I am an actress. I played in this theatre!" Half in tears, she flung out that she had played a real part, too, the nurse in *Shulamith*.

Adler turned on the doorman, his lips twitching. "And you dare keep her out?" he said in a terrible voice. "An actress? An actress who played the nurse in *Shulamith*?"

The mortified girl tried to run away, but Adler caught her hand, opened the door, and told her, laughing, that she could come to the theatre as often as she liked. She was soon part of the troupe and apparently acquitted herself well, for in a short time she was playing small parts. The girl came home one night, however, to face a terrible scene. Her father had discovered everything. He reproached her bitterly, and said her dead mother would not rest in her grave if she knew to what an end her child had come. Next day Dinah Shtettin, in tears, told Adler she could no longer be part of the company.

Adler would not have it. He went to see the pious father, told him he did not understand his daughter, and assured him she had entered an entirely honorable profession. The naive Shtettin had never in his life had such a guest. He was overwhelmed, confessed his ignorance of such matters, and agreed finally to come to the club and see his daughter perform.

Adler coached her for the occasion as the mother in *Uriel Acosta,* a character part traditionally played by a talented young actress. At the end of the play he brought the girl forward and told her to remove her wig. The audience answered with a burst of appreciative applause, and old Shtettin, bewildered but thrilled, accepted the situation.

The whole cast knew the girl was in love with Adler. She was cruelly teased, and suffered from the persecutions of Keni Liptzin, who was jealous of her youth and her position in the troupe as Adler's protégée.

Though she rose quickly, she probably did not earn much more than she had with the Gradners. A provincial English actor in these days was glad of three pounds a week, and the greatest London star got no more than ten. The Yiddish actors in London did badly even by these low standards. Adler himself, star and director of his company, earned about seven dollars a week in American money, and on this had to support his wife and child.

"Don't forget I was an artist, too!" he reminds us. "And that the artistic soul is worth more than a spit in the gutter! One can't go about like anybody at all. One has to dress with some style, wear a high hat, a cane. A bit of fun is also needed from time to time, and all this costs money. Things weren't easy, even for a star. And a star I was in those days, a bit befogged and clouded over, perhaps, but a star just the same!"

The fortunes of all the actors were soon destined to take an upward swing. At the end of 1885 a great piece of luck fell from the heavens. A butcher called David Smith saw Adler play, became his follower, his patriot, his patron, and finally got him and all the troupe out of the quagmire of the London clubs.

15

Smith's Theatre on Prince's Street

> Your sword may conquer mighty foes,
> But while I still draw breath
> My greater mission is to heal the sick,
> My greater, grander adversary — Death!
> GOLDFADEN: *Doctor Almasado*

Not far from Petticoat Lane, somewhat closer to the docks, another major avenue of Jewish street trade ran perhaps a third of a mile. Rosemary Lane was wider and airier than Petticoat Lane, less crowded, and its houses were taller and in better repair. But the small streets off the lane were narrower, dirtier, and poorer. Men with work connected with the river lodged in here, and by day these streets were loud with the cries of vendors calling their wares.

In one of these noisy, crowded, little passages, at No. 3 Prince's Street, the butcher Smith built Jacob Adler a theatre. Though Smith's playhouse was built like the ordinary London music hall, with an orchestra pit, a *parterre*, and a gallery, it was felt at the time that only a club could support Yiddish theatre in London. An appeal was therefore sent out for members and committeemen. A Mr. Kolinsky was appointed secretary, and the generous Sir Samuel Montagu accepted the post of honorary president. In keeping with the same idea, a room was set aside as a reading room, or library, members paid dues of a shilling a year, and officially the new playhouse was the Prince's Street Club. The audience, however, cared little for all that; they came to see the plays and actors they adored. And it is here in London that we find the first madly enthusiastic Yiddish public. In later prosperous years Adler recalled those early audiences of London and New York and longed for them:

"Where is the patriot," he wistfully asks, "who lived, flourished, screamed, whistled, hooted, wept, and laughed in those days? Dead as the mastodon, that patriot, his bones buried in the cold depths of earth! His high post in the gallery is empty, and the gallery, too, is empty, dark and cold, with wind blowing between the benches! No wonder it rots away and disappears! In the Yiddish theatre today we see order, decorum, politeness. Respectable people sit, well fed, finely dressed, those who have forgotten youth. How different it used to be! High in the gallery, holding to the sides of his seat, the young patriot sat, and high was his enthusiasm. No $3.50, no $1.50, no $1 could you ask of him. Ten or fifteen cents was the limit he could pay, and if extras were needed on the stage, he sat for nothing. The poor boy, by day a baster, a machinist, a puller for a tailor was the king, the soul, of our theatre. Without binoculars he saw the stage better than any critic. And no lady infatuated with a matinee idol ever followed so breathlessly every turn, every change of mood, every fall and rise of the voice, every cadence, every gesture!

"When we played well, how broad and free was his happiness, his triumph! And we, the actors, felt it, felt his love, a warm wave from the gallery to the stage, and because of this we had courage to go on, to strive higher. And if the gallery was quiet, the applause cold and lifeless, we knew the play was wrong, a failure, and that we must give another. The love of the gallery was our life. We needed it as water is needed by fish, as air is needed by all that breathes. Yes, that was the patriot as he used to be. He was the joy, the flame of our theatre!"

Among these "hidden saints" of the London gallery was a rawboned young Pole from a village near Warsaw. Boaz Jungvitz had come to London with 300 roubles in his pocket.

He thought such a sum would last at least a year. But his money was soon gone, and he hired out as a machinist. Young, as he was now called, went to anarchist meetings in Bernard Street, heard his first talk about capitalists and workers, and read *The Worker's Friend.* But his life, his happiness, was the Yiddish theatre, and many times the sixpence needed for food next day went instead for a gallery ticket to the Prince's Street Club. He adored the Gradners, but Adler was his god. He swore there was no greater actor in the world.

The roughhewn features and giant frame of this young man gave no clue to the charming mind of their owner. It is from the memoirs of this Boaz Young, later an actor himself, that we have some of our best insights into these early days of London and New York.

From what he and others tell us, these were times of extraordinary growth. Adler played his whole repertoire, and when he had exhausted it, found a new mine of material in the plays of Schiller, a dramatist instantly popular with the Yiddish audience. He had successes, too, in *Robert Diable,* in *The Silver King,* adapted from the London musical hit, in Bezelinski's *Madman for Love,* and in Goldfaden's *Dr. Almasado,* a play in which he first portrayed what he called the "Grand Jew"—a type he developed further in later years.

With a larger audience, the troupe gave performances every night except Friday, when they dared not play because of the rigidly Orthodox London Jews. The actors chafed under the surveillance of these men. "One would have thought our actors' faces were an insult to the high heavens!" Adler remarks impatiently. "Friday night we did not dare play for them. And on Saturday matinee, when they let us perform, we were forbidden to smoke a cigarette or light a fire even when the scene demanded it. We had to watch every turn we made, or in the middle of the play there would be a scandal!"

But these were minor annoyances. In the main the actors were in good spirits, and every night after the play the whole troupe would fall into some kosher restaurant, partake of food and drink, tell stories, and outdo each other with hilarious imitations. The three-year-old Rivke, or Nunia, as Adler's little girl was called, was a great success at these gatherings. This quaint little creature loved the jollity of these evenings. She laughed at all the stories whether she understood them or not, and many times morning light was coming through the windows when she was carried home, half asleep but happy.

Another nightly companion of the actors was the butcher, David Smith. Adler was extremely fond of his patron. He loved to make him laugh, played all kinds of tricks on him, and once went so far as to put a live lobster into his pocket.

With business better at the theatre, the idea began circulating that not only the star but other actors should also draw fixed salaries. This daring experiment resulted in a flood of new actors. From too few there were suddenly more than the troupe could use. Some of these new performers came, like Dinah Shtettin, from the Whitechapel shops, others from the amateur clubs.

Among the outstanding talents drawn from the clubs was Max Rosenthal, son of a wealthy Polish industrialist, who entered the professional theatre when the Gradners took him into their troupe. From the beginning there was something special, something quiet and beautifully modest about his playing. He had a certain "neurasthenic" quality, and excelled particularly when cast as an officer or an aristocrat. Rosenthal later played in America, where he was one of the Yiddish theatre's best actors and most intelligent directors.

"A star always had to be tall, with a handsome face and a powerful voice," says Boaz Young. "Rosenthal was none of these things, yet he was a star. His voice was not strong, yet he was heard. He did not play realistically, yet the biggest advocates of realism accepted him. He did not work on character, but made every character into Rosenthal. And all he did was beautiful, fine and creative."

Another product of the London clubs was Max Radkinson, son of the venerated scholar Michael Levi Radkinson, who did the first English translation of the Talmud. It was his lively, playful qualities, however, that brought the great *maskil*'s son to the London stage. He was a talented dancer, a born singer, and a comedian who for a time rivaled Mogulesko himself. In America Radkinson took the name Rudolph Marks. He was to play an important part in Yiddish theatre history not only as an actor, but also as a playwright and a successful writer of songs.

Among the *choristkas* in Smith's Theatre was the girl known as Hannale. This beautiful creature had been brought as a child from Warsaw to Paris. There her parents made a living as peddlers, and as soon as she was old enough, Hannale sold flowers on the Paris streets. When her father died, she and her mother left Paris and came to London, where Hannale joined Gradner's troupe. She was so poor at this time that Dinah Shtettin often had to lend her a dress or a pair of shoes.

"Oh, what a beautiful girl!" Dinah Shtettin would exclaim in later years, recalling this friend. "Such a figure! Such eyes!"

Hannale's enchanting voice and graceful, slender form soon drew attention. Adler, who felt she had the makings of a star, had her coached to sing Shulamith. She made her debut in this operetta, and it was at Smith's Theatre in London that she was billed for the first time as Miss Anna Held.

When the theatre closed a few years later, Anna Held went back to Paris, where she played with Max Rosenthal and later with Goldfaden. When Goldfaden's company failed, she went into French vaudeville. From there she went back to London, and then to Berlin. Wherever she went, she became the rage, and she was very soon one of the best-known vaudeville artists of her day. In 1896 Florenz Ziegfeld saw her in Paris, brought her to New York, and starred her in his Ziegfeld Follies. Here she sang "I jus' can't make my eyes behave" in her bewitching French accent, became the toast of New York, and, as all the world knows, soon married Ziegfeld himself.

Anna Held began a magazine article about her life with the gay but evasive statement, "I am *Parisienne—et voilà!*" Throughout her career, she carefully concealed her past. Sonya Nadolsky, her most intimate London friend, claims that when Jacob Adler had visited her New York dressing room, the enchanting star sent word she could not see him. If the story is true, Adler felt no rancor. He describes Anna Held as a friendly, sweet, and capable girl who possessed an unforgettable charm. "There was so much coquetry in her speech," he says, "she spoke each word with such sweet glances, looking at whomever she addressed with such graciousness and moving her clear white fingers in a manner so adorable, it was impossible to withstand her enchantment."

Another *choristka* in Adler's troupe was the charming Fanny Epstein. This girl had a remarkable history. A Hindu prince met her in London, fell in love with her, and took her off with him to India. Years later Fanny Epstein came back to London, wealthy and covered with jewels. She prospered for a time, played leading roles in Europe, and was well received by the public. It was her fatal generosity that ruined this actress. She gave away her money to every actor who asked for help, and in the end she had simply divided her fortune among her friends. Twenty-five years later, Boaz Young, visiting Warsaw, found her dying in a cellar, sick, old, and forgotten. Young looked up a few people who knew her and collected from them the few *zlotes* that kept her alive a few more days.

But it was not only amateurs and beginners like these who came into Adler's company. The greatest Yiddish actors also played at Smith's Theatre. For everyone came through London in those years. Every actor, every troupe stopped over for at least a performance or two that would fill up an empty purse. Some of these actors remained in Prince's Street, some went back to Paris or on to America. They ranged from stars like Mogulesko himself to actors who did not even have a name, whose word you had to take that they were actors at all, from "authorities" on the Yiddish drama like the great Professor Hurvitz to people who could not spell out a Yiddish or Hebrew word.

"But whether they were great or small," says Adler, "they came, thin, pale, depressed, this one in a battered high hat, this one with a soiled cravat, and one and all with a hunger—God help us! And though they all put up a front and talked big, anyone could see they had not come touring, but had fled for their lives as from a fire!"

Among those who played at Smith's Theatre was the famous Sophia Goldstein, and with her the gentle Socher Goldstein, already suffering from the tuberculosis that was soon to kill him. Yankele Katzman, Adler's old admirer, came. Zuckerman came, and Professor Hurvitz from Roumania. Kessler himself, with a big name now, came with the Finkel-Mogulesko troupe. Abba Schoengold came with the pretty, dark-eyed Clara he had married in Berlad. And all these actors played together, and played with fire and flame, at Smith's Theatre on Prince's Street.

In the Talmud we read that as the sun rises higher and more brilliant in the heavens, so much sooner the night must come.

The first shadows gathered when Yisrol and Annetta Gradner came back from Paris. They had no luck there, and returned penniless and sad. The friendship between Gradner and Adler had survived their rivalry; there was room for the Gradners in Prince's Street. But though he had his devoted public, Gradner could not endure a position second to another actor.

"I ask myself," said Adler, "why this rarely gifted man withered away so early. What force broke him? Why so soon fallen from his height while others, less gifted, made their way to the top?"

A few short years earlier the greatest star, Gradner at forty-six, was going downhill fast. He fell into speculation on the London Exchange, stayed all day at the Bourse, and late in the evening hurried back to play. In those days the unlucky man who lost on the Exchange had flour flung on him like a bridegroom. The unlucky rabbit ran, and the others ran after, whitening him again. Poor Gradner ran in one night, white as a miller. He was haunted by the fear of penury and tortured, too, with worry about his wife. When they returned to London from Warsaw, Annetta had collapsed with a heart attack, and the doctor warned her that the theatre would be her death. She played all the same, and the frightened Gradner watched from the wings. With every high note, every strong dramatic cry, the actors heard his low, terrified "Annetta! Annetta!"

For all his fears, he died before her. A kidney attack, a brief dreadful illness, and Gradner was gone. According to every written account of the time, he was a great actor, and for Adler he stood head and shoulders above the others, both as an artist and as a man. There is no question that if he had come to America he would have been one of the greatest stars. He was idolized in London. When Annetta made her first appearance after his death the entire audience rose in honor of his memory, and applauded a long time.

Annetta survived him no more than a year. She had never taken care of her health, never gave up the cigarettes she smoked incessantly. It is possible that after Gradner died she did not wish to go on. She was buried by his side in Stratford Cemetery. To this day no stone marks either of their graves.

Remembering Annetta Gradner, Adler wrote: "If ever there was an angel too pure for this world, it was she. Annetta, daughter of a poor cobbler, but honorably raised. Gradner met her in Kremantchuk, fell in love with her singing and brought her into the theatre. Audiences everywhere adored her. Her voice was small, but so full of feeling it brought tears to your eyes. Even in her gay songs she tore at your heart. People intrigued against husband and wife, tried to separate them. Impossible. Annetta was true, even when he was poor and alone."

After Annetta's death, the shadows fell fast. The child, the three-year-old Rivke, caught a chill, coughed, and fell into a fever.

"Croup," the doctor said. "The child has croup."

The English doctor told them what they should do, but the immigrant parents did not understand him. And the neighbor they called in to interpret also did not understand.

"What was her sin that she deserved it?" Adler demanded. "Why must it be little frail children who pay with their gentle lives for our ideals, our art? What higher wisdom, what justice is in it? Ach, the London poverty, the bitter poverty of the Yiddish actor of the 1880s! It was the fate of our Rivke, our little Nunia, to be dragged over the sea in a cattle boat, to grow up without care in the pauperish existence of our actors' life. In Russia my mother or sister would have taken care of her. In London, who was there? The mother had to run every night to the theatre to make a living. There was no money for a nurse, a servant. Somewhere under the hellish stage the child had to sleep while the mother and father left her to entertain the public. And after the performance? To wake her from her sleep, drag her again through the damp, windy London streets. . . . Is it any wonder that in the poor, cold room over Moishe Kibin's restaurant the weak, pale, affectionate child contracted a fever, coughed, choked, grew worse. . . ."

The parents sat night and day by the child's bed, listening to her heavy breathing and, when she awoke, reading in her eyes the childish pain and bewilderment. Mother and father sat together, but looked away whenever their eyes met. It was fear that did not let them look into each other's eyes. Worse than fear, the thought that it was their fault, that they had not taken enough care, that strong as they were, they had not saved such a fragile little butterfly.

The little girl's cough grew worse, she became confused, delirious, and from moment to moment the parents saw death coming nearer. Deep in the night hours Jacob bent over the bed and whispered in Yiddish, *"Rivkale, die derkennst mich?"* ("Rivkale, do you know who I am?")

In a small but clear voice, the child said in English, "Yes, Papa."

She did not speak again. Forty years later, as he remembered those two words, the throat of the seventy-year-old man closed, he turned away, and a wail like that of an animal broke from his lips.

The gentle little girl was soon gone, and the best days of Sonya and Jacob Adler went with her. Darkness had closed around them, and only darker still to come.

16

The Sinner

> From the day I began these memoirs I have trembled, knowing I must come to this moment. Do I dare to touch on this episode, the happiest in my life and the most terrible? How shall I make clear what happened, and what did not happen? And will it ever be understood? We live in a world where the moral code must necessarily apply to all situations, all circumstances, when a bass voice from above decides, "This is good, this is bad, this is right, this is wrong." And this is the tragedy of our life, that an unseen but indestructible division stands between us, that never can one human being know what goes on in the soul of another. Never. Never.
>
> JACOB ADLER

Remembering the events that once rocked Whitechapel, Boaz Young wrote: "In Smith's Theatre on Prince's Street were two beautiful girls who played small parts—Fanny and Jenny. Fanny, a blonde, had a Cinderella story. A Hindu prince fell in love with her, took her away to India, and made her a princess. Jenny was a brunette, slender, elegant, with two flaming dark eyes that said, 'Come—take me!' Jenny, too, got a prince, a prince who was afterward king of the Yiddish theatre. When she came to rehearsals in London, she would bring with her a three-year-old boy, the later well-known Charlie Adler, son of Jacob P. Adler and Jenny Kaiser."

They had met very soon after Adler came to London, and it was probably Sonya herself who brought them together.

The girl lived with her mother in the same lodging, and through the usual accommodations of poor people, lending and borrowing, she and Sonya became acquainted.

She was a girl of the London slums, born and raised in the poverty of Whitechapel. The poor dwelling, the shop, the simple relatives who brought her up, these were Jennya Kaiser's world. Her father was dead. Her mother is still remembered as a woman of queenly personality, but we have few facts about her. Mother and daughter were not close. By some accounts, Jennya feared the older woman.

She was very young when the actors came to London, seventeen at most, slender, of somewhat less than medium height, with eyes of deep black on a white mat background, dark hair, and the dazzling complexion of the London girl. She spoke Yiddish with a strong English accent, and her greatest passion was Yiddish theatre. "Sitting at the play," Adler says, "she found pleasure in weeping whole cups of tears, with never a care that she might injure those beautiful eyes!" Everyone who has described Jennya Kaiser has paused, remembering those eyes.

She came into the theatre as a *choristka*, but quickly rose to small roles. Boaz Young tells us she played "with more talent than schooling," which is surely better than if he had put it the other way around. Adler saw greatness in the young actress, but it was Jennya's simplicity, her open nature that he remembered best:

"She was honorable and honest, not because anyone had taught her to be so, but because she regulated her life by an inner standard of her own. Of the so-called higher ideals, she knew very little. Truth to tell, she did not bother her head about such things. She was open and truthful because it was her way, because in her nature there was no calculation, no shrewdness, slyness, guile, cleverness. Her goodness did not come from virtue or love of humanity, but from the simple, generous impulse of her heart. 'You want something of me?' she seemed to say. 'Why not? Here. Take it. I don't need it. It doesn't trouble me!' "

From their first chance meeting, Adler was aware of the wonder, the passionate admiration in those dark eyes. They met again; he ventured an uncertain greeting. By degrees the strangeness between them disappeared, and they stood face to face.

Among the women drawn into the orbit of Jacob Adler

there were two or three whose feeling for him ran deep. For these few, the handsome face, the actor's triumphs were less potent than something unguarded in his personality, something resembling a child's helpless trust that the world will do him no harm. This defenselessness, a quality often seen in the genius, awakened in them a passionate, protective pity.

A dangerous emotion. Jennya seems to have fallen in love at almost the first moments of their acquaintance. And without feminine tricks, without games, with that absence of coquetry he found extraordinary, she made him feel at once that everything was possible.

From the first, the wild course of this love terrified him. He was incapable of hiding anything from Sonya, and the matter, in any case, was soon beyond concealment. The sorry truth was clear enough to all the world. Both women were pregnant, and both would bear his child.

The blow to Sonya came at the best moment of their life together. After the birth of their child, Adler's great torment, his incessant need for women had lifted, fallen away. His life changed, he discovered a new happiness in their marriage. All through the last year in Russia, husband and wife were close as never before. This closeness had sustained them through the months in Riga, had helped them bear their exile. In London their union had reached a new perfection, for he had justified her faith in him as an artist, and he felt, with triumph, that she loved him as never before.

At just this moment, reality, like a force that could no longer be contained, shattered the illusion of their happiness. His tears, his plea that she possessed the best of him could not satisfy the proud love that would accept nothing less than every part of his soul. Sonya turned away, bitterly disillusioned with him and with all of life. It was perhaps his betrayal of himself she could not forgive. For he had not kept faith even with his passion for Jennya. In his unworthy fashion, he had trifled with others, too.

It was the old Talmudic division of *yaitzer hatov* and *yaitzer horre*, good and evil, spirit and flesh, upper world and lower. Though he longed for the happiness of the heights, life itself was in the lower world. Sonya was too pure. For all his despair, his heart went out to that other fallen being, his fellow sinner, his Jennya.

Years later, with only a little of his own time left, he understood better what he had felt for this girl:

"I loved her in all the ways a man can love, from the crudest to the most refined. I loved her really as a person, and to tell the truth for many years now I have thought of her with gratitude. I loved her as one loves a blooming young woman. I loved her as a comrade, a good brother. I loved her because she was not ashamed of our love and let the whole world see it. I loved her goodness, her delicacy, her daily motherly concern for me. I loved her simple frankness, her honesty never masked by a hair. I loved the stream of life that rushed from her. With every drop of my being, with my life itself, I loved her!"

For the puritanical age in which it was written, this was a reckless confession, the outpouring, one suspects, of a deeply disappointed man.

His time with Jennya was short. In the spring of 1885 Sonya gave birth to a child, a boy who was given the name Abram. Directly after this, the weakened woman fell ill with an infection. Her fever mounted, her condition took a turn for the worse, and in her delirium the sick woman called wildly, over and over, for her brother.

A frantic letter was sent to Russia in the hope that Alexander Oberlander's presence might work some kind of miracle. Oberlander set out for England, distraught over his sister's condition. The Tsarist police, convinced he was engaged in an underground operation, sent spies after him. Throughout Oberlander's stay in England, these men dogged his heels.

By the time he arrived Sonya had been moved to London Hospital in Whitechapel. There, day by day, she slowly sank. The doctors probably knew from the beginning that the case was hopeless, for Adler was allowed to visit her without hindrance and passed whole days and nights at her side. No one told him the truth, but he saw for himself that every day she grew paler, weaker, and more wasted.

In her twenty-seventh year, on Tisha Bov, day of sorrow and penitence, Sonya Adler closed her eyes on this world for the last time.

Her husband was not with her at her last moments. He had left the hospital a few hours earlier. By the time he returned, it was over. When they broke the news of her death, he bellowed like a maddened animal, tore at the dead woman, tried to waken her, to revive her, and with a cry of "Sonya, my So-o-nya!" fell to the ground, beat his head against the floor, wept, choked like a man who has taken a poison that has driven him mad, tore at his own flesh, tore at his hands.

"No, then I was no actor!" he said. "And perhaps, if you will, it was never acting, and the cry of Naphtali Hertz in the last act of *The Stranger* was only the memory, the echo dragged out of my soul, of that cry I gave at her bedside. They pulled me, led me, dragged me away from her corpse."

In the days that followed he was so broken by grief that those bitterest against him pitied him in spite of themselves. He had neglected everything during Sonya's illness. He was penniless, and had not even money to pay for her gravestone. It was a member of the Rothschild family who put up a monument for the sweet, unhappy lady remembered by all with such sadness.

"In a strange land my Sonya died (maiden name Oberlander, played under name Michelson, registered officially as Adler), and in the alien English earth she was buried, far from the Russia she loved. She left behind her two helpless children, one of them barely a month on the earth, the other already in his thirtieth year."

In his heart Adler had always hoped that he and Jennya would part friends some day, that the fever of their love would pass, and that he and Sonya would take up their life again. He could not believe she was gone, that he would have to live out his days without her. She had taken him from bad companions, from a worthless life. She had raised him up, given him an ideal, believed in him. Jennya had given him only happiness. Sonya had been his compass, his star. A man may forget his star, he may wilfully stray from his star. All the more terrible for him when he looks for it again in a sky grown dark.

For many weeks he saw no one. He sat all day alone, brooding over the past, picturing Sonya as she was when they first met, reliving that journey to Ekaterinoslav when Rosenberg had intrigued to separate them, remembering the reconciliation that came after. And from thinking always of the past, a deep melancholy awoke in him. "All this was," an inner voice seemed to say, "but is no more. Vanished. Flown away. Nothing can bring it back, no power on earth give it again into your grasp. And how beautiful it was, and how delicate!" Over and over he told himself that if only he had returned to the hospital in time, Sonya might have smiled at him again, given him a last embrace, murmured once again the old caressing "Yakob *dorogoi.*"

In time he began to think this had really happened, and that before she died, Sonya had forgiven him.

He was not allowed much time to mourn his dead. He had sown the wind, and now he reaped the whirlwind. There had been scandal enough over Jennya. Now a new storm broke, and with fury. Caught between opposing forces, he married Dinah Shtettin.

It is not possible, so long after the event, to unravel the reasons that led to this marriage, or to understand why he did not marry Jennya, whom he had greatly wronged and whom, in fact, he still loved. From differing accounts of the matter we find Adler's admission that he had been charmed by this girl who came with such fresh enthusiasm to unite her fate with that of the Yiddish theatre, and Dinah's confession that she would have "flung herself off a cliff" if Adler had bidden her. It is possible that the attentions of such a known libertine, however harmless, had damaged the girl's reputation. An outcry arose, and Adler for a time had to leave London. "But the scandal was growing," he writes. "The whole theatre colony was talking, the side that was more determined did not rest, and the wedding date was set."

It was no light matter in the Whitechapel of the 1880s to have compromised a young unmarried woman. Adler learned that Jennya's brothers had ordered her to go to the wedding and create a scandal.

"If you don't go, we will!" her brothers had said. "We will break his bones! We will kill him!"

"Go near him," said Jennya, "and I will throw myself in the river!" And she said this in such a way they believed her.

"Then speak to him," the brothers said.

"Very well, I will speak to him," said Jennya.

Adler, told of this decision, was minded to shut himself up in his room. The actor who enjoyed performing dangerous stunts every night on the stage was afraid of this eighteen-year-old girl.

She came on his wedding day, a shawl about her head, and in the stark, simple manner of that time, with the child in her arms. Adler caught sight of her as he was coming out into the courtyard of his hotel. His courage left him, and he fled ignominiously up the stair.

"Adler, come down!" she called.

"I am afraid," he answered.

"What are you afraid of?"
"You will do me some harm."
"Come down. I will do you no harm."
"Swear it!"
"I swear by my dead father."
With that he came cautiously down the stair.

She must have come with some last hope, but in his presence this too died. He stood at a distance and asked only what she meant to do.

"Nothing," Jennya said. The word was a mere breath, and with it she was gone. He called, went after her, but she had disappeared into the crowded street.

His friends hurried him on to his happiness.

"Food and drink are prepared. Friends are gathered. All is joyful. The rabbi intones the seven prayers, instructs the groom to put on the ring. 'Now you are anointed to me!' The goblet is smashed. *'Mazel tov!'* Man and wife!"

The days that followed could not have been cheerful ones for the bride. The new husband was torn with grief over his first wife, and by his own admission, still madly in love with another woman. He spoke to Jennya only once, a brief interchange. She ended it with a look of burning scorn and the words, "We are through!" Seeing her soon after on the arm of the handsome, talented Max Rosenthal, he felt all desire for life leaving him. He told a friend years later there were times he laid his bare heart against the floor, trying to find some ease from his pain.

And still he mourned for Sonya, and it was Sonya he felt he had truly loved. She had been his ideal. If she had a fault he had turned aside and refused to see it. All his life no other woman came up to her in his eyes.

The period of solitary brooding gave way to feverish activity. He hurried from one place to another, never resting, dreading the loneliness he had until now sought. And in this storm of action, his wound began to heal.

"The fear grew less, the ache weaker, the pain milder, until slowly, it was felt only as a quiet longing, delicate and almost sweet. Too strongly within my blood, my spirit, my whole being, life sang its song. I was thirty years old, and it was not my nature to die."

What the earth covers, the heart forgets. Only the young will find this Jewish saying cruel. Those who have survived a loss will recognize its truth. The heart forgets because it is no longer the same heart; part of it has died. Something in Jacob Adler broke in those London years. Even when he was reaching the height of his powers, that broken quality remained in his face, in his speech; it had become part of him. He had loved two women to the utter undoing of both. Yet he, too, had been helpless, and he does not seem to have greatly blamed himself. As he accepted others with their weaknesses and failings, so he accepted himself. It was not his way to analyze his life, but to live it.

His energies revived; he began to make the best of things. The newborn Abram had to have care, and he took a nurse for him. The young wife could not be altogether neglected. The theatre had to go on, and since Sonya, his leading tragedienne, had died, another had to take her place. That other was Keni Liptzin, whose rise thus began with the death of the woman who had been her dearest friend.

In the spring of 1886 a messenger came from America in the person of a Mr. Mandelkern. He was not the first emissary from beyond the sea. Moishe Chaimovitch, now established in New York, had several times sent agents, who came to London for actors and sometimes took back a star at a bargain price. Mandelkern, however, was an independent, energetic individual who, it was said, could "put a wall together with another wall, and make money out of both." He had not been sent by Chaimovitch, but by two Chicago tailors called Drozdovitch and Rosengarten. These men had seen Yiddish theatre, and felt it had business possibilities. They had heard of Jacob Adler from immigrants coming from England and wanted him to come with his company to Chicago. As inducements, Mandelkern was authorized to offer Adler ship's passage to America for the whole troupe, a contract from the two Chicago tailors, and a sum in advance.

The deal fell through. Adler dickered over terms, and while he did so, the sum Mandelkern had given him disappeared in the welter of his debts. Mankelkern either had no more to give or feared throwing good money after bad. It happened that the Finkel-Mogulesko troupe had just then come to London, penniless and with fresh memories of conditions in Russia. They made fewer demands than Adler, wasted no time thinking things over, but promptly accepted Mandelkern's proposition and left for America.

Adler took the disappointment philosophically. In truth, he did not greatly care. He had grown attached to London. Memories bound him to the place. And Yiddish theatre had picked up a good deal at that moment. Thus it came about that Mogulesko and Finkel went on to America while Adler remained another year in Prince's Street.

He might have stayed longer in England if not for a tragedy that rocked Whitechapel and ended, for years to come, all Yiddish theatre there.

The incident took place at Smith's Theatre on the night of January 18, 1887. A popular operetta, Hurvitz's *Gypsy Girl,* was being performed that evening. There was a full house, with a crowded orchestra pit and an even more crowded gallery.

Somewhat before midnight, with the play almost over, a slight mishap occurred on the stage. The burning of a house in the fifth act provided this play with its climax; and the illusion of flames was produced by igniting a harmless substance known as "Bengal fire." On this occasion a thread of smoke or a spark accidentally resulted, and a voice in the gallery shouted that most terrible of words, "Fire!"

What followed was the scene that takes place when human beings give way to unreasoning animal terror. Screams and shrieks filled the air, and a rush began for the doors. It took no more than a moment for panic to break out, with three hundred bodies pushing and struggling against each other for a way out of the trap.

The worst of the disaster might have been avoided if those in the hall had used the smaller exits provided. Unfortunately, most of the audience made for the main doors at the back of the hall. These doors were wide enough for general purposes, but were located only a step away from the foot of the staircase to the gallery. As a result, two streams of terror-stricken people came together at this one point, creating a mass so thick that no movement was possible backward or forward. A courageous few kept their heads, sacrificed themselves and saved others, but the greatest number were driven by blind instincts of self-preservation. The stronger ones pushed their way out, the weaker were suffocated, knocked unconscious, or trampled underfoot. And those at the front continued blindly to plunge on, pushing, struggling, and adding to the suffocation and trampling at the back.

According to newspaper accounts of the tragedy, and the London papers were full of it, the actors behaved heroically throughout. "Go back to your seats!" Adler shouted from the stage. "There is no fire! There is no danger! Nothing has happened!" He signaled the orchestra, the musicians struck up, and the actors, galvanized, began to sing and dance with all their might.

For a moment the audience was held mesmerized. Shouts and screams died down. All might yet have been well, but at that moment, the gaslights mysteriously went out, plunging the theatre into darkness. "Don't listen to him!" a terrified voice rang out. "Fire! Fire!" And the mad struggle began anew.

Some of those in the gallery made their escape by way of special exits giving on narrow "leads" twenty feet above the ground. Others, unable to push through the mass on the stair, prepared desperately to jump over the gallery railing. One woman had already thrown her coat over, and was about to make the leap. Adler cursed her from the stage. "You will fall and be killed, devil take you!" he cried. She jumped, and her screams of pain added to the chaos below. In spite of this example, another woman was already crawling after her, dress lifted and legs bared. "Shame!" one of the actors called. "A Jewish daughter with naked legs!" But apparently such was the fear that even the rooted instinct of modesty was forgotten. And throughout everything, the screams of "Fire!" never stopped for an instant.

When police and firemen finally entered, they found broken seats, broken benches, remnants everywhere of hats, bonnets, dresses, umbrellas, and seventeen people suffocated or trampled to death, most of them women and children.

All that night hundreds of frightened people gathered outside Smith's Theatre to inquire about the fate of relatives and friends. By morning, as word of the disaster spread, the crowd grew so dense that a force of police were sent in, and only those who lived or had business there were allowed to enter Prince's Street. Dr. Hermann Adler, son of the Chief Rabbi, spent the whole day with the families of the bereaved. Unsolicited donations poured into the offices of the *Jewish Chronicle,* and Sir Samuel Montagu came personally to the theatre to express his shock and sympathy.

The inquest was held in the reading room of the theatre, where the bodies of the dead were laid out—one old man, four children, and twelve women, most in their teens or early twenties. The seventy-four-year-old Mr. Isaac Levy of Goulston Street, oldest of the victims, was among those who had sacrificed himself to save others. His wife, too, was among the dead. Two of the victims were young expectant mothers, and another woman, a mother of eight, had perished together with her youngest son, a ten-year-old boy. The saddest case was that of nineteen-year-old Rachel Renalde of Catherine Wheel Alley. This girl was soon to have been married, and the money laid by for her wedding had to be used instead for her funeral.

"Poor, lonely, wronged dwellers of the London ghetto!" Adler writes. "A little pleasure they had wanted, a little make-believe joy and sorrow to help them forget the bleak winter night. A little happiness they had asked. For money—for a price."

By Jewish law, the dead must be interred as quickly as possible. Since burial had to be held over until after the inquest, Dr. Hermann Adler urged there be no further delay. Over the objections of some of the families, it was decided to proceed with a mass funeral directly after the inquest. At about six o'clock then, with darkness already falling, several hearses took the bodies from Prince's Street to the West End Cemetery. The procession passed in the main through a silent orderly crowd, but in Brick Lane, where crowds of old women lined both sides of the street, dreadful wailings and lamentations broke out. By the time the cortege reached the burial grounds, night had come on, adding a weird and terrifying touch to the already harrowing scene.

For many days a pall lay over the entire East End of London. The blinds of every house in Whitechapel were drawn in sign of mourning. Black crepe was draped over the front of the synagogue in Prince's Street, and the door left half open day and night, showing the dimly lit recesses inside.

There was talk of foul play, for someone had in fact gone down to the basement at the height of the panic and turned off the gas meter. Though a reward was offered, no clue to this mystery was ever found. Adler and the theatre owner, David Smith, were questioned, but both were soon dismissed. The authorities did not close the theatre; the Prince's Street Club had nevertheless received its death blow. The people of Whitechapel, gripped by a superstitious horror, refused to go near it. Yiddish theatre in London seemed to be finished.

"It goes without saying that a few loyal friends did not desert us," Adler recalled. "But what could we have from so few? Even in the best days the intake had been small. Now it shrank to nothing. No play, no actor, no special announcement could bring the audience back. The theatre stayed dark and forlorn, and so empty you could hear wolves howling in the gallery. Once again, as in Riga, the bitter question: 'What now?' And as in Riga, the answer came: 'Wanderer, go further!' "

The actors all urged Adler to make some decision. "Yankev sits in his tent," they said, laughing. "Time to go on to the next paragraph. Decide, Yankev! Make up your mind!"

But Yankev found it hard to decide. Russia was fenced off, and no return there possible. The news from Roumania and Galicia was not encouraging. No help could be expected from those lands. There remained, then, only France and America. Paris, the gay, glorious world city, drew the actors as with a magnet. A Jewish colony had already settled there, and people of their own kind, too, Russian, Roumanian, and Galician immigrants. These émigrés had found a tiny haven, a little oasis around the Place Montmartre to which they gave the name "The Hangout," where a faint thread of Yiddish theatre existed.

Adler threw off the dangerous fantasy. He had the example of Yisrol and Annetta Gradner, who had quickly come back, disappointed and sad. Paris, he was sure, was a grave. Only one gate was still open, America.

"From America we had heard only good," Adler writes. "In fact, the news was perhaps a little too good. We were experts ourselves in the art of bragging, and the successes reported by friends over the ocean were always discounted at least by half. The other half, however, remained. And there was one sign that overcame all doubts; of all those who had gone to America, none had ever returned."

Adler had from Mandelkern the address of the Chicago tailor, Drozdovitch. But Chicago, from everything one heard, was a city full of devils, murderers, and thieves. Only confused, unpromising rumors came from Chicago, while in New York there was Chaimovitch's troupe, and lately news that Mogulesko, too, had a theatre there.

Adler wrote a letter to Drozdovitch in Chicago and two more to actors he knew in New York. Yankev had decided. The path lay across the ocean.

The problem, of course, was money. They were all penniless, and most of them had long since pawned whatever of value they had. Friends and patriots were appealed to, an attempt was made to organize a farewell performance, but none of these efforts proved useful. Adler took himself once again to Crosby Square.

He was received this time with a surprising friendliness and immediate promises of assistance. The old Chief Rabbi, grasping that his grand-nephew was taking himself and his Yiddish theatre out of London, was ready enough to speed him on his way.

"In my later years," Adler said, "I understood the Chief Rabbi somewhat better. A pious man like my grand-uncle could not help but fear and distrust a Yiddish theatre. The truly pious Jew wishes to keep his Jewishness in only two places, his home and his temple. He does not want to parade it about, for this would give the Gentiles the idea that Jewish life is anywhere at all, like their own. Such a sternly religious man probably guessed, too, that a Yiddish theatre must at times touch certain things with a less than sacrosanct hand, that a wedding or funeral must be depicted and not for their own sacred purpose, but as part of a theatrical spectacle. Lastly, the great rabbi was always aware that Israel's enemies are about, ready to mock, to jeer. And where would they have a better opportunity than in a Yiddish theatre?"

But though Adler came to understand the Chief Rabbi of London, he never quite forgave him. His comments on this matter end on a rare sarcastic note: "All the same, blood is thicker than water! When I left London the great rabbi gave me, in his generosity, as much as thirty pounds!"

The size of the gift came as a disappointment, but it was enough to get the troupe across the Atlantic. Young Mrs. Adler remained in London; she was to join her husband only if all went well. Adler took with him his son, Abram, Keni Liptzin, now his leading lady, Volodya Liptzin, Shmuel Tobachnikoff (later called Samuel Tobias), the comedians Kempner and Baum, and Herman Fiedler. Alexander Oberlander, too, was once again part of the company; his wife and four children had joined him in London, and all of them were sailing.

A mood of wild, irresponsible gaiety seized the troupe as the day of departure drew near. Were they not going to fabled America where they would make fortunes, pick up gold in the streets? Adler joined in the laughter and horseplay and played practical jokes that kept everyone in high spirits. Beneath all, his mood was somber. He did not want to leave London. He had his two graves there in the Jewish cemetery. And this journey filled him with misgivings. They were coming unbidden to a strange country, uncertain of their welcome.

They sailed in February 1887, traveling like hundreds of other immigrants, in the steerage. Adler's thoughts carried him back to that other voyage, the first, from Riga. He had been young then, and full of hope. Between that journey and this a greater happiness had come to him and a greater grief than he would ever know again. Youth lay behind him, with the London years. Sonya and the child were dead. No path on earth would ever lead back to Jennya Kaiser. The boat plunged on through the dark Atlantic waters. He turned his face to the future.

Part III

AMERICA: THE GOLDEN YEARS

17

"Da Zdrastvuyet Amerika!"

> My blessings on you, fair new world,
>   On freedom your foundations rise.
> America, you are my love!
>   And if you say, "Give me your life,
> I need your strength, I need your blood,"
>   I will not ask for what, for whom—
> What you demand I'll freely give!
>
> MORRIS ROSENFELD, "Hymn to America"

Bathed in the impersonal, colorless daylight of the New World, a daylight already darkened by the electric elevated rails of the coming age, the Bowery cut its way a hundred years ago through New York's Lower East Side. Political bosses, saloon keepers, and underworld characters controlled this territory. Prostitutes roamed it, unmolested by the law, and the worst red-light district in the city flourished in its neighborhood. A harsh stretch of city asphalt, it ran uninterrupted from Chatham Square to Fourteenth Street. From end to end it throbbed with the brutal vitality of poverty and corruption, and its great commodity was entertainment.

The pleasures of the Bowery were to be found on every side, often on a surprisingly lavish scale. The Atlantic Garden, at Suffolk and Bayard streets, provided a German clientele with billiards, dancing, a twenty-piece orchestra, gold-framed mirrors, carved ceilings, crystal chandeliers, and a twenty-foot ballroom floor. Across the way, the Philharmonic Alcazar and Hotel added the inducements of fifty singing waitresses and daily concerts of comic sketches, music, song, and dance. Admission was free at both these pleasure palaces, and beer only five cents a glass.

The Bowery theatres were also within reach of all but the poorest. A good seat at the Thalia could be had for less than a dollar, a gallery ticket to some of the houses for as little as twenty cents. And the show itself ran on for hours. A typical bill at the Windsor featured the popular singer Paul Dresser, half a dozen variety acts, and as the main attraction De Wolfe Hopper in the full-length comedy *Four Hundred Wives*. Up the street, the National, a smaller "combination house," offered another long vaudeville bill, topping it off with *The Two Orphans, The Bandit King*, or some other melodrama of that day.

At Fourteenth Street the scene abruptly changed to one of opulence and glamour. Wallack's Theatre was already closed and dark; the beloved Lester Wallack had already deserted to one of the newer playhouses in the thirties. But the aristocratic Merton House Bar still flourished on the corner of Lower Broadway, and Fourteenth Street with its glittering row of theatres would remain a while longer the rendezvous and rialto of the New York actor.

Traces of a more brilliant period could be found on the Bowery itself. Popular touring companies, even great visiting stars, did not disdain its better houses. The century-old Thalia was the most beautiful theatre in the city. Brutus Junius Booth had played there, and New York connoisseurs still came down to see German greats like Possart, Barnay, and Sonnenthal. But the beautiful facade lay now in the shadow of the elevated tracks. The Greek columns of the Thalia rose in a squalor of beer halls, minstrel shows, waxworks museums, and one-night hotels, part of a past forgotten as the city pushed northward.

In this New World Moldovanka, on this midway of the poor, the Yiddish theatre was to have its third incarnation. Here it would take root, grow, and when its moment came, reach greatness.

Yiddish performances in America began in 1882, about the same time that young immigrants were coming together to form the first "dramatic clubs" of London. But while a dozen excellent players emerged from the Whitechapel clubs, the amateur efforts of New York for some reason produced only one. That one, however, was a star of the first magnitude, a star that shone unforgettably bright. So highly colored, so potent was this personality that to this day his name cannot be separated from the theatre he helped to create. For thousands of people even now, this one actor *is* the Yiddish theatre.

In 1882 Boris (Baruch) Thomashefsky was a handsome boy of fifteen with dark, curling hair, beautiful eyes, and a melting appreciation of all femininity, a figure already fluttering hearts among the green immigrant girls on East Broadway. Even at that age he had an extraordinary belief in his own powers, a trait often found in those who have shown exceptional promise as children.

We are forced to admit that early successes and his good looks had made him somewhat vain, with an image of himself that verged at times on the fantastic. This fault, coupled with his love of everything grandiose, might have drawn him far from reality. Something strong and steadfast in his character saved him from this. Early hardships gave him an understanding of life that never left him, and young as he was, we shall see that older men trusted and followed him.

This star of the future was born in the village of Asitniatchka, Kiev Province, the grandson of a village cantor. At four he already knew all the music his grandfather sang with the choir in the synagogue. On Saturday nights, at the Escorting Out of the Queen Sabbath, the cantor would stand his grandson on a table, and from this post the infant would sing whole Hebrew services, to the astonishment of the assembled guests. At five Boris created a sensation by appearing in the synagogue on Yom Kippur eve with a bandaged throat and a high fever, tugging wildly at the boy who was singing the *Adon Olam*,* and screaming that he, and he alone, must sing it.

A commotion broke out. Men shouted, women put their heads out from behind the screen in the gallery, and his mother called down to let the boy sing or he would kill himself. In the end his grandfather hurriedly threw a *tallis* over his shoulders, and the boy got through the service. He was carried home afterward, exhausted but happy. The old cantor, thinking he would forget, had jokingly promised to let him deliver this all-important prayer.

The incident was the talk of the town, and everyone predicted the boy would be a great cantor some day. His father, a man of more modern outlook, declared that little Baruch would bring glory to his people as an opera singer.

This father has a curious history. In his youth he had

---

* "Lord of the Universe," a prayer sung before the Ark of the Covenant.

studied for the rabbinate and was much admired for his piety. Nobody knew that while the studious youth pored over the Talmud, he was also secretly teaching himself Russian and German, and delving into forbidden books.

What he learned in these books changed forever the life of Pinchas Thomashefsky. His native village had become too small to hold him. Oceans and continents swam in his brain. And in all the village, he had not a soul with whom he could share the marvels he had learned. His friends would have recoiled from him in horror, for he had become an *Apikorus,* a freethinker.

One day he disappeared, vanished without a trace. He was off to the Caucasus, in search of life and adventure. He remained two years in that strange part of the world, squandered his wife's dowry there, and came home one day in the back of a wagon. His dark blue glasses, shaven face, and strange attire gave rise to a rumor that a great aristocrat had come to the town. When it was learned the marvelous visitor was the long-lost son of the cantor, the whole village came out in the streets and danced for joy. His wife fell on the wanderer's neck and forgave him. And his rich father-in-law gave the "naked aristocrat," as he was now called, a second and even bigger dowry.

A man like this could not remain all his days in Asitniatchka. When his son was eight years old, Pinchas Thomashefsky moved first to Zlatapolya, and then to Kiev, where he set up as a shopkeeper. His shop prospered, and the family, enlarged now by several other children, added to their income by taking in actors, choir singers, cantors, and musicians. Pinchas was among the earliest devotees of Yiddish theatre. He once traveled miles to see Mogulesko, went backstage on another occasion to shake hands with Jacob Adler, and in his spare time wrote a comedy called *Yankele, Young Scamp.*

In Kiev his talented son sang for the sugar and railroad magnate, Abram Markovitch Brodsky, a man so rich he was known as the Jewish Emperor. On the advice of Brodsky, Pinchas took the boy to Berditchev, where Reb Nissim of Belz, the most famous cantor of all South Russia, accepted him as a pupil.

After the Tsar's assassination in 1881, Pinchas Thomashefsky fell under police suspicion. As it happened, some young men from Kiev University took their meals in a student kitchen above the Thomashefsky shop. One day police came and made a search. They found a closet full of nihilist literature in the student restaurant and an illegal printing press in the cellar. The kitchen was padlocked, the peasant woman who owned it arrested, and three of the students sentenced to hang in the public square. Because Pinchas had loved these young men, and often talked with them, he was summoned to the office of the governor-general. When he refused to inform on his young friends, he was given twenty-four hours to settle his affairs and quit Russia forever. He left the next day for Galicia, not knowing whether he would ever see his family again.

Chaya Baila Thomashefsky sold what she could, gave away what she could not sell, and with her bundles of bedding, some tin plates and cups, and her four younger children, she set out for Berditchev to collect her eldest.

Young Boris was beside himself with excitement when he heard the news. To America? All the way from Berditchev to America? Who had ever dreamed of such an adventure? Reb Nissim, all his children, and the whole Berditchev choir came to the station to bid him good-bye, and the boy could not wait to be off. It was only as he was actually boarding the train that he broke down and sobbed. He understood at that last moment that he would never see these friends again.

Chaya Baila and her five children crossed the Russian border into Austria well after midnight in an ox-drawn wagon. They made the journey under burlap sacks, and several times quaked with fear as officials stopped their driver and questioned him. Next day they took the train to Brod in Galicia, where, to their great joy, they found Pinchas waiting for them on the railway platform.

They spent some terrible weeks in Brod until the Alliance Israelite Universelle, an organization of wealthy Western European Jews, sent them on to Antwerp. Here at last they took ship for America. The Thomashefskys crossed with one of the first great boatloads of 1881. They all suffered horribly from seasickness during the voyage, and Chaya Baila was convinced none of them would survive it.

On the fifteenth day Boris and his brother recovered and began exploring the boat. All the young people on those first ships were in wild spirits. America to them meant excitement, fun, a good time. Their elders, too, for all their cares, approached the other side of the Atlantic with a tremendous sense of renewed life and hope.

"Early on the twenty-second day," Thomashefsky writes, "we were awakened by the sound of footsteps running, a babble of voices, and the excited cry of *'Land!'* We threw on our clothes and rushed up on deck. It was already packed so thick with people we could hardly make our way to the rail. There was no skyline then, no Statue of Liberty in the harbor, but through the rising mist we could see the long shoreline of New York. Everyone was shouting, pointing, laughing. Men threw their hats in the air for joy, and from a thousand throats the shout went up, *'Da Zdrastvuyet Amerika!*—Long live America!' "

A month or two before the Thomashefskys arrived, a boat from Hamburg had brought a young firebrand called Abraham Cahan to these shores.

Cahan wrote: "Those who came later had an idea, even if it was a mistaken idea, of America. They had received letters from relatives or friends in America. Some of these relatives and friends returned to Russia and told tales there of the new land. But for us who left Russia in 1881, a letter from America was an object in a museum, a visitor from such a place impossible even to imagine. For us this was truly a land mysterious and unexplored. The sight of the most familiar object, a cat, say, filled us with amazement. 'Look!' we cried. 'There are cats in America! Just like at home!' At every step we realized we were no longer in the ordinary world, but in *America*!"

No doubt the Thomashefsky family as they disembarked at Castle Garden felt something of the wonder Cahan describes. This hexagonal building, once the city opera and civic center, was now the government clearinghouse for immigrants. Hundreds of people milled through the main hall, filling it with an ear-splitting racket. Confusion piled on confusion, for little here could be understood or put right. Newly arrived immigrants ran about inquiring for the relatives or *landsleit* who should have met them. Others searched for lost belongings. The Thomashefskys, stunned by the noise, gazed on the scene, frightened and lost. They had no one at all in America. They sat on their bundles until two men came up and asked them if they wanted a cheap hotel. These were agents hanging about the immigration center on the lookout for small commissions. Pinchas gratefully accepted their help.

Immigration was relatively light in 1881, and the officials at Castle Garden detained no one. The Thomashefskys were simply registered and allowed to leave. Porters picked up their baggage, and they followed it outside, where several families like themselves had already been rounded up. Their two guides commandeered an express wagon drawn by two huge horses, boxes and bundles were piled on, and everyone crawled up after them.

A group of young dockside loafers watched the scene, laughing and imitating the gestures of the foreigners. The Thomashefskys laughed back politely, not altogether sure how these Americans felt about them. They were soon to be enlightened, for as the wagon moved off the whole crowd ran after with loud jeers, speeding it on its way with a shower of rocks.

"A fine beginning!" Pinchas remarked with pain. "Stones in Russia, and here more stones. The Jew, it seems, has one fate everywhere, to be pelted with stones."

"Those are loafers, trash!" his guides assured him. "You have come to a great land, a land where there are no pogroms! You will never regret coming to America!"

It was a smaller, more intimate New York taking in these immigrants. Above the fifties the numbered streets stopped entirely, and a mile further, city pavement gave way to open fields and farms. Yet rumors of things to come were everywhere. Brooklyn Bridge, not yet open to the public, already made its giant leap over the river. Trains roared over the elevated tracks, shattering the peace of the streets below. The sense of change, of a relentless building, tearing down, rebuilding, demolishing were in the very air.

The Jewish quarter as yet took in only a few blocks around East Broadway. This was a neighborhood occupied by tailors from West Poland, old-fashioned folk drawn by the German Jewish garment centers on Hester, Canal, and Grand streets. The sight of these people, the women wearing shawls, the men with beards and *yarmelkes,* gave comfort to the families coming in on their wagon.

The Thomashefskys reached the end of their journey at Falk's Hotel, a few doors from the corner of East Broadway. Pinchas took two rooms for his family, they unpacked, and began to settle in.

An hour later the fourteen-year-old Boris came out on the stoop, and after hesitating a moment, ventured out into the street. He went no farther than the corner, where a sign announced the office of the *Judische Gazetten,* at that time the only Yiddish paper in New York. Here he encountered a boy his own age, the son of the publisher, Sarasohn. They exchanged a shy word or two, and the young foreigner went back to his hotel, courage in his heart. He had made a friend in America.

Pinchas, who had strong radical leanings, had shipped out of Antwerp with a group of Kiev socialists who called themselves the *Am Olam*, the Eternal People. These idealists wanted to found Communist colonies in the new land. One such collective had already been created in Kansas, and an Odessa *Am Olam* had also founded a short-lived Jewish colony in Oregon, where the town New Odessa still bears the name they gave it. The Kiev *Am Olam* had less luck. Ideological differences split the membership, and a disapproving letter from the First Internationale in Switzerland sank the whole enterprise. These followers of Tolstoy did not till the earth of New Jersey as they had dreamed, but went instead into the sweatshops of the Lower East Side.

The wheel of fortune turned sharply in America. Education and learning counted for nothing here. Tradesmen and laborers went into the savage pushcart life of Hester Street, fought their way up, became contractors, shop owners, great manufacturers. Intellectuals and professionals preferred the factories, certain they would soon get out again. Most of these men were lost forever in the sweatshops.

Not destined to be a farmer in the New World, Pinchas Thomashefsky became a shirt operator. Since he had to help support the family, Boris got a job in a tobacco factory. Here he and the other tobacco cutters, greenhorns like himself, sat at long tables rolling the self-igniting cigarettes by which the German Jew Jacoby hoped to make his fortune.

Now in all these shops there were immigrants who at home had given up food and drink to buy a ticket to the Yiddish theatre. Homesick in their bleak new life, they sang as they worked. Singing broke the dreary sound of the machine, and those who knew the theatre songs best acquired a sort of fame in the factories. Jacoby did not mind the singing. He enjoyed it. And it made the work go better when the boys sang.

In this factory on Chatham Square the Yiddish theatre of America came into being. "Opposite me," Thomashefsky recalls, "sat a dark boy called Rosenblum, a tailor's son. Next to him on the bench was a red-haired boy called Abe Golubock. Rosenblum said he had been an actor in Russia, but we did not believe this. Who would give up such a glorious life to be a tobacco roller? Later I found out Rosenblum had been an extra at the Marinsky in Odessa. But whenever he began to sing the red-haired boy, Golubock, would make a face. *'Nyet! Nyet!'* he cried angrily. 'It doesn't go like that!' And he would repeat the song a bit differently. Golubock had a brother in Russia who was really an actor. We all had great respect for him because of this!"

One day Abe Golubock brought news. His actor brother had left Russia and was playing Yiddish theatre in a London club. Then and there the young tobacco worker unrolled a poster that had come in the mail. The poster announced that Leon Golubock, the world-renowned comedian with a gold medal from the Tsar, would play both the Buba Yachna and Hotzmach in Goldfaden's *Witch* and would dance a Kamarinska in the third act. It further proclaimed that Madame Soore Krantzfeld, the Adelina Patti of the Jewish stage, would sing the role of Mirale.

The poster caused such excitement that all work stopped. Jacoby himself took an interest in the wonderful news. But Abe Golubock's pride was masking a heavy heart. The fact was, his brother was suffering hunger and want in London. He had sent a letter with the poster, begging Abe to find a rich American who would bring him to New York with his troupe. In his distress, Golubock showed this letter to Boris Thomashefsky.

Now this young man had from earliest childhood looked upon himself as a celebrity who wanted only an opportunity to be recognized by the world. His practical sense, always acute, told him if he found means to bring over these actors, he would surely have a place among them. He promised Abe Golubock he would do what he could.

That night Thomashefsky dreamed he stood on a vast stage. The Golubock brothers led him forward, presenting him to the applauding audience as a great new star.

He had foretold his future with remarkable accuracy.

On the corner of Essex and Hester streets, swinging doors opened into the dark, friendly, noisy beer saloon of Frank Wolfe. This German Jew, thoroughly Americanized, was prosperous enough to wear diamond rings on his fingers and diamond studs in his colored shirts. Like most saloon keepers, he had a certain influence. Political business was often settled in saloons of this kind, where aldermen, police inspectors, and other such people could be found. A great many things were "straightened out" at Frank Wolfe's saloon, and the sign across the window proclaimed him, with some justice, as the "Friend of the Working Man."

There is no Jewish law that prevents a pious man from keeping a tavern. Wolfe, a good Jew, held an honored place on the board of an Orthodox synagogue on Henry Street, and it happened that young Thomashefsky earned a little extra money by singing in the choir of this particular synagogue on Friday nights. Wolfe and his wife had taken a fancy to the handsome boy who sang so well, and once or twice had invited him to dinner at their home.

That Friday night, when the services were over, Thomashefsky told Wolfe about Abe Golubock and his brother, the Yiddish actor in London. "Is there such a thing as Yiddish theatre?" the German saloon keeper asked in surprise.

"Certainly!" Thomashefsky answered. "In Russia and Roumania they have had it a long time. Now in London they have begun to play Yiddish theatre."

After some thought, Wolfe told Thomashefsky to bring around his friend, and the meeting with Abe Golubock took place soon after. Wolfe was interested in the idea, and seven steamship tickets were eventually sent to London, along with a sum for the actors' expenses.

Some weeks later Leon Golubock and his troupe arrived, and Frank Wolfe, Thomashefsky, and Abe Golubock were at Castle Garden to meet them.

A more dilapidated and forlorn group had never come down those gangplanks. They were all pale as wax from the ocean crossing, dazed by their arrival. The shapeless hats and shoes of the men were painful to see, and their woebegone prima donna, Madame Krantzfeld, hardly looked better.

Of all this company, only the seventeen-year-old comedian Leon Golubock had actually played some parts in the Russian provinces. The rest were amateurs picked up in London. Golubock's troupe consisted of his older brother, Miron; Madame Krantzfeld, daughter of a small-town cantor; Rafael Boyarsky, son of a theatrical costumer in Moscow; a cool, aloof boy of the Warsaw streets called Simon; and a Mr. and Mrs. Spector, two young nihilists who had been expelled from the Russian *Gymnazia* and who after years of wandering had found their way to London.

The saloon keeper behaved handsomely. Within a week

the actors were so changed no one would have known them. Dressed in Prince Albert coats and high hats, with money in their pockets, they walked through the Yiddish quarter like kings. Already they had followers, awestruck admirers who fought for a place beside these great ones on the pavement.

Wolfe intended to make a splash. He took the Thalia, handsomest of the Bowery theatres, engaged their twenty-four-piece orchestra, and brought in the fifty singers of the synagogue choir. Thomashefsky was to lead this chorus and to sing an important solo in the second act. Rehearsals were held at No. 7 Hester Street, and a notice in the *Judische Gazetten* announced that on August 12, 1882, the Hebrew Opera and Dramatic Company would present *The Witch*, an opera in five acts and eight scenes, words and music by Avrom Goldfaden.

These preparations were in the meantime causing disquiet in certain quarters. A group of concerned German Jews had come together in a body known as the Hebrew Immigration Aid Committee, an organization formed with the purpose of assisting newly arrived fellow Jews from Eastern Europe. Worried by reports of the coming theatrical performance, the members made some inquiries. They learned that Goldfaden's *Witch* depicted an old Jewish woman as a sorceress and a Jewish peddler as a swindler and thief. Feeling such a play would bring discredit on the Jewish community, they sent a message to the Golubock brothers asking them to come to their Committee headquarters on State Street.

The Golubocks together with Thomashefsky appeared at ten the following morning. They were admitted to a dark basement room, where the Committee received them seated behind a long table, a scene that scared them half to death. These stern men had worked their way up in the American business community through their honorable dealing and unremitting industry. They had only impatience for these actors with their absurd high hats and their more absurd plans. And indeed, though the hearts of the Immigration Committee genuinely ached for their unfortunate brothers from Eastern Europe, they often failed to understand them. "There was no common language," Abraham Cahan tells us, "and the inner language was even more different. The whole outlook was not the same."

After asking a series of questions, a white-bearded official gave the actors a severe lecture. "Go out into the country and become peddlers!" he told them sternly. "Find decent work, and don't bring shame on your people with this foolery you call theatre."

The actors left like criminals, with lowered heads. They were crushed by the ruin of all their hopes. They thought if they did not obey the Committee they would be sent back to Russia!

When they confided their fears to Frank Wolfe, he laughed and the whole saloon laughed with him. "The poor Russian Jews should have as little to fear from that murderer the Tsar as you have from the Committee!" Wolfe told them. "This is America! The President himself cannot harm you here! Rehearse! Put on your play! And if you succeed you will make good money, and bring over your relatives, too!"

Thomashefsky never forgave the Immigration Committee, and even tried to blame them for what subsequently happened. Other actors, however, flatly contradict his story, and since he himself tells three different versions of it, we may assume that the Committee had nothing to do with the failure of the first performance.

At the last moment, the play was for some reason switched from the Thalia Theatre to the Turnhalle,* a small German hall just off the Bowery. The last-minute change lost the troupe a good part of their audience, but in the general disaster that followed, this hardly mattered.

Apparently Madame Krantzfeld had become hoarse during rehearsal. Since she could not sing, she simply did not appear. By nine-thirty, the overture had been played again and again, and the audience was becoming angry. At ten, Wolfe and the frantic Thomashefsky took a carriage to her home on Forsythe Street, where they found the prima donna in bed with a towel around her throat. She was prevailed on to dress and come to the theatre, but by that time matters had gone too far. People were shouting and demanding their money back, and some of the rougher ones were threatening to break the chairs.

The situation was desperate. The orchestra leader had gone home and taken the music with him. Madame Krantzfeld refused to sing without the orchestra. A quarrel broke out backstage. Salty Russian and Yiddish curses were exchanged. In the end the Golubocks simply pushed her out onto the

---

* This curious little building, now called the Manhattan Plaza, is still standing at 66 East Fourth Street.

stage. Instead of singing, she declaimed. At this final insult a pandemonium of whistles and catcalls arose. Thomashefsky, trying to lead a disorganized chorus, felt nothing but relief as he saw the audience walking out of the hall. Wolfe left without saying good-bye to the actors, and for several days they were ashamed to show their faces on the street.

Nevertheless, two months later Wolfe had found a butcher on Bayard Street who was willing to go in with him, and the two of them financed a week of performances, again at the Turnhalle. Thomashefsky still had his boy soprano, and since they had no prima donna, it was he who sang the feminine leads. He had some personal success, and by the end of the run had made up his mind that, come what may, he would remain an actor.

At the end of that year he was trying to get the National Theatre for the troupe. The manager, a Roumanian Jew named Michael Yomen, advised him to try the Bowery Garden over the way, where tickets were ten and fifteen cents. "The Litvak there is losing his shirt," the manager remarked. "He's tried everything, and every rehearsal costs him money. He might do business with you."

Formerly a beer hall, the Bowery Garden was now a hangout for sailors, prostitutes, and derelicts. The hall, long and narrow with a flat, ungraded floor, was furnished with rows of chairs fastened together by wooden strips. The stage, however, was deep, better than the one at the Turnhalle. The owner, B. Levy, distracted by business problems, listened to Thomashefsky because his mother had seen the troupe at the Turnhalle and liked it.

Levy agreed to let the Yiddish troupe perform on weekends, but before drawing up the contract asked whether so young a man had a right to sign for the others. "The actors trust me," Thomashefsky answered. "They will do as I say."

Overcome with gratitude, the troupe made him their director. Thomashefsky went to work, and soon showed his organizational ability. He built up the cast with amateurs from the *Am Olam,* and brought in others from Jacoby's factory. He had his pick of beauties, too, for every pretty girl in the quarter asked nothing better than to be an unpaid part of his chorus.

The troupe soon acquired a playwright in the tailor Israel Barsky. This original man, besides running his tailoring establishment, contributed to socialist periodicals in Europe and was editor of a Yiddish *Am Olam* newssheet. When Wolfe, discouraged by small audiences, took his money out of the venture, Barsky became the troupe's financier as well as their dramatist.

They opened with Barsky's first play, *The Madwoman*. Here a father opposes his daughter's marriage to an artist and wants instead to marry her to a wealthy but evil man. The daughter refuses. The father puts her away. She goes mad. The artist goes into the world, makes his fortune, comes back, and marries the girl, now cured of her madness. In the meantime the father has lost his money and gone blind. A beggar now, he sings beneath his daughter's window. She recognizes him, takes him in, he is cured of his blindness, and the play ends.

The Madwoman was not much more absurd than a half-dozen melodramas on the boards that season. Wallack opened his new theatre with *Youth,* a story of villainy in high society, noted by the critics as "the best in town for the sailing of the troops and the battle scenes." Other hits that years were *The Ticket of Leave Man, The Silver King,* and *Lights O'London,* all gloriously innocent of anything resembling an idea. Downtown the fare grows more lurid, with *The Strangler of Paris* at the Union Theatre, *The Two Orphans* at the Windsor, and *Coney Island, or Little Ethel's Prayer* at the Park. Barsky's melodrama had in fact been inspired by these Bowery thrillers. His *Madwoman* should be noted, moreover, as the first Yiddish play to be written in America, and the first, too, with an American setting.

After two more plays by Barsky, Pinchas Thomashefsky pulled out his old Kiev manuscript, and *Yankele, Young Scamp* reached the stage at last. It was followed by *Rothschild's Biography*. Pinchas, who had written the play, took a character part, and Boris played Rothschild, the penniless young ragpicker in the first act, and later, the great financier, intimate of kings. Their next production was *The Pogrom in Russia,* a play by Boris himself.

The engagement at the Bowery Garden came to an abrupt end midseason because of a split between the Thomashefsky and Golubock factions. A scandalous love affair between Thomashefsky and a pretty chorus girl aggravated the situation, and Levy put them all out. A troupe of Chinese acrobats took over their weekends performances.

Thomashefsky got the troupe a theatre in Newark,

but only four people turned up to see them. A one-night stand in Philadelphia proved even more disastrous. The German theatre owner, Alexander Kost, advertised them only in the German papers. The audience, hearing a language they did not understand, walked out one by one, and the actors found themselves playing to the empty walls. After a painful scene, Alexander Kost drove them out of his theatre. The actors realized later that Kost, fearful of competition in his city, had simply played them an ugly trick.

They played next in a hall over a saloon on Avenue D, but had to give it up when they discovered a brothel on the floor above. They were once again without a theatre, and the actors all came to Thomashefsky, cursing him because he could not keep up the troupe.

One after the other, they dropped off, went back to the sweatshops. The Thomashefskys themselves were almost evicted from their home. An East Side peddler who had liked Thomashefsky in *Rothschild's Biography* saw their furniture on the street and paid their rent.

Boris, looking for work, heard about a job in a sweet caporal factory on Hudson Street. As he walked into the shop a voice boomed out, "Hello, Thomashefsky!" Abe Golubock was the shop foreman. His two brothers, comedian and tragedian alike, sat rolling cigars. A rueful reunion.

They all worked in the Hudson Street factory until the spring of 1884, when the manager of the National Theatre sent a messenger asking Thomashefsky to "come over and talk business."

Michael Yomen was having second thoughts about the Yiddish actors. He had lost part of his audience to the Bowery Garden the year before. Now, with the slow summer months looming ahead, he wanted to get these customers back. He asked Thomashefsky if he could put on a new sketch every week, none of them longer than a half-hour, none with more than five actors, and all with songs and dances. Thomashefsky told him he could begin at once. He and Michael Yomen shook hands on the deal, and Thomashefsky rushed back to the Golubocks. They kissed him in their joy. "Let it be vaudeville, as long as it is theatre!" they exclaimed.

And so we find a sketch called "Shmendrick's Wedding" sandwiched between "Parker and His Dogs" and "The Bowery Belles," and a week later, following "Lost in a Pullman," an act of Goldfaden's *Recruits*. This combination of Yiddish and

American vaudeville on the same bill has greatly perplexed historians of this theatrical period, and George Odell, in his monumental *Annals of the New York Stage* concludes, mistakenly, that the "Hebrew players" must have performed on the roof.

The American vaudeville actors spent all their money on good times. They liked the freehanded Thomashefsky, and it was a gay season. Once again the actors bought themselves Prince Alberts, high hats, elegant canes. The Thomashefsky family moved into better rooms on Eldridge Street, and Michael Yomen, pleased by bigger audiences, was planning to let the American actors go the following season and to feature only Yiddish theatre.

Suddenly, like "thunder from a sunny sky," all this fine time came to an end. Boyarsky came into the dressing room one night and said with a frightened look, "Have you heard, Boris? Real actors are coming. What shall we do?"

It was true. The troupe of Maurice Heine (formerly Chaimovitch), after their brief stopover in London, was now en route to America and would arrive in ten days. Handbills advertising the "Russian Yiddish Opera Company" were already on the street.

Thomashefsky tried to tell the scared actors there was room for two Yiddish troupes in New York. Barsky, more experienced, laughed at him. "Pack up, children!" Barsky said. "You will soon be rolling cigars, pressing shirts!" He warned the actors to have no false hopes, but to get themselves jobs. "Forget theatre!" Barsky said, throwing salt on their wounds.

The new troupe gave their first performance on May 23, 1884, at the Turnhalle, and played there twice a week until late in July, when they moved into the Oriental Theatre. This was nothing more than Levy's old Bowery Garden, renamed in hopes of attracting the Chinese population now coming into the quarter. Because an Oriental Bank had opened next door, the hall continued to be called the "Oriental" until it closed some years later.

It was only Heine's little provincial troupe that had crossed the ocean, but they played with sincerity, and they were liked. Jewish critics were surprised at their competence, and an anonymous letter in the *Judische Gazetten* pleaded with the orchestra to play more softly so as not to drown out the "electrifying voice and speech of Madame Heine."

And, indeed, that passionate voice, even when it was cracked and old, haunts the memory of those of us who knew it.

By mid-April of 1885 the new troupe was drawing such crowds that the New York *Sun* sent a man down to see what was going on. A review of *Bar Kochba* appeared in that paper soon after, under the heading, "A Quaint Hebrew Drama." The *Sun* critic found the opera "badly constructed, wordy, and without ingenuity," but devoted two enthusiastic paragraphs to the Goldfaden score.

Thomashefsky was sick with jealousy. "I did not go to see them," he admits. "Their success broke my heart." He became ill, took to his bed, and told himself he would die rather than go back to the tobacco factory. This is the lowest point of his entire life.

His own troupe had collapsed. Barsky left for a farm near Cleveland, and the others, too, gave up and got themselves jobs. The Thomashefskys spent the summer in a New Jersey town called Rarington. Boris dreamed, took piano lessons, fell in love with his piano teacher, and told himself to forget the theatre. All the same, in the fall he and Pinchas were trying again. Making up a troupe of their own family circle, they went off into the uncharted regions of Philadelphia, scene of their humiliation at the hands of Alexander Kost.

How they fared there is unknown, but a year later Thomashefsky was back in New York, still an actor. Feeling like a stranger in the city, he checked into the Continental Hotel on Broome Street. He took in the show that evening at the Oriental Theatre, and afterward went to a cafe with some of the cast. They had heard something of his amateur theatricals and apparently there was some unkind laughter at his expense. The eighteen-year-old director defended his actors with hot pride. "You would be only too happy to have a comedian like Leon Golubock," he retorted. "And a character actor like Leon Spector you do not possess at all!" Characteristically, it was Thomashefsky who picked up the bill that night and paid for everyone.

For all his defiance, he knew he could not compete in New York with the professionals. He spent the next days seeking out his old Turnhalle company. Miron Golubock was working as an insurance agent, Spector and his wife owned a shirt factory, Boyarsky managed a hat store on Division Street. They were all doing well, making money. Yet every one of them gave up what he was doing and went in once again with Thomashefsky.

The newly formed company left for Philadelphia, then went on to Washington, Baltimore, Boston, Pittsburgh, and Chicago—first of the Yiddish actors ever to play in these cities.

In June of 1886 a bombshell fell on Heine's troupe at the Oriental. The *New Yorker Staat Zeitung* reported the arrival of the Jewish Operetta Company of Roumania under the direction of Siegmund Mogulesko and Maurice Finkel. "This troupe," the *Staat Zeitung* noted, "consists of twenty gentlemen and ten ladies, all of them artists well known in Europe."

If Thomashefsky had been there, he might have known a bitter pleasure. Heine and his actors read the news with consternation.

They would have to dig in now, and fight for their life! The great Mogulesko had arrived!

18

The Magic "Professor"

> When the lion roars, the tiger gnashes his teeth, the leopard springs and bites and fire rains down from the skies, then shall justice triumph at last, and the Jewish nation shout, "Shema Isroel Adonai Elohenu!"
>
> *Fragment of Hurvitz operetta*

In spite of the notice in the *Staat Zeitung*, it was only Mogulesko and Finkel who were brought over by Mandelkern that June. Mogulesko wanted to play in New York. The two Chicago tailors Drozdovitch and Rosengarten had no theatre there, but to satisfy Mogulesko told him they were leasing the National on the Bowery.

Mogulesko trusted everyone. He knew nothing about business, and he had been in America three days. He signed a paper agreeing to play in any theatre and any city his managers would stipulate. After signing the agreement, Mogulesko was given a small advance. Since it was only part of what he needed to bring over his troupe, he had to go back to London and give a series of desperate "last performances." By late summer he had raised enough to come back to America with his company.

In his cast were Finkel; Mrs. Annetta Finkel; Sam Adler, a clever actor who later had an important career in Europe; the playwright Joseph Lateiner; Siegmund Feinman, a man respected for his superior education; and David Kessler, billed at that time as a romantic lead.

Drozdovitch and Rosengarten, to gain time, booked the troupe for two weeks at Terrace Garden, a German theatre on Lexington Avenue and Fifty-eighth Street. News of these performances created enormous excitement on the Lower East Side, and in spite of the fact that the theatre was so far uptown, the opening on October 13 brought an audience overflowing into the street.

Mogulesko had chosen as his first play Offenbach's *Bluebeard*. David Kessler sang the lead in this operetta, and Mogulesko himself played Papaloni, a minor role with no songs or dances. In making this modest choice, Mogulesko was following the European tradition, in which the leading actor does not necessarily take the spotlight at his first performance, and will often present himself simply as part of his ensemble.

A Jewish audience in Paris, London, or Odessa would have understood this. But the men and women at Terrace Garden that night were already an audience of Americans. They had come to see the star, and they wanted no one else. Halfway through the first act the growing resentment found expression in an angry voice shouting, "It's not Mogulesko!" Others took it up, and shouts of "It's another actor! It's not Mogulesko!" were heard on every side. Mogulesko had to come out after the second act and promise the audience he would appear in a bigger role the following night. The audience left dissatisfied, and a rumor got around that the performances at Terrace Garden were a swindle, with an impostor masquerading as the star. *Bluebeard* was hastily removed from the boards and in its place *Coquettish Ladies* by Sheikevitch was announced, to be followed by Offenbach's *La Perichole*.

Coquettish Ladies was one of Mogulesko's great successes, but he played it to an almost empty hall. Even those who came hardly applauded. This cold reception worked so on Mogulesko that the following week when they put on the Offenbach operetta, he would not go on, and the whole run at Terrace Garden was a failure.

David Kessler never forgave Mogulesko for the insult he had personally suffered there. "We had a full house for our first play," Kessler wrote. "Only Mogulesko was dissatisfied. An angry, capricious man! When we put on *Perichole* he was 'sick' and would not play. We all knew the cause of his anger, that his role was too small, but he would not say this openly. We begged, we pleaded—no use! At nine o'clock the audience was stamping, 'boo-ing,' but still it was 'No!' Another actor who hardly knew the part had to take his place. The audience was ice-cold and hardly moved their hands at the end of the play."

With the end of the Terrace Garden run, Mogulesko discovered he had been tricked. His managers had no theatre on the Bowery, and were demanding he bring his troupe to Chicago. Mogulesko did not want to leave New York. He refused to go, and in the end the Chicago men got a court order and took possession of his costumes.

For three months after that the actors could not play at all. It was a bad time, worse than anything they had known in Europe. Some of them went without food for days at a time.

They were rescued by Yechiel Schreiber, owner of a cafe on Canal Street. Schreiber had helped Thomashefsky's troupe in their worst days. How he held out his hand to the Roumanians.

They had made a useful friend, for the cafe owner was one of the most popular men in the quarter. He was generous, he was known to be honest, and most important, he was active in a score of the lodges and *landsmanschaft* societies * already numerous on the East Side. Benefit performances were already a feature of the American theatrical scene, and Schreiber, with his contacts, was just the man to organize such evenings. Businessmen began to take an interest, and Louis Levy, an East Side lawyer, looked into Mogulesko's legal problems. Levy, who saw at a glance that the Chicago men had taken advantage of his client, took the case to court and won it. The actors were at last free of Drozdovitch and Rosengarten.

Levy, together with a glass merchant named Ludwig Roth and another man named Goldman, leased the National Theatre for a year, and opened it on January 7, 1887, as the Roumania Opera House.

It must be admitted that the troubles of Mogulesko had come as a blessed reprieve to the actors at the Oriental. Silberman and Heine had wasted no time. A notice in the *Judische Gazetten* announced that the Oriental had been equipped with steam heat, electricity, better seats, better scenery, and in fact now offered "all the improvements of the best New York theatres." In addition, Heine and Silberman promised the public

---

* Immigrants with no relatives in America were sometimes brought over by a *landsman*, a friend, or even an acquaintance who had grown up in the same town or village. The bond between these people often lasted a lifetime, and it was common for them to band together in societies.

an enlarged cast and fourteen new productions in the coming season. Most of the new productions never materialized.

After Mogulesko's failure at Terrace Garden, the Oriental troupe began to feel they might survive. They had their small, devoted public, passionately loyal to such favorites as Max Karp and Heine. And Madame Heine in particular was adored to the point of idolatry.

It was in fact only the love of the public that kept this actress from leaving the troupe and going back to Odessa. Conditions in London had shocked her dreadfully, and New York was hardly better. The Oriental was ill-equipped, filthy, the dressing rooms unheated and freezing. Heine, who had promised everything as a lover, had turned into a husband who held the purse strings in an iron grip. There were continual quarrels in the house about money. The young actress was growing in power with every role, but the husband was chary even of praise.

Heine probably sensed a strength he could not control much longer. He did not like his wife's popularity, and as soon as he could afford the expense, sent Max Karp to London to bring back the famous prima donna Sophia Goldstein.

The young wife, a stoic by nature, took her humiliation in silence. Sophia Goldstein had grown in beauty over the years. She possessed the most remarkable feminine voice ever heard in the Yiddish theatre. And she was surrounded by legend as the first actress ever to appear on its stage.

The new star made her New York debut in *Bar Kochba*. She was hailed by the critics, but got a cool reception from an audience that had adored Mrs. Heine in the same role. Violent debate soon broke out between the "patriots" of the new prima donna and the old, and the battle waxed so fierce that people who never went to the theatre were aware of it.

The two actresses at first played on different evenings. After a month of this, Heine insisted that his wife appear with her rival in *Zhidovka*, Lerner's adaptation of *La Juive*. Sophia Goldstein had known a great triumph as the Rachel of this play. But when Mrs. Heine came onstage as the unimportant Princess Avdotya, a storm of protest broke out, and such was the uproar that the curtain had to be brought down.

Madame Goldstein refused to appear again, and soon after left the Oriental for the Roumanian troupe. Max Karp, who was in love with her, followed. These were bad losses for

Heine. But Sara Heine had more power now with the husband she had begun to fear as a formidable enemy.

The Roumania Opera House opened late in the season with *Rashi, or the Persecution of the Jews in France,* a spectacular opera in five acts and twenty-eight scenes with music by Mogulesko. This new *Rashi* had little in common with the historical drama by the learned Katzenellenbogen. It was, in fact, the work of Moishe Isaac Hurvitz-Halevy, the self-styled "Professor" who had once competed in Bucharest with Goldfaden. Hurvitz, just over from London, was now official playwright of the Roumanian troupe.

Heine and Silberman countered the success of *Rashi* with *Tisza Eslar,* a Lateiner play based on a sensational trial still fresh in Jewish memory. The "Tisza Eslar affair" had created a stir of anxiety a year or so earlier when a rabbi in that Hungarian town was accused of a ritual murder. The play had strong audience appeal, and became the model for a series of *zeit bilder,* timely dramas based on actual events.

The Lateiner play had barely begun its successful run when Hurvitz presented not one but two full-length dramas on the same subject. *The Trial at Tisza Eslar* and *The Conspiracy at Tisza Eslar* were shown on two successive evenings, an intriguing novelty. Hurvitz himself played the defense lawyer, thundering away at each performance to bursts of excited applause. And the Roumanians had the further advantage of Mogulesko as Mauritz Scharf, the thirteen-year-old boy tricked into giving evidence against his father.

The long and bitter feud between Hurvitz and Lateiner dates from this incident. It was a struggle in which Lateiner usually came off second best, for Hurvitz could turn out plays like lightning, one after the other, and in addition had spies who kept him informed of everything his rival was doing. Thus it came about that Lateiner had barely set to work on *Solomon's Judgment* when Hurvitz was already presenting *King Solomon,* an elaborate operetta that completely overshadowed it. Lateiner, rushing to complete the first act of *Don Isaac Abarbanel,* was shocked to find the other theatre already advertising *Don Josef Abarbanel.* The two plays were about different men living in entirely different epochs, but their names were alike, and this confused a public knowing little or nothing of either.

Lateiner at least stuck to facts in his "historical operettas."

Hurvitz had no such scruples, and would mix together the events of three centuries without a qualm. What he lost in historical accuracy he gained in sensational curtain lines. Lateiner's efforts to keep up finally ruined him, for he lost the plodding craftsmanship that had been his only quality.

According to Abe Cahan, it sometimes happened that a play by Hurvitz was not ready, an act or so still unwritten by opening night. "Never mind," Hurvitz would say. "Put it on. We will see." And instead of a fourth act, Hurvitz would come out dressed as a Turkish sultan and talk any kind of high-sounding nonsense that came into his head. Cahan writes: "A minute before the curtain went up, Hurvitz would say to Weinblatt or Feinman, 'Whatever I say, nod your head!' Hurvitz is the Sultan, Weinblatt the Prime Minister. The Sultan speaks. The Minister nods his head. And the public accepted it!"

Hurvitz, who lived in high style, loved best of all to ride about in an expensive carriage. According to Cahan, he once borrowed $500 from one of his servants and used the money to buy a spider phaeton and four horses. "At times the theatre was failing, the actors going hungry," Cahan relates, "but Hurvitz sat with a coachman and footman in gold braid and had himself driven through the streets of New York like a Roumanian prince!"

The actors laughed at the "Professor" he had attached to his name. Those who had known him in Roumania even dared address him as "Professor Apostate," a sly reference to his days in Bucharest as a missionary. But Hurvitz's title was regarded with awe by an audience described by one critic as "the most naive public on God's green earth." Some of these people had never seen even the outside of a theatre until they came to America. What happened on the stage was absolutely real to them. We are told that in Thomashefsky's theatre in Baltimore, when a second act curtain rose on Jewish prisoners freezing in Siberia, groans and wails went up in the audience, and some old women took off their shawls and threw them to the actors on the stage. The character actress Bena Abramovitch, playing a housewife, was startled one night by a woman who came down to the footlights and asked her for a glass of water. When Hurvitz started the first afternoon performances, an old man complained at the box office that week after week they advertised only "Matinee." He had already seen "Matinee" and wanted to see something else.

To this audience, Hurvitz with his Germanized Yiddish and his portentous air must have seemed like some awe-inspiring magician!

The theft of *Tisza Eslar* which began the rivalry of Hurvitz and Lateiner also ushered in the era of the "patriots," a term that goes back to the Russian theatre. We have already seen the Oriental audience divided into enemy camps when Sophia Goldstein challenged the supremacy of Madame Heine. Now, with the coming of a second troupe, partisan passions flared up with astonishing force. Pitched battles were actually fought between the patriots of the Oriental and those of the Roumania Opera House. And these fiery struggles were soon raging around rivals within the same troupe. When Kessler replaced Mogulesko as the shepherd boy in *King Solomon*, Mogulesko's patriots created such an uproar that Kessler was forced to leave the stage. The theatre managers had to come out and shout above the clamor that those who did not wish to see Kessler could leave and get their money back. Mogulesko's patriots were prepared for this, and a mass march to the box office was organized. Kessler's supporters did not take the insult in silence, and blows were struck and blood spilled in the fight that followed on the street.

Patriots dressed like their idols, copied their manner and their speech, and had their own meeting places, usually a saloon near the theatre. They were a familiar sight on the street, where they often stood about for hours disputing and bragging about their favorites. Boaz Young, recently arrived in New York, soon found his way to these stage-mad circles. Young talked incessantly of London, of the Gradners, Max Rosenthal, and especially of his own idol, Adler. "He will cover them all," Young declared. "Just to look at him is worth the price of admission." He was so obsessed with his idol that the others called him "Adler," a name that stuck to him for years.

Handbills soon appeared on the street, each troupe trading insults with the other. The wildest slanders and accusations were used in these campaigns. Both companies were already stealing actors from each other, and often a player lampooned in one handbill would be praised to the skies as soon as he had crossed the street to the other theatre. Insulting couplets were also written into the texts of plays and sung from the stage itself. A certain part of the public took a keen interest in this war of words, but in the end both troupes suffered, for the better audience, seeing the two theatres intent only on destroying each other, stopped going to both.

In the spring of 1887 the Fire Department inspected the Roumania Opera House and ordered Mogulesko to put in new doors and fire escapes. The theatre had to close down for these repairs, and the troupe could not finish the season.

Mogulesko heard that an actor called Thomashefsky was taking in $15 a week in Philadelphia. Since he rarely earned that much himself, he sent a letter asking Thomashefsky to come to New York and "talk things over." Thomashefsky took the next train to New York. He was in a fever all the way, thinking Mogulesko was going to make him an offer.

Mogulesko, however, talked about his own troubles. A short season and a bad one. Now repairs that would take months, and he and his actors without a penny for the summer. He had sent for Thomashefsky in hopes that he would arrange some performances in Philadelphia.

Thomashefsky immediately saw the possibilities of the situation. He went back to Philadelphia, and announced to his audience that Mogulesko was coming with the smash New York success, *Coquettish Ladies*.

The Roumanians opened a few nights later, and were cheered to the rafters by a packed house. "Who needs New York?" Mogulesko said delightedly. "Philadelphia! That's a city!"

In *Coquettish Ladies,* Mogulesko appeared in three different characterizations. In the first act Golman, a young pimp of the Odessa streets, is carrying on an affair with a married woman, an accomplished coquette. In the second act Golman returns after eighteen years in the army, an old, used-up soldier and a drunk. In the third act his former mistress, together with her daughter (also a coquette), drives a virtuous stepdaughter out of the house. This homeless girl seeks out Shprintze the Matchmaker, a gossipy old woman who places servant girls. Shprintze sings couplets, defeats the evil plot of the two coquettes, and ends by making a match of it between the virtuous girl and the hero, a wealthy dentist.

Mogulesko, playing the young pimp of the first act and the old drunk of the second, appeared in the third as Shprintze the Matchmaker.

Sixteen-year-old Bessie Kaufman, soon to be Boris Thomashefsky's wife, saw the play in Philadelphia, and wrote: "I saw one actor, one genius, one Siegmund Mogulesko. He did not play Golman; he lived it! On the stage the young criminal of the Odessa street, fire in every movement. . . . With every glance of his eyes, you saw his soul! And in the last act, Shprintze! Not the flaming boy, not the old drunk, but Shprintze herself, a real Shprintze from home! Hard to tell it was Mogulesko, not a 'her,' but a 'him'!"

Abe Cahan, who saw the play later in New York, was thrilled by the great performance: "From the moment Shprintze the Matchmaker was seen, the whole theatre did not stop storming and thundering with applause. The Yiddish quarter talked of nothing but the wonders Mogulesko showed in playing three different characters, and all of them great. A born genius he was, and his personality was as marvelous as his art. His talent and charm lit that foolish play with rays of divine fire. He bewitched us with his singing and his acting alike. His every turn was loved. From that day on I was his most ardent patriot!"

The Roumanians played in Philadelphia until the summer months and then toured the nearby towns. By the fall the repairs of the National were completed, and they went back to New York.

Thomashefsky saw them go with a sigh of relief. He had been worried the whole time that they would stay in Philadelphia and compete with him.

19

The Revolt Against Goldfaden

> There were strikes everywhere, one heard of them all over the country. I believe there was something in the American air that caused them, for in London, no matter how bad things had been, we had at least stayed together.
>
> JACOB ADLER

In January 1887, Abba Schoengold, regarded at that time as the greatest dramatic actor in the Yiddish theatre, arrived in New York. He was warmly welcomed by the Roumanians, and was talking terms with them when their offer was unaccountably withdrawn. Finkel became unapproachable, and Schoengold got only embarrassed evasions from the rest of the cast. He could not fathom who in the troupe had opposed him, and it was some time before he understood that he had been dropped. He was stunned by the blow.

With no other alternative, he accepted a place in the Oriental company, a comedown that marks the beginning of this actor's tragic decline.

He was not the only one to meet with reverses. In February of the same year, not long after the tragedy at the Prince's Street Theatre, Jacob Adler and his troupe arrived. Both Yiddish theatres had been sent word they were coming, but the New York actors cold-shouldered them. Though the troupe waited a long time at Castle Garden, no one from either theatre appeared.

"Not one of the Yiddish theatre family found it needful to

greet forlorn wandering colleagues come for the first time to a strange land," Adler writes. "We went outside onto the grass, we looked in every direction, hoping for one face we knew, for the sound of one familiar voice. No one came, though in both troupes were actors I knew well, some I had even reckoned as friends. For this behavior there can be only one explanation, the terrible poverty of the Yiddish theatre in those days. Both troupes probably thought of me as another burden they would have to carry. They knew, too, that swimming along with the big fish were a whole shoal of little fish. They feared, I suppose, that with our coming, their poor little fish pond on the Bowery would grow even more crowded and muddy."

The troupe passed through New York without so much as a look at either of its Yiddish theatres. Adler had the address of Drozdovitch the tailor, and he and his actors left New York the same day they arrived. They got to Chicago in time to share the tailor's Purim feast, and over the haman cakes and wine, Adler and Drozdovitch talked business.

Matters went well enough, and in a short time the troupe was installed in the Madison Theatre, a house in the heart of the Jewish quarter. They had some success there, but after Passover Adler tells us things began to "fall on the buttered side." The small Chicago audience had seen all their plays, and the actors had nothing new to give them.

Affairs went downhill with frightening speed. Though Adler and Keni Liptzin earned little more than the others, they were blamed. Bad feelings developed, ending with a split in the company. Half the troupe left to give their own defiant performances in a neighboring hall, and Adler had to find amateurs to fill out his cast.

"One can easily imagine what came of all this," he writes. "In the cramped little Jewish quarter of Chicago, where not even one theatre could remain on its feet, two were now competing. And competition in those days meant insults, slander, couplets sung from the stage, leaflets on the streets. Our competitors plastered the whole quarter with posters against us, and I can't say we were altogether innocent of the same tactics. If both sides did not go to greater lengths, it was because even slander costs money, and money neither of us had. We tormented each other a little longer, each driven by his need, and naturally both fell. Finished, Yiddish theatre in Chicago. We both went under."

The actors scattered. One got a job driving a hackney cab, another as a messenger for an insurance firm. Oberlander and his wife fell back on the usual resource of the impoverished Yiddish player, a small, poor restaurant in the Jewish quarter.

Adler himself walked the hot Chicago streets, trying to raise money to go on. His friends lived in different parts of the vast city, and there were days when he walked miles from one to the other. Often when he got there he refused the food they offered, ashamed to let them see how badly he wanted it. A diamond merchant by the name of Kean would have backed the troupe, but the offer came too late. The actors had scattered to the four winds, and could not be reorganized.

Always at Adler's side through the hopeless Chicago days was the motherless Abram, Sonya's child. One night while Adler and Kean were talking late in a wine cellar, the boy fell asleep on a bench. The sight awakened Kean's pity. "You can't raise him like this, Adler, without a home or a mother," he said with reproach. Kean offered to take the boy, bring him up properly, and see that he got an education. The Keans were fine German Jews, kind people with an orderly home and children of their own. When Adler left Chicago, his son remained there with the Keans.

The Oberlanders also stayed on. Of those who had sailed with him from Riga, only Keni Liptzin was still at his side—the only one left of the old days, the time with Sonya.

Adler's return to New York went all but unnoticed; far more important people had arrived. Spivakovsky had found his way over the ocean, and with him, on the same boat, Avrom Goldfaden.

The actors were excited by Goldfaden's arrival. The Roumanians, especially, wanted their old master to see how well they played, and how they had prospered in their new home. The whole troupe went to meet the boat, a gala performance of *Shulamith* was given in Goldfaden's honor, and he was formally invited to enter the Roumanian company as an honored guest.

The actors apparently thought adversity had tempered that imperious nature. They were in for a shock. Goldfaden informed them in icy tones that he would enter their theatre only as its director and head. "I must have my own troupe," he said. "I can be part of no other."

The Revolt Against Goldfaden

"At these words," writes Kessler, "we got frightened as sheep who see the wolf. The big actors saw they would once again be nothing more than Goldfaden's employees. The small actors were scared, too. They were used to the old troubles. They did not want new ones."

The Roumania Opera House had not been leased to the actors, but to Levy and Roth, who had put up several thousand dollars as "key money." Goldfaden convinced these men they would do better with him as head of the theatre. The marquee was accordingly changed to read Goldfaden Opera House, and a production of *Bar Kochba* was announced under his personal supervision.

Rebellion broke out. An emergency meeting was called, and the actors declared in hot speeches that they would rather die of hunger than be Goldfaden's slaves as they had been in Russia and Roumania. When the managers threatened to organize a new company, it was open war. Max Karp, Sophia Goldstein, and the Finkels sided with Goldfaden. The others walked out in what may well have been the first actors' strike in America.

Their action was in the mood of the times. This was the era of Debs, the era of the first great railroad strikes. Although the mere suspicion of unionism meant blacklist in 1887, strikes and riots raged throughout the country, and the Jewish labor movement, in a first lusty infancy, was a force making itself felt on the Lower East Side. Street meetings were held there twice a day, the mood was militant, and the orator on his soapbox like as not a fiery young revolutionary just over from Russia.

The strike went on for over a month, a bitter struggle marked by clashes with the police. Kessler himself was arrested four times, taken to the Essex Street police station, and each time bailed out again.

"Though we were not organized, we were steel and iron!" writes the actor Leon Blank. "I cannot remember a better strike. The public struck with us! Hundreds of people joined us on our picket line, and patriots gave out handbills denouncing the scabs!"

An anonymous set of verses distributed during the strike has been preserved in the memoirs of Boaz Young. Since it is the only one of these compositions to survive, we set it down in the original Yiddish:

> "Mogulesko, unser lieben
> Mit sein Compagnia, fartrieben,
> 'N scabs, *velcher a 'shtick' sichen
> Seinen auf sehr platz farblieben.
> Aveck, bahelfer, fin dem ort
> Vie es hobn geshpielt kinstler dort!
> Azoi sugn alle, umetum—
> Fin New Yorker Publikum!"* *

Goldfaden rode the storm as long as he could, and then gave in. Friends of the strikers bought out Levy and Roth. The marquee was changed to read Roumania Opera House again, and the victorious actors came back.

As often happens, however, both sides had lost. The company could not make up its deficits. A new owner, Frank Pillings, bought the house and reopened it as the National Theatre. The Yiddish actors were out.

Goldfaden's position was also desperate. He had received no royalties from either of the theatres for the use of his plays, and when he tried to write new ones, he found he no longer had his old talent. The edict against Yiddish theatre had hit Goldfaden harder than anyone else; it had struck him down at the height of his creative life, and he never recovered. He put on a few performances around New York, and a little later tried to start a dramatic school. But though the Yiddish press supported him, nothing he touched succeeded.

Abe Cahan ran into him now and then in the office of a literary weekly called the *Folk's Advokat*. Cahan was usually pleased to chat with him, for the playwright was lively, intelligent, and always interesting. What struck Cahan most forcibly was how strongly Goldfaden had *felt* the Yiddish actor of that time. Though he himself had rarely acted, his speech, his way of dress, his whole manner showed this influence.

"He was very sharp in his criticism of Hurvitz, Lateiner, and Sheikevitch, playwrights who had taken his place in the theatre," Cahan said. "At times he used expressions that could not be printed. But he spoke with humor, often with a smile. He still called the actors 'Dovid' and 'Moishele' as he had when they came to him, mere boys, to learn their trade. He said they

---

* "Mogulesko, whom we love,/Driven out with his troupe,/And scabs, seeking a piece of money/Remain here in their place./Away, low slaves, from this spot/Where artists have played!/So say we all, yes, everywhere—/We, the New York public!"

were ungrateful, that he had taken them from deepest poverty and ignorance, that it was he who had 'made them into human beings.' "

How Goldfaden managed at this time is unknown. According to the peppery Bessie, he came to Boston at one point "With torn shoes." What happened between himself and Thomashefsky is recorded by neither, but Goldfaden was soon back in New York, and once again in financial straits.

The Roumanians, without a theatre, were saved by an organization called the Order of David's Harp. This society, formed by Hurvitz and Yechiel Schreiber, brought together the world of the lodges and the world of the Yiddish theatre. Subscribers paid a membership fee of two dollars. For this they were promised the equivalent in theatre tickets, seven dollars a week in the event of illness, $500 as a dowry for an eldest daughter, and $700 in the event of death. Hurvitz went from lodge to lodge, making a German speech everywhere about David and his heavenly harp. The theatre chorus went with him, psalms were sung, and thousands of people joined.

Through David's Harp, the actors were able to lease a theatre at Eighth Street and Fourth Avenue owned by John Poole, an actor who occasionally had written sketches for Tony Pastor. The Roumanians opened at Poole's at the end of August 1887, and Hurvitz organized a giant procession with music, horses, streamers, and flags. Trumpets blew, the chorus sang, Hurvitz made speeches, and patriots ran about telling everyone of the glory and riches of the new Order.

Abe Cahan, now writing for the New York *Sun*, had a journalist friend who wanted to see the parade, and the two men joined the crowd on Canal Street. The parade, starting at Schreiber's Cafe, was to march from there to the new Yiddish theatre on Eighth Street. "In the front row," writes Cahan, "greeted with loud 'Hurrahs,' came Hurvitz himself, a short, thickset man with dark hair, a little Spanish beard, a high hat, and streamers across his breast. Beside him, also with a high hat and streamers, his minister and second-in-command, Yechiel Schreiber. The parade had been organized like some great festival of the people, and Hurvitz and Schreiber were cheered all the way."

Cahan turned away from the spectacle, depressed. "This is what the masses want!" he told himself. "Give them Tammany politicians and Hurvitz!"

David's Harp collapsed almost immediately. Hurvitz bought himself a carriage and four horses, built himself a house in the country, and there it ended. The subscribers howled, and Hurvitz was openly denounced in the press as a thief, but nothing could be done.

The Roumanians opened with a crippled cast. Hurvitz had to lie low until the hullabaloo died down. Sophia Goldstein and Max Karp, just married and in disgrace as strikebreakers, had to go back to the Oriental. Finkel, also a strikebreaker, was out entirely—without a theatre for the rest of the season.

With Finkel out, Heine was quick to see his chance. Deserting Silberman at the Oriental, he joined Kessler at Poole's. With him he brought Sara Heine, Abba and Clara Schoengold, the playwright Lateiner and Max and Sophia Karp, now forgiven for their part in the strike. For the first time the two troupes played together.

Naturally, there were collisions and clashes. Schoengold, who had gotten small parts from Silberman, got no parts at all at Poole's. Kessler could not bring himself to give so much as a place on the stage to the actor once so far above him. The two men finally had it out, and strong words were exchanged. After this Schoengold went back to the Oriental and played whatever Silberman gave him. If there was an ache in his heart for his lost career, nothing on the subject is known to have passed his lips.

Another more serious clash took place between two actresses already met in combat. Kessler, starring in *Bar Kochba,* had to choose between two prima donnas, one with a more remarkable voice, the other with a finer dramatic gift and a more classic style. Kessler chose Sara Heine to play the heroic Dena, and cliques immediately formed, throwing their support to one side or the other.

Kessler and Sara, lost in their parts, were barely aware of the storm. These two shared an ideal unknown to any of the others. Each of them had trembled before a vision of art, fearing to fall short, to be found unworthy. Sara had studied dramatic art in Odessa with the Viennese director Gritzkopf, and the standards he had set were always before her. Kessler had studied nowhere, but reached instinctively for the highest.

The cast was amazed to see the surly, angry Kessler, so rough and impatient with his actors, turn gentle as a child with his new leading lady. She liked his character; he loved her presence. She had faith in the crude, unformed Kessler; he discerned, under the glitter and show of the actress, the more dazzling flash of intellect. This was not easy to see, and few indeed, saw it, for she was a woman of simple, direct emotions and entirely unschooled all her life in everything but art.

A friendship of this kind was dangerous, and especially so for the woman. Ever since the days of Rosa Friedman, certain virtuous ladies of the Yiddish theatre had been careful to draw a line between themselves and the whores. No middle ground existed; every actress fell on one side of this line or the other. The least misstep, a glance, a mere innocent smile, was enough to expose the sinner to innuendo, insult, and actual persecution. Only with care could even an old and ugly woman escape slander in this rigidly puritanical theatre. The beautiful Sara Heine, adored by the public, failed even to guard herself.

The whole company was aware that violent quarrels were going on in the Heine household, that there was talk of divorce, and that Heine in one of his rages had thrown his wife's photograph to the ground and trampled it. Sara soon felt the change in her position, for of all the women in the troupe, only the little soubrette Clara Schoengold remained at her side. This gentle creature, so devoted to her husband and children that no whisper of reproach ever touched her, refused to desert her friend.

The marriage was somehow patched together. Sara feared a divorce that would cost her both her sons. The friendship that had raised such a storm came to an end, and the incident was closed. It left her with a lifelong contempt for all respectability. And she never forgave the mean jests and sly insults that had once embittered and poisoned her youthful heart.

In the fall of that year three people went back to Europe. Spivakovsky was the first to go. He would undoubtedly have become a leading actor had he remained, but he did not like America and would not stay. "No matter how much better it may be here," Spivakovsky said, "it is dearer to me there!"

Goldfaden followed. He stayed a time in London, then went on to Paris, where in a letter to Sholem Aleichem, he expressed hope of having good business. Notable in his Paris cast were Max Rosenthal and the soon-to-be-famous Anna Held.

Goldfaden had a good house at his Paris opening, but the cashier ran away with the money. Sometime later he is writing desperately to his publisher, Dineson, urging him to sell his poems at any price. "The Frenchman has been here twice for his rent," he writes. "I do not ask for clothing or food."

In a letter to Sheikevitch, he complains of asthma attacks and says he is spitting blood. "My disease shows how the hardships I have gone through in the Yiddish theatre have affected me. I was always healthy, of healthy stock, but so be it! Because of my illness, I must not become excited or overstrain my nerves."

Later that year, we find him recovered and in Lemberg. Here he wrote one of his last plays, *Times of the Messiah*, a piece containing some bitter autobiographical references to his days in America.

The actor Kalman Juvelier, in the Lemberg cast, tells us that Goldfaden was particularly good at explaining to the actors the inner motivation of their roles. "Scenic imagination he also had in plenty," Juvelier adds, "and in spite of the limited means at hand, the father of the Yiddish theatre was often able to achieve remarkable effects."

The leading lady of the Lemberg troupe was a young singer named Bertha Kalisch, later to be renowned on both the Yiddish and the American stage. This actress found in Goldfaden none of the arrogance and pride others have described. She declares, on the contrary, that the actors in Lemberg loved him, and that he had only to appear for the whole theatre to "light up with his presence."

The Lemberg engagement ended in a quarrel with the owner of the theatre. Money was owing to Goldfaden, but the company was hard pressed, and he left without asking for it. After this he seems to have gone into actual want. Walking at night through the Yiddish quarter of Lemberg, and hearing behind lit-up windows his own songs, he asked in his bewilderment, "Don't they know, as they amuse themselves and give their parties that the composer is wandering about on the streets without even bread to stay his hunger?"

The proud nature was bending at last, learning its bitter lesson.

Of the three who left America, Adler was the last. After endless trouble, Keni Liptzin was taken into the Roumanian troupe, but neither of the companies wanted Adler. Finkel did not like him, and he could not come to terms with Silberman about his parts. He wandered about for a time, gazing at the sky between the first tall buildings of New York, and at last went back to London.

His youthful bride was waiting for him there, but it was the thought of Jennya Kaiser that had drawn him back like a rope. Jennya was a leading lady now with a troupe of her own. Yiddish theatre had picked up again in London, yet Adler did not stay. Perhaps some hope he had sank again. We know that he visited Jennya and saw his son, and after that left for Warsaw, where his wife apparently joined him. He remained in that city two years, receiving there a very great acclaim.

At the end of that time he had grown too famous to be ignored. When he returned to London in 1889, both Heine and Mogulesko were waiting to take him back to America.

20

Russian Soldier, Jewish King

> Don't forget there were no moving pictures yet where people could see for ten cents a production that had cost millions. Yes, I was the only one who dazzled the public with electric lights of every color, glittering palaces, gold and silver toys. I always did better than my competitors! Girls, women, everyone ran to see Thomashefsky!
>
> BORIS THOMASHEFSKY, *My Life*

Heine had gone all out to advertise his new star. Adler arrived in New York to find posters splashed with the words "Greater than Salvini!" and proclaiming that the *Nesher haGadol* — the Great Eagle — had flown to the shores of America. The phrase "Greater than Salvini" angered Adler, who did not want it thought he made such a claim. Because his name had been linked to the world-famed Italian tragedian, he opened in a comedy, *The Beggar of Odessa.*

It was apparently destined that every major Yiddish actor should stumble on the threshold of his American career. The Beggar, a legend in London, failed completely in New York. The audience, expecting a tragedy, was puzzled by the comedy lines, and scene after scene went by in a deathly silence. As the first-act curtain fell, hissing was heard; and the manager of the theatre, in a panic, rushed out and told the audience he had been deceived in Adler, an untalented, third-rate actor.

Though a whisper started in the cast that the London star was "not for New York," there were a few who saw the worth of his performance. Sara Heine, who had played his daughter, came to his dressing room to express her respect and admiration. If we are to judge by later events, her gesture made an impression on an actor feeling all the smart of his ill usage.

Adler made a second appearance later that week in a play called *Under the Protection of Sir Moses Montefiore*. Once again he suffered a failure.

"He did not succeed," writes Boaz Young, "until he appeared with his own handsome, naked face and in the uniform of *The Russian Soldier*, or *Moishele Soldat*. Adler played his role with high melodrama, shouted beyond human strength, and when the curtain fell the walls shook with applause."

The Russian Soldier was such a success that Heine grew uneasy. He had agreed on a partnership with Adler on his performances, and now began to regret the division of such large profits.

Soon after this, Finkel, forgiven for his part in the strike, came back to Kessler at Poole's. Heine, ousted, did not go back to the Oriental. Instead he got the backing of some businessmen, closed a deal with Frank Pillings, and took a five-year lease on the National. Yiddish theatre was entering a new phase. From now on Heine and Finkel would vie for supremacy, with Silberman hanging on, a poor third, at the Oriental.

The battle soon grew hot. Finkel, with more stars, put Heine out of the National and brought his own company in. Heine, far from beaten, brought off his major coup. He stole Mogulesko, and with this greatest star, got the Thalia, the best theatre on the Bowery. Adler, his dramatic star, took Abba Schoengold out of the Oriental and finally gave him some parts worth doing.

Schoengold was at this time already showing signs of the eccentricity that gained such a hold over him in his later years. One of his peculiarities was a mania for adding to his costume. No matter what he was playing he would put on side whiskers, a plume, a cloak, a scarf, a sword. He had a special passion for medals. Adler tells us that when he appeared in London as Bar Kochba, he was so covered with tin decorations he looked like a man in armor. Adler, who loved him, describes him as the best "second man" he ever had. But the "second man" is not the leading man. Schoengold played Da Sylva in *Acosta*, the Cardinal in *La Juive*, both great parts, but second.

La Juive, especially, was a bone in his throat. Adler, playing the Jew, Eleazar, had so many pious speeches that the audience had barely left off applauding before they began all over again. One night, in the big prison scene, Schoengold as the Cardinal suddenly exclaimed in deep tones, "Do you think it is easy for me to ask you to give up your faith? Know then, that I myself am a Jew forced to hide his Judaism." As the audience sat breathless at this revelation, Schoengold whipped a prayer shawl from under his red robe, wrapped it around himself, and crying in a heartrending voice, *"Shema Isroel, Adonai Elohenu!"* he made a terrific exit.

When Adler asked in amazement how he had allowed himself such a liberty, Schoengold replied, "Do you think you will always have the whole delicious little goose to yourself? Give me for once a taste of the gizzard!"

Adler played at the Thalia until the spring of 1890, when a violent quarrel broke out backstage between himself and Heine. Adler, holding up the curtain, insisted that Heine live up to the terms of their partnership. Heine, with more than one reason to dislike his star, temporized. As the two men argued, the curtain went up and an actor called Laibish Gold came onstage in Adler's role. Adler left the theatre immediately.

The following night Kessler came into the Thalia and took over Adler's role. Heine had guaranteed him $15 a week if he would leave Finkel.

Adler, after brooding for some days, sent a letter to Boris Thomashefsky.

This young man was no longer an unknown quantity. He had acquired a power in the profession, for he was creating what would later be "the road" for the Yiddish actor. Kessler, Mogulesko, and Keni Liptzin had all played to his audiences in several cities, and both the Oriental and Roumanian troupes had toured under his management in the summer months.

Receiving Adler's letter, Thomashefsky came at once to New York. He found the London star at the Occidental Hotel on Broadway and Broome Street. Young Mrs. Adler had finally joined her husband. She arrived in New York in her ninth month of pregnancy, and soon after gave birth to a daughter, a little girl she named Tzirale (later Celia). The hotel room was full of actors visiting her.

"It made my heart ache," Thomashefsky writes, "to see the great Adler with his beautiful, clever eyes staying in this run-down hotel. He sat and joked, his majestic form in a torn silk jacket, his feet thrust into out-of-shape slippers. He made everyone laugh, but in spite of his jokes, I felt his heart was bitter."

The young mother sighed, displeased that her husband talked so lightly, and at last said in a weak voice, "Yakobshe, what good are these jokes? Mr. Thomashefsky came from Philadelphia on business."

Adler put on a high hat and a handsome coat, and took Thomashefsky to a Jewish restaurant on Canal Street. He wanted to play *Uriel Acosta* in Philadelphia. The two men got along well, and quickly reached an agreement.

As they were parting, Adler with some abruptness told Thomashefsky he wanted Sara Heine to play the role of Judith. "She is the only one with the figure for it," Adler said. "And she plays it well." Thomashefsky was surprised, but without indiscreet questions agreed to engage her.

Thomashefsky's cast in Philadelphia was made up largely of his own family. He had married Bessie Kaufman a year before, starting her in the troupe as a soubrette and soon after making her his leading lady. The new Mrs. Thomashefsky had not yet developed the voluptuous figure or the famous "chesty" voice of her later years, but she was bright with blonde beauty, she dressed herself exquisitely, and had a willful, heady charm all her own. She was already a strong box-office draw. Sara Heine, recognizing a creature female as herself, got along very well with Bessie Thomashefsky. And in fact, these two remained good friends all their lives.

Little Emma, youngest of the Thomashefsky sisters, had taken Bessie's place as comedienne of the troupe, sharing her scenes with another child actress called Sabina Weinblatt. Two other sisters of Thomashefsky filled out the cast as character actresses, and their husbands had been pressed into service, too, one as company prompter, another as cashier. Pinchas himself was still on hand, his son's right-hand man in the matter of new plays for the public.

New plays were, of course, the problem. Pinchas did what he could, and Thomashefsky himself turned out a number of musicals, some of them decided hits later in his career. When the supply ran low, Thomashefsky would go to New York, visit one of the Yiddish theatres, and come back with a couple of tunes and a "theme." Bessie tells us that when the company played the Chelsea in Boston, Thomashefsky made a trip to see the Lateiner success *Judah Maccabee*, and came back with the plot scribbled on the back of an envelope.

"Since he had the plot," says Bessie, "he and Pinchas could

fill in the prose. Music they scratched together from other plays. Boris wrote one or two new songs, and in three days' time, father and son are ready with a new masterpiece for the Yiddish theatre."

This kind of fare was good enough for Thomashefsky's humble public, but he wanted to make a splash with Adler's *Acosta*. He took a good theatre on Halstead Street, and was excited to see well-dressed people in the audience, some in evening dress. Adler had a triumph in Philadelphia. Ladies threw flowers to him from the boxes, and after the play young people waited outside the theatre and gave him an ovation at the stage door.

Philadelphia was a wide-open city at that time, and there were parties and suppers after every performance. Sara Heine was gay as she had not been since she left Russia, and Adler, too, was in the best of spirits. "Thomashefsky understands business" he told his companion joyfully. "He will make us rich!"

Gossip about these doings was soon circulating in the profession, and disquieting rumors were beginning to reach Mrs. Dinah Adler. She came to Philadelphia one day unannounced and in an excited state of mind. Apparently she did not find her husband in his own room, and a violent scene erupted in the little Jewish hotel on Pine Street. Adler had to leave town to prevent a great scandal. Mrs. Heine moved into a furnished room and remained there in seclusion. She had never gotten over the horror she had felt when her husband trampled on her photograph, and she was resolved now to have her freedom.

Thomashefsky gave out handbills explaining that illness had obliged his star to leave the cast. Fortunately, Dinah Adler, who had played some performances in New York, stayed on as a guest star in her husband's place. This allowed Thomashefsky to finish the season. He was thinking of a vacation at the sea when a letter came from Chicago. "Take Sonya and come," Adler wrote. "I leave everything to you. Chicago is a good city for Jewish theatre, and we can do well here."

"This I knew without him," Thomashefsky remarks with some annoyance. "I had already played several times in Chicago, and always with success."

All the same he gave up his vacation plans. He and Mrs. Heine traveled by coach to Chicago, and all night the enamored Sara talked only about Adler. She was madly in love and declared she was going to divorce Heine and marry him.

The reunion of the lovers was marred by an unfortunate occurrence. By mistake Thomashefsky and Sara got off the train at the first Chicago stop. They found themselves at six in the morning in the stockyards, with not a horsecar, a carriage, or a living soul as far as the eye could see. There was nothing to do but walk, trusting to luck. Both of them were carrying heavy valises, and Sara had also brought a hatbox. They had to pause every few steps, put down their luggage, and rest.

After wandering in this miserable way for an hour or two, they came on a policeman who told them they were only a short distance from their hotel. Borne up by the hope of food and rest, they toiled on. As they turned the corner of Twelfth Street, Thomashefsky saw a tall silk hat moving about on the street. He was about to call out, but stopped himself in time. Adler was not alone. He was deep in talk with a young woman.

Thomashefsky tried to steer his companion to the other side of the street, but as the hotel was in plain view ahead of them, he did not succeed. There was no way to prevent the meeting, and in a moment the four came face to face. Mrs. Heine gave a startled scream, the girl took fright and ran away, and the two actors had a job between them to quiet a hysterical, shocked, and badly disillusioned woman.

They managed to get her into the hotel, but Sara insisted she was returning at once to New York. Since she would not go to Adler's room, Thomashefsky got her another. Here she had hysterics, wept for her wounded feelings, and flung tearful reproaches at her lover. In the end, hurt and helpless, she gave over and forgave him, but her love had received an injury from which it never entirely recovered.

Thomashefsky was shocked at how badly Adler had managed his affairs in Chicago. He was living in a wretched back room of the hotel, with a broken bed, a broken chair, a candle on the table, and nothing but a transom to admit the light of day. He had not been able to get a theatre, had not found anyone to help him. "I thought he was a businessman," Thomashefsky said. "I found out you could not depend on him. A great artist, a tried and tested actor who knew every trick of the trade. He liked to tell humorous stories, to play practical jokes, to sleep late, but in business—a child!"

Thomashefsky looked up a saloon keeper who had backed him before, but the man had put his money into some other venture. Things looked bad. Thomashefsky's troupe was waiting in Philadelphia, and unless he found a theatre they would break up for the summer.

At the last moment Adler took Thomashefsky aside and told him with some embarrassment that Mrs. Heine had some pieces of jewelry. Adler could not ask her himself, but felt they might raise some money with these valuables. "Tell her she will get them back as soon as we begin to play," Adler urged. "And that the troupe will also give her a beautiful present."

Thomashefsky went to Sara's room and found her packing. Since they could not play, she was going back to New York. After hearing Thomashefsky out she silently gave him a ring and two bracelets. He says the jewels fetched $800 at the pawnshop, but Thomashefsky's lordly sums must always be greatly reduced. Whatever the amount, it got them a good theatre, the Standard, for the two summer months.

They hurried back with the good news and found Sara in tears over her jewels. "The bracelets and ring were not from you," she said to Adler in tones of deep reproach. "It was my husband, Chaimovitch, who gave them to me. From you I have had nothing—only trouble and pain."

Adler did not answer. And truly, he was a cause of grief to every woman who loved him.

They played all summer at the Standard and in the fall moved back to Halstead Street. Hurvitz joined them there, and they had a success with his new play *The Johnstown Flood*.

They were looking forward to a good season when two visitors appeared: Henken, the German manager of Poole's, and Adler's old London friend Mandelkern. They had come with a proposition: Finkel had taken the National, and Heine was in the Thalia. Poole's was standing empty. They wanted Adler to come in.

Thomashefsky felt they were doing well and begged Adler to remain in Chicago. But Adler, more than anything, wanted to compete with the actors who had not allowed him to play. He and Sara left for New York with Henken and Mandelkern. Thomashefsky played on in Chicago, but his successes there gave him no pleasure. He felt he was lost in a backwater, and longed to be with the greats of New York.

His moment was at hand. Some weeks after Adler's departure, a telegram arrived with the message: "Come immediately. You and entire family engaged at the National Theatre." It was signed by Maurice Finkel.

Three days later the whole excited Thomashefsky family was in New York. As soon as they arrived, Thomashefsky left the others at a hotel and went to the theatre. It was strange to remember, as he approached the National, that it was here he had played Yiddish vaudeville with the Golubocks. The Bowery had changed since those days. The Germans were prospering, moving uptown; it was becoming a Jewish neighborhood. Three Yiddish troupes were now giving nightly performances—Adler at Poole's, Heine at the once-German Thalia, and the Roumanians at the National. The Oriental was closed and dark; its days as a theatre were over.

Thomashefsky was pleased to find the Roumanian cast assembled to greet him, but his pleasure vanished when he learned the reason for this welcome. Kessler had left the company and gone in with Heine at the Thalia. Thomashefsky was needed to replace him. Posters were already out, announcing that the following night "Thomashefsky, America's Favorite," would appear in Lateiner's operetta *David ben Jesse*.

"But Mr. Finkel and greatly respected colleagues," Thomashefsky said in despair, "I do not know *David ben Jesse*. I have never even seen it! Why have you done this to me? Why didn't you tell me?"

"Too late!" said the laconic Finkel. "You have already been announced. You will have to play it."

Actors crowded around, pleading with him not to refuse. Finkel gave him the score, sat him down with the fiddler, and promised him a dress rehearsal the following afternoon. Everyone tried to give him courage, and the great prima donna Sophia Goldstein, now Sophia Karp, came up to him and urged him not to give up. "Study, Thomashefsky!" she said. "Learn the role. Don't let yourself be shamed after Kessler!"

"And what Sophia did not say in words," the susceptible Thomashefsky adds, "she said with her beautiful eyes!"

Perhaps Sophia's eyes inspired him, for in fact he did well at the dress rehearsal and was applauded by the whole cast. Even Finkel gave him a rare *"Molodyets!"* He qualified it, however, by adding, "But it is the audience tonight who will be your judge and jury. And God have mercy on you if their verdict is 'No'!"

At these words Thomashefsky went ice cold, and his nerve left him completely. He revived a little as he dressed for the performance, for indeed he looked extremely handsome in Kessler's costume.

In this operetta, the young shepherd David makes his entrance, singing, into the palace of King Saul. Thomashefsky had often played to a well-filled theatre, but never in his life had he walked out onto such a stage:

"On the throne, Max Karp as the King. Seated beside him, the Queen—our beloved Bena Abramovitch. On one side of the throne, the Minister and the High Councillors—Siegmund Feinman, Max Abramovitch, and Abba Schoengold. On the other, the Princess—Sophia Karp. On the steps, the Jesters—Rudolph Marks and Siegmund Mogulesko. Near them, the Soothsayer—Maurice Finkel. And in addition to this stageful of stars, twenty or thirty extras and chorus members!"

Thomashefsky took heart, made his entrance, and was encouraged at the end of his solo by applause from both audience and actors. "Because a singer I was!" says Thomashefsky. "If you were not a singer you were not the pupil of Nissim of Belz!"

The song once over, the dialogue began. This took place in German, for both Lateiner and Hurvitz considered Yiddish a language proper only for comic scenes. King Saul had the first line: "Say, youth, who art thou?" To this Thomashefsky was required to answer in German, "I am David ben Jesse of Bethlehem." Instead, the nervous actor answered, "I am David ben Jesse of *Bais Lacham*," lapsing at the last word into his own language.

The mixture of German and Yiddish in one speech was a rare gaffe, and hilarity broke out in the audience. The actors, too, were choking with laughter. Thomashefsky, without faltering, said, "Oh, great king and all your kingly family! You need not wonder at my words, for in Chicago that is how we Jews speak German!"

He was surprised by a crash of applause from the audience. The actors joined it. They, too, were heartily sick of the absurd *Deitchmerish* they were forced to speak, truly a jargon that was neither Yiddish, German, nor anything else.

Thomashefsky went through the rest of the evening without a blunder, and after the third act Feinman took him out before the curtain. In a ringing speech, he told the audience that it was this same Boris Thomashefsky who as a fifteen-year-old boy had raised the curtain of the Yiddish theatre in America. "And tonight," Feinman concluded, "we welcome him into our Yiddish theatre family. Now and forever, Thomashefsky is with us!"

Pinchas and Chaya Baila, in their box, wiped away tears of

joy, the audience responded with stormy applause, and the curtain went up on the cast, all with flowers in their arms. Mogulesko and Rudolph Marks led the new young David forward, and Schoengold, Max Karp, and Finkel brought him a great harp made of flowers.

He had made a debut to be remembered.

Both Kessler and Adler soon realized they were faced with a serious threat. Kessler was directly affected, for he had been the king of these historical operettas. Adler suffered as well. He had to take the better plays off the boards in order to keep up with the competition.

Thomashefsky does not conceal his satisfaction at these triumphs: "The Yiddish theatre of that day stood on Lateiner and Hurvitz!" he declares. "To look like a star, an actor had to wear slashed doublets, golden crowns, cloaks of satin. All of us did it! Kessler wore a hat with a long feather, bare feet, and a shirt with red patches. Adler, to outdo him, wore a bigger hat with three feathers, a naked throat, a spangled throw over his shoulders, and to make it more realistic, he put on chains, bracelets, and long Turkish earrings. I soon showed both of them I could play that game! I put on a crown, a sword, chains, bracelets, silk hose in three colors, and three cloaks instead of one! If they had thunder, I had lightning. If Kessler sang the Evening Prayer, I sang the Prayer for the Dead. If they shot with arrows, I stabbed with daggers. If they killed six of the enemy, I killed all of them with one blow. If they came in on horses, I came on with three horses and a golden chariot. And believe me, next to me they looked like plain foot soldiers!"

Abe Cahan, recalling how he began to see Thomashefsky's picture and posters on the East Side, writes, "In those days heroes, even biblical ones, wore short jerkins that displayed their legs, and Thomashefsky's legs were the finest in the Yiddish theatre. An operetta at the National would run month after month, while Kessler and Adler had to change their program every week."

The fact is that Thomashefsky thoroughly enjoyed these spectacles, while Adler and Kessler looked down on them. Kessler in particular loathed them. Surveying himself one night in a full-length mirror, he broke out cholerically, saying, "All day long I am a human being, I speak like a human being, act like a human being. At night I must dress myself up like a turkey, like an idiot! If I went out in the street like this people would throw stones at me for a lunatic. Here they shout bravo!" Kessler expressed this disgust even on the stage. In the love duets, he would stand as far as possible from the prima donna, singing, "I love you, no, no, no!" or "Thou art not mine, I am not thine!" In the most heroic scene he would wipe his nose on his sleeve. He often substituted unprintable words for those in the text. The audience did not catch these interpolations, but the actors did.

Once, in *A Father's Curse,* a melodrama by Siegmund Feinman, Kessler came out of his dressing room in an outlandish costume and began tearing strips from a newspaper and pasting them to his forehead. The actors watched nervously, but nobody dared question him. Siegmund Feinman was in agony. Not only was he the author of *A Father's Curse,* but he was also playing the father, and he foresaw some antic that would ruin his play. And, in fact, in the scene where the father pronounced a curse on the villains about to execute his son, Kessler, instead of reading his lines, began to bark like a dog. He left off to say in a disgusted tone, "A play! An audience! Come, father! Finish it up! Fall on my neck and let's pull down the curtain!"

The curtain fell, and some scattered applause came from the bewildered audience. Feinman was furious, but Kessler burst into demonic laughter. "Did you hear them?" he demanded. "Do they deserve anything better? I barked like a dog, meowed like a cat, and they applauded!"

Critics commented sharply that Kessler had no respect for the public. The new playwright Seiffert wrote resentfully, "If Kessler does not like a role, he does not have to play it. But he has no right to behave hatefully and prevent other actors from playing."

In the summer of 1891 Sara Heine secured a long-sought divorce from her husband. The marital ties of Jacob and Dinah Adler were legally dissolved soon after. Maurice Heine did not speak to his former wife again for forty years. It was different with the unhappy, deceived Dinah Adler. She remained Adler's friend, and even continued to play in his troupe, billed as "Madame Dinah" until some years later when she married the actor-playwright Siegmund Feinman. She was from first to last the innocent victim of her own affections. Though Siegmund Feinman, best of men, brought up little

Celia Adler as though she were his own child, Dinah Feinman never forgot the man to whom she had first given her heart.

The two divorces were handled with some tact, but there was nothing quiet or discreet about the wedding that followed. Adler took the Atlantic Garden for the occasion, champagne flowed, the whole Yiddish theatrical and newspaper world came to celebrate, and the new Madame Sara Adler, who loved nothing better than a show of splendor, was in her element at last.

Their union, though rocked by storms, endured. With this new "Sonya," Jacob Adler buried his dead, put away the memory of the past, and took up his life again.

Theatrically, too, it was a new beginning. Poole's opened in the fall of 1891 as the Union Theatre. Adler's first offering was Zolotkev's *Samson the Great,* a play Salvini had done. He followed this with *Quo Vadis* and then *La Juive.* He was through with the operettas, the only Yiddish actor to dispense with the old repertoire entirely and to rely on classics and modern European plays.

"For to live forever with jest and song," he writes, "was hardly my idea. The time had to come when our theatre would touch on the deeper places of life, when plays of a more serious kind would find a place on our stage. And this task of deepening our theatre, of so to speak, 'tragicizing' it, fell, in great measure, on me. Here I was forced to stand alone. Those who have grown into the old way, those to whom the old is not only a material good but also a spiritual income must oppose the man who brings the new. This is the fate of the innovator, the reformer.

"I was weak as a singer," Adler continues. "I had not a good voice, nor, I confess it, a very good ear. But is this why I turned away from the operettas and leaned toward purely dramatic plays? I think not. From my earliest days on the stage I gave first importance to those roles where the actor works not with his feet, but with his face, voice, eyes; not with jests and comic antics, but with the principles of art; not to amuse the audience with tumbling and *salto mortales,* but to awaken the deepest emotions of their soul."

The Union Theatre drew such good audiences that Kessler, Mogulesko, and Feinman were all soon playing there. Adler had caught the pulse of the times. The new press, speaking for the intelligentsia and the labor movement, was demanding a Yiddish theatre that would be an educational force among the masses. Abe Cahan, in particular, kept up a savage barrage against *shund* (trash), accusing Hurvitz and Lateiner of turning the stage into a circus and of preventing better playwrights from approaching the theatre. Such attacks seriously damaged the prestige of these playwrights. It is not the first or the last time a group of intellectuals, running counter to the trend of the day, have ended by changing it.

The power held by Hurvitz and Lateiner was also being seriously weakened at this time by the growing prestige of certain actors. In his article, "Yankev P. Adler as Artist and Man," the critic Rothbluth writes: "In those first years, when the whole repertoire consisted of foolish operettas and badly adapted European plays, a repertoire without an idea, without even a language, actors like Adler, Kessler, Mogulesko, Thomashefsky, Sara Adler, Keni Liptzin, Bertha Kalisch, and Bessie Thomashefsky showed their artistry. Even in bad, senseless plays, a moment of power, a lightning flash of talent held the simple audience electrified, and astonished those intellectuals who occasionally fell into a Yiddish theatre. These early actors were giants, miracle workers. And their miracles were performed not for material gain, but out of limitless love of their art."

Certain feats of acting have become legends in the Yiddish theatre. Leon Blank relates that Kessler, weary of heroics, begged for a "bit" usually given to an extra, that of an ancient Hebrew warrior. The hoary general, his victories long forgotten, silently follows a group of soldiers across the stage and exits after them—nothing more.

Kessler's performance held the actors hypnotized. Leon Blank writes: "We saw the old soldier, ready to die for his flag. And such was Kessler's magic that we saw all the others, too. We saw that one was a coward, that another was heroically brave. We saw how they had fought around him, how they had died around him! And the audience understood! They felt the greatness of it! A thunder of applause at his exit. Kessler was happy that night as I have never seen him. And truly, it was one of his finest moments."

Reviews of the day constantly refer to extraordinary acting. Abe Cahan writes that when Adler came on as Samson with his jawbone, the audience "sat paralyzed, afraid Samson would destroy the world with his terrible strength." Keni Liptzin, playing a double role in Morris Rosenfeld's *Rachel and*

Leah, transfixed the poet-playwright with her "hair-raising transition from holy beauty to devilish laughter." Thomashefsky himself did not understand his own success. An old cracked phonograph record of his voice rings to this day with how the man belonged, heart and soul, to his people. It was for this he was loved, not for his fine legs.

A great audience already existed—an audience of Zionists and socialists, working people and intellectuals, rich and poor. Patriotic about America, nationalist in their devotion to the promised *Palestina,* remembering always the lost home, the lost life, the *shtetl* of their past, this public was waiting for the curtain to go up on the true Yiddish theatre. All that was needed was a man who would find for that theatre its subject and its voice.

Since everything was in readiness for him, this man now stepped forward.

21

A New Lear

God said, "Jacob my child,
Have no fear, my own dear child,
Amalek, Baal, and others, too,
Vanished as into a lake,
But you, my only child,
Remain a people now and forever!"
"Enough of torment," Jacob cried.
"Raise up your child as you have promised!"
"Be not afraid, Jacob, my true servant!
No one asking me for justice goes forth without it.
Have no fear! Keep my law!
And laugh at their armies and their might,
For I will smite them, yes, I will scatter them
When the time comes!"
                Song, *The Yiddish King Lear*

In the spring of 1886 Abe Cahan had found a printer who let him use his press and gave him a corner of his shop as an office. Here Cahan and a man called Rayevsky got out a sheet they called *Die Neie Zeit—The New Time*. The paper lasted only a few weeks, unable to compete with the ultra-Orthodox *Judische Gazetten*.

A year later, in the aftermath of the tragic Haymarket riot, the German editor of the Chicago *Arbeiter Zeitung* was hanged as a spy. A tremendous upsurge of radical feeling followed this event. Abe Cahan joined the Socialist Labor party, and together with a fiery, young orator named Louis Miller made a second try at a socialist newspaper.

In honor of the martyred Chicago editor, the new weekly

was called the *Arbeiter Zeitung.** It sold for three cents a copy, and was an immediate success. Cahan had a way of explaining socialist theory in the light of Talmudic ideas, a technique extremely effective in allaying the doubts of his Jewish readers. Philip Krantz, an editor Louis Miller had brought over from London, quickly recognized that Cahan had the more popular touch. The bluff, genial Krantz put an end to the growing tension in the editorial office by making Cahan unofficial editor. Circulation immediately jumped from three thousand to seven thousand. Within a year, half a dozen Yiddish dailies and weeklies were holding their own along with the *Arbeiter Zeitung.* Cahan had created a mass reading public who could not get along without their Yiddish newspaper.

Intellectuals of every shade of opinion began to gather around the new press, and a remarkable literary era began. Stories, novels, and poems were coming from Y. L. Peretz in Poland and from Sholem Aleichem in Russia. Eliakum Zunzer, whose songs were loved in the wine cellars of Odessa, opened a print shop in New York and wrote for the anarchist *Frei Folk's Stimme (Free People's Voice)* and the literary *Folk's Advokat (People's Advocate).* Morris Rosenfeld wrote his heart-rending poems of the East Side ghetto for the *Arbeiter Zeitung.* And so dense and so vocal was the gathering of Russian-born novelists, journalists, poets, and philosophers on the Lower East Side that the center of the Jewish quarter was laughingly known among them as "East Broadway-skaya Oolitza."

In 1891 a remarkable newcomer found his way to the socialist contingent of this colony. Jacob Michailovitch Gordin, the man destined to revolutionize the Yiddish theatre, had been in turn a farmer, a journalist on Russian newspapers, a worker in the shipyards of Odessa, and an actor in a traveling Russian company. The son of a well-to-do merchant of the Ukraine, he had been brought up in the spirit of the *Haskala,* a modern, enlightened spirit strongly colored nonetheless by Jewish tradition and belief.

A radical tendency and a fiercely inquiring mind carried him further than this. At twenty Gordin formed a society called the Spiritual Biblical Brotherhood, which denied all dogmas, denied the hereafter, opposed the rituals of marriage and circumcision, and demanded that the Scriptures be reevaluated as moral rather than religious doctrine. The Spiri-

---

* *Workers' Newspaper,* later issued as the *Jewish Daily Forward.*

tual Biblical Brotherhood, angrily attacked in the Yiddish press of Odessa, was disbanded in the repressions following the assassination of Alexander II.

The members tried next to found a Jewish farming colony. Profoundly affected by the teachings of Leo Tolstoy, Gordin felt his people would find their salvation in a return to the soil. When his group was refused permission to buy land, Gordin went off by himself to a remote village and worked for three years as a farmer.

Following this we find him acting as unofficial editor of the *Elisavetgrad News* and contributing powerful stories of Jewish life to the *Odessa Messenger* and the Jewish magazine *Sunrise*.

Some years later, he is again attracting the attention of the police as head of a Tolstoyan Circle, a group that gave Bible readings to the peasants, interpreting the scriptures in the light of Tolstoy's ideas. The readings were stopped by the police, and Gordin, in danger of arrest, left Russia. He came to America with the old *Am Olam* plan of forming communistic Jewish colonies in the New World.

His arrival created a stir on the Lower East Side, for he was a journalist and writer who had made something of a mark on the Russian literary scene. He was, besides, a man of extraordinary presence, outstandingly handsome, with the flowing beard of a prophet, a head of thick, dark, curling hair, wonderful eyes, and with something about his whole, tall, stalwart person suggesting pride, honor, and intellect.

His sketches, dealing with Jewish life under the Tsarist terror, soon were appearing in the *Arbeiter Zeitung*. Newspaper work, however, did not bring him enough money to support his wife and family, and Philip Krantz advised him to try his hand at a play for the Yiddish stage.

It was this London editor who brought Gordin and Adler together in the meeting that was to open the great era of Yiddish theatre. Adler had just produced *Titus Andronicus, or the Second Destruction of the Temple, Judith and Holofernes,* and *Hymie in America,* the last a comedy by Rudolph Marks. He had heard of Gordin as a great writer, a follower of Tolstoy. He went to the appointed place as a thirsty man goes to water.

"We met in a wine cellar on the East Side where the Yiddish intelligentsia used to gather," Adler relates. "As usual, I spoke of my great need for better dramatic material. I had in my pocket a German play of some kind, and I gave this to Gordin, saying, 'Here is a ready-made subject. Perhaps you could make a play for it for the Yiddish theatre.' Gordin, with a fine gesture, gave the book back to me with the words, 'If I write a play for you, it will be a *Yiddish* play, not a German play with Yiddish names.' "

The journalist went home and wrote his first drama, *Siberia*, in one inspired spurt of energy, feeling, he says, "like a scribe at work on the Sacred Scrolls." He had drawn his plot from an item in a Russian newspaper. An innocent man is sentenced to exile in Siberia for a crime he did not commit. On the way the prisoner escapes, joins his wife and children in another part of Russia, takes another name, and begins a new life. Years pass. He has become a respected, useful member of his community when a competitor, jealous of his success, discovers his secret and betrays him to the police. Torn from his family, the innocent man goes out once again into exile.

The cast at the Union Theatre did not like *Siberia*. There were no heroic scenes, no nationalistic speeches, and they did not understand the realistic dialogue. "What kind of prose is that for an actor?" one of them asked afterward with disapproval. "My grandmother can also talk so!" And Mogulesko, who had heard about the Biblical Brotherhood, muttered, "This Jew with his black beard, strikes me as an anti-Semite."

Adler went ahead with the play over the objections of the cast. He believed in it.

Gordin stayed away from the theatre all week. When he came to the general rehearsal on Friday, he discovered that Mogulesko had written comic songs and couplets into his part, and had inserted a whole section of the opera *Hernani* into the second act. When the playwright objected, Mogulesko answered indifferently, "A play must have music, no?"

Gordin rose to his feet, his eyes flashing. "I will not allow it!" he shouted. "By what right have you done it?"

Mogulesko flared up. Tempers mounted. Kessler and Max Karp sided with Mogulesko. Others joined them. Adler, defending Gordin, was shouted down. The quarrel rose to a height, and Mogulesko, in a rare outbreak of anger, cried, "Away, anti-Semite! Your breath should not be near our theatre!"

Gordin left the theatre, and did not come to the premiere of his play.

The audience, accustomed to sensational effects, was bored by *Siberia*. Halfway through the second act, laughter was heard, followed by actual hissing and "boos." Adler was in despair, and when the act was over, came out before the curtain. His presence produced a silence, and in a voice shaking with emotion, he addressed the public in a historic speech.

"Disgraced and lowered I stand here, *gospoda*," Adler said, "my head bowed in shame that you do not appreciate the masterpiece of the great Russian writer, Jacob Michailovitch Gordin. *Gospoda*, if you would open your eyes and your ears, if you would open your hearts and your understanding, believe me, you would not laugh at this play, but would give it your most serious attention."

His words had an effect on a certain part of the audience, and they broke into applause. "Because of this," Leon Blank writes, "the third act went better. The scene where Adler pleaded with Kessler not to betray him to the police made a strong impression. And in the last act, when Mogulesko, playing the servant, came to the line, 'Master, we are parting!' he burst into real tears, and he could not go on. And the great artist played the scene in such a fashion that weeping was heard throughout the audience."

Because of this success, Mogulesko apologized to Gordin. The others did the same. And when he came to see his play the following week, actors and audience joined to give him a warm reception.

Siberia did not draw the public, but it got a good press and created intense curiosity in the profession. Bessie Thomashefsky writes: "We all heard that in the Union Theatre there was a strange play where the actors talked as though they were in their own home. Everyone was curious about the play, and even more curious about the new writer. There were different opinions about the play itself, but everyone agreed that Gordin was a man of intellect, a real judge of theatre. Because of this some of the actors were frightened of him."

Siberia ran only two weekends. Gordin's second play, *Two Worlds*, had an even shorter life. His third effort was turned down. Either Adler did not like it or he could not overrule others in the company. Gordin, in need of money, took the play to Finkel.

"In the Thalia Theatre we are rehearsing a little masterwork by Lateiner," Bessie Thomashefsky relates. "As we are at work, Finkel's assistant tells him a Jew with a beard wants to see him. 'Tell him to come back on Purim,' Finkel answers, and goes on with his rehearsal. The assistant comes back a second time, breathless. 'Mr. Finkel—it is Gordin!' A moment later Gordin walks in, a tall, broad-shouldered man with a flowing dark beard, a neat, shabby dark suit, a wide-brimmed black hat, a walking stick. He wants to sell us a play called *The Russian Pogrom*. He comes back next day, reads us the play. We sit, listen, whisper. We decide to take the play."

Gordin was paid $60 for *The Russian Pogrom*, and offered an additional $5 a performance if he would play the role of the *pristav*, the police lieutenant. He accepted on condition that he had final say on everything connected with the production. According to Bessie, he came to every rehearsal and decided on everything, even the costumes. He played his own role in Russian, with not a word of Yiddish. When Finkel tried to put a song into the first act, he walked out, taking his manuscript with him. The actors brought him back, and Finkel promised to take the music out. "If you must have a song, I will get you the authentic White Russian music," Gordin said.

The actors were surprised by a good house on the opening night. The playwright dressed with the others, made up with the others. When he made his entrance in the second act, the public stood up, waved handkerchiefs, and shouted, "Hurrah for Gordin!" The actors were astonished, Gordin himself forgot his lines and stood dazed, muttering, "*Shtoh?* What is happening?"

He had only one short scene, and it was marked by a startling incident. The Russian *pristav* enters a Jewish home. The mother of the house hates and fears the police officer, but hoping to placate him, sets food and drink before him as a bribe. The veteran character actress Bena Abramovitch played the scene admirably, wished the *pristav* "Good appetite" in trembling Russian, but as she turned away added, *sotto voce* in Yiddish, "Choke on it!"

Gordin's fist crashed down on the table. "*Stop!*" he thundered out. "*That is not in the text!*"

The actors onstage were terrified. The audience, too, sat in startled silence.

Pogrom had a moral success, but was a box-office failure. "It was a pleasure to do a fine play with artistic dialogue," says Bessie, "but the real supporters of the theatre, the great, almighty public, did not come."

In the fall of 1892 this notice appeared in the Yiddish press: "The Union Theatre, under the sole artistic direction of Jacob P. Adler, has been reorganized with the aim of driving from the Yiddish stage all that is crude, unclean, immoral, and with the purpose of lifting the Yiddish theatre to a higher level. The Independent Yiddish Artists Company will present to the public only beautiful musical operas and dramas giving truthful and serious portrayals of life."

Thus Adler informed the public that he would stand or fall with Jacob Gordin.

The feeling in the profession was that he was committing suicide. Mogulesko, Kessler, and Rudolph Marks left him and joined up with Hurvitz at the National. Some of Adler's actors deserted with them. Adler had to fill out his cast with players from Europe. He was even forced to take in some amateurs.

He and Sara were living at this time in a tenement on St. Marks Place. On a cold autumn morning, a tall, rawboned, fair-haired young man was seen to approach this building. After hesitating at the entrance, he walked away, circled the block, and came back again. Boaz Young, three years an actor with an amateur group, was getting his nerve up to ask Jacob Adler for a job. He finally summoned enough courage to enter the house and knock at Adler's door.

A woman in a dressing gown whom he recognized as Sara Adler answered the knock, asked him what he wanted, and calling in a voice full of gaiety and love, "Yakobchik, there is a young man for you," led him into the dining room.

A first child had recently been born to Jacob and Sara Adler, and the father was sitting at the cradle. The little girl, a month old, was sick with a form of colic that had already killed a number of infants. Adler's eyes were sad as he gazed at her.

"What is it, young man?" he finally asked with a sigh. "You want to be an actor, I suppose."

"Half an actor I am already!" Young replied. "In your theatre, if you will take me, I think I might become a whole one."

Young was surprised at his own boldness, but Adler seemed to like his answer. Since Young said he had sung the role of the father in a performance of *Shulamith*, he was told he could "help out" in the chorus, and he was put down for a salary of $7 a week.

Some weeks later, when Young came to rehearsal he found the stage deserted. Henken, the German owner of Poole's, also owned the saloon next door, where Young joined the

A New Lear

entire cast seated around a table. Adler was reading them *The Yiddish King Lear,* a new play by Gordin.

"It will be on the poster from Friday to Saturday," one of the actors predicted. Berl Berenstein grumbled that he had no comedy scenes. Shmuel Tobachnikoff, the juvenile, complained that there was no place for him to do a number. "And what kind of part is it for Adler?" Tobachnikoff asked with a shrug. "To play an old man, an ordinary old Jew in a long coat and a *yarmelke*?"

But Adler remembered a song in the Odessa wine cellars about an old father turned away by his children. He remembered how grown men had wept at that song. And he felt the play would be a success.

Gordin had reset Shakespeare's tragedy in the Russia of the nineteenth century. His Lear is not a king, but a Jewish merchant of wealth and authority, a patriarchal type perfectly familiar to his Russian-Jewish audience. To Adler, this "king" had immediately suggested the Uncle Arke of his youth, loved, feared, and obeyed by all the Adler clan. And he felt from the first reading that this play, this role, would decide his fate in the theatre.

The complaints of the cast soon died away; it was clear from the first rehearsals that Adler was going to do something extraordinary with this part. "Every actor caught the spirit," Sara tells us. "And if any of us clung to the old, bad, undisciplined way, parading himself before the public, striving for cheap laughter, cheap effects, it only reminded us all the more how great was the change taking place before our eyes."

On opening night Adler, already in his costume and makeup, stopped at Sara's dressing room, and said, "Come and see what kind of audience we have tonight!" Sara, looking through the opening in the curtain, saw a theatre packed with a new kind of audience. The entire Russian-Yiddish intelligentsia had turned out to see Gordin's play. Even the gallery was different tonight, filled with a tense, subdued excitement.

The curtain of *Lear* rises on the Purim feast of Gordin's merchant-king. At the head of the decked table, surrounded forty-strong by family, friends, and retainers, truly a little "court," we see the great Dovid Moishele, patriarch and ruler of his family.

"I have in my life witnessed ovations for great artists," Sara writes. "In Odessa especially, such demonstrations could rise to remarkable heights. Adler's Russian-Yiddish 'king,' discovered onstage as the curtain rose, created just such a moment. From the orchestra to the gallery, the theatre crashed! His character had 'taken' before he had spoken a word. And this was nothing to the scenes that came later. He was not an actor, but a force! All of us played with inspiration, but the great figure in his play Gordin had given Adler, and the triumph that night was his own."

The play's action closely follows that of Shakespeare's tragedy, with the characters, even to the Fool, given their modern counterparts. Dovid Moishele is a lofty soul, but he is blinded to the darker realities of life by his power and wealth. Like Lear, he is weary of his duties and decides to divide his fortune among his children. "Kent" tells him he is making a mistake, and the story of Shakespeare's *Lear* is recounted to him as a warning. Unheeding, the aging merchant entrusts his fortune to two unworthy daughters and disowns the third, who will not stoop to flatter him. Milder in spirit than Shakespeare's king, Dovid Moishele feels the youngest daughter will repent and come back, and the first act ends on a note of union, with all voices raised in triumphant song.

The curtain rises again on a darker mood, and the somber domestic tragedy begins to unfold. As Gordin's Lear is not a king but a merchant, so his two wicked daughters are not queens but monstrous housewives. Ignorant, grasping, their energies confined to narrow household concerns, they have only one passion, the hoarding of their wealth. These women and their husbands have long hated the rich father on whose bounty they exist. Now we watch them intrigue to rob him of every vestige he possesses. Step by step, the proud old man is driven back onto the naked cutting edge of life. Shakespeare's Goneril and Regan strip their father of his court. Gordin's frightful daughters bring him almost to death, for in their wolfish greed they deny him the very food that keeps him alive. For one brief moment the father rises up in wrath. With all his old terrifying authority, he demands the keys of the coffer containing the 70,000 roubles of his fortune. Quailing, his daughters yield up the keys. But Dovid Moishele is nobler than his children. Scorning to go back on his given word, he flings the keys back at them together with his contempt.

The play remained in Adler's repertoire for almost thirty years. Those who saw it at the end, this writer among the rest, have since traversed the greater part of their own lifetimes. They remember anger like crashes of thunder, scenes mounting in epic strokes to the moment when the old king, crying aloud his grief, goes out to beg his bread on the street. That cry for alms, that *"Shenkt a neduve der Yid-dish-er Ken-ig Leeeee-ar!"* echoes still across the gulf of fifty years and more.

Ten years after the first performance, when New York critics began taking an interest in the downtown theatre, the following review appeared in the November 1902 issue of the magazine *Theatre*: "The Lear of Adler is . . . a modernized Russian-Hebrew comedy of manners into which the old patriarch and his three daughters are transported in all their emotional picturesquesness, and with surpassing dramatic effect. It is a poignant drama of domestic life, vividly true in its portrayal of middle-class Jewish characters and customs under the Russian monarchy, but world-appealing in its broad passion, tenderness, irony, and intensely human flashes of fun. No finer acting has been seen in New York than Adler's gradual transition from the high estate of the Hebrew father, distributing his bounty in the opening scenes, to the quavering blind beggar of later developments."

Lear meant more to Adler than a mere triumphant performance. With this play the Yiddish theatre, speaking with its own voice, touched at last the universal. The cardboard villains, the plots and counterplots have vanished. It is the dark forces in the human soul that bring on human tragedy. Gordin, teacher, leader, fighter, had taken the greatest possible subject for his theatre—the audience itself. Their dilemma, their struggle, their wisdom and their folly were his grand theme. His stage was to be a platform on which they saw their own lives, saw in powerful human terms the depths to which they could sink, the heights to which they could rise.

For Adler this was the moment of light, the great fulfillment. With Gordin's *Lear* he had come, together with his theatre, out of falsity and into truth.

22

The Great Three-Way Combination

> **SHIMEN**
> Will you come with me, Lemach? We will live together in the city. I will take care of you. And doctors will cure you of your illness.
>
> **LEMACH**
> (*weeps*) Then why did you go away and leave me? (*backs away*) Let me be as I am! Let me be mad! If you make me well and I tell what I know, you will all go mad!
> *The Wild Man*

Adler came out of Poole's, took the National Theatre, and put Gordin's name on the marquee as his dramatist. After several near-failures, the playwright came through with his first original masterpiece.

In the Yiddish *Lear*, a father is brought low by ungrateful children. In *The Wild Man*, Gordin took as his theme the destruction of children by a father.

The play is set in the dark, unenlightened home of the merchant Schmil Leiblach. One of the sons, a student, has escaped this unhappy house. A second has turned into a worthless gambler and drunkard. The third son, a weak epileptic, has been so stupidly, senselessly beaten to "cure" him of his weakness that he has grown up a semi-idiot. This third son, known to the town as the "Wild Man," is the central figure of the play.

From the first curtain rise, when the idiot boy is discovered playing with his own gigantic shadow, the note of terror is struck. From there the action builds to the inevitable tragedy. The father in his dotage has married a woman of the town, a singer in a cabaret. The new wife comes into the dark, unhappy home, bringing with her Vladimir Varabaitchik, her lover and pimp. These two make love behind the old man's back, squander his money, and turn his house over to riots and drunken parties. The besotted husband sees nothing. The young wife rules him, and a daughter who fights her influence is turned into the street.

As the family structure cracks, the idiot boy grows worse, his actions more uncoordinated, his words more whirling. "I, too, want to marry, like my father," he babbles. Nobody listens or understands that the Wild Man, no longer a child, is madly in love with his stepmother. The play comes to a terrible climax. With the whole house asleep, the sick boy reveals his love to the frightened Madame Zelda, his sexuality finally finding its release in the act of murder. Raising high the knife over her body, the idiot cries in his mad joy, "Father! Father! I have married!" In another moment he has cut his own throat, and the curtain has descended, ending the play.

Finkel gave a brilliant performance as the dark-souled Schmil Leiblach, himself the victim of a brutal, materialistic environment. Sara Adler shone as the daughter fighting to protect her home. But the triumph once again went to Adler, who as the twisted, pitiable Wild Man was established once for all as the greatest star of the Yiddish stage.

The Wild Man was pirated by actors for decades. An epilogue was even added in which the worthless son reforms, the father comes to his senses, the daughter is rescued from the streets, and the idiot boy is cured. It is this bastardized version of the play that Franz Kafka saw in 1910. The melodramatic excesses of the production are noted in his diary of that year, but he was impressed by the play, adding, "But Gordin knows what he is doing . . . . The action moves forward, and the obviously great powers of the author begin to work."

With the success of *The Wild Man*, a strike broke out at the National over the issue of fixed salaries. Yiddish companies, as in Russia, still operated on shares, or, as they were called, *marks*. Adler had chafed against the injustices of this system in his youth. The star and manager of his own theatre saw things from a different position. Adler's successes in *Lear* and *The*

Wild Man did little for the small players in his troupe. Boaz Young, bringing home seven dollars after eight performances, wrote: "He took for rent, for costumes, for electricity—there was nothing left for the actors!"

Gordin, the socialist, walked out with the strikers, took up their cause, played a benefit for them at the Thalia, and wrote articles in the *Arbeiter Zeitung* against "Adler's exploitation." It was a short-lived struggle, and a losing one for the actors. After a few concessions were made, Gordin and Adler patched up their quarrel, and the striking actors came back.

We may say in Adler's defense that it was hard, even with a success, to come out ahead at the National, a small house with only seven hundred seats. After the strike he did even worse. Gordin, now the company dramatist, had to grind out plays like any hack, and the theatre suffered a string of failures. Adler was learning what many a theatre man has learned before him, that an unsubsidized theatre cannot exist on art alone. Forgetting rivalries, he joined David Kessler at the Windsor.

Kessler was glad of the new forces, for he had recently lost two of his actors. After years of neglect, Albert Schoengold had turned his back on New York, and gone out on the road as his own master. He took with him the original Odessa manuscript of *Uriel Acosta* and a pirated copy of *The Yiddish King Lear*. Like Thomashefsky in the early days, he formed a troupe around his own family. The gentle Clara, mother now of four children, was no longer young or pretty, and her husband took another leading lady. Clara Schoengold died a few years later, and Sara Adler, who loved her, never again gave more than a cold nod to the actress who had replaced her.

As for Rudolph Marks, he had given up the stage for good, a disappointed, embittered man. He had been cruelly used by Finkel and had never had luck in any other company. His naive plays—*Lost in New York*, *A Sailor in Distress*—had passed their vogue. As a comedian he had always been overshadowed. "I look like Mogulesko, I am small like Mogulesko and have a voice like Mogulesko," Marks said, "but when we begin to play, everyone knows which of the two is Mogulesko!" He took back the name Max Radkinson, and became a lawyer. His part in the history of the Yiddish theatre, however, was not yet played.

Adler and Kessler, joining forces at the Windsor, drew up a joint contract. Adler was to play the comic roles in the historical operettas which were Kessler's mainstay, and the two stars would alternate in the Gordin repertoire with which Adler was now identified.

After four failures at the Windsor, Gordin wrote *Shloimke Charlatan*, a piece of theatrical bravura with a leading role to make any actor's mouth water. The hero of the play has been done out of his inheritance by a scheming older brother. He leaves home, becomes in turn a soldier, a juggler, a singer, an actor, and after twenty years comes home, a drunkard and vagabond. He plays tricks for the village children, juggles, produces an egg out of the air, and in a brilliant monologue, an actor's showpiece, tells them the whole sorry story of his life—all for a bit of whiskey. But wreck though he is, Shloimke is better than his respectable brother. Since he can regain his fortune only by soiling his hands, he gives it up. The curtain falls as the ragged figure takes himself off to the thrilling "Rat-tat-tat-tat" of his own mock army drum.

Adler and Kessler both were dying for the role, and drew lots for the right to the first performance. Adler won. He played the lead on opening night with Kessler in a minor role. The following night Kessler had his turn at the lead. Adler never played it again. Kessler's performance could not be followed; it was too great. His Shloimke was a figure so hypnotic, so full of extraordinary invention and play that the audience released its tension in salvos of bravos at every great speech, every great curtain scene.

The playwright Leon Kobrin wrote: "Kessler's Shloimke was not a charlatan, but a man who has learned to take poverty and injustice with a laugh, a jest, a trick. Under the clown's mask, the buffoonery, one saw the deep loneliness of a human being who had it in him to be good, useful, and who became useless and bad because life had crippled him."

Kessler's admirer, the critic Asherovitch, wrote, "The desire to do something original, something new, is a deep part of the creative artist, and this desire Kessler always had." Because a fellow critic accused Kessler of not knowing his lines at the first performance, Asherovitch wrote: "Even if he did not know his lines, he knew the character, knew the inner feelings of a man who has learned life's hardest truths, who in his fallen state still looks with irony on others, who laughs out of a bitter heart, weeps only when he is alone, and will let no one near him to see the truth of his soul. Shloimke often talks nonsense, but Kessler's very gibberish was so inventive that one remained hypnotized by the sheer brilliance of his word play."

Shloimke Charlatan marked the turning point of Kessler's career. From that time on he was regarded as equal to Adler. And there are critics who feel that in the Yiddish theatre Kessler's was the greatest talent of all.

After *Shloimke,* Kessler and Adler often vied with each other in the same roles, and it is interesting to compare them. One may say that Kessler was at his greatest when he portrayed the elemental passions, while Adler's whole personality suggested the power of intellect, of enlightenment. It would be wrong, however, to restrict either one of them to such categories. Kessler gave one of his most memorable performances as the aristocratic Prussian father of Sudermann's *Heimat.* Adler was known for his "inner" quality, and was often best of all in moments of simple human feeling.

The sun had already risen on that extraordinary stage. Now, with the appearance of Bertha Kalisch, the moon rose.

The prima donna, not yet thirty years old, was brought over from Roumania by Joseph Edelstein as a new attraction. Slender, queenly, with classic features, dark hair, and wide-set tragic gray eyes, the new prima donna brought a nobility to the shoddiest melodrama.

Madame Kalisch had studied singing in her youth at the Lemberg Conservatory. As a child she had seen Annetta Gradner and had never forgotten her. When Goldfaden came to Lemberg she entered the Yiddish theatre as his leading lady and after his quarrel with the theatre owner, went off with him to Bucharest. Here her name reached the impresario of the Roumanian National Theatre, and she was taken on a trial basis to sing the lead in the operetta *The White Lady.* Anti-Semites who came to the theatre planning to insult her threw flowers instead. She was bidding fair to become a successful artiste in spite of her unchanged faith.

Her success, however, aroused jealousy in the theatre, and a tenor in the company warned her not to drink water or to sniff flowers sent by strangers. She became frightened. When Edelstein offered her a New York engagement, she left Bucharest in the middle of the night, breaking her contract, and with her husband and her small daughter came to America.

The new star at first played only singing roles, but soon showed her dramatic gift. For a year or so she alternated with Sara Adler in such popular successes as *Camille, Madame X, Madame Sans-Gene,* and *Zaza* and in literary classics by Shaw,

Gorki, Ibsen, and the great French feminist Brieux—a repertoire superior to that of any stock company of that day.

Bertha Kalisch was a widely read woman, equally at home in Yiddish, Hebrew, Russian, and German. Within a few years she spoke an English of such purity that Harrison Gray Fiske was able to star her on Broadway. From that time on Madame Kalisch played on both the Yiddish and the American stage. In the Yiddish theatre she had a following among the more educated public, and some of her greatest patriots were the actors themselves.

Gordin had brought the intellectuals into the Yiddish theatre. The public, however, like every public, remained unpredictable and essentially indiscriminate. Art and *shund* alike were food for its huge appetite. Just across the street from the Windsor was the Thalia, where Thomashefsky reigned. And between these two playhouses there was continual war.

Hurvitz got his own back after *Shloimke* with the operetta *Rouchel*. This play, a run-of-the-mill affair, was made famous by a song. "Eli Eli" was sung by Sophia Karp in a scene where a Jewish girl was stoned to death in a marketplace. Originally Hurvitz had written a long monologue for the scene, but Sophia, the world's worst study, could not learn it, and two days before the opening, Thomashefsky persuaded Hurvitz that a "number" would do as well. Thomashefsky himself supplied the text, a half Yiddish, half Hebrew version of the psalm, "My God, my God, why hast Thou forsaken me?" The chorus master, Jacob Sandler, set this to music. "Eli Eli," swept the immigrant population of America, and crossing the ocean, became famous throughout Europe. The song had become the national anthem of the Diaspora.

Years after it was first sung on the Yiddish stage, the vaudeville headliner Belle Baker, once herself a child actress in the Yiddish theatre, sang the now world-famous song on the American stage.

The Windsor had just recovered from "Eli Eli" when Thomashefsky had one of the biggest hits in all Yiddish theatre history. As *Alexander, Crown Prince of Jerusalem,* Thomashefsky spoke German, wore tights, played romantic love scenes with Sophia Karp, and drew capacity audiences at every performance.

"Who among the older Jews does not remember how the whole East Side stormed when Thomashefsky played *Alexan-*

der, *Crown Prince of Jerusalem?*" says Abe Cahan. "He was twenty-two at the time, tall and strong, with a wonderful sculptured form. A handsomer prince could not be imagined. Shopgirls gave up the necessities of life to buy tickets to this play."

In truth, Thomashefsky could not be outdone. His overwhelming masculinity was balanced by a softness even more dangerous. His well-known susceptibility crossed the footlights with fatal impact. He appeared like a magical figure amid glittering palaces. His unique diction, with its rolling *r*s and liquid *l*s, brought colors into Yiddish never before heard in that language. He saw himself, the world, and the Jewish destiny as matters of high romance. He was, in fact, a personality impossible to resist. Years later, Stella Adler, asked to describe the actor adored by her family, replied simply, "He looked like a king, he lived like a king and played like a king."

Alexander, Crown Prince of Jerusalem ran all season. Women besieged the box office, and a sensation was invariably produced when the handsome star, wearing tights, came onstage declaiming: *"Vie geflogen komm ich, Mein Geliebte, hier tzu dich!"* *

The entrance never failed to evoke an outbreak of feminine hysteria. At one matinee, a woman rose from her seat screaming, "He is my King, the glorious Alexander!" The lady had to be removed from the theatre as she was beginning to tear off her clothes.

The long lines at the Thalia box office could not be anything but painful to the troupe across the street. Thomashefsky soon suspected that plans were being made for some sort of theatrical coup. He was quite correct. One night Adler announced that he and Kessler would present the greatest tragedy ever written—Shakespeare's *Othello,* with Kessler and himself alternating as Othello and Iago. And Adler added that Othello was no crown princeling of Jerusalem, but a part that only an actor could play.

The speech was reported the same night to Thomashefsky. Stung, Thomashefsky went out before the curtain and announced he would play Hamlet.

Once he had announced it, he had to carry it through. The playwright Seiffert made a translation in twenty-four hours. Keni Liptzin was brought in to play Ophelia, and Thoma-

---

* "As on wings I come, My beloved, here to thee!"

shefsky engaged the German director of the Irving Place Theatre, who coached him in the role, and advised him about costumes, wigs, and scenery.

Rehearsals of *Hamlet* took three and four hours longer than any other play. The actors could not make head or tail of the text, and asked each other with groans what Shakespeare had wanted of them. Adler, who loved a fight, made curtain speeches every night, ordering the audience not to go near the Thalia, and Hurvitz, hurt by all the fuss, came to his star one day and said, "Thomashefsky! I will write you a better play than Hamlet!" — a remark that caused a roar of laughter along the East Broadwayskaya.

Thomashefsky writes, "At the last rehearsal I felt I was breaking! I had seen Edwin Booth in the play, and had once even traveled from another city to see him. The thought that I must play Hamlet was terrible!"

To the surprise of the company, the play was a success. The audience, in fact, was so enthusiastic that at the final curtain a call for the author went up. This demand was repeated after every performance, and one of the actresses finally suggested impatiently that they put makeup on some actor, send him out to take a bow, and be done with it. "Instead we used to ask them to forgive us," Bessie writes, "but Shakespeare lived far away in England and could not come to see his play."

The story, invariably told whenever the subject of Yiddish theatre comes up, may deserve a closer look. To begin with a call for the author is usually heard only on opening night and, to give away a theatrical secret, it is usually started by one of his friends. In this case, it occurred at every performance, and the friend, we will agree, can hardly have been present.

Now, if this audience had never heard of *Hamlet*, neither were they obliged, as the rest of us are, to be thrilled by it. Nobody had told them it was better than any other play. They did not know the famous lines, could not pick out the famous speeches. Yet they shouted for the playwright — and at every performance! Apparently these untutored immigrants, many of them seeing theatre for the first time in their lives, recognized in the play an unequalled tour de force of passion and intellect, and in their enthusiam, tried to call out the author.

Actually, it is hard to imagine a finer response, or one that would have pleased him more.

"We did excellent business with *Hamlet*," Bessie reports briskly, "and played it for three weeks running." *Othello*, too, had a fairly good run. Neither play remained in the standard Yiddish repertoire.

One night Thomashefsky received a message that Adler wanted to speak with him privately. They met at the Central Park Casino, a restaurant not usually frequented by the Yiddish actors. Adler complained that he was suffering at the Windsor, that the classical plays he and Kessler presented had no success, and that business was not what it should be. "He offered me a three-part combination," Thomashefsky writes. "Adler—Kessler—Thomashefsky—and we three will tear up America!"

Thomashefsky, offered a full partnership, talked the matter over with his manager, Joseph Edelstein, and decided to accept.

"In your wildest fantasy," says Thomashefsky, "you cannot imagine what happened in New York. Speculators bought up the tickets and sold them at ten times the original price. The Bowery from Canal Street to the theatre was beleaguered by the crowds, and mounted police had to be called out to see that those with tickets got in."

Thomashefsky never admits to anything but triumph. From other actors we learn that the three-way combination made no such furore. "The audience was not ravished," one actor drily observes. Another remarks merely that "extra benches did not have to be brought in."

It soon became clear, moreover, that one stage is not large enough for three stars. Sara writes: "The moment Kessler came into the troupe, he made it clear he would play only the big roles. At first we thought he could be laughed out of it, but once the actors had their lines and we began to really rehearse, that was the end of the *kibitz*. Kessler did not care about the interpretation of the play; he would sit on the side and give Adler a free hand with that. But as soon as it came to his scenes, a storm began. It got so that the rehearsal without trouble was like heaven. A wrong word, a wrong movement, and it came to scandals, shouting, and even blows. Kessler was not just a strong-tempered man, he had a fiery character. His soul kindled even at rehearsal. At times he became so enraged with the actors that I wondered how a human heart would take it. I was afraid he would kill someone, or drop dead himself of heart failure."

Kessler never understood that the weaker players did not have his powers, and that his demands were torture to them. The wife of one of these men, desperate, sought him out one day and told him her husband came home every night weeping from his insults. "Mr. Kessler, we curse you!" she said. "Our children curse you!" Kessler burst into tears, kissed her hands and begged her to forgive a sick unhappy man.

He could not control these rages, and actually Kessler cursed and swore at the actors even when they pleased him most. "May he burn!" he would exclaim happily. "but the son of a bitch really played that scene."

His salty wit and rough manner were famous in the profession, but Kessler was understood by no one. The theatre was the dark side of his life. Ambition drove him without rest. Adler's fame rankled; he thought himself the greater of the two. He had wronged Abba Schoengold, and it was on his conscience. His biographer, Asherovitch, tells us that during a joyful party onstage, while other actors sang and entertained, Kessler remained on the side, lost in his thoughts, troubled, despairing. When the others tried to include him and insisted he give them a song, he came forward and with tears in his eyes sang the *Mismor l'Dovid*.* There was something tragic in his character, something apart from the others.

At the Windsor the three stars drew lots to decide who would take the lead in each new play. But though Kessler was willing to share honors with Adler, he did not by any means intend to give the same rights to Thomashefsky. When Kessler starred in *Virginius*, Thomashefsky offered as a favor to direct and also play a small role in the third act. "I did not want my husband to direct," Bessie writes. "I knew beforehand that there would be trouble. If Thomashefsky called rehearsal at ten, Kessler came at one. If he made it twelve, Kessler came at three. As soon as Thomashefsky came onstage, Kessler began making faces and imitating him. He played with hate, croaked himself hoarse. Thomashefsky was fresh, alert, made a good impression in his small part."

Kessler lasted no more than three weeks as part of the great combination. He and Adler joined forces several times in later

---

*The Psalm of David

years, but the partnership never lasted. There was an unexplained personal coolness between these two men. They respected each other, but they did not get along.

After Kessler left the Windsor, a notable event occurred. The great German actor Morris Morrison appeared there, playing in German in the Yiddish-speaking cast. Thomashefsky had met Morrison some years back in Chicago when the celebrated actor, in a pitiful condition, sought him out. Because the director of the German theatre in New York had made anti-Semitic remarks, Morrison walked out and soon after left New York. Penniless, he had spent months working as a laborer on a farm. He was ashamed to go back to Germany.

Thomashefsky, shocked by his condition, loaned him some money and arranged a performance for him at the Standard Theatre. Morrison played in German with brilliant success, but the money this performance brought him was soon gone. One night Thomashefsky asked him if he would play Yiddish theatre. Morrison began to weep hysterically and ran into the kitchen. "Boris, you want to ruin me!" he screamed. Some days later, without a good-bye or an explanation of any kind, he disappeared.

Now, years later, he showed up in New York, sought out Thomashefsky and told him it was Yiddish theatre or suicide. Morrison, an incurable gambler, had lost everything at cards. He looked like a tramp and was living on the Bowery. Adler, thrilled to have him, gave him star billing at the Windsor, playing Iago to Morrison's Othello, and Da Sylva to his Acosta. In the Dumas Play, *Kean,* Adler played the role of Kean's manager, a part requiring him to open a door in the second act and to say in reproachful German, *"Herr Kean, the public is waiting!"* For this one line Adler wore a derby, a wig, a costume that made him look half his size, and a roar went up at the sight of him.

Morrison toured in his famous German roles after he left the Windsor, but in the end could not support himself and was forced to come back to Thomashefsky. In his last years he relied entirely on Yiddish theatre.

Renowned in his day as the "Emperor-actor" of the German stage, Morris Morrison died in 1910. He was buried, as he had wished, beside Mogulesko.

Boaz Young, describing Adler during his years at the Windsor, writes, "Adler never copied his last performance but played his part a little differently each time. He liked to have music in his scenes, and this was criticized as not realistic, not modern. But Sir Henry Irving used music for his entrance in *The Bells*. In the Chinese theatre, too, cymbals crash when the hero enters to 'wake up the gods.' Adler knew how to be natural through artistic means. His warmth, his fire he took from the everlasting sun."

Of the actor's personal life, Young writes, "He never drank, never touched tobacco, never touched cards. Theatre!"

This is hardly the carefree, pleasure-loving actor of the early days. Adler, his hair already turning white, is emerging as a figure altogether more formidable. He is beginning to be feared. He is beginning to be hated. There were actors who felt he kept them down. The demands he made on himself were taking a toll. He had sudden, unexplained attacks of hysteria, morose moods when everyone around him fled his company.

Young tells of one of these outbursts on the road in Chicago, when for some reason he lingered a moment at Adler's dressing-room door. The master of makeup was beginning to mix colors on a painter's palette, and Young was hoping for a glimpse of how he worked. "What are you spying on me for?" Adler lashed out wrathfully. "There will be time enough to steal from me after I am dead!"

Pressures, it is true, were mounting at this time. Adler's career was soaring; his personal life was once again in ruins.

It was Thomashefsky who unwittingly had brought about the new crisis. The Windsor management had adopted a policy of bringing over new stars each season from Europe. Thomashefsky, Adler, and Edelstein all had agreed to take turns at this task. Thomashefsky took it into his head to import a certain Medvedyev, a well-known Russian opera star.

This Mikhael Medvedyev had never been subjected to the restrictions of other Russian Jews. He lived in Moscow, where he was accepted in the best society, traveled freely to Berlin, Vienna, and Bucharest, and regularly went on tour in his own land. He belonged to a small wealthy group untroubled by difficulties even during the worst anti-Jewish campaigns. He was eager to see America, and to everyone's surprise, he accepted Thomashefsky's offer.

Hundreds of Jewish immigrants who had admired the singer in Russia went to meet him at the boat, and a great success was predicted. Since he neither spoke nor understood Yiddish, Thomashefsky arranged a concert, the first half of the program to be devoted to operatic arias, the second to folk songs.

Though the first concert drew a packed house, Medvedyev had no success in America. The Yiddish audience of that day was not accustomed to concerts, and did not care for them. After the first, they stopped coming. And though he tried his best, Medvedyev could not learn to speak Yiddish.

The handsome tenor, in the meantime, was stirring up gossip by his unconcealed admiration of Adler's wife. Confronted with angry questions, Sara admitted everything. Adler's incessant infidelities had broken her and ruined her life. She had found a man who respected and loved her. She wanted a divorce. And having spoken, Sara openly made plans to leave for Russia with her lover.

For Adler the sun had gone out. He could not be faithful to her, but as an actress and as a woman, he adored his wife. He fell into a terrible state, became ill, and could not play. Gordin, worried, begged Sara to remain in New York at least until the end of the season, and to this she finally agreed.

Concerned for Adler's health, Sara failed to notice alarming symptoms of her own. She came to a performance one night with a pounding headache and a fever. During the first act she grew weak, her knees trembled. She was trying to get to a chair when she felt liquid welling into her mouth, saw blood on her white dress, and fainted.

A specialist was called the following day, and the worst fears of the family were confirmed. Tuberculosis. A dread word. The case, however, was light, and Sara was assured it could be cured. Two days later, however, a second hemorrhage occurred, and it became clear the illness was more serious than had been suspected.

Some weeks later she was taken in a wheelchair to Grand Central Station. She was on her way to a sanitarium at Saranac Lake. She parted from Adler quietly, without drama. She had been told emotional scenes might be her death, and she was a woman greatly minded to live.

Adler went on as best he could, but it was a bad time. According to Thomashefsky, the theatre remained dark more often than not.

That spring it was Adler's turn to search out new actors, new faces for the public. He was in Europe a little over a month, and when the ship brought him back into New York harbor, he was sighted, granite-faced, at the rail. "Sonya is living?" he shouted harshly.

"Sonya is living!" came the answer. "Living and well."

He took the news with a bitter joy, for he had lost her just the same, and he knew it.

Sara spent six months in Saranac, and another three at a sanitarium in Lausanne. From there she went to Berlin, where a renowned specialist pronounced her cured.

Medvedyev joined her in Berlin, but letters from America were reaching her daily, and the moment of decision found her boarding the boat that took her back across the Atlantic. She could not live with the thought of Adler lost, without a home, his pride broken.

She took her place again at his side and continued at regular intervals to bear his children. Her peasant strength and iron will had pulled her through, and she was never again to know a day's illness. But the old life was over, the old happiness shattered. She had loved greatly and her love had all but killed her. From now on she went her own way. She had her duties as Adler's wife, her obligations as his partner and helper in the theatre. Her life she now regarded as her own, to do with as she wished.

Sara had turned the tables. To the end of his days, Adler loved her jealously and with passion. She never loved him again as she had loved him once.

23

The Meeting in Odessa

> NIKITA
> Mother, O mother! Don't bury it! Don't you hear? It is crying! It is still alive!
>
> MATRENA
> How can it be alive? You have crushed it flat. You have smashed the whole head.
>
> NIKITA
> But it is crying! I hear it still! (*shuts his ears*) I have forfeited my life, I have forfeited it! Where shall I go? (*he sits on the porch steps*)
>
> The Power of Darkness

At this time Thomashefsky and Adler both lived at 85 East Tenth Street. Adler had rooms on the second floor, Thomashefsky on the third. A dumbwaiter, worked by ropes, connected the two flats. Every morning Adler would come into the kitchen in his bathrobe, open the dumbwaiter door, put his head out into the shaft and call deeply, "Thomashefsky, a black year on your head! Thomashefsky, the devil himself go into your bones!"

Thomashefsky remained discreetly silent. He had bested his partner somewhere on the field of love.

Having cursed Thomashefsky, Adler turned his attention to his children. The little ones were not yet of school age, but the oldest girl, Fanya, had to be wakened and dressed. At school Fanya was Frances Adler. At home her father and everyone else called her Nunia. Her teacher had told her she must appear in class with her hair properly braided and tied with ribbons. Since nobody ever bought the ribbons, her father braided her hair every morning with two strips torn from the bedsheet. But if the day were rainy or cold he had not the heart to wake her at all.

In spite of her American birth, this odd child, thin as a scarecrow and with enormous eyes, spoke the broken English of an immigrant. Her Yiddish accent and outlandish clothes made her the laughingstock of the school, and she was happy only when playing with the props backstage.

One summer her father took her to a fine resort hotel where every afternoon a crowd of little girls in organdie dresses played with their hoops on the lawn. Told to make friends with these children, she went up to them and in her absurd mixture of Yiddish and English faltered out, "Maybe you want *shpielen sich mit mir?*"* The whole little crowd scattered with screams of laughter, and the girl turned to see an unforgettable look on her father's face. Taking his daughter by the hand, Jacob Adler said humbly, "Come, Nunia, I'll take you home."

When life on Tenth Street did not please Nunia, she would get on her bicycle and go to her grandmother's. Sara had brought over her parents after her marriage, and the old couple were greatly bewildered by this change in their life. Mrs. Levitzky did not understand the endless crisscross of New York slum streets, each like the other. She longed for her old home in Kiev, where every ghetto lane had its own life and character. She grieved for her husband, the old Zayde Ellye, who sat all day in a dark shop cutting theatre tickets. Nobody knew he had been a king in his youth, a horseman, owner of the greatest riding stables in Odessa.

The old people had been settled in their own dark little rooms on the East Side. But with them had come that tart-tongued Rouchel who had been their mainstay in Russia. Rouchel was to be a famous personage, for it was she who came into Adler's home as its ruler and guardian, who saw to it that kosher laws were kept in his kitchen, and that every Friday the roast goose and Sabbath *challa* were laid out on the dining room table. Rouchel was an *agunah,* a deserted wife, and as such could never marry again. At thirty she looked fifty. But there was something radiant, something of holiday about her whole immaculate person. She loved Adler onstage and off,

---

* "Maybe you want to play with me?"

watched over him like a mother, and it was Rouchel who brought up his children, and later, his grandchildren.

When Nunia was eight years old, a great event occurred in this household. The legendary "brother in Chicago" materialized as a real boy. The Chicago Keans had kept Adler's son for more than ten years. He was fifteen, now, they could do no more for him, and sent him on to his father's care.

Sonya's Abram was now Abe Adler, a tall young man, aristocratically lean and fastidious to a fault. He was very handsome, but one of his eyes drifted upward, the result of a childhood injury. This perpetual wink, which made him entirely irresistible, gave him the greatest distress throughout his youth.

The first sight that met this well-brought-up boy was a child with tangled hair jumping up and down and shrieking wildly for her *"shilkene dresh."* Nunia was demanding to be adorned in her brother's honor. Everyone got up at a different hour in this house, everyone ate at another time. Nobody gave the new brother a room. He slept every night in another bed. "Guests" arrived and stayed for days and weeks, with no one very clear who they were. Whole pieces of furniture disappeared and turned up on the stage. The boy quietly christened his new home "Matteawan.[9]" He treated the children like puppies, troublesome but amusing, robbed them regularly of their allowance money, and told them that Chinamen grew on trees, hung there by their pigtails, and fell off when they were ripe. They believed everything he said. All the children, and above all, Nunia, had fallen madly in love with their older brother. And indeed, the aloof, sporting Abe, later his father's manager and advance man, was to be the most-loved member of this family.

Several years later, a second brother was to make his appearance in this house. This startling new addition came from England. Charles Adler went directly from the boat to the theatre, and coming up to the box office, said, "I want to see Jacob Adler—my father."

The dramatic appearance of Adler's son made a sensation, and a legend arose that he had arrived with a gun, determined to force his father to recognize him. The story, like so many others, is untrue. Adler had twice been to London, and had both times seen his son. Charlie Adler had come to America on professional business. A gifted dancer and for several years a member of a Russian ballet company in London, he had been engaged by the Ringling Brothers as a bareback rider. He was on his way to Chicago.

The Adler girls made a great fuss over their English brother. Sara, who did not like her husband's children with other women, deliberately turned her elegant back on him. The young man stayed only one night in his father's house. In the morning, Sara, seeing he was not planning to remain, came up to him and tried to make amends for her rudeness.

In the fall of 1899, Thomashefsky learned that Miner's People's Theatre, old home of Irish-American melodrama, had failed. The troupe had vacated, and the house was standing empty. American theatre was no longer possible on the Bowery; it had become an Italian and Jewish neighborhood. Thomashefsky, always alert for an opportunity, went to see Miner. Rudolph Marks, now a lawyer, completed the deal, and three days later the lease was signed.

Adler did not want to leave the Windsor, and wept when he saw the workmen carrying out the scenery. "Thomashefsky, we have done so well here," he said pitifully. "Why must we go to another theatre?" Edelstein and Thomashefsky laughed at him. They said he could have better business at the People's, a house farther uptown, in a better neighborhood.

Thomashefsky threw a gala party at the first rehearsal. There were masses of flowers, a table stretched the whole length of the stage, the orchestra played catchy theatre songs, and Thomashefsky made a speech. Adler tried to speak too, but was overcome by emotion.

The People's opened with *Sonya of East Broadway*, a play by Leon Kobrin, a young writer sponsored by Gordin. Thomashefsky had his own separate premiere. He had signed a contract that he and Adler would never appear on the same evenings.

"We went into the People's with our right foot," Thomashefsky writes. "Good business, and every year better! Edelstein was a canny man; he put a stone on every dollar he made. Adler was the same. I was the only one not worried about a fat bankbook. I spent my money and enjoyed it."

In the years that followed, the Thomashefskys lived high. They kept a carriage and horses, a twelve-room house on Bedford Avenue in Brooklyn, a bungalow at the sea that had electric lights, a garden with a fountain, and goldfish, and another twenty-acre house in Hunter, New York, where he built an outdoor summer theatre called Thomashefsky's Paradise Garden. Each of the Thomashefsky boys had his own Arabian horse, and Thomashefsky's dressing room at the theatre was fitted out with golden mirrors, blue tapestries, lamps of every color, and marble statuettes.

Adler had no need for these luxuries. Though he loved fine clothes, he did not understand them and wore whatever his tailor advised. A dreamer by nature, he was not particularly conscious of his physical surroundings; he would have lived in the same tenement for the rest of his life had Sara not taken him out of it. When she moved the family to a brownstone on East Seventy-second Street, Adler went with deep misgivings. He had no faith in this new way of life, and did not think it would last.

The days of poverty in the Yiddish theatre were ending nonetheless. And with the new prosperity came unrest and division.

When the United Hebrew Trades Council held its first meeting in 1888, the only two Jewish unions were the organized typographers and a small union composed of the Yiddish theatre chorus. The actors had sent delegates, but were rejected. Since they were paid on the shares system, they were branded as capitalists.

In 1900 a new struggle broke out, a battle embittered by emotions that had rankled for years. The small players had no standing in the profession. They worked a seven-day week, with no days off, played matinee performances on both Saturday and Sunday, put in long unpaid rehearsal hours. They could be hired and fired at will; they were subjected to abuse and insult. Kessler, in his rages, had even been known to strike his actors.

Their greatest grievance, however, was the absence of a fixed salary. From week to week these people did not know what they would be paid. In a holiday week they might take home twenty to forty dollars; if business happened to be bad, they might get no more than two or three.

In former years, Kessler, Mogulesko, and Feinman had jumped at a guarantee of fifteen dollars a week. Now the big stars were beginning to make fortunes. Rebellion was brewing. The small actors wanted an end to the system of marks. They wanted to be united with their fellow workers under the protection of the now powerful Hebrew Trades Council.

In this last desire they were helped by Joseph Barondess, a

The Meeting in Odessa

great figure in the Jewish labor movement. Barondess, among the founders of the Hebrew Trades Council, took up the cause of the actors and got them accepted.

The strike spread rapidly to every other Yiddish theatre in the city. When police broke up their picket lines, the actors linked hands, lay down on the street-car tracks, and swore they would not budge until they won their conditions. Yiddish theatres outside New York supported the strike and refused to send scabs. Thomashefsky, Adler, and Edelstein had to play with wives of musicians, dressers, and even with people off the street. "Everyone played but the actors," as one player wryly remembers.

After a few weeks, Thomashefsky weakened. One suspects that this best-hearted of men could not bear to have the actors dislike him. "At first we were against them, but then we were sorry," is the comment of this hard capitalist.

Adler and Edelstein gave in soon after. The actors won their demands, and twenty years before the formation of Actors' Equity—in December of 1900—the Hebrew Actors Union of New York received its charter from the American Federation of Labor. A year later, Local 2 came into being, with jurisdiction over all theatres outside New York, and soon after Local 3 took over vaudeville houses and music halls.

Though the small actors earned, on the whole, less under the new minimum wage then they had before, they were proud of their union, proud of their status as independent workers. Fixed salary became the policy in every city in America. For good or for ill, the Hebrew Actors Union had become a controlling factor in the Yiddish theatre.

In the spring following the actors' strike, Adler took a trip to Russia to see his family. He was accompanied on this journey by his wife and the eight-year-old Nunia. They stopped in London for a few performances at the Pavilion Theatre, went on to Germany, and from there, by train, crossed the border into Russia. They entered illegally. There was, in fact, no other way; everyone who came back had to do so by bribery.

Odessa was beautiful as ever, but changes were there all the same. The genial Feivel Abramovitch was no more. And Hessye was old now and very frail.

Adler's sister, Soore, was a married woman now, and her brood of golden-haired children were in a fever of excitement to see their uncle, the actor from America. Adler's photograph hung in the best room of the house, and everyone in Odessa knew he was rich and famous.

He had come intending to take the family back with him, but could not carry out his plan. Hessye had lived in Russia all her life and said she meant to die there. No plea, no argument moved her. She was resolved in her decision, and when mother and son embraced at parting, both knew it was for the last time.

Adler has recorded one incident of this visit to Odessa:

"Walking in the street one night, my eye was drawn to a singular figure— a beggar with a stick, his beard wildly overgrown, a vacant idiotic look in his bulging eyes, and a shivering hand outstretched to the passersby.

"I took him in with one sharp look and called out, 'Rosenberg!'

"He peered at me and said, 'Ah, so it is you, Yankele!'

"It was impossible to talk with him. His tongue was lamed, his thoughts confused. But a gleam of the old intelligence slowly lit in his eyes. 'You've done all right over there in America, Yankele,' he said with a knowing look. 'So share, eh, with an old comrade?'

"I pulled out everything I had, Russian roubles and American dollars tumbled together. But at the sight of the money Rosenberg seemed to change his mind. He stole a look at me, laughed uneasily and muttered, 'Up to your old trick, eh, Yankele? Stage money!' And with that he took himself off.

"I ran after him shouting, 'Rosenberg! Wait! These are American dollars! They are better than your Russian roubles!' But it was no use. Lame, half paralyzed, he still moved with an amazing agility. I looked a long time, but did not find him again.

"It was our last meeting, and that was such a meeting that better it had never been. The memory of it has stayed with me the rest of my life like a leaden weight on my heart."

He asked everywhere for his friend, but people did not want to talk about Rosenberg. Adler had come at a terrible time. Russia was nearing the 1905 revolution. Every Jewish family had known tragedy. Pogroms were raging. Friends had joined the underground and been arrested, exiled, murdered. In these days when human beings were tested beyond the limits of their strength, Rosenberg had done some deed that could not be forgiven. No hand was held out to him. He had been cut off from the Jewish community.

Shortly after he returned to America, Adler heard that Rosenberg had fallen sick, been taken into the Odessa hospital, and died there.

The eight-year-old Nunia carried back memories of a *datcha* by the Black Sea, of the wild countryside outside Odessa, of the wonderful stone-blind grandmother. She taught the children at home the droll names of the Russian cousins—Manya, Fanya, Vanya, Sonya. She longed for the day they would come to America and she would see them again.

Adler came home exhausted and ill. He could not play, felt unable to go on, and asked Thomashefsky to release him from his contract.

Word spread that Adler was leaving the stage.

Thomashefsky had always talked him out of these moods, but this time things looked serious. He and Edelstein drew up a contract, offering their partner the sum of ten thousand dollars on condition that he did not appear again in New York.

This document made a bad impression. Adler found that after all he did not wish to give up the theatre just yet. He stopped talking to Thomashefsky, and in his anger decided he would play again, and moreover, what no one else would dare to play.

For Adler, for all Russians of his class, the name of Shakespeare himself dimmed beside that of Tolstoy. No writer, living or dead, could stand with the great nobleman, friend of the peasant, friend of the Jew, friend of all mankind. Rejecting a new play by Gordin, Adler chose as his next production *The Power of Darkness*, a tragedy of peasant life. It was the first production in America of any play by Tolstoy. This was the era of the happy ending, and the greatest writer of the modern age was unknown here as a dramatist. The play, one of the strongest in the whole of dramatic literature, is seldom produced on any stage, for it cannot be done without very great actors.

Photographs of Adler and Tolstoy appeared on the posters, and the notice in the press read, "*The Power of Darkness* by Count Tolstoy is true art, not false, not imitative, not distorted." According to Thomashefsky, these words were aimed at Jacob Gordin. The cause of their quarrel, however, is unknown.

Thomashefsky writes: "Adler and I were still living then in the same house on Tenth Street. For some reason we were not talking at the time, but from my dining room window I could see the room where he worked. Coming home late after the theatre, I would see him at his desk, writing, erasing, going over the translation again and again, often until daybreak, his whole soul in Tolstoy's great work."

Thomashefsky, curious as to how rehearsals were going, found the actors nervous and angry. Because the play had so large a cast, a number of them had to double in their roles. Mogulesko played two parts, some of the smaller actors had taken three and even four. They had consented to this not so much for Adler's sake as out of respect for Tolstoy, and now there was resentment.

"Adler doesn't know himself what he wants!" the actors complained to Thomashefsky. "One day he tells us to take the speeches quietly, calmly, the next he shouts that he wants strength, feeling!"

Adler, it is true, had aspirations for this play as for no other. He wanted perfection, and was making this demand on a superb but undisciplined cast, used to running through their parts at rehearsal and performing only on opening night. It was a bad system. Thomashefsky knew it himself and when actors assured him they would be "fine at the performance," he would answer drily, "Yes, very fine! They will cry when they have to laugh!"

On the day of the general rehearsal Thomashefsky received a phone call from the theatre. "Thomashefsky, come quickly!" Adler said. "You will have to play my part tonight! I cannot do anything with these coachmen, these amateurs, these charlatans!"

"I did not wait for him to insult each actor personally, but ran to the theatre," Thomashefsky writes. "This is what I found. Adler was running through the lobby. After him ran Mrs. Adler, after her Edelstein and his wife, and after them a whole squadron. Everyone was shouting, 'Adler! Mr. Adler!' The 'sides,' the actors' roles, were falling on the floor of the lobby. When Adler saw me, he threw the play and all the parts on the floor. 'Devil take them, these lackeys, these bathhouse attendants!' he exclaimed. 'Now they don't want to double in their parts! The stagehands are bringing in the scenery, the property people carrying in trunks, sacks—all this when I have to rehearse. I cannot, I cannot anymore!' He turned to me. 'Thomashefsky, take the play, take my part, rehearse with them. To hell with it. I'll be a tailor, a shoemaker, a doorkeeper, I can't live this way!' And he began to weep hysterically."

Thomashefsky saw at a glance that the situation on the stage was truly bad. Scenery and props were coming in, the actors were in a defiant mood, there was talk, angry laughter, no order anywhere.

Thomashefsky took Adler into the office, spoke to him until he was calmer, and finally suggested they sit together on the stage. "You will sit at the table, I will sit next to you," Thomashefsky urged. "If an actor or actress does not play as you wish, if a scene is not as you conceived it, tell me how you want it, according to your feeling, your taste, and I will see that it is done. But I beg you, speak to no one. Only to me!"

Edelstein, Mrs. Adler, and her brother, who was the cashier, all begged him to do as Thomashefsky said, and Adler finally consented.

Thomashefsky quieted the actors, reasoned with those who did not want to play double roles, and quickly established order. Once or twice, when an actor objected to some piece of direction, Adler sprang to his feet and Thomashefsky had to hold back his arm, raised for combat. The rehearsal proceeded in this way until Adler was calm enough to take it over himself.

He had, in fact, created a miracle, for nothing like this picture of peasant life had ever been seen on the Yiddish stage. The whole cast achieved heights. Adler played Nikita, the gay seducer, drawn deeper and deeper into sin and crime. Anisya, the peasant woman who poisons her husband to marry Nikita, was played with blood-chilling reality by Sara Adler. The second-act curtain, with a cast of 60 onstage and all dancing, drew ovations, and at the play's end was heard that sound that marks only very great triumphs— the long, sustained roar of every voice shouting in tribute.

The Yiddish press hailed the production and the ensemble playing was praised as something equaled only in the Russian theatre. Gordin came to the opening, sent flowers afterward, and acknowledged that the cast had played like artists.

For once the whole profession rejoiced at a success they felt as their own. "There was joy in the box office," Thomashefsky writes, "but an entirely different joy than was felt when we did other plays. An entirely different audience came. Not the kind of customers to whom we were accustomed. Not the girls and pretty little women who used to run to my performances! The Russian-Yiddish intelligentsia came!"

A review of the play in the magazine *Theatre* said: "Tolstoy's somber drama *Power of Darkness* was presented recently on the Bowery by the members of the Yiddish Theatre Company, Mr. Adler being seen in the role of Nikita. Gloomy and depressing as is this masterpiece of Slavonic literature, the play was admirably performed, and the stage management little short of a revelation. Would that some of our managements, and our actors, too, made the pilgrimage to the Bowery to receive lessons from this gifted Jewish actor, who is unquestionably one of the great players of our time. If Adler could act in English and perform in a Broadway theatre, he would be idolized; unfortunately, he is not sufficiently versed in the vernacular. Yet, for that matter, neither are Bernhardt, Salvini, or Duse, to whose class Adler belongs." *

Thomashefsky and Adler were friends again, and remained friends to the end. Their partnership, however, was drawing to a close. When Adler took over the Grand Theatre a year later, they had come to a parting of the ways.

The Grand was to be the scene of Adler's crowning achievements. But the struggle for possession of this much-disputed theatre ended in events that were to rock the Yiddish theatre world to its foundations.

* *Theatre*, November 1903, Vol. I, p. 8.

24

A Tragedy on the Yiddish "Theatre Street"

> A canny man, Finkel. A farsighted, quiet man. Too quiet for my tastes. Never joked with the actors, never gave any of us a smile or a good word. But on my sister Emma he smiled! And for her he had a good word!
>
> BORIS THOMASHEFSKY, *My Life*

Emma Thomashefsky, youngest of the star's sisters, had first danced out onto the stage at the age of five. At twelve she was going to public school in Philadelphia and playing nights in her brother's theatre.

Emma shared her comedy scenes with another child actress called Sabina Weinblatt. Every play in those days included a turn for this charming pair, who brought a world of life and gaiety onto the stage. Both of them sang, danced, marched around at the finale waving Jewish and American flags, and according to the composer, Rumshinsky, these two delightful children often turned a failure into a hit. Frequently they played sweethearts, alternating each night as the boy and girl. The types they portrayed—a little servant girl, a village youth who courts her—were closer to the audience than the high-flown heroes of the play, and Emma and Sabina were greatly loved by the provincial Yiddish public.

Of the two, Emma Thomashefsky had the finer gift. She was pretty, graceful, and she had a delightful alto voice. But it was her warmth and life that made her a favorite. When she was on the stage, the audience never wanted her to dance off again.

Emma's promise was fulfilled in the years that followed in New York. At seventeen, she blossomed out with a remarkable flowerlike beauty. She had all the potent Thomashefsky charm. Her every move on the stage was adorable. Actors loved her warmth, her sense of fun, and those who knew her in the later, tragic years describe her even then as gay and undaunted. Thomashefsky took pride in her talent and fostered it in every way. She began getting bigger parts and everyone predicted a great career.

One night Finkel, talking over a new play with Thomashefsky, referred tenderly to the young girl as "our little Emma." Thomashefsky was disturbed. Finkel, well into his forties, had already divorced a wife with whom he had two children. He was, besides, a man of abnormally gloomy, silent disposition, disliked by almost everyone in the profession.

From the beginning, Finkel had been something of an enigma. A number of actors place him with the original Goldfaden troupe in Jassy, but Mogulesko insists he came in later. No one is quite sure when he appeared; there seems to have been something shadowy about the man in those early days.

He made himself respected soon enough. He was a capable *regisseur*, an organizer who could be entrusted with the most serious business matters. When Yiddish theatre in Russia was forbidden, it was Finkel who went to St. Petersburg for the permit that allowed the desperate troupe to give "German concerts." He was three months about the business, but when he came back the permit was in his hand. He could be depended on to carry through the most difficult commission, and his honesty was proverbial. He had never been known to break his word.

With all these virtues, he had no friends. His icy temperament repelled those around him. He had life and death powers over the troupe, and no one knew better how to humiliate and break anyone who dared to oppose him. An actor is defenseless against the cruelty of his *regisseur*, and there were people in his company who hated him to the grave and beyond.

His coldness was a byword in the profession. Mogulesko was present in a Russian town when a newly engaged extra asked him for a rouble in advance, faltering out that for two days he had not eaten. "Bad!" Finkel said, but offered nothing further.

The story became famous, and Mogulesko used that laconic "Bad!" in the melodrama *The Jewish Heart*.

Finkel's talent as an actor was acknowledged by all. Adler rated him as excellent; Bertha Kalisch said that in his own genre he was beyond compare. He was especially good in the historical operettas when something strange and a bit chilling was needed. In such roles Finkel's distinct, monotonous delivery and large, fixed eyes created an uncanny effect. But his abilities were by no means limited to such parts. In Gordin's plays he created types so realistic and original that other actors were afraid to follow him.

As a director, he is remembered chiefly as a disciplinarian. It was Finkel who authored the "First Statute," a list of eighty-two rules governing the actor's behavior during rehearsal, during performances, and even afterward at the cafe. This "First Statute" hung in every dressing room, and every actor had to sign it along with his contract. To disobey any article of it meant instant dismissal, and once he made a decision, Finkel never reversed it. He was known in those days as the Czar of the Yiddish theatre. His word was law. Even stars feared him.

This was the man who courted the seventeen-year-old Emma Thomashefsky. And her brother saw with dismay that the girl was excited by his interest. Finkel was talented, brilliant. In his own way he could be counted handsome. He had unlimited powers over his actors. He directed, acted, composed songs for the theatre. To the young actress, full of budding ambition, he must have seemed an almost godlike being.

Thomashefsky, worried as he was, did not think matters could be serious. Finkel, he felt, was too cold by nature to fall in love, especially with so young a girl. Thomashefsky was mistaken. Finkel had married his first wife for practical reasons. Emma was the first real passion of his life, and he meant to have her.

The two of them were seen walking on Broadway, riding in a carriage in Central Park, and these meetings were reported to Thomashefsky. Questioned directly, Emma flung herself into her brother's arms and, in a flood of tears, admitted that Finkel had asked her to be his wife.

Thomashefsky, beside himself with worry, called the family together in an emergency meeting. His parents, brother, and sisters gathered in the office of the Thalia. As soon as she heard of the proposal, Chaya Baila wailed out that this was the end of her child. "An old man!" she wept. "And stingy, too! Nobody can get a nickel out of him!"

Finkel was summoned to the office and informed that Emma's family did not approve of his courtship and would not give their consent to such a marriage. Finkel, as was his custom, remained silent. When Thomashefsky demanded an answer, he said coolly, "My answer you will permit me to owe you!"

With that he withdrew.

The family remained at a loss. Pinchas, now president of a Brooklyn synagogue, had to leave for Friday services. The others also had business. They disbanded without making a plan. Thomashefsky, too agitated to go home, remained in the empty theatre.

At seven, actors began coming in for the evening performance. Thomashefsky was full of his trouble, and the matter was soon known. The cast agreed, without a dissenting voice, that the fresh, happy, talented girl must be saved from this marriage. A meeting was actually held, and a vote taken. It was unanimously decided that Finkel must end his courtship of Emma Thomashefsky or leave the company.

Thomashefsky was chosen to deliver this decision. The actors waited in a small smoking room backstage. Thomashefsky stationed himself at the stage door, and when Finkel arrived, gave him the company ultimatum.

Finkel made no reply, but walked into the smoking room and asked the assembled actors if they had heard what Thomashefsky had just said.

"We heard it," one of them quietly answered.

"And is it true?" Finkel demanded.

With one voice the response came: *"It is true."*

It was the first time Maurice Finkel had ever faced a battery of actors solidly united against him. It was not, however, to be the last. He turned white, told Thomashefsky he would send for his things, and left the theatre.

The actors waited tensely. Those last words had an ominous ring. The entire wardrobe of the theatre was Finkel's property. If he claimed it, the performance that night would have to be canceled.

Sure enough, a small army of boys appeared at the stage door for the costumes. Thomashefsky sent them back with the message that he would deliver everything the following Monday. Finkel, probably out of consideration for Emma, carried the matter no further.

Patriots sent to spy out the situation were soon going back and forth across the street. They reported that the manager had gone directly to the Windsor Theatre across the street, and was now deep in conversation with Kessler. This news was followed by worse. Kessler had announced from the stage that the great Maurice Finkel was now a member of his troupe. This was no more than expected, but Kessler added that another splendid artist would soon grace his stage—the beautiful and popular young actress, Emma Thomashefsky.

"At this news," Thomashefsky related, "I felt the ground fall away under my feet. I rushed to Emma's dressing room and found her crying with Sabina Weinblatt. When I told her what had happened she was frightened to death. She cried harder than ever and told me she knew nothing about it, that Finkel had never so much as mentioned the Windsor Theatre."

An extraordinary scene followed. Thomashefsky led the frightened girl out before the curtain, had the houselights turned on, and asked permission to bring up a matter that concerned the well-being and happiness of his family. He then asked the audience to witness his sister's oath that she would not join Maurice Finkel at the Windsor Theatre, would not accept from him or anyone else an engagement there.

The overwrought Emma swore.

For weeks after, Thomashefsky was flooded with letters of advice from the public. The incident was the talk of the whole theatre-going community.

Finkel played a week or two at the Windsor and then dropped out of sight. Thomashefsky began to hope things had simmered down. He was wrong. One morning Emma was gone. Later that day a telegram arrived. Emma and Finkel had married, and were both engaged for the season at the Arch Street Theatre in Philadelphia.

The Thomashefskys had to accept the situation.

Some months later, Thomashefsky and Sophia Karp guest-starred in *Romeo and Juliet* at the same Philadelphia theatre. Emma met her brother on the stage, fell on his neck, and wept. "A murderer I never was!" says Thomashefsky. "I wiped away her tears and forgave her." Emma called out joyfully to her husband. Finkel came up on the stage, his hand outstretched, saying, *"Sholem al Isroel*—All Jews at peace!" The two men were reconciled.

Thomashefsky found his sister in love and happy. The newly married couple lived well. They had a three-story house on a fine street near a park, and two servants served them at dinner. "Finkel liked a good brandy, wine, good Roumanian dishes, he was a Roumanian," Thomashefsky observes. "He treated Emma beautifully, but more like a father than a lover. He was too old for love, too old for Romeo."

The marriage, for all Thomashefsky's fears, worked out surprisingly well. Emma's star was rising. She was always in demand. She had dramatic ability and began to play leads. Her husband had the sole management of her affairs, and made a good thing of it. This was the era of the big star-manager combines. For a long time Finkel rode the crest of the wave.

It was the actors themselves who finally deposed this "Czar." His downfall was accomplished at the time the other actor-managers became, perforce, members of the newly formed Hebrew Actors Union.

Among all the managers, Finkel was the most hated. His stinginess was notorious, his terms the worst in the profession. He owned the wardrobe of his theatre and gave himself an extra mark for it, thus forcing his cast to pay him for their costumes. He was loathed for his humiliating discipline, and for his detestable "First Statute."

His destruction was engineered by the actor Rudolph Marks. Finkel had always disliked this young man because of his prestige as the son of the great scholar Radkinson. His dislike deepened, it is said, when he noticed a certain tender emotion between him and Emma Thomashefsky. Rudolph Marks had left the theatre rather than endure Finkel's persecutions. Now lawyer for the Hebrew Actors Union, Marks led the "revolution" that brought about Finkel's downfall.

In some way Finkel had been led to believe the union would blink at certain undercover arrangements in regard to the new minimum wage. Rudolph Marks exposed the kickbacks, and when a vote was taken on Finkel's admission into the union, a thunderous "No!" came from the membership.

Some people felt that Finkel had been deliberately misled and had suffered an injustice. But he had no real friends. No one stood up for him. He was eventually allowed into the union, but as a mere actor. The public humiliation broke him professionally, and is said to have caused the fatal rift with his young wife.

The marriage would probably not have lasted much longer in any case. Finkel was in his fifties, while Emma was barely twenty-eight. After ten years of marriage and three children, she was more beautiful than ever. Her ability in dramatic roles was being recognized. As her husband's influence and prestige waned, she must have resented his hold on her.

Finkel put up a desperate fight to keep his position. In 1903, in spite of his damaged prestige, he was one of the builders and founders of the new Grand Theatre, the first playhouse ever built specifically as a Yiddish theatre. Here Finkel hoped to combat the growing popularity of Gordin's new "realism." But by now he was running against the tide. The historical operettas of Hurvitz and Lateiner were no longer bringing in audiences accustomed to something better. Finkel had a disastrous season, and had to close before the first of the year.

A rough battle followed for possession of the new theatre. Zukor-Loew wanted it as a moving-picture house. Adler had title to it, but some technicality about possession arose, and Sophia Karp, one of the original owners, refused to quit the premises. This prima donna had known only a few good years as Thomashefsky's leading lady. In every other company she had been kept down. She was associated in everyone's mind with the Hurvitz-Lateiner operettas, now going out of fashion. Deathly afraid that Adler would put her out and no one else would engage her, she slept in the dressing room, spent days and nights wandering about the icy, unheated theatre, and finally came down with the pneumonia that killed her. Her death was a shock to everyone, and masses of people followed her coffin, weeping over her untimely end. This was the first of the great Yiddish theatre funerals.

The battle for the Grand went on. Adler learned that Finkel had hired an Italian street gang to frighten him off, and was advised that an Irish gang was standing by ready to do battle for him. Instead of calling on these allies, Adler entered the theatre forcibly by smashing the glass door of the lobby with his cane. Finkel asked the police to arrest him, but they refused. Though the case was carried to the state supreme court, Adler retained possession.

Finkel was out. He and his wife had no theatre for the rest of the season. Emma got work with various companies; every troupe was delighted to have her. Finkel received no such offers.

Husband and wife were growing apart. She had her life in the theatre. He sat at home. Actors who had flocked to Emma's house after the play made excuses now. Finkel's leaden silence made them too uncomfortable. Emma had to come home alone each night to the dark gloom of her husband.

The final blow came when Finkel found out from a third party that Emma had accepted an engagement with Adler for the coming season. A terrible scene took place. Finkel accused her of black treachery. Emma declared she had a right to save herself from misfortune. As the quarrel reached a height, she took her three children and left the house.

The marriage, according to rumor, was already on the verge of a breakup. Emma's name was persistently linked with that of Adler's juvenile lead, the young matinee idol David Levinson, and it was generally believed she would marry him as soon as she was free. Whether or not this is true, she left her husband's home and went with her children to a summer hotel near the town of Ferndale in the Catskills. After several days, Finkel followed her there.

The long vacation season in the Yiddish theatre began with the first hot days in spring. A number of actors were already resting and relaxing in this pleasant spot, among them, Jacob and Sara Adler, vacationing with their children.

Finkel would have done better to have stayed away. His presence caused frightful embarrassment. His wife ignored him. She was surrounded by her friends. The humiliated man, avoided by everyone, had to keep up a pretense at an interest of his own in the company of a child.

The twelve-year-old Nunia was to remember the great Finkel only as a thin little man with enormous sad eyes who spent hours with her every day playing a simple game called ticktacktoe. She knew he was connected in some vague way with Emma, but she never saw them together.

On an afternoon in June, Emma and some of the actors, David Levinson among them, decided on a walk down to the village. Emma was taking her three children and Nunia and her four-year-old sister Julia were also invited. Nunia was all excitement. Just to be near beautiful, gay Emma Finkel was the greatest happiness any child could imagine. A walk with her meant ice cream sodas, fun, giggles, warmth.

She was hurrying with her little sister to join the others when Finkel gently caught her arm. "Don't go with them, Nunia," he said. "Stay here today. Stay and play ticktacktoe with me."

She was to remember the appeal all her life. "But who would stay with him," she said, recalling it, "if they could be with her!"

With a hurried excuse she ran off to Emma, who knew how to make children love her.

Finkel immediately set out, taking a short cut, and before the little party had gone any distance on the road, they came face to face with him. "Where are you going?" he asked, barring his wife's way.

"What harm is it to you?" Emma answered with cold indifference.

The others, uneasy, walked ahead to let them talk, but after a moment Emma brushed past her husband and went on. As she joined the others, Finkel drew out a revolver and fired it five times in succession. David Levinson, struck by the first bullet, uttered a terrible cry. Emma fell, flame spurting from her body. Finkel then raised the revolver to his right temple, and sent the sixth bullet through his own brain.

Nunia uttered one long, piercing scream and ran for her life.

In the hysteria and commotion that followed, the little sister was forgotten. Hours passed before a search was made. The four-year-old girl was found wandering around on the deserted, darkening road near the dead body of Maurice Finkel.

The event came as a shock to the whole Yiddish theatrical world and caused a stir in both the Yiddish and the American press. Levinson was ruined; he had been wounded slightly by the first bullet, and his name appeared in every newspaper account of the affair. He could not show himself on the New York stage and was forced to play in other cities under an assumed name. Though he returned years later, he did not regain his former prominence.

Emma Finkel never walked again. One of the bullets had hit her spine, paralyzing the central nervous system. A wealthy Philadelphia lady who loved her left her home and family and spent two years taking Emma to every specialist in Europe. No one could do anything, and the sick woman was brought back to America, still bedridden. For ten years she was nursed by her two daughters with a devotion that was the marvel of the profession. After that she had improved sufficiently to get about in a wheelchair, and a benefit was arranged for her.

The composer Joseph Rumshinsky gives us a description of this performance: "The audience had not seen her since the tragedy. When she was wheeled out onto the stage they sat frozen with horror. I had written a song for her, a little melody with the refrain, 'Little birds, don't forget me!' When Emma Finkel sang those words it was the Yiddish public she meant. Such an emotion broke out in the theatre, such sobbing and wailing, such a burst of loyal, heartbroken applause, that for a long time the play could not go on."

After this Emma appeared in benefit performances every few years, always to a packed house. In Zolarterevsky's play *Raymond,* she played the role of a woman in a wheelchair. "She had a little drinking song," Rumshinsky relates. "She had to repeat it four and five times. The audience would not let her go."

Actors who knew Emma in these years invariably speak of her as gay and full of spirits. Celia Adler and her sister, Mrs. Ludwig Satz, lived for a time in the same house, and often took their children to see Mrs. Finkel. "The children danced for her, showed her all their tricks, and basked in her laughter and approval. It was a pleasure to go there," Celia Adler said, "for we were the whole time laughing and enjoying ourselves."

As the years passed and hopes for her recovery faded, Emma's emotional life centered on her son and two daughters. She was convinced that nobody could be more gifted, more exceptional, and that their talents would certainly be recognized. "My children will be great," she would say dreamily. "My children will be rich! The whole world will talk and write about my children!"

At times when the family was pressed for even the smallest sums, her daughters teased her. "*My children will be great, my children will be rich!*" they could chant together, laughing. Emma could not be shaken in her belief. She had transferred to them all the ambitions she had once had for herself.

And her children, in fact, did remarkably well. Abe Finkel was for many years a well-known Broadway director. Lucy Finkel became a prima donna on the Yiddish stage and in later years worked closely with Gertrude Berg on the popular radio program of the thirties, "The Goldbergs." Bella Finkel, the younger daughter, had a notable acting career and married an actor soon to be known as Paul Muni. Thus, as Emma had predicted, wealth and fame came to her children.

She rejoiced in their success and for years kept a book in which she carefully pasted every article, every review, every mention of her two daughters, her son, and her famous son-in-law, Paul Muni. No item was too small to be preserved in this book. And here she also wrote the whole story of her own tragic life.

Emma Finkel died in 1923, at the age of forty-six. As she had wished, her book was placed on her heart and buried with her.

Maurice Finkel's son by his first marriage changed his name to Fenn and married the actress Bertha Gersten. A daughter of the same marriage was for a number of years the pianist of the Bucharest Opera House, and was killed during the Nazi occupation. Sabina Weinblatt married the actor Max Rosenthal, and played successfully for many years on the Yiddish stage.

25

Shylock on Broadway, Tolstoy on the Bowery

> He hath disgraced me and hindered me half a million; laughed at my losses, mocked at my gains, scorned my nation, thwarted my bargains, cooled my friends, heated mine enemies, and what's his reason? I am a Jew.
>
> *The Merchant of Venice*

Recollecting the role that was to bring him world fame, Adler wrote: "In the course of my long career I have played simple Jews, Jews who were poets and dreamers, Jews who were clowns, fools, *schlimazls*, unfortunates. In all of them I had pleasure. But true happiness, the proud happiness of the creative artist I knew when it was given me to create the Jew of high intellect, proud convictions, and grand character.

"I am not a historian; far from it, but my understanding of the Jew in history is as follows: He is a patriarch, a higher being. A certain grandeur, the triumph of long patience, intellect, and character has been imparted to him by the sufferings and traditions that have been his teachers. Not only can he go through life; he is rooted in life and has grown strong in it. And so he has much joy, much reality, much blood in him. All this must be seen in his bearing, his figure, his appearance. Weighty and proud his walk, calm and conclusive his speech, a man of richest personal and national experience, a man who sees life through the glasses of eternity. So I played him, so I had joy in him, and so I portrayed him as Shylock. My pride in him reached those who saw it. And this was our mutual triumph."

The first sympathetic portrayal of Shakespeare's Jew was that of Edmund Kean in 1847. Almost every actor after him has played Shylock as at least part hero. Sir Henry Irving's interpretation, considered the greatest until that of Jacob Adler, went far in justification. Irving's Shylock was morally superior to the Christians around him, and was driven to cruelty only by their more cruel persecutions.

Adler scorned justification. Total vindication was his aim. In an interview published in the magazine *Theatre,* he said: "The idea I wished to convey was that Shylock from the first was governed by *pride* rather than revenge. He wishes to humble and terrify Antonio in return for the insult and humiliation he has suffered at his hands. This is why he goes so far as to bring his knife and scales into the court. For Shylock, however, the desired climax was to refuse the pound of flesh with a gesture of divine compassion. When the verdict goes against him, he is crushed because he has been robbed of this opportunity, not because he lusts for Antonio's death. This was my interpretation. This is the Shylock I have tried to show."

The magnificent contrast of the jesting Venetians and the grave, deliberate Jew is Shakespeare's achievement. Adler's Shylock coming slowly over the bridge of the Rialto was its realization.

Music was written for the Yiddish production by the talented Joseph Rumshinsky. This is no longer the fashion, but nothing brought home the difference between the Jew and his adversaries so well as the carnival theme of the Venetian masquers and the somber Hebraic cello line that prefigured the entrances of Shylock.

The performance itself is best described in terms of certain departures from the text. Jessica's balcony scene, as Shakespeare wrote it, ends with her elopement with Lorenzo. But no actor in those days would dream of robbing the audience of the scene Shakespeare left out—Shylock's return and discovery that his daughter has eloped with a Christian.

Sir Beerbohm Tree ran up and down the stage, calling for his child and throwing ashes on his head. Irving simply went up to the door of his house, knocked, knocked again, and waited as the curtain slowly descended. Neither was admonished for what modern-day audiences would find unthinkable—the addition of anything whatever to the play.

Adler unlocked the door of his house, entered, and called his daughter—first with a low, sure call, certain of a response, again with mounting fear, and at last in powerful, vibrating cries of biblical wrath. Following a pause, he came out of the house, seated himself on a low bench. Nothing was heard as the curtain fell but the rasping sound of tearing cloth. His child is dead. The Jew is rending his garment.

In the courtroom scene every gesture was calculated to make clear that Shylock did not intend to go through with his bargain. Adler whetted the knife against his shoe, but his audience laughed, knowing well it was not *they* who thirsted for blood. When the verdict went against him, commanding him to give up his fortune and turn Christian, Adler tottered and the words "Give me leave to go from hence,/ I am not well," were delivered in the tone of a man near death.

His overthrow was completed with Gratiano's jeering speech:

In christening shalt thou have two godfathers.
Had I been judge, thou shoulds't have had ten more,
To bring thee to the gallows, not the font.

On these lines, Gratiano brutally took the Jew's arm and forced him down to the very earth. Shylock, crouching, sobbing, was the very picture of the terrified ghetto Jew. But the moment passes. He begins to right himself again, to find himself again. He rises, shakes the dust of this court and its justice from his sleeves, and in the full pride of his history and his race, makes his exit.

Adler reached the high point of his performance at this final moment, and both Yiddish and American critics have lingered over it:

"Not always does he humble himself!" the Yiddish critic Alter Epstein writes exultantly. "Not always bow his head before the mighty ones of the earth! There comes a moment when the emperorlike figure rises to its height and we see him in his true magnificence. And how we thrilled, how fierce the beating of our hearts as, arms folded on his breast, with a burning glance of scorn, he slowly left the hall!"

Adler's Shylock made an unprecedented impression on the theatrical world, and was so universally acclaimed that two years after the production on the Bowery, Arthur Hopkins induced him to play in a Broadway production.

The play opened at Proctor's Fifty-eighth Street Theatre in 1903, Adler speaking his lines in Yiddish with an English-speaking cast. Frank Gilmore, later the first president of Actors' Equity, played Antonio. Portia was played by Meta Maynard.

The review in *Theatre* reads: "Adler's Shylock is a highly impressive creation, not only from the artistic but also from the racial viewpoint. The Jew of Venice, as he represents him, is indeed avaricious and vindictive, but above all, he is the passionate, proud, and scornful vindicator of Israel as against the despiteful usage of the Christian merchant and his friends. 'Hath a dog money?' Shylock asks, and loses his 3,000 ducats primarily for the sake of Antonio's humiliation in borrowing the money from him, and the legal forfeit of the pound of flesh gives the Jew his overwhelming triumph, dearer to him even than gold. Despoiled by the court in which he has asked for justice, he casts one look of ineffable contempt upon his persecutors, then walks off in superb, silent dignity, a martyr-type of his nation. This was the keynote of Adler's conception, which he projects with fine picturesqueness and force throughout. His rich, sonorous voice can scarcely be matched on the stage today unless we hark back to the elder Salvini. Romantic tragedy is undoubtedly his forte, though his range is as wide as Irving's or Coquelin's." *

The Arthur Hopkins production was repeated at the American Theatre on West Forty-second Street two years later, with the New York *Herald* calling Adler's performance "that rare dramatic experience on Broadway, the coincidence of a great actor and a great play." †

Adler did not appear again on the American stage. He had been recognized there as an artist on par with the greatest. His name had been coupled with that of Sir Henry Irving, and there were critics who considered his interpretation the more powerful of the two. He had done this as a Jew, and in his own language. His dearest wish had been fulfilled. He went back to his own stage.

A number of important critics and intellectuals were now taking that stage very seriously indeed. In *Hudson River Bracketed*, Edith Wharton, describing a supersophisticated New

---

* *Theatre*, November 18, 1903, Vol. III, p. 160.
† New York *Herald*, May 16, 1905.

York set, writes with some annoyance that "they all knew what was going on downtown at the Yiddish theatre." And Lincoln Steffens, in his *Autobiography,* calls the Yiddish theatre the best in New York.

Reviews began to appear in the New York press, and Broadway actors began looking in on the theatres of the Bowery. S. J. Kaufman, columnist for the *Globe,* fell in love with Jacob Adler and brought everybody down. John Drew came backstage one night with red roses, and Kaufman had to explain to Adler the identity of this overwhelming admirer. In years to come actors like Jack Barrymore, Ruth Chatterton, Madge Kennedy, and Richard Bennett came often to the Yiddish theatre, as did critics like Stark Young and George Jean Nathan. Broadway actors who had to repeat the same lines of the same play month after month were intrigued by the repertory system the Yiddish players had brought from Europe. Critics found the plays stronger and more interesting than the theatrical fare uptown. We are dealing with an age when except for classical revivals and Shakespeare productions, nothing could be found from one end of Broadway to the other but light, popular entertainment. The American theatre, as we now understand the term, had not yet come into existence. Light comedy or sentimental melodrama were the order of the day. It would be twenty years before Eugene O'Neill loomed up from "beyond the horizon" to create what we now know as the "American drama."

There was no dearth of talent on Broadway; indeed, this was the era of exceptional talent. But while uptown audiences were flocking to see *Alias Jimmy Valentine* and *The Heart of Maryland,* the East Side ghetto Jew was feasting on Tolstoy, Gorki, Ibsen, Strindberg, and Shaw, to say nothing of wonderful pictures of Jewish life by Jacob Gordin, Sholem Asch, Osip Dymov, Leon Kobrin, and others.

The Yiddish theatre had entered its best period. New talents began to emerge, new actors who challenged the supremacy of the stars. Adler discovered an obscure comedian named Ludwig Satz who became part of Adler's company, and immediately made a name for himself. The former watchmaker, Morris Moskovitch, joined the ranks of leading players, and in Gordin's *God, Man and Devil,* shared honors with Kessler himself. Another newcomer, Gustave Schacht, brought about an actual crisis in Adler's theatre. As Chayutin, the eccentric, nearsighted tutor of Gordin's *True Power,* Schacht had such a

Sara Adler and her children Stella and Luther in Tolstoy's *Kreutzer Sonata*.

David Kessler in *Yankel the Blacksmith*.

Bertha Kalisch

Max Rosenthal and Sabina Weinblatt in *Bought and Paid For* by Eugene Brieux.

Unknown melodrama circa 1910. (Left to right) A. Schrage, Jacob P. Adler, Sara Adler, Frances Adler, Joseph Schoengold.

Sara Adler in Tolstoy's *Resurrection*.

Katusha Maslova, Act I.

The Prison Scene, Act III.

Stella Adler
in *The Beautiful Lady*.

Julia Adler as Jessica
in the David Warfield production
of *The Merchant of Venice*.

Frances Adler and Joseph Schoengold
in *The Wild Man*.

The Adlers in *The Wild Man*. (Left to right) Julia, Jay, Luther, Charles and Abe Adler.

April 2, 1926. The Funeral of Jacob P. Adler.

Jacob P. Adler

Maurice Schwartz as Mordecai Mazze in Laivick's *Rags*.

Luther Adler as Tevye in *Fiddler on the Roof*.

Celia Adler and Paul Muni in the Ben Hecht pageant, *A Flag Is Born*.

success that the audience would not let him leave the stage. "They forgot the play and wanted only Chayutin," Sara writes. Adler's patriots finally started a fist fight in the theatre, and Adler took the part away and gave it to someone else.

Schacht was something new in the Yiddish theatre. He had mined for gold in South Africa, edited a Yiddish newspaper in Johannesburg. He challenged Adler in the press to a theatrical duel: a competition in all the leading roles with the critics to judge between them. There was great antagonism after this between Adler and Schacht, and people were surprised when year after year Adler continued to engage him. "He is a good actor," Adler would answer curtly. "I need him."

At about this time, a young immigrant by the name of Avrom Moishe Schwartz began hanging around Mogulesko's stage door. Schwartz spent all his money on the Yiddish theatre. Soon he found that although he admired Mogulesko, he was equally excited by Kessler and others. "My patriotism took another tone," Schwartz writes. "I began to feel I must not be a blind slave, a patriot among patriots, but I should admire every great actor. And the Yiddish theatre at that time was full of great actors. I liked Siegmund Feinman. I fell in love with Thomashefsky's artistic speech; he also pleased me by his fine, proud figure. I liked Elias Rothstein and the comedian Torenberg. But among Mogulesko's patriots, the name of other actors was not allowed."

Schwartz began his career with a recitation at the Delancey Street Dramatic Club, and then got his first real job with a small company, giving one performance of Zolatarevsky's *Twentieth Century* in Bridgeport, Connecticut. He came home from Bridgeport with six dollars. His family made fun of him, a quarrel developed, it came to blows with his father, and Schwartz left home. After playing some amateur performances at Teutonia Hall (the old Turnhalle), he got an offer from the Auditorium Theatre in Cincinnati. He was to receive a salary of eight dollars a week, with an extra dollar for taking on the duties of stage manager.

"To be a stage manager meant shoving scenery and furniture around, packing and unpacking before and after the show, and helping the extras with their makeup. But I liked it because I learned the technical side of the theatre. The man who was supposed to direct was careless, and so I became unofficial director, too. That is to say, I knew nothing about directing, but because of practical problems began to do things that were intelligent."

The actors were annoyed by the demands he made on them, but Clara Rafalo, star of the troupe, let her director go and put Schwartz at the head of the troupe. He got a raise in salary and managed to save up thirty dollars. With this sum he bought ten almost new projectors from a stranded American company. The young director began experimenting with lights.

In 1912 Esther Rouchel Kaminska, known as the Duse of the Yiddish Stage, came from Warsaw as a guest star. She saw Schwartz in Philadelphia, and it was Kaminska who told David Kessler about a young actor who was "all fire and flame," and who, she predicted, would have a great future.

Kessler came to Philadelphia, looked Schwartz over, and engaged him to play the lawyer in his production of *Madame X*. With this first professional appearance in New York, the long career of Maurice Schwartz began.

Up to this time men had dominated the scene. Now came the era of the women. Bertha Kalisch as the Magda of Sudermann's *Heimat* gave one of the great performances of all Yiddish theatre. Keni Liptzin, too, had become a force to be reckoned with. In her middle years Liptzin did not look like the same woman. Every trace of the commonplace had been burned out of that face by the white heat of her ambition. She lived only for the theatre, and working on a role, forgot everything, walked about in a daze, her eyes looking into another world. Her Medea is said to have "scorched the boards," and in Gordin's *Mirale Efros*, originally titled *The Yiddish Queen Lear*, Liptzin was hailed by Yiddish critics as a star equal to Kessler or Adler.

Sara Adler came into her own in Tolstoy's *Resurrection*. In this play Adler's Prince Nekhludoff was overshadowed by the simplicity and grandeur of Sara's Katusha.

Sara, so much the "actress" in life, never brought anything to the stage but truth. The innocent, happy peasant girl, seduced by Nekhludoff in the first act, the prostitute, condemned to hard labor in the second, were both encompassed with the delicacy and strength that were uniquely her characteristics.

Gordin had dramatized the Tolstoy novel in a spirit of prophecy that foreshadowed the Russian Revolution. Tolstoy himself suggests this; he does not marry Katusha to the prince who is sacrificing himself for her, but to the revolutionist, Simonson, who loves her. In the closing scene of the play,

Nekhludoff and Katusha go their separate ways. The prisoners, singing their somber Russian song, pass slowly across the stage, up a ramp, and into a great white light symbolizing Russia's hope. Last in the procession are Simonson and Katusha—a smiling Katusha, resurrected from the dead, waving farewell to the man she has redeemed by her forgiveness.

The twelve-year-old Nunia Adler, watching the opening-night performance, rushed backstage as soon as the curtain fell. She had the strange idea that if she got there soon enough, all those magical people would still be going on with their lives. But the stagehands were already striking the set. Katusha, Simonson, and the Prince had vanished.

Sara followed *Resurrection* with a second great performance in Gordin's tragedy of immigrant life *The Homeless*. Here she played the role of Mrs. Bathsheba Rifkin, a simple Russian Jewish housewife whose husband leaves her for a woman of intellect, a woman of the new time. For the "homeless" of Gordin's title were that first generation of immigrants, alienated from their children, lost in a world they did not understand.

The deserted wife in this play has a breakdown. After years in a mental institution she comes home to find that her husband has remarried and her son no longer remembers or needs her.

Gazing through the tenement window at the falling snow, Mrs. Rifkin remembers her home in Russia. Her illness is taking hold again, and she believes she can go back. She no longer sees herself as the pitiful abandoned wife, but as the great archtypal Mother despoiled of her awesome Place.

Neighbors call for help, but when the ambulance comes Mrs. Rifkin has become a child again, circling, laughing, happy in her belief that she is going home. "Yes, lady," the young American doctor says with deep compassion, "I'll take you home!" Eerily circling, clapping her hands with a child's ecstasy, whispering over and over, "I am going home! I am going home!" Mrs. Bathsheba Rifkin dances away forever.

Keni Liptzin produced her own version of *Resurrection* some years later. But no actress, no matter how gifted or ambitious, ever dared follow Sara Adler as the simple Jewish housewife of Jacob Gordin's *Homeless*.

In 1907 as a result of contracting diabetes, Albert Schoengold lost one of his legs. Thomashefsky had started a magazine, an eight-page sheet called *The Yiddish Stage*. Hearing of Schoengold's misfortune, the great-hearted Thomashefsky made this appeal to his fellow actors:

"Children! We have a brother— a star who shone bright in our heavens. Can we let him perish of hunger? I am speaking of Abba Schoengold. He is poor, he is sick. He has lost one of his legs. The handsome Schoengold can no longer walk! Benefits are played for him in music halls. Do you hear? Do you understand? Do you feel? For Schoengold, benefits in music halls?"

Schoengold had been going downhill even before his illness. The death of his wife had taken its toll, and a second marriage to the actress Anna Sherman had kept the family together only a short time. His children were grown now; they had gone about their own careers. He continued to play on the road after the loss of his leg, but bad luck plagued him. He was seen one summer in a Toronto company that gave only one performance every two weeks.

Boaz Young, who now had a troupe of his own, ran into Schoengold on one occasion in Boston. Young describes the actor as the wreck of his former self, but with traces of the old extraordinary beauty still in his face. Falling into talk with Young, Schoengold said: "I feel like a stranger now in the theatre. Above all, I feel estranged from my colleagues. Times have changed, yes, very different times. How does it go? New birds, new songs. Young people are coming up. I am old, and my song is sung." After a short silence he said, "You cannot imagine what it is like to know every day that death is coming nearer, and that no power on earth can stop its approach."

In the winter of 1908, Schoengold, playing a performance in Montreal, went into the wardrobe room backstage. While searching through the costumes, he was felled by a heart attack. He was found dead some minutes later.

A legend arose that Schoengold had died on the stage, and for one brief day the Yiddish press was once again full of his name.

"He was among the first pioneers of our theatre," one journalist wrote, "a man who made a path for future generations. But he died well. He died on the stage, a death all actors might envy. To his last breath he did not get off the war-horse on which he had done battle for so many years."

In a more bitter and angry eulogy, the actor and playwright Moishe Schor wrote: "In his fifty-three years he lived more than other men in a hundred. He had been dead a long time—dead as a man, dead as an artist, dead to the public for whom he once played. He brought to art a fresh young life, and was old before his time—gave everything and was forgotten—lived for the world, and died alone."

These were big years for Yiddish theatre. The stars were moving uptown; their wives and daughters wore diamonds. The road for the Yiddish actor stretched from Canada to California, and every city with a substantial Jewish population had its permanent professional company. Actors visited these theatres as guest stars and made fortunes. Adler got a thousand dollars a performance on the road, and Sara went to Paris every spring to have her gowns made by Worth.

The Adler family moved to 137 East Seventy-second Street, a four-story brownstone with a fountain, a garden, and an elevator. Sara furnished her sitting room in the period of Louis Quatorze, with carved pieces, rich hangings, and satin wall paper.

The top floor of this establishment was turned over to the eldest daughter. At fifteen Nunia Adler had bought herself a gown with a train. Her father gave her a carriage of her own with two blue-ribbon horses, and every night Harry the coachman drove her to the opera. At seventeen the plain girl blossomed out with a haunting, original beauty. She was too slender and tall for the fashion, but her hair and eyes more than made up for these defects. Her wit and the fun of her company would have brought her admirers had she possessed no beauty at all. She had inherited from one grandmother a fiercely loving heart, from the other, a devastating way of speaking her mind. Even Adler was afraid of this strong-willed girl. Sara gave way to her in everything.

The family had lived for several years in the brownstone on East Seventy-second Street when it was rocked by a domestic explosion. There were violent scenes, accusations. The scandal reached the New York press, and Adler, furiously jealous, moved out, taking his five children with him. There was talk of divorce, but after a year of separation, husband and wife were reconciled. The brownstone had either been sold or somehow lost, for the reunited family moved now to an apartment on Lenox Avenue.

Separations and reconciliations had, however, become the pattern. A year later there was another quarrel. Sara left the house and formed a troupe of her own at the Novelty Theatre in Brooklyn. The seventeen-year-old Nunia promptly stepped into her mother's roles, and Sara was never to forgive her for it.

Frances Adler, now her father's leading lady, performed with a competence and poise unusual in so young a girl. And in time Adler came to depend on her advice as well, for she always told him the blunt truth. When Adler clowned on the stage, amusing the actors with jokes and asides, he received a note reading, "Papa! Onstage they are laughing with you. Backstage they are laughing at you!"

When he amused himself with a flirtation and put on trivial plays, Nunia warned him to watch his step—a very great actor had come to town. Sara had brought Rudolph Schildkraut over from Max Reinhardt's company in Germany. Jacob went to the Novelty Theatre and watched the German actor give a great performance. He did not change his plans that season, but the following year he put on his entire repertoire and got his audience back.

When Nunia was eighteen, her father took her on the road, and the played a week of performances in Glickman's Palace Theatre in Chicago. A robust young man in the company played six character roles that week, all letter perfect, and all excellent. Adler, distracted by weaker actors in the cast, hardly noticed. Nunia was dazzled.

This remarkably able actor was Abba Schoengold's son, who was playing in Chicago that season with all his brothers and sisters. Celia and Sadie Schoengold were the soubrettes of the troupe. Ben, oldest and handsomest of the boys, played juvenile leads, and Sam and Freddie, the youngest, filled out in smaller roles. But it was the second son who had inherited the voice and the talent, and who was the mainstay and pride of this family.

Joe Schoengold had grown up on the streets of New York, had fought with Jewish street gangs against gangs of Irish and Italians, had watched boys he knew grow up as criminals and others become lawyers and great judges. As a child he had traveled with his father's troupe on the road, but when his mother died he was sent back to New York. For a time he lived with strangers, dark-souled, brutal people who left him with a lifelong conviction that human nature at bottom is more bad than good. He ran away, worked as a printer's apprentice for ten cents a day, lost his job, slept in the backyards of New York and Brooklyn. One morning he awoke with a pillow under his head; some woman had felt sorry for the homeless boy.

At eighteen he and his brother Ben were part of a Yiddish troupe in San Francisco. Galli-Curci was singing that winter at the San Francisco Opera House. Her manager, an excitable little man named Bergelman, heard Joe Schoengold sing and offered him a place in Galli-Curci's chorus. The diva and her troupe were soon leaving for New York and then for Italy. Bergelman painted a picture of a great future, firing the young man's imagination.

Schoengold, under contract to the Yiddish troupe, had to leave town secretly. Tiptoeing through the house with his valise early in the morning, he changed his mind. The sight of his sleeping older brother stopped him. Ben was a helpless boy who would have had a hard time of it alone.

Schoengold later played leads with Keni Liptzin on the road. Liptzin would have engaged him in New York, but the union prevented this. Young actors were not allowed to play in New York until they had done their three-year stint on the road. Schoengold, disappointed, remained at loose ends until Elias Glickman offered him a place in Chicago. From the first he played big parts—Bar Kochba, Avesholem, all the heroic leads. But during the day, this unusual young actor spent his time in the Chicago public library, devouring history, philosophy, fiction, educating himself.

When Adler went down the list of the Chicago cast, considering which of them he should bring back to New York, Nunia said, "Why are you leaving out Joe Schoengold? He was the best one of all!"

"Yes, he was good," Adler agreed thoughtfully.

Schoengold had done his three years' apprenticeship, and amid the rejoicings of his brothers and sisters, he came to New York. He played in Adler's company, took voice lessons, threw high Cs around the basement of the theatre, and knocked around town with Abe Adler. "Do you want to go up to Matteawan?" Abe would ask him. "That's when it was fun!" Stella Adler remembered. "When Abe came and brought Joe!"

Joe came often. He could not, in fact, stay away. Many people were attracted to the laughing Adler clan, and wondered at times what drew them so strongly. It was, of course, Odessa that drew them. The spirit of that city lives on for generations.

For Joe Schoengold the unconventionality of the Adler household was perhaps its greatest charm. The house was lively, always full of people, and there were so many pretty girls! Alexander Oberlander had settled in New York, and Abe Adler was soon to marry beautiful Esther Oberlander, youngest of his daughters. Jacob Adler's sister, Soore Levovsky, had come to America, and she and the "Russian cousins" were always in the house. The seventeen-year-old Fanya Levovsky had ambitions for the stage, and her blue eyes and ravishing red-gold curls had already won her parts on Broadway. Then there were the Adlers themselves, mettlesome young eaglets all. Julia, the "musical one," sang like a lark, had the best figure and the greatest natural fire. Jay, black sheep of the family, was a man-about-town, living a life of pleasure, with the feminine sex large in his scheme of things. There was Nunia herself, brilliant, original, witty. And Joe grew particularly fond of the two smallest Adlers, the towheaded young loner Luther, and his sister, a laughing little blonde witch called Stella.

All the young people wanted Joe Schoengold to marry Nunia and were conspiring to bring this about. Only Jacob and Sara were not pleased; they had grander plans for their daughter than a poor young actor. They told her she was making a mistake. Nunia laughed. They warned her she would live to regret it. Nunia played "Hearts and Flowers" on an imaginary fiddle. She wanted Joe Schoengold, and there was no doing anything with her once she made up her mind. Plans were made and the date set for the ceremony.

A week before her wedding Nunia brought Joe Schoengold to see her grandmother, now ill and in the hospital. "Buba," Nunia said with pretended cheerfulness, "This is my intended, my *chussen*."

"He is not your *chussen*," said the dying Pessye Levitsky. "He is your husband."

It was true. The Young couple had already been secretly married at City Hall.

The official wedding took place at Palm Gardens. The bride wore a diamond tiara, the gift of her father. Sarah gave her diamond earrings the size of hazelnuts, and other jewels were lavished on her. Every personage of importance in the Yiddish theatrical world was invited, and when the festivities were over the newlyweds settled down in a home of their own in Mapleton Park. Nunia took up embroidery and, to the admiration of her family, devoted herself to being a wife and mother.

Joe Schoengold played with Adler, with Kessler. He had his father's dramatic strength; he could play anything. A favorite with the public because of his powerful and beautiful baritone tenor, Schoengold soon formed a company of his own. New York critics were impressed by his performance in Sigmund Romberg's *Maytime,* and Romberg, who loved his voice, starred him on Broadway in his operetta *The Magic Melody.* The show flopped, but Schoengold's big song was a hit, and one day two gentlemen from the Metropolitan Opera appeared. They offered Joe Schoengold $35 a week on condition he would give up his bombastic shouting roles in the Yiddish theatre and devote himself for six months to being coached for his first operatic appearance. Re-named Guiseppe Orabello, he was to make his Metropolitan debut opposite Rose Ponselle.

"But Joey," said Jacob Adler's spoiled, petted Nunia, "an hour every day in a limousine comes to $35 a week!"

Schoengold, in love with his beautiful young wife, gave up the Met without too great a struggle. It was only in later years that he thought with regret of the life that might have been. At the time, his career was growing and a great future seemed to lie ahead. He was a star, drawing his $400 a week. A family man now, with a wife and two little girls, Joe Schoengold was a pragmatist, an American. Yiddish theatre was booming. The Met could wait.

26

Gordin's Theatre: The Apex

ROSH HAYESHIVA
Let all see with whom Elisha ben Avuya passes the time on the holy Sabbath! With a degraded, fallen woman! (*seizes Beata*)

BEATA
Let me be! If all men passed their time with us as he has done with me, there would be no degraded, fallen women!

Elisha ben Avuya

We have improved the theatre so much of late that in order to understand the theatre of Adler and Gordin we must first put back a great many things we have discarded.

Let us remember, then, the proscenium that defined the stage, the footlights that separated it from the audience, the curtain that concealed it, the flat painted scenery, the musicians in the pit, and, above all, the little semi-circular prompter's box.

Adler's benefits always drew a capacity house. A deafening racket in the lobby and in the theatre itself, a vast hum of pleasure. People crowd the aisles, chatting, laughing, new arrivals constantly adding to the press. There is excitement, anticipation, a certain tension, too, for the gods are about to speak.

At a given point the orchestra strikes up. The air vibrates

with the brassy, Middle-German music we think of as distinctively "Yiddish." Pulses quicken. New arrivals hurry down the aisles. A long wait. Presently the houselights go down. A sibilant "Shhhh!" sweeps through the darkened theatre. Coughs. Whispers. At last a light turns on in the prompter's box. This is the magic signal. Immediately, the curtain rises.

If the play tonight is like a hundred others, the first act will take place in Russia and the second—another world, another *planet*—America. The audience never tires of seeing its own great experience reenacted.

A responsive audience. Such tributes are heard nowadays only at the opera. The applause redoubles for Adler's solo bow—Adler always *runs* out for this, thrilling the public with the lightening impulse still his from earliest childhood.

Every great star will be called back twenty times and more after a strong performance. For Adler blessings are added. "May you live long!" the emotional voices shout. "May you have good health, may you have good fortune."

Applause and shouts die down only as houselights go on and Adler, his cast onstage, comes forward to make his curtain speech. Waves of warm applause punctuate his words, "I have played for you as I have played for your fathers. . . . Here in our new land, our new home, we do not forget. . . ." Several of his children are in the cast, and he presents them to the audience. He presents his son-in-law, Schoengold. Schoengold's two small daughters are in the box, and the grandchildren too receive ringing applause.

Because the writer and her sister were applauded that night, they were both to remember it well: the theatre, the box, the white-haired grandfather moving about the stage, a figure vigorous, perfectly balanced. He brings forward the members of the cast with words of praise for each. Solomon and Annie Manne, who first brought him to the Whitechapel clubs, go back to the London days. Others have been with him longer still. Fishkind, Katzman, Aaron Schrage, once a folk singer in Odessa. Repeated the words, "forty years and more," Adler breaks down like a child and cannot go on.

The audience goes home at one in the morning. Outside the theatre some twenty or thirty men and women line up at the stage door. A long wait in the bitter cold night. Adler emerges at last, his family and friends around him, a silken happiness in his eyes. Fervent prolonged applause from these impassioned patriots. Before entering the automobile at the curb, Adler takes off his hat in a beautiful, simple gesture of respect. Somewhere offstage, David Kessler growls, "And he makes his hair even whiter than it is!"

And, indeed, Adler was loved by the downtown public for his white hair. The remarkable nobility of his appearance had not diminished with age. Jay Adler tells us that once outside Proctor's Fifty-eighth Street Theatre, a group of girls in white confimation dresses came up to his father, curtsied before him, and kissed his hand. A priest on the church steps watched them, laughing. "They thought you were a cardinal," he explained.

A multitude of jokes and legends have sprung up around him through the years, and it would need the pen of a Proust to trace the distortions of time. The picture emerging is of a clever actor, a bit of a showman. This image is foreign to those who knew him. They remember a man who had very few opinions, never argued, never criticized, never talked about himself unless to tell a humorous story.

When Mogulesko died, Adler delivered the eulogy. He fainted at the end of it. His children did not know he had fainted; they did not even know he had spoken. The magazine *Theatre* has recorded an incident unknown to anyone in his family.

He was extraordinarily humble about his own achievements. Nunia once asked him what he thought of himself as an actor. He said hesitantly, "If I had been educated, I might perhaps have been—a good actor." He was always conscious of his lack of schooling and all his life had the fixed idea that if only he had gone through the Russian *Gymnazia* he would have been a greater artist.

He was known to be generous, and for years anyone in financial straits was advised to "see Adler." A young law student, later a prominent east side attorney, came to him one day in a sweat of anxiety. He had gambled away his tuition money, his parents' life savings. "And if I give you the money," Adler asked gravely, "You will gamble with it again?"

"No, Mr. Adler!" the young man tensely answered. "No! I will not gamble with it again!"

Adler silently wrote out the check and handed it to him.

It must be admitted that his innocence sometimes led to a

blunder. For years he kept a wretched composer on salary because of a single remarkable piece of music. It was the *William Tell Overture..*

After he appeared on Broadway as Shylock, some American actors invited him to a symposium on Shakespeare. He did not want to accept, fearing to expose his ignorance. His family told him he need not speak and urged him not to refuse. He sat in on the symposium, heard nothing new, and was irritated by an English actor who rose with an air of importance and kept saying, "Ah, Shakespeare...ah, Shakespeare!" but added little more. Adler came home, disillusioned. "Ah and bah I also could have said," he remarked drily.

He is often accused of theatricality because of the concentration he brought to every action of his daily life. The writing out of a check, the putting on or off of his hat and coat, the mere adjustment of a pair of spectacles—nothing was so small as to be done without care, without a certain attention to form. He had never mastered English, and when he spoke it, every word or phrase was charged with his intense effort to make no blunder, no shameful slip, but to pronounce each word properly, if possible even beautifully.

Playwrights were often annoyed by this insistence on "beauty." "God knows that in life and in the wings of the theatre he did not always use the finest language," Leon Kobrin comments irritably, "but on the stage, everything not 'beautiful' was written out of the text. His changes often spoiled the liveliness of the dialogue. At times he labored so with his mighty pen that the whole original feeling of the play was lost!"

It is true that Adler disliked anything ugly on the stage. Watching a fellow actor portray a coal miner in a dirty, blackened costume, he turned away, offended. "One does not bring dirt onto the stage," he said with scorn. "Put *paint* on your costume if you want it to look soiled!" In *The Beggar of Odessa* his appearance was so hilarious that the audience rocked with laughter at the sight of him. Yet, according to those who remember him in the play, his whole person was spotless and beautiful to see.

At home he was good-humored, composed, a nature perfectly balanced and at rest. He filled the house with dogs, cats, canaries, and plants, told humorous stories, and played tricks that made his children laugh. But he was not talkative, and kept many things to himself. His friend Louis Miller, editor of the socialist *Varheit,* said to him one day, "You are too silent these days, Adler. You hardly speak. It is not good." Stella Adler, hearing this, was frightened.

He was getting on, getting older. The doctors did not like the condition of his heart; his old obsessive fears about it had come true. He put his last drop of strength into every performance, and Sara told him he would kill himself if he continued in this way.

Writing about Gordin's play *The Russian Jew in America,* Adler says: "I had a particular love for this early play by Gordin, reading into it much autobiographical of Gordin's life, and also of my own. As Gordin originally wrote it, the Russian Jew does not die, but lives, an old, broken, disappointed man. Later Gordin wrote an epilogue that showed the death of the Russian Jew. Dying, he has a vision, a hallucination. He lives through his whole life again, pictures of his old home appear before him, Russian fields, Moscow, pictures of America, too. And he dies in the strange land, singing quietly, 'Moscow, my Moscow, city of cities, streets of gold . . .' I played this scene with such tearing inner emotion that my wife, Sara Adler, became frightened that something would happen, a misfortune with my heart, long, long a broken, damaged thing. Each time I played this scene she stood in the wings, and just as Gradner used to call to his sick Annetta that she must not forget herself, must not injure her health, so Sara Adler stood behind the paper wall of the Windsor Theatre, calling warningly, 'Adler! Adler!' "

In his later years, the whole East Side looked upon him as a father. There was not a mobster or thug in the area who would have laid a hand on him. A profound respect surrounded his very name. Of all the actors, he was the most prized by the public, the most loved.

In this latter part of his career, Adler one day received the following letter from Lausanne, Switzerland:

> To a Great Artist, Master of the Jewish Stage—Mr. Jacob P. Adler, New York.
>
> Incomparable Master!
>
> I send you through my friend, Jacob Sapperstein, a play which I have composed from several works written by me twenty years ago. I have worked a great deal on this play, and put into it a very great content.
>
> As I worked on the main character, the hero, I had you in

mind, Great Maestro, because only an artist like yourself is capable of creating and showing the soul of this character. Great Master of the Stage! In my play you will find none of the effects on which the Jewish public has for so many years been nourished. You will find no soul-tearing scenes, no corpses in cribs, no demented women, no patriotic songs or nationalist speeches, no transient boarders seducing innocent maidens, and no vulgar jokes. You will find only a simple Jew, father of five daughters, an honest, clean, wholesome, and greatly suffering character who, with all his misfortunes, will make the public laugh from beginning to end.

The four acts of the play are four little tragedies, and together they make up the long, tragic life of a Jewish family. My present title is *Family Pictures in Four Acts*. As you will see, the play is neither comedy nor tragedy, but has elements of both.

Read into it, think into it, and you will see that you can show marvels. Without pretense, without empty effects, you can show yourself in all your largesse, and create a role that will evoke healthy laughter, deeply felt sighs, and perhaps, from time to time, a quiet tear.

I would like to think of this role as your crowning performance before you part with your profession. Pray God, not soon. Amen.

Your ardent admirer,
Sholem Rabinovitch
Sholem Aleichem

The play in question was, of course, *Tevye the Dairyman*. Though Sholem Aleichem had written it for Adler, it was the as-yet-unknown Maurice Schwartz who was to bring the works of this genius to the Yiddish stage. Adler was essentially an actor of the romantic school, and did not feel the part was for him.

Fifty years after he refused it, his son Luther Adler played his inspired Tevye in the Broadway musical *Fiddler on the Roof*.

There was a saying on the Lower East Side that when Adler and Jacob Gordin walked arm in arm down the street, "the earth trembled." One would like to imagine these two as the closest of friends. The facts are otherwise. The men who had between them created the "golden era" of their theatre were seldom on friendly terms. Too often they were bitterly opposed.

Adler had a respect for Gordin akin to reverence. "He is my rescuer, my Messiah!" he once said passionately to Leon Kobrin. "Without him I would have had no life in the theatre!" This affirmation, however, was not enough. A man may revere another, and yet feel himself an equal. Gordin's pride allowed of no equality with an actor, even a great one.

Abe Cahan, himself a man of extremely imperious character, complains continually of Gordin's arrogance, asserting that the slightest criticism would send him into rages, and that at times he went so far as to threaten the offender by lifting his cane. Gordin's temper and pride made him enemies in the Russian colony, but Cahan admits these were outnumbered by his friends:

"He was witty and could make an excellent joke," Cahan writes. "In the company of friends he was always gay and companionable, and very warm and hospitable in his own home. At a party or a New Year's ball his tall figure, proud face, and flowing beard were always the center of a large, admiring group."

Thus Cahan, whose complaints about Jacob Gordin are always balanced by a reluctant admiration.

Pride was undoubtedly Gordin's overmastering sin, but it was a pride based on a standard of honor few men set themselves. Radicals relying on Gordin's friendship soon discovered they had caught a bear that could not be caged. Gordin could be captured by no party; the spirit of truth was too strong in him. Though his main support came from the progressive movement, he never hesitated to attack anything he considered harmful or stupid.

His play *The Russian Jew in America* created an uproar in radical circles because of the character Huzdik, a militant unionist who ends as the boss of an anti-union shop. In the first act Huzdik defends a stupid union ruling with the words, "It doesn't have to make sense; it's the majority resolution!" — a line that drew a knowing laugh from the audience. When later in the play the former militant fighter, now a boss, delivered the line, "Everything would be fine if not for the union!" Abe Cahan rose from his seat in the theatre thundering in Russian, "*Eto lozh!* — It is a lie!"

Cahan's break with Gordin began with this incident. Cahan wrote a sharp review, reprimanding Gordin for showing only the "negative aspects of unionism." Gordin attacked Cahan in a curtain speech and stated in the press that his plays were above Cahan's criticism. Cahan answered that if this was Gordin's position, he would not in the future review his plays. The two men were brought together, but the reconciliation did not last. Cahan refused to recognize Gordin as a literary force in the Yiddish theatre. Gordin would accept nothing less. The rift was permanent.

During one of his lectures before a socialitst group, a former Russian army officer accused Gordin of expounding on Molière and Shakespeare, but doing nothing for the Yiddish theatre. Because of this criticism, Gordin founded the Yiddish Frei Folk's Buehne, Yiddish Free People's Theatre, a dramatic group where talented younger actors could dedicate themselves to the better drama.

Gordin was the heart and soul of the new workers' theatre. He brought in the best teachers and lecturers, gave performances of his plays for their benefit, raised money for them, and drew around himself a committee that worked with equal dedication. According to Leon Kobrin the cream of the intelligentsia came to Gordin's lectures. Kobrin writes:

"He was not the greatest speaker in the world. We had better ones on the Jewish street, and what Gordin said many of us had already heard, perhaps even said ourselves. What made it important was that *Gordin* said it! The younger writers looked up to him, and when he walked among them he was like an apostle of biblical days with his disciples. When he left the Folk's Buehne, every important intellectual left with him."

This is the best, most creative period of Gordin's career. The public looked upon him as their leader and teacher. The actors adored him. He gave them parts that brought out all their talent, lines to say drawn from the inmost truth of Jewish life and gorgeous with wit and wisdom. They cared more about Gordin's opinion than that of the most important critic. Bertha Kalisch writes that for her every word he uttered was "a piece of Torah."

For a number of years his influence was so all-pervading that *shund* was forgotten. Actors and audience alike had acquired a taste for fine theatre, and "better plays" brought not only honor but income, too. Everyone wanted to play Gordin. Everyone wanted to play the classics.

Kalisch and Kessler made history in Sudermann's *Heimat*, Kessler as the aristocratic Prussian general, Kalisch as his daughter, the errant Magda immortalized by Eleanora Duse. Keni Liptzin's marriage to Michael Mintz, owner of the Yiddish *Herald,* gave her financial independence, and her name became associated with Gordin and better theatre. She took her own theatre, and produced plays by Ibsen, Hauptmann, Hugo, and Andreyev. As the Jewish matriarch of Gordin's *Mirale Efros,* Liptzin created a figure of such authority as to set a standard for every actress who afterward attempted the role.

Mirale Efros was perhaps the best-loved and most popular of Gordin's plays. Abe Cahan, comparing Liptzin's performance with that of Esther Rouchel Kaminska, who played it during a visit to New York, preferred Liptzin's "impressive declamation" to the more realistic performance of the visiting Polish star:

"Liptzin's pride, her humor, her mastery, her shrewd, practical sense, all this was from Shakespeare rather than from Lithuania. She was not proud like an ordinary woman, but like a Lear. She did not go about the stage like a rich housewife of Grodna or Berditchev, but like a queen. In stage technique, in the mechanical means that help a melodramatic performance, Liptzin was more expert than Kaminska. Melodrama was the core of her *Mirale Efros.* But whatever one may say about the faults of her playing, her *Mirale* was among the outstanding interpretations created on the Yiddish stage."

Thomashefsky, fired by ambition, produced a number of fine plays during this period. As an actor, he was apparently at his best in the dramas of Leon Kobrin, and in *Lost Paradise,* he did some magnificent character work. Indeed Thomashefsky had only to play a character part to show himself as an outstanding dramatic talent. Jacob ben Ami declares that at his best, he was only a little under Kessler and Adler.

Thomashefsky was making his mark as a director too at this time. A production of Zangwill's *Children of the Ghetto* received an excellent press. And singled out for special praise by New York critics was young Celia Feinman, daughter of Jacob Adler's marriage to Dinah Shtettin. Celia, in a moment of rebellion, had taken the name of her stepfather, Siegmund Feinman. Later, however, she took back her own name, and it was as Celia Adler that she became an important force in the Yiddish Art Theatre movement. At this earlier period, she was already extremely popular. She had pathos and charm, she had an irresistible talent for comedy, she was frankly of the people and the people took her to their heart. She is the only one of Adler's children who was to achieve stardom on the Yiddish stage.

America: The Golden Years

New playwrights were coming to the fore. Sholem Asch shocked the Yiddish world with his *God of Vengeance,* a play closed by the police because of a lesbian scene in a brothel. Osip Dymov, a Russian playwright, wrote his brilliant, stylized *Bronx Express,* and followed it with *Slaves of the Public,* a spoof on the Yiddish theatre with two little comedy playwrights strongly suggesting Hurvitz and Lateiner. And things in Europe, too, were beginning to pick up. In 1908 the Russian edict against Yiddish theatre was lifted. The playwright Peretz Hirschbein formed the Vilna Troupe, which toured with plays by Sholem Aleichem, Sholem Asch, David Pinsky, and Jacob Gordin. Hirschbein himself later came to America, and his idyllic comedies of village life, *The Forgotten Corner* and *The Lonely Inn,* were to bring an important new direction to the Yiddish theatre.

Though Gordin's popularity reached its high point with *Mirale Efros,* the Yiddish theatre itself finds its apex in *Elisha ben Avuya,* a play set in the early Christian era and, in the tradition of *Acosta,* with a heretic as its hero.

The strange light of the *Haskala,* a light half Hellenic, half biblical, plays over this drama. Elisha ben Avuya loves life, beauty, and art. We find in his character the nobility of Lessing's Nathan the Wise, the generosity of Timon of Athens. In his personal beauty and love of beauty the character was inspired by Adler, for whom it was written. In his uncompromising integrity, his suicidal code of honor, Elisha is Gordin himself.

Elisha reads Homer, decorates his garden with Greek statues, plays host to Roman aristocrats, and allows his daughter to adorn herself and live for pleasure. Christianity he rejects as inimical to life, but he is equally opposed to a narrow interpretation of Judaism. Like Gordin, he is an atheist and even dares to dispute with the rabbis on the existence of God. Yet he remains unalterably Jewish, and can be conceived of as nothing else.

Elisha is tricked out of his fortune, betrayed by his Roman friends, and condemned by his own people. His daughter runs off with a Roman soldier. His wife deserts him. Only Toivye Avyoini, Toivye the Poor Man, remains faithful. When he turns to the fallen woman, the beautiful Beata, who had loved him, he is rejected. Beata has become a Christian and renounced all happiness in this world. Toivye Avyoini brings back Elisha's daughter, but too late; he has already taken poison. The rabbis solemnly denounce him as a heretic who will not come to eternal life, but his disciple, Rabbi Meir, "cries to the heavens" that Elisha will live forever. His daughter weeps over his body. Beata goes her way to a nunnery and church bells offstage toll in the Dark Ages.

The play failed when Adler first produced it. "Put it on after my death," Gordin told him. "It will be a success." Gordin had advised him well. After the playwright's death, *Elisha* ran for a year. To his children, Adler is identified with this role as with no other.

Goldfaden had come back to America in 1903, a man broken by illness and failure. He was welcomed with deference, and the actors gave a benefit for him at the Grand Theatre. After that, the three main theatres gave him only a small sum each week and a benefit once a year. This was barely enough to sustain him and support his family. The Yiddish theatre was thriving, and in a letter to Y. L. Peretz, Goldfaden writes bitterly about the wealth of the theatre he had created. "But I do not complain," he concludes. "My mission in life is accomplished. I have given to my people a Yiddish theatre. I ask nothing more."

Goldfaden made his last try as a playwright with *Son of His People,* based on George Eliot's novel *Daniel Deronda.* Though the play was written in a serious vein, Thomashefsky insisted it needed music. When Goldfaden disagreed, Thomashefsky had another composer supply the songs. Arguments broke out, and some officious underling took it upon himself to tell the father of the Yiddish theatre that he was in his second childhood and should not meddle with what he did not understand. Goldfaden turned white, left the theatre. He died soon after the opening.

Gordin survived him by only a year, and like Goldfaden, his career ended with a failure. *Dementia Americana* was a savage satire on the runaway real estate speculation in Brooklyn and East New York that ended by ruining thousands of small investors. The play poured merciless ridicule on these once-poor immigrants who had forgotten their heritage in the "dollar madness" of America. The playwright who had spared no convention, no prejudice, had turned his laughter and scorn on his own public.

Dementia Americana got an adverse press. Critics felt Gordin was wrong to laugh at the misfortunes of people who had in some cases lost their life savings. Thomashefsky produced it against his own better judgment, and for Gordin's sake he kept it running a few weeks.

Gordin died in 1909 at the age of fifty-eight. In the eighteen years he had been in the Yiddish theatre he had written seventy plays, a good dozen of them masterpieces. He had purified the language of the stage, ridding it of the corrupt Germanized diction that had plagued it. He had lifted the Yiddish theatre to a height it had never known before. His death came as a shock to the whole downtown world.

Cahan was shaken. Though he had attacked Gordin as a dramatist, he had never failed to acknowledge the incorruptible integrity of his character.

Because of their lifelong rift, Cahan felt he should not write the eulogy. He gave this task to A. Lessin, an important colleague on the *Jewish Daily Forward*. Lessin's piece recalled the happy days when Gordin had worked on the staff, lingering on the first impression he had made there:

"How one longs to see once more that giant figure with the great brow and the good, thoughtful eyes, that face from which shone out a proud, majestic, broad, and rich nature. What a personality this was! What an example to all men! We hardly dared speak to him. Of Yankev Gordin one always expected something great. One could do no less, and he expected it of himself!"

On the same page Cahan's editorial declared that Gordin had worked in the spirit of Tchernyshevsky and Dobrolyubov, that he had devoted his life to progress, to light, and to the betterment of the Jewish masses. Cahan called on those masses to honor his memory.

Gordin's last published work, in the form of a feuilleton, was a sort of fable in which the Jewish nation was represented as Jehudith, his bride and spouse. "Jehudith had a child," Gordin wrote, "a neglected, sick child growing up in squalor and dirt. I took this child for my own. I wiped off her dirty little mouth, dressed her in decent clothes such as are worn by happy, cared-for children, showed her her charm, her talents. I gave gifts to the child as well. My gifts were perhaps of no value, but they were the best I had; I have given better ones to no one else. And for all that I had done the mother hated me.

She hated the gifts I had given her child. She hated the good, decent clothes in which I had dressed her, and put her back again in the old filthy rags. Nevertheless, I continue to love the child. And though today Jehudith and I have nothing to give one another, we remain one body and one soul. She concerns herself little with me, yet she is my love. I know that when I fall, her friends, bought for a few groschen, will dance on my body and she will look on, indifferent. The day I die is the day she will forget me."

The words were bitter truth. No man of genius has ever been more brutally consigned to oblivion, no writer so idolized during his lifetime so totally neglected after his death as Gordin.

One wonders, reading his plays, why this man was not good enough for his critics. He gave the stage strong themes, authentic characters, progressive, daring ideas. His prose has the rise and fall of his own heart's beat, and only a few of the greatest can make that claim. The public continued for twenty years to love his plays. Yet all this was not enough. Gordin is "good theatre, but not literature." And though Cahan does not deny that the dialogue is interesting, it fails to satisfy him. "Realism" was the catchword of the day, and like all catchwords, it made wise men foolish. In his insistence that Gordin's characters "say clever things such people would not be able to say," that "they speak with the playwright's words, not their own," one hardly recognizes the intelligent Cahan. If this is a sin we will have to throw away Shakespeare, Ibsen, and Shaw along with Gordin!

David Pinsky, a far less interesting playwright, accuses Gordin of building his characters around certain actors, a weakness again that Gordin shares with some distinguished predecessors. Shakespeare had Burbage. Ibsen would allow no one to play Nora at his Swedish premiere but Betty Hennings, a woman known as the Duse of Scandinavia. Gordin dares to create a heroine in love with a Russian officer, pregnant with his child, and prevented only by his death from turning Christian and marrying him. He is asking a Jewish audience to rise above their own highest moral law, but knows that Bertha Kalisch has only to step on the stage to make them understand and weep for her.

As time went on, it became the fashion to downgrade Gordin. In later years he was pushed aside entirely. A more ethnic concept of the Jew was replacing the old heroic image. Peretz

Hirschbein's *Forgotten Corner* had become the formula for critical success. Every play with a rural setting, every play about village Jews was automatically "art." Every play about big-city Jews in the modern world was somehow "not art." Hirschbein himself was pilloried when he attempted a more universal play.

Many American critics also prefer this later period to the first. They are intrigued by the faraway, poetic settings, charmed by the picturesque *klein shtetl* types. It is easy for the world to contemplate this Jew, so witty, so lovable, so permanently in his "forgotten corner." It is less easy to gaze into the tranquil eyes of Albert Einstein.

Gordin, more than any other, is the playwright of the *Haskala*. The hero of the *Haskala* is Einstein.

27

Shund

> To our house there came one day a cousin,
> Pretty as the sun, the little greenhórn,
> Rosy cheeks and lips, a laughing glance,
> Happy little feet that longed to dance.
> This little cousin never walked, she sprang!
> We never heard her talk, for joy she sang!
> Hair that fell in golden locks and curls,
> And teeth—a row of perfect little pearls!
> I took the cousin in to my "next-door-ke."
> A neighbor had a millinery "store-ke."
> The first day, and the job is in her hand—
> May it only live, Columbus's great land!
> *Popular Yiddish song*

Between 1905 and 1908 almost a million immigrants came through Ellis Island. These people, survivors of frightful pogroms, did not want a serious theatre, but one that amused them. A tremendous audience for light entertainment came into being. With the failure of *Elisha ben Avuya* in 1907, Gordin was losing ground. *Dementia Americana* the following year signaled the reaction. Jewish vaudeville had become the rage, variety stars began attracting the public, and dozens of music halls sprang up, cheap cafes where customers sat at tables and were served drinks while they watched the performers on the stage. A battle began between the music halls and the theatres, and actór-managers began looking about for plays that would bring back the public.

Bessie Thomashefsky writes: "At the Thalia Kessler, Kalisch, and Moskovitch were still playing Gordin. Well, they had made their reputations with Gordin, so who could blame them? But at the People's Theatre Thomashefsky and I were making fortunes. Very soon the Thalia began to envy our big houses. They threw away the art, threw away Gordin, and began delivering the goods to 'Moishe'—the great almighty public!"

Bessie had summed up the mood of the times. While Gordin's last play, *Dementia Americana*, failed, the Windsor Theatre put on Lateiner's melodrama, *The Jewish Heart*—and against all predictions, the Lateiner piece was the hit of the season.

Other theatres were quick to follow the new trend. Thomashefsky's *Minke the Servant Girl* coined money, and his next production, *Dus Pintale Yid* by Seiffert, had a sensational forty-week run. Both were cheap comedies of the old-fashioned type. *Shund* had once more become the standard theatrical commodity.

A hunt began for any kind of trash that would satisfy the market, and on stages throughout the country innocent maidens were seduced by villains, mothers searched the earth for their lost infants, and heroes were saved in the nick of time from the electric chair.

Though the Adler family laughed until their sides ached at the wild improbabilities of *shund*, one cannot remember it now without affection. It was always warm, often professional and talented, and it gave a legion of lesser actors a livelihood and a life. The melodramas of Libin and Sheikevitch were, in fact, excellent of their kind. They were simply *Lebensbilder*—pictures of life—plays with strong situations, their avowed purpose to evoke the tears and sympathy of the public. And, in fact, it is a gloomy theatre that does not have refreshingly innocent plays of this kind.

Shund at its best came close to being good theatre. At its worst it outdid the wildest of the Bowery thrillers. Anybody could get together a cast and make a living of sorts, and unbelievable excesses were committed. A well-known actress produced *Romeo and Juliet*, but since she was the star and it was her theatre, she advertised it as *Juliet and Romeo*. Two actors without the ghost of a cast traveled with *Joseph and His Brothers*. A man called Rabinovitch had no play at all; he simply sat at a table, took a pose indicating deep thought, and delivered a rehash of speeches from *Elisha ben Avuya* and *The Yiddish King Lear*.

Luther Adler saw a typical "sketch" on the road with an actor called Hyams. A mother sits rocking a cradle and weeping. Her child is dying. Enter the doctor—Hyams. He takes the child's pulse and sighs, "The end is near." The mother speaks up. She knows that her child is dying, but has heard that the doctor has a wonderfully sweet voice. She begs him, before her child dies, to sing her a little song. The doctor consents, comes down to the footlights, and switching to Americanese, addresses the orchestra leader with a brisk, "Okay, Professor! Shoot!" The orchestra strikes up, and Hyams sings, "A Mother Is the Best of All Things."

Jewish girls sold into white slavery in Chinatown provided a favorite theme. The cast of one thriller used to go up to the roof of the theatre in the hot months, take off their wigs, and play cards. One of them, so the story goes, forgot the time until the stage manager shouted up the stair that he was "on." Snatching from the table a Chinese pigtail, the actor clapped it on his head and ran down to the stage. Since he also wore a long white beard, the audience roared. To save the situation, the actor exclaimed, "You think because of my beard that I am a Jew. But in my heart"—tearing off the beard—"I am a Chinaman!" To this day anyone indulging in peculiar behavior in the Adler family is told, "In your heart you are a Chinaman!"

Adler stubbornly resisted the epidemic of *shund,* and his son developed a phobia about the swarm of would-be playwrights bringing their "literary" plays to the Grand. "Does your drama have in it something deep? Is it cultural, psychological, and historical?" Abe Adler would ask in scholarly German. If the answer was yes, the unhappy playwright was treated to such a flood of pure American profanity that he fled for his life.

Adler sometimes gave in and produced a tearjerker. After two fine plays failed, he once put on a melodrama entitled *The Living Orphans.* The play was an instant success. On the opening night Adler brought the author out before the curtain and made the shortest speech of his career. "You and this man," he told the audience, "are ruining the theatre!" The author blushed as though he had been paid the greatest compliment. And the following night Abe Adler sent a note to his father's dressing room that read: "Make all the speeches you like. We're booked six months in advance."

In the summer of 1911, the New York *Herald* respectfully

carried an item noting that the Tolstoy estate had given Jacob P. Adler first American rights to the posthumous play *The Living Corpse*. The premiere of this play caused something of a stir in the New York theatrical world, and in November of the same year, this review appeared in *Theatre* magazine:

"The sensation caused by the Russian and French productions of Count Leo Tolstoy's posthumous drama drew a number of Broadway notables to the Thalia Theatre last week to watch the performance of *The Living Corpse* which Jacob P. Adler had the courage to present to his clientele at that house on November 3rd. Throughout his admirable impersonation, and throughout Fedia Protasoff's fall from revelry to penury, Mr. Adler kept burning that spark of nobility that was finally to end his pitiful existence. Although a pistol figures in the dramatic theme, the tragedy never flared into melodrama; it was played by the entire cast with too much gravity and sincerity. Mr. Adler particularly met the serious demands of the play with a sensibility the more affecting in that it never descended into hyperbole."

As Protasoff, the aristocrat who seeks oblivion among the gypsies and becomes a "living corpse," Adler relived the Odessa nights of his first love with the gypsy girl, Bronya. The critic Alter Epstein found the performance wanting, the character not fully realized. Kobrin, who translated the play, was enthralled by Adler's performance:

"Not one loud cry! How softly and dreamily he told his drinking companions the story of how he became a living corpse! In every move, every turn, you saw the Russian aristocrat! And in the courtroom scene, when he met his aristocratic wife, now married to another, how he looked at her! How his eyes begged her to forgive him! What a silent, mute play this was, how full of soul! Even his suicide did not break the quiet of his performance. Silent as a shadow he took himself off, and then offstage — the shot!"

In 1919, when John Barrymore appeared in this play (*Redemption* on Broadway) Adler took a box and brought the family. Barrymore was so handsome that the eccentricities of his style went almost unnoticed. In the suicide scene his body made a convulsive leap upward, and then collapsed. The Broadway audience expected death scenes to be romantic, and laughter was heard. Adler was angry at the laughter. He thought Barrymore's interpretation very fine, and after the play went back to tell him so. "How could you do this to me, Mr. Adler?" Barrymore broke out, unnerved. "I couldn't play tonight!" Adler's presence in the box had thrown him off in his performance.

It is clear from the success of *The Living Corpse* that *shund* had not altogether triumphed. If Gordin's supremacy had lasted only a few years, the reaction was equally brief. The new immigrants grew more refined in their taste. The craze for music halls subsided. Vaudeville, though it continued to be popular and lucrative, ceased to dominate the theatrical scene. Adler had allies now in the women. Sara Adler, Bertha Kalisch, and Keni Liptzin all fought valiantly for "good theatre." A balance was eventually reached, and together with the audience demand for simple entertainment there was a return to the better type of plays. In the end both tastes had to be served. In this respect the Yiddish theatre was like all others.

Whether they specialized in art or *shund,* the theatres downtown were the cultural center of immigrant life. Every public event found its echo on the stage. When news of the Kishinev pogrom horrified the world, the three-year-old Stella Adler stood center stage, arms thrown wide, and in a voice that carried to the farthest gallery cried:

> Jews, for the love of mercy,
> Give of your charity!
> For the dead, burial—
> For the living, bread!

This poem by Shimen Frug about the Kishinev massacre was so effective that Adler went from lodge to lodge with it, raising money for the survivors. At the last two lines Adler would come down from the platform and go through the audience, stovepipe in hand, repeating, "For the dead, burial—/For the living, bread!" People wept and emptied their pockets. Women with no money to give threw their wedding rings into his hat.

There were songs and plays about the fire at the Triangle shirtwaist factory, the Mendel Bailis trial, the sinking of the *Titanic*. When America entered the war in 1917, stars on the East Side sold thousands of dollars of Liberty bonds. Actors raised huge sums for the Red Cross, and the roar of the

Broadway audience at George M. Cohan's "Over There" found its echo downtown as the American flag was unfurled on every Yiddish stage.

For the actors it was a rich life, warm and essentially intimate. The profession was so interconnected by marriages, divorces, and love affairs as to resemble some great quarrelsome family. It was rare that a Yiddish player married outside the profession. When they did, the wife or husband was drawn into the theatre one way or another and inevitably was shoved "on" in some emergency. Actors were married on the stage, and their children were brought on as soon as they could walk. Pearlie Schoengold made her debut at the age of two, and created an uproar when she addressed Adler as "*Zayde*," a mistake that brought shouts of laughter and a rain of coins from every part of the house.

Every important player in those days had his patriots who defended him against all others. Bertha Kalisch, playing weekday nights in Liptzin's theatre, was cheered at her curtain call by a publicity man named Ben Gilman. A group of Liptzin's followers immediately converged on him with the words, "In this theatre only Liptzin is cheered!" When Gilman cheered again, he was lifted out of his seat, roughed up, and finally for some reason thrown up the stairs into the gallery. "I've been thrown downstairs before in my life," he told Luther Adler. "To be thrown upstairs was something new."

The devotion of patriots could be a nuisance. One such admirer came to every performance of *Lear*. Each time Adler came to the line, "Will no one here give me even a piece of bread?" this emotional man would come down the aisle, wailing, "Mr. Adler! I'll give you bread! Come with me! Children are no good. To hell with them!"

There were individuals whose attachment to an actor was so strong they gave up their professions to serve them. Such men became in effect his supreme patriot who led all the others. Boaz Young tells us that when Regina Prager died, her most devoted patriot, Gimpel by name, followed her coffin, crying, "How will I live without seeing her face? How will I go on without her beautiful voice?"

"And four days later," Young writes in big, scary capitals, "GIMPEL DIED!"

Adler's patriots were named after his famous roles. A fiery quarrel broke out one day between two of them. "I am Moishele Soldat!" one of them, fists raised, reminded the other.

His rival, squaring off for battle, retorted, "And I am the Wild Man!"

A sensation was produced when Kessler's chief patriot, known to the East Side as "Goulash," changed his colors and came over to Adler. This caused such a flurry downtown that a full-page story about the event appeared in the New York *Globe*. Goulash, whose real name was Harris, functioned for years as Adler's "front man," an important post in the theatre.

Adler was not the only Yiddish actor to appear on Broadway. In 1911 David Kessler made his try in a play by Sam Shipman called *The Spell*. He had a disastrous failure. Kessler's English, without a trace of foreign accent, would pass muster on any New York stage today, but was not good enough for an age when diction was the prime requisite. The play itelf was weak, full of drawing-room talk, the part not in Kessler's best genre.

Abe Cahan, present at the opening, writes defiantly: "I can't deny that the first performance at the Majestic was a bad one. Kessler was crude, raw, unpolished—well, he wasn't good. All the same you saw on the stage a human being made of flesh and blood and full of feeling. In spite of his imprisonment in a language not his own, there were moments when I wanted to get up and shout, 'Better this unrefined, uneducated Kessler than a thousand of your cultured Shakespearean talking machines!' "

According to Cahan, Kessler was better at his later performances, but this was too late; the reviews were brutal. Kessler went back to the Yiddish theatre.

The following year a contractor named Johnson built a new theatre for him on Second Avenue. Happy as a boy, Kessler vowed he would give only good plays in his new "temple of art." He opened with Gordin's *God, Man and Devil*, and Mayor Gaynor was present as his guest of honor. In his curtain speech Kessler said, "I told Mr. Johnson the contractor that if I did not have a new theatre I would go back on the American stage. My friend Mr. Johnson got frightened! 'Dave, my boy,' he told me, 'You are staying on the Yiddish stage!' And he built this temple of art to keep me there!" Mayor Gaynor joined the laughter and applause of the audience.

The first season at Kessler's Second Avenue Theatre was gayer and more lively than anywhere else, and the box-office take higher. Other managers wondered if the Bowery was not played out. They began to look toward Second Avenue, a wide, clean, prosperous street with no elevated tracks overhead and without the derelicts and saloons of the Bowery. Within a few years, half a dozen theatres had gone up, and Second Avenue, alive and twinkling with the lights of marquees, had become the center of Yiddish theatre in New York.

At this time, with business booming and money rolling in, Mogulesko became increasingly troubled by a certain hoarseness of the vocal cords. His doctors assured him his voice would come back, but Mogulesko had dark thoughts. Convinced he would never sing again, he took up the study of the drum and decided to make a living as a drummer.

The news of his illness spread, and hundreds of people came to his door inquiring after his health.

With time the hoarseness improved, and Mogulesko's return was announced in *The Immigrant*. Though everyone assured him he would have a triumph, Mogulesko studied the part as though he had never played it before. He was terrified he would lose his voice in the middle of the performance, disappoint the public, cover himself with shame.

He opened to a packed house, the people full of joy at his return. And a miracle took place. Mogulesko's voice came through, clear and beautiful as before his illness.

In *The Immigrant*, Mogulesko played the peddler Feivel Pavolye, Feivel Watch-Your-Step. This little man is taught by a friend to stand up to his wife, be a man, assert himself. He tries to obey, tries to stamp his foot, but in midair the foot begins to tremble. And this trembling of the foot was so exquisite that for a whole season the East Side wanted nothing else. "The Windsor Theatre is standing on Mogulesko's foot," the actors said, laughing.

In the last act of *The Immigrant*, Mogulesko, tiny, frail, laughing, indomitable, sang the greatest of his songs:

> Lift up your pack, little Jew!
> Carry it—never grow weary!

A great wave of strength went out to that struggling immigrant audience from the little comic figure on the stage. Mogulesko had come back to give them laughter, and with laughter they could face anything.

A miracle, by its nature, occurs only once. Though Mogulesko played again, his voice rasped. The audience did not notice or care, but the sound of it was torture to him. At times when the audience out front was laughing and applauding, Mogulesko was weeping in the wings.

As his illness progressed, he was unable to play regularly, and no theatre could engage him. Since he had no savings, he had to give benefit performances. These not only taxed his strength, but brought him very little income. He behaved as though he needed nothing, played benefits for other actors, but his inner despair was great. Mogulesko drank, and at times he drank too much.

The whole profession was heartbroken at his trouble, for he was greatly loved. In spite of his success, he had remained simple as any old-fashioned small-town Jew. His modesty was the marvel of the theatrical world. When he played with other comedians, he composed songs for them, built up their effects, became enthused over anything good they created. In his own art he had remained supreme; no one dreamed of challenging him. Like Chaplin, he pleased everyone, the simplest audience as well as the most demanding critic. His plays died with him, for no other comedian ever attempted them. He created unforgettable characters in Gordin's plays, but actually he preferred Lateiner and Hurvitz. He liked to improvise, to sing and dance, and was hampered by a character already created by the author.

Leon Kobrin feels that Mogulesko typified the essence of the Yiddish comic spirit: "The Yiddish comic spirit loves a dance. Mogulesko danced. And when he danced the *chosid* at his holiday, the Jew himelf danced, the whole Jewish nation was joyful when Mogulesko danced! The Yiddish comic spirit loves a song. Mogulesko sang the songs he himself composed, the songs of his heart. And they are *their* songs—they sing them long after they leave the theatre. The Yiddish comic spirit loves a peppery joke. Mogulesko delivered such jokes with an air so natural, so innocent, as to make them irresistible. His illness could not destroy his spirit. The creative power so alive in him found, in spite of everything, a way to express itself. When his throat choked, Mogulesko sang with his face, with his movements. When his last strength was gone, one foot moved—and laughed!"

In January 1914, he appeared for the last time. Right after the performance he went home, took to his bed, and did not get up again. On February 4, fully conscious to his last moments, he died. Just before the end he said with a smile that he had an engagement in the other world, adding more seriously, "When I am called, see that I am given as I deserve from the Yiddish public."

American journalists were amazed by the thousands of people that came to his funeral, the extraordinary chanting of solemn Jewish dirges broken by snatches of his comic songs, the cries of "Alas, Mogulesko—an angel!"

"Tributes to Irving, Joseph Jefferson, and Mansfield were carefully planned and organized. It was different with Siegmund Mogulesko, when a whole people spontaneously poured out of sweatshops. Measured by the number of sincere mourners crushed around the cortege, Mogulesko's fame was greater than any actor who ever lived!" *

The Yiddish theatre roared on. After a quarrel with his manager, Adler gave up the Grand and took a theatre at Eighth Street and Fourth Avenue. A Russian troupe headed by Paul Orleneff and his wife, Alla Nazimova, gave Sunday performances of Chekhov's *Cherry Orchard*, Ibsen's *Brand*, *The Devil* by Andreyev, and Hauptmann's *Sunken Bell*. Adler used to instruct his audiences to come and see the "fine Russian actors." All the intellectuals of the Lower East Side crowded into Adler's theatre to see these Sunday performances. Orleneff, head of the company, was a short, stocky man, blond, full of vigor, a magnificent player. Kessler, watching him in Ibsen's *Ghosts*, turned away with tears in his eyes, muttering, "And I dare to call myself an actor."

In later years, when Nazimova became a star of the American stage, she wrote: "It was not so bad down on Fourth Avenue! We did not make money, but we played the classics. . . . The intellect of New York you will find on the East Side. . . . They may lack, for the present, the material things of life, but the future is theirs!"

After two years, Adler left the Eighth Street for the People's Theatre. One night he called Luther and Stella into his dressing room and introduced them to a tall lady in a Greek tunic. The lady, seeing a little blond girl and boy, kissed them and began to weep. Adler murmured in Yiddish, "She lost her children!" It was Isadora Duncan. She and her troupe were to give Sunday night concerts at Adler's theatre.

* *Theatre*, July 1914, Vol. II, p. 27.

Isadora was at this time at the height of her career, still wealthy and still wearing the jewels given her by the millionaire Singer. Contrary to all reports, she was extremely beautiful and spoke with an exquisite diction. She adored Jacob Adler, threw roses to his box at the end of her concerts, and asked him, as she had asked others, to have a child with her. Apparently Jacob and Sara were once again separated at this time, for the Adler girls begged their father to marry Isadora. The family was all mad for the great dancer. Julia Adler, in particular, never missed a performance or a rehearsal. One day, seeing her at the back of the theatre, Isadora asked her why she did not join the dancers on the stage. "But Miss Duncan, I don't know how to dance," Julia said.

"Oh, just listen to the music and think beautiful thoughts, and you will dance!" said Isadora.

In 1917 a Mr. Bronstein, just arrived from Russia, took rooms in the Bronx. He lived quietly, read a good deal, and spent some evenings at the Cafe Royale on Second Avenue. He occasionally dropped in to see a Yiddish play, and after a performance one night, went backstage and had a chat with Adler. After some conversation, Mr. Bronstein said he was returning to Russia. "And what will you do there?" Adler asked. "We are going to overthrow the Kerensky government," his visitor replied. Adler nodded quietly. He was quite used to revolutionists from Russia, and their plans did not surprise him. Mr. Bronstein left America shortly after. Adler heard of him next as Leon Trotsky.

When the news of the Russian Revolution broke, Adler took his daughter Stella to the giant socialist rally at the Hippodrome, and received an ovation when he appeared in the box. Though he had always thought of himself as a socialist, this had never interfered with his passionate devotion to his new country. Most of the Yiddish actors shared both these loyalties. Freedom from the Tsar was all the socialism they required.

It was a good life in America for the actors. There were steak dinners after the play. There were the exciting train trips of "the road," the long vacations in the mountains or at the sea, the trips abroad every year to London, Paris, Carlsbad. Best of all was coming home for the new season. No city in the world with the tempo, the excitement of New York. Giant figures were on the scene in those days, giant talents.

Rachmaninoff at Carnegie Hall, Caruso and Farrar at the Met, Pauline Lord and the Barrymores on Broadway, Chaplin down the street. . . .

Nunia and Joe Schoengold, ardent Caruso fans, often went to the opera. On one occasion Caruso gave such a performance that they remained in their seats after everyone had left, still banging their umbrellas and screaming bravos. Caruso came out, looked around the house in surprise, then gave a laugh and a wave to the two adoring lunatics in the gallery.

One night, instead of Caruso, a handsome young man appeared on the stage. Caruso had been taken ill and could not sing. Such a thing had never happened before. Nunia felt a little chill go over her, a sense of cosmic scenery being shifted.

After staying for an act or so, the young couple got up and left, disappointed. Nunia did not want to go home. There was still time to catch her father's last act, and they took a taxi downtown.

They were surprised there by an extremely bad performance. Nunia hurried backstage as soon as the curtain fell, and asked her father what was wrong.

He looked up helplessly and in a high, trembling voice said, "I am imitating myself . . . imitating Adler, I can't anymore. I'm too old."

Caruso ill, her father old . . . That was the moment, Nunia said, when she knew that "everything was over."

28

Final Appearance

> No, my Shakespeare! For me, the Jew, your answer is not enough. My life has been no brief moment, no tale signifying nothing. When I measure it with the measure of my feelings, it has been an eternity, an ocean.
>
> JACOB ADLER

The decline of an era can best be seen in the birth of the one to come.

With Adler and Kessler still seemingly at their height, the actors of the newly formed Yiddish Art Theatre gave a matinee one day with nine people in the audience. Maurice Schwartz made a speech afterward to the almost empty house, thanking those who had come for their belief and devotion. "And if you like," Schwartz ended with a smile, "we can all go out now and have dinner!"

Several minutes later his stage manager knocked at his dressing room door. "Mr. Schwartz!" he called in a tone of alarm. "They are here!"

His audience had accepted the invitation.

Two men had collaborated in the idea that would produce the second great era of Yiddish theatre. Jacob ben Ami, thoughtful, modest, a student by nature, provided the idealism needed for such an undertaking. Maurice Schwartz contributed the organizational ability, the sound commercial sense, and the personal force that made it a reality.

The two could not have been more different in temperament, in point of view, and in theatrical background. Ben

Ami had his roots in the Hirschbein Troupe of Odessa. These were dedicated drama students who emerged a few years later as the Vilna Troupe and made a powerful impression on New York with their extraordinary stylized production of *The Dybbuk*. Sara Adler, playing with Schildkraut at the Novelty Theatre, heard about Ben Ami as an interesting actor who was also extremely handsome. She brought him over from London to play the lover in Tolstoy's *Kreutzer Sonata*. Ben Ami arrived late and found Ben Schoengold playing the role. He refused to take the part away from another actor, even though Ben Schoengold, gentlest of men, fully expected to be replaced.

At no point in his career can one imagine Maurice Schwartz with time or patience for any such fine-drawn gesture. Unlike Ben Ami, Schwartz had grown up in the rough and tumble of the professional theatre. Energy and ambition made a way for him, and in 1919 he was able to take the Irving Place Theatre with a company of his own. He engaged Ben Ami in a troupe that also included Ludwig Satz, Celia Adler, Bertha Gersten, and Joseph Schoengold. Most of these actors had been stolen from Kessler.

Yiddish actors, from the greatest to the smallest, always had one benefit performance every season, an evening from which they took all profits. Ben Ami, given a choice of plays, chose Peretz Hirschbein's gentle study of rural life, *The Lonely Inn*.

"You will make thirty dollars with this play," Schwartz told him.

Ben Ami insisted and put his own money into the production. The play brought something new, fine, poetic, into the Yiddish theatre, and critics raved.

On Ben Ami's advice, Schwartz followed this success with two more "literary" plays—*Love's Crooked Ways* by David Pinsky, and Peretz Hirschbein's charming *Green Fields*. The critics once again were enthusiastic, but after a first spurt of interest, the audience stopped coming.

The following year Ben Ami took the Madison Square Theatre on his own. He engaged the painter Joseph Foshko, first scenic artist of the Yiddish theatre, and brought in a German director, feeling himself too young to direct.

Joseph Schoengold asked to be released after the first rehearsals. The discussions about character and the emphasis on theory seemed to him childish.

Ben Ami had a successful season with plays by Sholem

Aleichem, Hauptmann, Tolstoy, and Osip Dymov. His own work attracted such notice that the Broadway producer Arthur Hopkins offered him the lead in a modern-day version of *Samson and Delilah*. Ben Ami refused, feeling he could not desert his troupe. A quarrel with his backer, however, ended with the loss of the Madison Square. Still torn by a sense of loyalty, he told his close friend Lazar Fried (husband of Celia Adler) of the Hopkins offer. Fried did not believe his ears. "You must be a complete idiot to refuse this!" he exclaimed.

Ben Ami had a distinguished success on Broadway. From that time on, like Bertha Kalisch, he divided his career between the Yiddish and American stage. After he left the Madison Square Schwartz came in, reorganized the company, and called it Maurice Schwartz's Yiddish Art Theatre.

Although he had waited until he saw commercial possibilities in an art theatre, Schwartz never afterward deserted the idea, and it is on those strong shoulders that the Yiddish theatre was carried into the future. As an actor he had the presence and authority that instantly mark the born star. In comedy he was superb, and his Sholem Aleichem portrayals, particularly, were unsurpassed. Schwartz produced over a hundred plays in the course of his career, and it was his work that brought the word "director" into the lexicon of the Yiddish theatre.

These triumphs, however, were not quickly achieved. It was not easy for a newcomer to make his way, for the older stars were still at the top of their power and popularity.

Adler, his moment of weakness forgotten, played eight times a week, went over to London every spring, and in the summer swam and rode horseback to get himself in condition. In addition to all this, he had begun to write his autobiography and sat up late every night at this task. This history, entitled *Forty Years on the Stage*, appeared, chapter by chapter, for three years in Louis Miller's socialist paper, *Die Varheit*.

In the summer of 1919 differences arose between Adler and the Hebrew Actors Union. Complaining that Adler monopolized the best talents, the union refused to give him Joseph Rumshinsky, a composer for ten years his close associate. Adler refused the man they offered, closed the Grand and made plans to play the entire coming season in London.

He was completing his *Varheit* memoirs at this time, and in one of the closing chapters we find these angry words: "And now I hear the old Spivakovsky is sick in London, and must come in his need to strangers! Is this how it ends for a pioneer of our theatre, one of our first and best actors? See, then, the end of Spivakovsky, who gave his life to our theatre!"

Adler's old friend and rival had indeed fallen on bad times. It was many years since he had turned his back on America, and the decision had not been for the best. He had met only difficulties when he returned to Russia, and since then had apparently lived out his life in the cities of Central Europe, playing as he could with whatever actors he could keep together.

A Spivakovsky Troupe toured for some years with success and even fame, but time passed and his actors scattered. Spivakovsky went on, but conditions were difficult and sometimes desperate. Actors who saw a performance of *Shulamith* in Warsaw tell us he sang his role in a red blanket under which his boots and black trousers could be seen.

At the close of the first World War he came to London. Yiddish theatre was in full swing in that city, but Spivakovsky found every door closed. The actors would have nothing to do with him because of a rumor that while he was in Russia he had renounced his faith—become a convert. There was a grain of truth to the story. Spivakovsky had in fact received a paper in Russia that allowed him to play in cities where Yiddish theatre was under a ban. This was a legality, a conversion without substance, but it was not forgiven. The actors looked upon him as an apostate and a traitor. They cut him dead.

Since he had to make his living he gave performances with amateurs. When even this resource gave out he simply sat all day in the actors' cafe in Whitechapel, asserting perhaps by a stubborn presence his right to be there. In the end he fell sick and had to go into the hospital. He had almost no visitors and a journalist friend, outraged by the neglect of his colleagues, finally published an angry appeal on his behalf.

At this a change of heart was experienced. Actors began to say that an injustice had been done. A number of them came forward, and a performance at the Pavilion Theatre raised some money for the sick, rapidly failing man.

It is at this point that Adler, preparing to take his company to London, got news of his illness and wrote the bitter comment that appeared in the *Varheit*. There must have been letters, too, for Spivakovsky knew he was coming and repeatedly said that Yankev Adler remembered their friendship and would look after his family. Adler went directly from Victoria Station to the hospital, but was met there with the words, "Too late."

He played in London all that winter with very great critical and public acclaim. Adler was at the height of his fame at this time, and London received him like a king. According to his son Charles, the theatre was mobbed at every performance, with people waiting two days on the street for tickets to see him.

In spite of this success, it was neither a good nor a happy time. He and Sara were divided as never before, and his memoirs almost recklessly reveal an anger and disappointment with all of life. The cold and damp of London affected his health. He was bitter about the death of Spivakovsky, identifying himself in some strange way with the broken actor who had ended his days discarded by the world. Pressures in his theatrical life were mounting; he was playing up to and beyond the limits of his strength. One night he pointed to a woman backstage and asked with fear how she had come there. He had mistaken a strange woman for Keni Liptzin.

Once again the crisis passed. In the spring he was back in America and in recovered health and strength. A grand reconcilation took place between himself and Sara, and husband and wife played together all the following season. Adler had the makings of a troupe now in his own family. When he put on *The Merchant of Venice*, Nunia was his Portia, Stella his Nerissa, Julia played Jessica, and the sixteen-year-old Luther did service as Lancelot Gobbo.

In the summer of 1920 Adler rested in the pleasant town of Pine Hill, New York. Several of his sons and daughters spent this vacation with him, and Joe and Nunia Schoengold, together with their two little girls, took a cottage of their own down the road. Pearlie and Lulla Schoengold had once been applauded by the audience, and were growing up in the entirely mistakan idea that they were celebrities. They liked to go to their grandfather's because everyone there made a fuss about them, because the porch was covered with glorious pink roses, and because they could play all day in the cool orchard behind the house.

It was an easy, happy summer, with a constant flow of guests from New York. Handsome Joseph Schildkraut stayed on for weeks, carrying on a determined but unsuccessful flirtation with Julia Adler. Jay came with a moody, difficult boy called Jed Harris. Adler rested and relaxed. There were big plans in the wind, talk of a return engagement of *The Merchant* on Broadway that fall.

One afternoon, Dr. Held, physician to all Yiddish actors, paid Adler a visit. The doctor sat cross-legged on the grass. Adler, in the best of health and spirits, lounged in a hammock strung up on the lawn and chatted with him.

An hour later the children in the orchard became aware that something was amiss. Hysterical voices were heard from the house, stifled cries of agony, and the sound of women weeping. Stella, sobbing, took the older girl into a little room at the back of the house and told her to pray for her *zayde*. Pearlie clasped her hands and prayed with all her might. Her sister played on under the trees, never knowing that inside the house the all-powerful grandfather lay helpless between life and death.

Dr. Held stayed at his friend's bedside all that day and night, but there was little he could do.

Headlines in the Yiddish press next day carried the news to the shocked downtown world: JACOB ADLER FELLED BY PARALYTIC STROKE.

The first of the "farewell performances" was given a year later at the Manhattan Opera House. Months ahead, Nunia, working with the efficiency of a general, began rounding up the Broadway celebrities that would ensure its success. No one refused her. Jolson came down. Will Rogers came down. Richard Bennett, Leo Ditrichstein, George Jessel, headliners from the vaudeville world and theatrical greats, everyone was there for "the Old Man."

Adler, as advertised, played the first act of Gordin's *Lear*. Since this takes place around the festive Purim table, he could remain seated throughout his time on the stage.

After this first benefit, "farewell performances" and "positively last appearances" were advertised every year. When more money was needed, the paralyzed man got on a train and went out on the road. He would play the first act of *Lear*, and another actor would take his role for the remaining acts. In 1924 Adler improved somewhat, and in Toledo, Ohio, he attempted *The Stranger*. In this Gordin play, based on the Enoch Arden story, Adler had a second-act entrance described as the greatest moment of all Yiddish theatre. Since he portrayed a man broken and ill, he felt he could play all four acts. According to the Toledo *Blade,* ten thousand people came to the theatre hoping for tickets. But when Adler appeared there was such weeping and such ovations that he broke down, weeping aloud, and the curtain had to be drawn.

People of sensitivity were shocked to see the sick man paraded in this way before an audience, but it could not be helped. Several years later a blind Bertha Kalisch would be led around the stage in the tragic "last performances" that were her only livelihood. The Yiddish audience did not come for the Broadway celebrities, but for a last glimpse of the idols they adored.

The Old Guard was disappearing fast. Keni Liptzin had died in 1918. In her later years she was capricious and hysterical. She screamed if someone brought her the wrong dress or the wrong wig, had spasms when she played, fainted, had convulsions. It was impossible to engage her. Her husband, Michael Mintz, had pawned all he had to keep her theatre going, and in 1912 Mintz lost everything and shot himself.

"I was a weak woman," Liptzin wrote, "but I had the spirit of Mirale Efros in my blood. I have played good plays in every city and I have paid back every penny of Mintz's debts. Now I am alone and homeless. My only consolation, my only happiness, is the stage, but I sit idle weeks and months because my theatre has been taken away from me."

She was obsessed with the idea that enemies had caused her illness, and when she was dying said to Kessler, "It's all up with me, David. They've put the evil eye on me now, and Mintz is gone. There is no one to take it away."

In her last hours Liptzin spoke in a commanding voice, and referred to an actor as "Kalman," the name of her steward in *Mirale Efros*.

Kessler himself died two years later. While rehearsing at the Lyric Theatre in Brooklyn he was suddenly felled by an attack of violent abdominal pains. His collapse had a fearful effect on the actors; they felt they had seen a giant fall. They wanted to cancel the performance, but Kessler felt better next day and insisted he could go on. While playing the last act he fell unconscious. He was taken by ambulance from the theatre to the hospital, was operated on the following morning and died the same day.

After Kessler's death all bad news was kept from Adler. The newspapers were hidden when Caruso died. The suicide of a loved relative was also concealed, and one night he startled his family by asking why this friend was not there. Somebody found a hasty explanation, and a short uneasy silence followed.

"I suppose he is already under the earth," Adler said. Nobody contradicted him.

The stroke had left his mind and his speech unimpaired. On "good" days he could get from one room to another unsupported and raise both arms to the level of his head. On bad days he remained in his room or sat in an armchair by the window. A man was engaged who read to him and took him out every afternoon for an outing along the Drive. In 1925 Louis Miller asked him for a continuation of his memoirs. The old socialist *Varheit* was no longer in existence; Miller was making another try at newspaper publishing with the short-lived *New Varheit*. Since Adler could not sit at a desk and write his memoirs, the critic Joel Entin came to the house three times a week to write out the London memories he dictated.

From time to time he was taken to a concert or a play. One afternoon at Carnegie Hall a shabbily dressed lady rushed up and kissed him. On the way home Adler said sadly, "I think it was Duncan, and I hardly spoke to her!"

When the Moscow Art Theatre came to New York, Adler insisted on paying his respects to Constantine Stanislavsky. Luther and Nunia drove with him to the hotel, but when he got there he was too weak to get out of the automobile. Word was sent up, and a few minutes later Stanislavsky, in his bathrobe and slippers, hurried out of the hotel. The two men exchanged some words in Russian, and impulsively embraced. Stanislavsky wept, and Adler wept with him.

On another occasion Luther drove with his father to the Sherry-Netherland Hotel, where Jack Barrymore met them for lunch. Barrymore was moody, and spoke bitterly about the theatre, the public, the whole game. "Don't give them your heart!" was his cynical advice. He had just signed a picture contract. He talked about the money he would make, the yacht he intended to buy for his fishing trips.

"You are no good," Adler said quietly. "You are a bum."

Barrymore laughed. After a rather dark silence he spoke of something else. If Adler's judgment hurt him, he did not show it.

Visitors came often to the apartment on Riverside Drive. Max Wilner, the young bouffe comedian, came to see Jacob Adler, danced to amuse him, slid across the room on the polished floor, his dancer's feet magical, witty. Adler laughed. He loved it. The young performer reminded him of Laizer Zuckerman.

Mrs. Dinah Feinman came one day, sat with him for an hour, and when the tired man was led back to his room, rose to go with tears in her eyes. Julia Adler took her to the door, where she cried and said, "I loved your father, and I love him still."

When no one came, Adler sat alone in his armchair gazing out at the river.

From time to time he raised his voice to ask for something, and his "Sonya!" was heard in some distant room of the big apartment. Sara, hearing her name, would appear in the door, the scowl she always wore for him on her face.

That scowling face was what he wanted.

"Sonya," he would say, articulating with difficulty, "What will be—the end of it?"

"The end will be—" impatiently, forcefully, "that you will get well, that you will play again—and that will be the end of it!"

Once again reassured, he would turn back to the window.

New names were twinkling from the marquees of Second Avenue. Samuel Goldenberg. Celia Adler. Aaron Lebedeff. Ludwig Satz. A whole generation of Jewish women wept over Jennie Goldstein's seduced and betrayed shopgirls. Molly Picon sang, danced, an irresistible scamp and waif. She ran for four years in a little Cinderella story called *Tzipke*. Schwartz was beginning to loom as a big name, a big force. Actors crowded nightly into a Cafe Royale humming with life. Everyone loved the playwright Willie Siegel, who laughed at his own *shund*. On the East Side, phonograph records of Caruso mingled with the bouncy Yiddish strains of "Columbus, I Have No Complaints." America had entered the heady prosperity of the twenties.

Adler sat at his window. The hurly-burly of the theatre downtown came to him only as a faint echo.

Every weekend the grandchildren, Pearl and Lulla, were brought to see him. Pearlie knew that their *zayde* was sick now. The younger child took it for granted that he sat alone and silent all day. It was only as she grew older that she remembered those years and wondered what the thoughts of the kingly old man must have been in his armchair looking out over Riverside Drive.

Out of the yellowing pages of an old newspaper, his thoughts, in the fullness of time, were revealed:

January 17, 1925, *New Varheit:*

A cold, windy day. I sit in my armchair looking out at the frozen Hudson. Thick gray fields of ice lie before me, cut through here and there with long, broad, dull green cracks, a sign that in this place the water had struggled with its icy enemy. The eastern shore is low and flat, but in the west, sharp and bold, the thickly wooded Palisades rise toward the sky. Mountain on mountain, tower on tower, a long, mighty, fortressed wall. Am I not in Moscow? Is it not the Moscow River that spreads out, frozen, before me? And that wall, so gray, so high, is it not the Kremlin that in barbaric times protected the Winter Palace from the approaching Tatar hordes? Russia! My thoughts carry me back, and pictures of the past mix and mingle in my mind. The assassination of Alexander II. The ascension to the throne of Alexander III. The suffocating reaction that followed. The ukase against our theatre that sent our lives crashing around us in ruins. I must describe all this while my mind and imagination can still give it form and color. I must set it all down, for it belongs not to me, but to future generations.

January 24, *New Varheit:*

On February 12 of this year, Avrom Lincoln's birthday, I will reach my seventieth year. The best of my life, the most satisfying, is fading. My dressing room I see once a year, at most twice. My public, too, I see seldom, that public I have feared so much and still love so dearly. Far from my public, far from my dressing room, how gray and pale are now my days!

Old I am as an artist, and of the companions who started out with me, only I remain. Where are they now, my true ones of yesterday? Where is Goldfaden, my rabbi, my teacher? Where is Mogulesko, the young companion whose career flowered together with my own? Where is Gordin, the wise man, the sincere, the playwright in whose characters my talent unfolded like the petals of the rose? Where is Keni Liptzin—fate brought us together in that faraway village of Russia, and in the great city of the new world we were not parted. Where is David Kessler—though we were competitors we loved one another. Better than anyone he understood and appreciated my art, and knew, too, that better than anyone. I understood and appreciated his. Where are they all? The black Kassamann has laid them all away and left me here all alone, the last of my generation.

Old as I am, I have my memories of the Yiddish stage, memories I must set down so that, dipped in blood, lit with the tears of a living witness, the world may know how we built, out of the dark realities of Jewish life, with our blood, with our nerves, with the tears of our sleepless nights, the theatre that stands today as a testament to our people.

His children were all busy with careers on Broadway. Jay Adler played with Schildkraut in an English translation of Sholem Asch's *God of Vengeance.* Julia was Jessica to David Warfield's Shylock, and the following season Belasco starred her in a comedy called *Rosa Machree.* Luther got the coveted role of Laurette Taylor's son in *Humoresque.* Stella, after playing the lead in Karel Capek's play *The World We Live In,* left Broadway to study in a small group experimenting with the ideas of Constantine Stanislavsky. She was roundly laughed at by her brothers and sisters for a seriousness they considered unprofessional.

As for Adler's niece, the little "cousin from Russia" was Francine Larrimore now, a reigning star on Broadway and soon to be the heroine of such successes as *Chicago, Brief Moment,* and *Let Us Be Gay.*

The life of this family still centered around the sick man on Riverside Drive. From day to day hopes for his recovery rose and fell, and everyone talked of how things would be "when Papa gets better."

It never occurred to any of us that he could die.

Passover came early that year. Adler sat at the head of the table. He led the prayers with much of his old strength, joked, and told stories as he used to do. The family rejoiced, but that spurt of power was his last. Several days later when Nunia came to visit him, he was too tired to leave his room. As she was leaving, Nunia stopped at his door. "It's not very nice, Papa," she said reproachfully. "I come to see you, and you don't come into the living room."

"I will do-o-o it!" he answered in the strongly emotional broken English so peculiarly his own. "I will do-o-o it next time!"

The "next time" he had promised never came. Two days later he was helped to the dining room for his midday meal. He waited, and then, with the impatience of a sick man whose meals are the only events of his day, raised his voice and asked for the soup. Sara, helping Rouchel in the kitchen, answered that it would soon be ready. After a silence his voice was raised again. "Where have they taken the child? Why do I never see Pearl?"

"They will bring her soon," Sara answered.

Moments later the women heard a frighteningly heavy thud. Sara ran into the dining room, calling his name. He had fallen heavily from his chair to the floor, blood streaming from the nose and mouth. Sara screamed and called wildly for a doctor.

"Have you no eyes?" Rouchel said from the doorway. "Don't you see the human being is dead?"

He died during the week of Passover. There was no need to sit *shivve* or to cover the mirrors in the house. There is a blessing on all who die at that time.

There were eulogies and editorials in the American press. Leo Ditrichstein compared Adler's Lear with the Othello of Salvini and the Hamlet of Booth. *The New York Times* declared that with his demise the heroic age of the Yiddish theatre had come to an end.

For the downtown world, his death had a different meaning. Adler had never left his people, never set himself above them. For forty years he had given them only what was greatest in himself. He had created for them and for the world an image of the Jew at his highest. It was not the actor they had lost, but the man who, through the years of their poverty and darkness, had held up before them an ideal.

The men who give us that light are mourned with a very deep grief. Twenty-four hours before the funeral, masses of people were gathering at the Hebrew Actors Club, where the body lay in state. By eleven that morning the crowds had become so dense that the doors had to be closed to all but the family and members of the union. Thousands had already filed past the bier, and the streets outside were black with those hoping to be admitted.

By the following day, fifty thousand people had poured into the streets in what *The New York Times* called "a demonstration on the Lower East Side seldom equaled in the history of New York." Other New York papers estimated that as many as a half million people had gathered during the two days his body lay in state. Buttons were sold with Adler's picture and the words, "We Mourn Our Loss." His photograph and the same legend were displayed in store windows. Most stores were closed during the two hours of the funeral procession. A squad of twenty-four mounted police and more than a hundred patrolmen were stationed along the route of the procession. Cries and laments were heard as the pallbearers brought the coffin out of union headquarters, and the police had trouble keeping back the crowds surging forward in their effort to come nearer.

Jacob Adler had lived out his time, done his share, like all of us, of good and harm. He was perhaps a very great sinner, but like that other Jacob, also a man human and frail, he had the blessing.

Services were held on the stage of Kessler's Second Avenue Theatre, and afterward hundreds of mourners, weeping and wailing, followed the cortege down the Bowery, going on foot through Grand Street, Forsythe Street, Delancey Street, and over the Williamsburg Bridge to the Mount Carmel burial grounds in Brooklyn. Every girder of the bridge was hung with men watching silently to see the hearse go by. And all that hour the church bells of New York rang out to mark the passing of a great Jew.

It was 1926, another kind of time.

Epilogue

The Theatre of the Heart: A Heritage

A stir of interest rippled through the profession two years later as the family got together in a production of *The Wild Man*. All the Adlers took part in this play. Joe Schoengold played the dark-souled father and also directed. Jay turned in a stunning performance as the slippery Varabaitchik, the role originally played by Mogulesko. The slender, petite Julia, in a feat of character acting, played Shiffre the cook. And Abe, watching young Luther Adler rehearse the role created by his father, said quietly, "I think the boy is star material."

The Adlers could have formed a permanent company, but the pull of individual careers proved too strong. They dispersed.

In the late twenties, Yiddish theatre was going strong. There were twelve companies in New York, two more houses showing Yiddish vaudeville, and fourteen theatres on the road. But the wheel was turning now on its own momentum. The immigration quota passed by Congress in 1922 had stopped all but a trickle of incoming Yiddish refugees. Young American-born boys and girls were flocking to the movie palaces on Broadway. They did not care for Yiddish plays or Yiddish actors. The language itself was dying. What Adler had once sighed over as a "theatre of youth" was becoming a theatre of the older generation.

Stars of the Yiddish stage turned to the American theatre. Ludwig Satz had a successful run in the comedy *Potash and Perlmutter*. Nellie Casman sang her famous "Yossel" at the Palace. Nunia played a witty Helena in the Boston Repertory production of *Midsummer Night's Dream*. And Muni Weisenfreund, greatest of the younger players, flashed across the theatrical scene, bringing to Broadway the electric intensity of the Russian actor. After *Four Walls*, Weisenfreund was signed by Fox Films. Within a few years he had won international fame as Paul Muni.

Stella was for a time Maurice Schwartz's leading lady. Her stay in the Yiddish theatre was short and left with all Jewish actors a memory of her heartbreaking beauty and great sweetness of character. In *Wandering Star*, based on Sholem Aleichem's novel about the Yiddish theatre, her performance was described by a fellow player as so ethereal as to seem "no more than a perfume on the stage."

Stella left Schwartz to enter the Group Theatre, where Luther Adler soon joined her. Both of them gave performances in the Group that have come down as legends to a younger theatrical generation.

Among the Adler family only Celia and Nunia still relied on the Yiddish theatre. Abe was a well-known Broadway manager. Jay went on the road with Sidney Kingsley's *Dead End*, and then left for Hollywood. Charlie Adler, between trips back to England, performed as a dancer in vaudeville. His wife, the daughter of Gustave Schacht, was beautiful, she had a voice, and for many years Charles Adler and Emily Earle toured as headliners on the American vaudeville stage.

Julia Adler retired after her marriage to the painter Joseph Foshko. She returned to the stage only once, in 1939, to play Bessie Berger in the Group revival of Clifford Odets's *Awake and Sing*. Julia did not appear again. The Adler family, too, has its lost talents.

In 1932 Schwartz, by a fluke, had one of the longest runs in New York with I. J. Singer's mystic *Yoshe Kalb*. The American and Yiddish theatre alike lay in the deadly grip of the Depression. Out-of-work actors pounded the pavements, looking for any kind of job. One after another, the houses on Broadway and Second Avenue closed.

A score of "little theatres" came into being. The Theatre Collective. The Theatre of Action. The Theatre Union. The Yiddish Artef. Left-wing groups where dedicated young people worked without pay, happy to keep their hand in, learn their craft.

Down in the night-blooming, din-filled cafeterias of Greenwich Village you could always find the disinherited kids of the thirties, Abe Adler's son and Joe Schoengold's daughters laughing away the nights together, and dreaming of a better world under the red banner of the revolution.

At sixteen Pearlie Schoengold had stepped into a lead role when Stella Adler left the cast of *The Wild Man*. She gave an uncertain, timid performance, but thrilled the audience with a flood of power in the difficult emotional scenes. Now jobs were scarce. She joined the Theatre Collective. Her sister worked for a season with Schwartz, then studied with Benno Schneider, the Russian director of the Artef. Abe's son dreamed and schemed, produced a road show of *The Front Page*, tried his hand at a play, ran a little movie house, lost it again.

If there is such a thing as rebirth, Rosenberg lived again in Allen Adler. Like Rosenberg, he had a speech defect. Like Rosenberg, he had an army of lonely men who followed him through the mad adventures of his days and nights. Allen gave everyone a devastating nickname, found the hilarious bend in every soul, uncovered a madman behind every variation of the human facade. A dozen times success was in his grasp. As many times he could not resist the mad caper, the insane jest that sent his plans crashing about his ears. During the brief years given him, he threw his laughter into the teeth of life. He died young, and only those closest ever guessed the longing of that wild romantic heart.

The bad years scarred the younger people lightly. The older ones found them harder. Joe Schoengold lost everything in the stock market crash of 1929, and never quite got back on his feet.

In 1933 Schoengold organized a company and took it to South America. He had played Buenos Aires before and had a big following there, but this time the luck turned. It was the little comedian Menashe Skulnick who was called back time after time, the applause redoubling each time he took a bow.

Skulnick relates that Schoengold came into his dressing room afterward, laughing. *"You did it!"* Schoengold exclaimed, pointing at him. "I couldn't do it, but *you did it!*"

Skulnick was amazed. "I could hardly believe my ears!" he told Abe Cahan. "Any other actor would have been dying of jealousy! From that time on, Schoengold split his profits down the middle and made me his partner!"

Along with his father's talent, Schoengold had inherited his lofty indifference to the ups and downs of a dog-eat-dog world. He had long ago lost his illusions about the theatre. Like his father, he had chosen the road, preferring good money in Chicago, Boston, and Philadelphia to the risk of stardom in New York. A touch of vanity would have served him better than all his realism. During the Depression years the road dwindled and died. Schoengold came back to find he had been away too long.

One way or another, he managed. He was an actor respected as one of the best. A whole profession loved him for his strength, his sanity, and the joy of his presence. He hung on, made his deals, survived.

Nunia had long ago lost her diamonds in the dressing rooms of a hundred cities. Her father had once put away three thousand dollars in her name, but she had forgotten the city and did not remember the name of the bank. She had come down in the world, but she did not much care. There were still cheap rooms in pleasant enough streets. Joe came home as always, smiling and with huge bags of good things to eat. The kids came around. Abe came with Allen. Celia came. Everyone played casino or fan-tan. Nunia talked of the old days, cried a little sometimes, and remembered her father.

Sara Adler had her own little apartment on University Place. She took rhumba lessons, hobnobbed with her old friends, and every year Nunia organized a benefit evening for her.

When she was far into her seventies, Sara performed all four acts of Gordin's *Homeless,* with Zvee Scooler in the role of the husband. She still moved around the stage like a poem, and played her part just as she had played it forty years before. She had staged and directed the entire production, and afterward went to the Cafe Royale and stayed there until four in the morning.

In her last years she lived with Stella, married at that time to Harold Clurman. She had her two rooms in the apartment with Pretty Boy, her beloved cockateel, the mahogany desk from East Seventy-second Street, the portrait of Sarah Bernhardt on her dressing table.

One day Nunia, visiting her, said in a sad voice, "Have you heard, Mama? They have closed the Cafe Royale."

"And when will they open it again?" asked the undaunted Sara.

And for a short time, they really did open it again.

When she went to the hospital for a cataract operation, Stella asked her in the cab if she was afraid.

"If you are afraid of the bear, you do not go into the woods," Sara calmly answered.

When she was recovering, Luther came with his son, Jacob Adler, and told his mother the young man had been admitted to the Massachusetts Institute of Technology.

"Oh, I am afraid for him!" the still-thrilling voice answered. "I am afraid for clever people in this world!"

In 1939, when she had passed her eightieth year, a Golden Jubilee evening was given in her honor. Harold Clurman, Abe Cahan, Sylvia Sidney, married at the time to Luther Adler, and Reuben Guskin, manager of the Hebrew Actors Union, gave testimonials from the stage, and Sara played the great third act of *Resurrection*. Actors of the Group Theatre were present on the occasion. Morris Carnovsky commented that except for the supreme art of Eleanora Duse, he had never seen a greater performance.

She died in 1953 at the age of ninety-three. She had survived her husband by almost twenty-five years.

Many very old people came to her funeral. The great critic Sholem Perlmutter spoke the eulogy, and a gray-haired patriot, one of the last, exclaimed in his solemn broken English, "The last pillar of our theatre has fallen."

He was himself its last pillar, if he had only known it.

Visitors taking a certain path in Mount Carmel Cemetery in Brooklyn will come upon a remarkable life-size eagle of rough dark granite. Carved by the sculptor Aaron Goodelman, this bird hovers aloft, a single work of art in a sea of tombstones.

Under those wings Sara Adler was laid to rest. And there Allen, Abe, and Nunia also sleep.

Yiddish theatre is still played here and there about the world. In Israel it is having a revival. The New York actors have a season today of about eleven weeks. Every year Joseph Buloff, Jacob ben Ami, or David Opatoshu put on something fine. Let us give homage, too, to the dazzling gifts of Leo Fuchs, to the beloved Jacob Jacobs, to lovely Miriam Kressyn, to Seymour Rechtzeit, Nellie Casman, Stan Porter, Bruce Adler—all the gallant little band.

A hundred years have gone by since Avrom Goldfaden took the first actors out into the provinces of Roumania. Since that time the world has changed past recognition. We have a stage today that probes without a tremor into the most fearful crevices of the human soul, and we are so intent on Truth that we have gone a long way toward enthroning ugliness. Now that we have had our Theatre of the Absurd, our Theatre of Cruelty, our Theatre of Violence, we may want to remember the actors who, against such great opposing forces, built together a theatre of feeling, a theatre of the heart.

Everyone has his own Yiddish theatre. For some it is the comedy of Ludwig Satz or Menashe Skulnick, for others it is the romantic stance of Boris Thomashefsky or the impressive effects of Maurice Schwartz. For the Adlers, the Yiddish theatre will always mean the plays and the actors of Gordin's time.

Not long ago a young avant-garde composer was present at a gathering of this family. The talk that evening went back for some reason to that other time, to the theatre of Gordin's day. "But what's the use?" someone said, giving up with a sigh. "Nobody knows now how it was."

"But I do know!" the composer said. "*This* is how it was!" And walking over to the piano he found with one hand a succession of chords.

He had played the slow movement of Beethoven's Rasoumovsky Quartet in E Minor. Nothing could be further from Yiddish theatre, yet for a moment no one in the room spoke. For our young friend had really understood. In the slow, brave march of those chords, one somehow finds them—Gordin, Kessler, Thomashefsky, Liptzin, Kalisch, Adler—all the lives that make up the story.

Words may fail, but music never. These pages can tell only a part of it. Those who want the innermost truth of "how it was" have only to listen to that music, speaking as it does of all hope, all human endeavor—and then they will have it.

The End

Bibliography of Sources

Adler, Celia. *Celia Adler Recalls*. New York, Celia Adler Foundation and Book Committee, 1959.
Adler, Jacob P. *Forty Years on the Stage, My Life Story and the History of the Yiddish Theatre*. Die Varheit (in Yiddish), April 30, 1916–February 28, 1919.
———. *My Life*. Die Neie Varheit (in Yiddish), April 1–July 30, 1926.
Adler, Sara. *My Life Story*. Jewish Daily Forward (in Yiddish), September 11, 1937–March 31, 1939.
Asherovitch, M. *David Kessler and Muni Weisenfreund* (in Yiddish). New York, Forward Association, 1930.
Beck, Ruth Torton. *Kafka and the Yiddish Theatre*. Madison, Wisconsin, University of Wisconsin Press, 1971.
Black, Mary. *Old New York in Early Photographs*. New York, New York Historical Society, 1973.
Cahan, Abraham. *Pages of My Life*, Vols. I–IV (in Yiddish). New York, Forward Association, 1926.
Clurman, Harold. *The Fervent Years*. New York, Alfred A. Knopf, Inc., 1945.
Dimont, Max I. *Jews, God and History*. New York, Simon & Schuster, 1962.
Dubnow, S. M. *History of the Jews in Russia and Poland from the Earliest Time until the Present Day*. Philadelphia, Jewish Publication Society of America, 1916–1920.
Finestein, Israel. *A Short History of Anglo-Jewry*. London, published for the World Jewish Congress by Lincolns-Prager, 1957.
Gartner, Lloyd P. *The Jewish Immigrant in England*. Detroit, Michigan, Wayne State University Press, 1960.
Gordin, Jacob. *Dramas of Jacob Gordin* (in Yiddish). The Friends of Jacob Gordin. Place of publication and date unknown.
Gorin, Bernard. *History of the Yiddish Theatre* (in Yiddish). New York, Literarisher Verlag, 1918.
Hapgood, Hutchins. *The Spirit of the Ghetto*. New York, Funk & Wagnalls Company, Inc., 1965.
Hodder, Edwin. *The Life of a Century*. London, George Newnes Ltd., 1901.
Kafka, Franz. *Dearest Father, Stories and Other Writings*. New York, Schocken Books, 1954.
———. *Diaries 1910–1913*. New York, Schocken Books, 1971.

Kessler, David. *How I Became an Actor* (in Yiddish). *The Day,* January 7–27, 1917.
Kouvenhoven, John A. *Columbia Historical Portrait of New York.* New York, Harper & Row, 1971.
Lifson, David. *The Yiddish Theatre in America.* New York, Thomas Yoseloff, 1965.
Liptzin, Sol. *Eliakum Zunzer, Poet of His People.* New York, Behrman House, 1950.
MacGowan, Kenneth, and William Melnitz. *Golden Ages of the Theatre.* Englewood Cliffs, New Jersey, Prentice-Hall, Inc., 1959.
Margoulieth, Moses. *History of the Jews in Great Britain.* London, Richard Bentley, 1857.
Mayhew, Henry. *London Labour & the London Poor,* Vols. I and II. New York, Dover Publications, Inc., 1968.
Mosse, W. E. *Alexander II and the Modernization of Russia.* New York, The Macmillan Company, 1958.
Odell, George C. D. *Annals of the New York Stage,* Vols. XI–XV. New York, Columbia University Press, 1927–1949.
Sanders, Ronald. *The Downtown Jews.* New York, Harper & Row, 1969.
Seth, Ronald. *The Russian Terrorists.* London, Barrie and Jenkins.
Sholem Aleichem. *Wandering Star.* New York, Crown Publishers, 1952.
"Stepniak." *Russia under the Tsars.* London, Ward and Downey, 1885.
Thomashefsky, Boris. *My Life* (in Yiddish). New York, Trio Press, 1937.
Thorn, John, Lockyer, and Smith. *A History of England.* New York, Thomas Y. Crowell Company, 1961.
Timbs, John. *London and Westminster.* London, Richard Bentley, 1868.
Young, Boaz. *My Life in the Theatre* (in Yiddish). New York, Ykuf Verlag, 1950.
Young, Stark. *Immortal Shadows.* New York, Hill and Wang, 1958.
Zangwill, Israel. *Children of the Ghetto.* Philadelphia, Jewish Publication Society, 1862.
Zeiger, Marvin. *History of the Yiddish Theatre in New York City to 1892.* PhD. dissertation for the Graduate School of Indiana University.
Zunzer, Miriam Shomer. *Yesterday.* New York, Stackpole Sons, 1939.
Zylberzweig, Zalmen. *Encyclopoedia of the Yiddish Theatre* (in Yiddish), Vols. I–VI. Mexico City, Hebrew Actors Union of America, 1969.

Outline History of the USSR. Moscow, Foreign Languages Publishing House, 1960.

Index

Abramovitch, Bena, 252, 236
Abramovitch, Max, 252
Actors' Equity Association, 287
Adler, Abe (Abram; son), 194, 203, 236, 282, 334–335, 357, 360
Adler, Allen (grandson), 359, 360
Adler, Reb Avremele Fridkus (grandfather), 8, 11–12
Adler, Bruce, 361
Adler, Celia (Tzirale; daughter), 246, 254–255, 302, 326, 345, 352, 358, 360
Adler, Charles (son), 191, 284–285, 348, 358
Adler, Dinah Shtettin (second wife; later Feinman), 179–181, 196–197, 203, 246–248, 254–255, 352
Adler, Feivel Abramovitch (father), 5–8, 12, 65, 81, 143–144, 161
Adler, Frances (Fanya; also called Nunia), 282–283, 287–289, 300–301, 313–317, 348, 349, 351, 354, 357–360
Adler, Dr. Hermann Marcus, 164, 201
Adler, Hessye (mother), 6–12, 17, 23, 57, 65, 71, 80, 144, 287–288
Adler, Jacob P.:
 acting standards of, 16–17, 102–105, 113–114, 258–267, 320–323, 334–336, 341
 acting style of, 68–80, 137–141, 168–172, 184, 260–272, 289–292, 304–308, 327–328, 335
 critics' response to, 255–257, 267, 291, 292, 305–308, 321, 335
 early jobs of, 9–15, 18–21, 24–31, 56–62, 67, 71
 early romances of, 14–15, 22, 23, 24, 28–29
 first United States visit of, 235–236, 243
 home life of, in Russia, 5–7, 11–12, 143–144, 287–289; in the United States, 283, 284, 286, 316, 321
 influences on, *see* Goldfaden, Avrom; Gordin, Jacob; Gradner, Yisrol; Rosenberg, Yisrol; Russian theatre; Tolstoy, Leo
 and Kaiser, Jennya, 191–197, 204, 243
 labor views of, 81, 87–92, 126–129, 269–270, 287
 last years of, 343, 348–356
 London career of, 161, 163–190, 198–204, 346, 348
 marriages of: first, *see* Adler, Sophia Oberlander; second, *see* Adler, Dinah Shtettin; third, *see* Adler, Sara Heine
 memoirs of, 346, 347, 353–354
 musical ability of, 17, 113, 255
 personal characteristics of, 7–15, 21–23, 28–30, 76–77, 198, 278, 318–323
 political sympathies of, 14–15, 23, 122–123
 professional relations of, *see* Goldfaden, Avrom; Gordin, Jacob; Gradner, Yisrol; Heine, Maurice; Hopkins, Arthur; Kessler, David; Rosenberg, Yisrol; Schoengold, Abba; Spivakovsky, Jacob; Thomashefsky, Boris
 schooling of, 8–9, 82–85, 320
 sobriquets of, 13, 172, 244
Adler, Jacob (grandson), 361
Adler, Jay (son), 316, 348, 354, 358
Adler, Julia (daughter), 300–301, 316, 342, 347, 348, 354, 357, 358
Adler, Luther (son), 316, 323, 334, 348, 354, 357–361
Adler, Rabbi Nissim Hillel, 161, 163–165, 203
Adler, Nunia (daughter), *see* Adler, Frances
Adler, Rivke Vera (the first "Nunia";

365

daughter), 143–144, 184–185, 189–190
Adler, Sam, 225
Adler, Sara Heine (third wife):
  as an actress, 222–223, 256, 269, 310–311, 313–314, 336, 345, 360–361
  first marriage of (to Maurice Heine), 228–229, 240–241, 244–250, 254
  second marriage (to Adler), 254, 265–266, 270, 279–281, 285, 287, 313–314, 348, 352, 354, 357
Adler, Sophia Oberlander (Sonya Michelson; first wife)
  Jacob Adler's courtship of, 15, 62–77, 80, 87–95
  Jacob Adler's marriage to, 95, 106–125, 137–144, 163, 168–169, 191–197
Adler, Soore (sister), *see* Levovsky, Soore Adler
Adler, Stella (daughter), 274, 316, 340–341, 348, 349, 354, 358, 360
Alexander II, 4–6, 26, 118–123
Alexander III, 145–146, 147, 353
Alexander, Crown Prince of Jerusalem (Hurvitz play), 273–274
Alliance Israelite Universelle, 211
Am Olam, 219
"Angel, The" (Goldfaden poem), 38
Annals of the New York Stage (Odell), 222
Apology for the Honorable Nation of the Jews and All the Sons of Israel, An (Nichols book), 156
Arbeiter Zeitung, 259
Arch Street Theater, Philadelphia, 297
Artef Theatre, 358
Asch, Sholem, 326–327, 354
Asherovitch (critic), 271, 277
Ashkenazim, 158–159
Auntie Sosya (Goldfaden play), 37
Awake and Sing (Odets play), 358
Azmirov (Odessa reviewer), 25, 97

Bain, Cheikel, 111–117, 130, 145–148
Baker, Belle, 273
Banker Tyrant (Hurvitz play), 54
Bar Kochba (Goldfaden opera), 102, 223, 228
Barondess, Joseph, 285–286
Barrymore, John, 308, 335–336, 351
Barsky, Israel, 219–223
Becker, Simche, 173
Beggar of Odessa, The (play), 169–171, 178, 244
Belasco, David, 354
ben Ami, Jacob, 326, 344–346, 361
Bennett, Richard, 308, 349
Berenstein, Berl, 265

Berl of Brod (vagabond singer), 15
Beygun, Lipitz, 68
Bezelinsky (playwright), 103, 184
Bigamist, The (Lilienblum play), 103–104
Blade, The, Toledo, OH, 350
Blank, Leon, 49, 237, 256
Bluebeard (Offenbach operetta), 226
Booth, Edwin, 355
Boris Godunov (Moussorgsky opera), 113–114
Bowery Garden Theatre, *see* Oriental Theatre
Boyarsky, Rafael, 216, 222, 223
Breindele Cossack (Goldfaden play), 52, 63–64, 69–70, 82–85
Brendel, Dorothea, 34
Brief Moment (Behrman play), 354
Brieux, Eugene, 273
Brodsky, Abram Markovitch, 56, 210
Bronx Express (Dymov play), 327
Buloff, Joseph, 361
Busy Doings of Yeklein, The (play), 32

Cafe Royale, 342, 350–360
Cahan, Abraham, 212, 217, 258, 259
  on Adler, 256
  on Gordin, 324–325, 329, 330
  on Hurvitz, 230, 239
  on Kessler, 339
  on Liptzin, 327
  on Mogulesko, 233
  on Thomashefsky, 273–274
Camille (Dumas play), 272
Capricious Daughter, The (Goldfaden play), 118
Carnovsky, Morris, 365
Caruso, Enrico, 344, 350, 352
Casman, Nellie, 357–361
cellar singers, 15–16
Chaimovitch, Moishe Heine (*see also* Heine, Maurice), 173, 176, 198
Chaimovitch, Sara Levitzkaya (*see also* Adler, Sara Heine), 173–176
Chatterton, Ruth, 308
Chicago (play), 354
Children of the Ghetto (dramatization of Zangwill novel), 326
City Theatre, Odessa, 15, 24–26
Clockmaker's Hat, The (play), 54
Clurman, Harold, 360, 361
Cohan, George M., 337
Conspiracy at Tisza Eslar, The (Hurvitz play), 229, 231
Coquettish Ladies (Sheikevitch play), 226, 232–233

Daniel Deronda (George Eliot), 328

Index

Daughter of Hell, The (operetta), 41
David and Goliath (Berman play), 33
David ben Jesse (Lateiner operetta), 251–253
Dementia Americana (Gordin play), 328–329, 332–333
Desolate Isle, The (Goldfaden play), 47
Dinman, Simche, 46, 48
Ditrichstein, Leo, 349, 355
Dr. Almasado (Goldfaden play), 182, 184
Don Isaac Abarbanel (Lateiner play), 229
Don Josef Abarbanel (Hurvitz play), 229
Dresser, Paul, 208
Drew, John, 308
Dumb Bride, The (Goldfaden operetta), 44
Duncan, Isadora, 341–342, 351
"*Dus Pintale Yid*" (Goldfaden poem), 36, 38
Dus Pintale Yid (Seiffert play), 333
Dybbuk, The (play), 345
Dymov, Osip, 327, 346
Earle, Emily, 358
Edelstein, Joseph, 272, 276, 285–289
Eighth Street Theatre, 341
Eisenberg, Annie, *see* Manne, Annie
"Eli Eli" (song), 273
Elisha ben Avuya (Gordin play), 327–328, 332
Entin, Joel, 351
Epstein, Alter, 306, 345
Epstein, Fanny, 186–187
Ettinger, Dr. Solomon, 35

Father's Curse, A (Feinman play), 254
Feinman, Celia (Adler), *see* Adler, Celia
Feinman, Dinah, *see* Adler, Dinah Shtettin
Feinman, Siegmund, 235, 252–255
Fiddler on the Roof (Broadway musical), 323
Fiedler, Herman, 168–170, 203
Finkel, Annetta (Schwartz), 51, 72, 116, 225
Finkel, Bella, 302–303
Finkel, Emma (Thomashefsky), 247, 293–303
Finkel, Lucy, 302
Finkel, Maurice (Moishe):
   as actor and director, 16, 269, 295
   in actors' strike, 237, 240, 245
   and Adler, 72–73, 243, 300
   character of, 72–73, 295
   children of, 302–303
   as folk singer, 16, 30, 38, 47, 147
   and Goldfaden, 51, 115–116, 237
   and Gordin, 262–263
   marriages of, 116, 293–303
   suicide of, 300–301
   and Thomashefsky, 250–252

Fishkind, Avrom, 68–69, 108, 145, 319
Fiske, Harrison Gray, 273
Flying Dutchman, The (opera), 44
Folk's Advokat, 259
Forgotten Corner, The (Hirschbein play), 327, 330
Forty Years on the Stage (Adler), 346
Foshko, Joseph, 345, 355
Foshko, Julia, *see* Adler, Julia
Four Walls (Broadway play), 358
Freig Folk's Buehne, 325
Frei Folk's Stimme, 259
Fried, Celia Adler, *see* Adler, Celia
Fried, Lazar, 346
Friedman, Rosa, 44, 47, 50, 55
Frug, Shimen, 336
Fuchs, Leo, 361

Garrick, David, 170
Gersten, Bertha, 303, 345
Gilman, Ben, 337
Gilmore, Frank, 307
Glebova, Madame (Odessa actress), 23–25, 29
Glickman's Palace Theatre, Chicago, 314
God, Man and Devil (Gordin play), 338
God of Vengeance (Asch play), 326, 354
Gold, Laibish, 246
"Goldbergs, The" (radio show), 302
Goldenberg, Samuel, 352
Goldfaden, Avrom:
   and Adler, 15–17, 30, 70–74, 114–118, 123–129
   character of, 52–53, 73, 96, 236
   as director, 242
   early career of, 35–55, 62
   effect of ukase on, 146–147
   last years of, 241–242, 328
   as playwright, 97–108
   recitation style of, 38
   United States career of, 236–238, 328
Goldfaden, Naphtali (Tulya), 67, 68, 74–77, 87–94, 106–108
Goldfaden Opera House, *see* Roumania Opera House
Golditza, 48
Goldstein, Jenny, 352
Goldstein, Socher, 39–42, 47–49, 187
Goldstein, Sophia, *see* Karp, Sophia Goldstein
Goldstein brothers (*see also* Bain, Cheikel), 13
Golubuck, Abe, 214–218, 221
Goilubuck, Leon, 215–218, 221
Golubuck, Miron, 216, 221, 223
Gordin, Jacob Michailovitch, 104, 259–273, 279, 310–311, 323–333, 362

Gorin, Bernard, 45, 51, 333
Gorki, Maxim, 273
Gradner, Annetta, 49–50, 86, 161, 166–169, 187–189
Gradner, Yisrol:
  early European career of, 16, 38–42, 47–50, 55, 86–87
  London career of, 148–150, 161, 165–169, 177–179, 187–189
Grand Theatre, 292, 299, 334, 341, 346
Granny and Her Granddaughter (Goldfaden play), 42, 49, 63
Granovsky, Chaya Soore, *see* Schoengold, Clara
Green Fields (Hirschbein play), 345
Gritzkopf (Viennese director), 101, 240
Group Theatre, 358
Guskin, Reuben, 361
Gypsy Girl, The (Hurvitz operetta), 199

Hamlet, Thomashefsky's production of, 274–275
Harris, Jed, 348
Hartenstein, Jacob, 141–143
Haskala ("The Awakening"), 17, 33–35, 44, 327, 331
Hauptmann, Gerhardt, 346
Hebrew Actors Club, 355
Hebrew Actors Union, 286–287, 346
Hebrew Opera and Dramatic Company, 217
Heimat (Sudermann play), 310, 325
Heine, Maurice, 222–224, 227–229, 240, 244–246, 254
Heine, Sara, *see* Adler, Sara Heine
Held, Dr. Isidor, 349
Held, Anna (Hannale), 185–186, 242
Hennings, Betty, 329
High Commission for the Revision of Current Laws Concerning the Jews, 146
Hirschbein, Peretz, 325–326, 329–330
History of the Yiddish Theatre (Gorin), 45
Homeless, The (Gordin play), 310, 356
Hope of Israel (Menasseh ben Israel book), 157
Hopkins, Arthur, 305–306, 346
Hopper, De Wolfe, 208
Humble Addresses to the Lord Protector (Menasseh ben Israel book), 157
Humoresque (play), 354
Hurvitz, Moishe Isaac Halevy, 53–55, 187, 229–231, 239–240, 250, 273, 275, 325
Hymie in America (Marks play), 260
Immigrant, The (play), 338
Independent Yiddish Artists Company, 264

Intrigue, The (Goldfaden operetta), 41
Irving, Sir Henry, 304, 306

Jacobs, Jacob, 357
Jessel, George, 349
Jew, The (Richard Cumberland play), 159
Jewish Chronicle, 200
Jewish Daily Forward, 259, 328
Jewish Heart, The (Lateiner play), 295, 333
Jewish Operetta Company of Roumania, 224
Jignitza Theatre, Bucharest, 42–43
Johnstown Flood, The (Hurvitz play), 250
Jolson, Al, 349
Judah Maccabee (Lateiner play), 247–248
Judische Gazetten, 213, 258, 329
Judith and Holofernes (play), 260
Juive, La (Scribe play), 101, 104, 245–246, 255
Jungvitz, Boaz, *see* Young, Boaz
Juvelier, Kalman, 242

Kafka, Franz, 269
Kaiser, Jennya, 172, 191–197, 204, 243
Kalisch, Bertha, 242, 256, 272–273, 310, 325, 330, 336, 346, 350
Kaminska, Esther Rouchel, 310, 325–326
Kaplan, Shimen, 132
Karp, Max, 174, 223, 228, 237, 240, 252–253, 261
Karp, Sophia (Goldstein) (Soore Siegel)
  in Europe, 41–42, 49, 187
  in the United States, 228, 237, 240, 273, 299
Katzenellenbogen (playwright), 104, 229
Katzman, Jacob (Yankele), 61, 64–65, 77, 87–90, 108, 187, 319
Kaufman, Bessie, *see* Thomashefsky, Bessie
Kaufman, S. J., 308
Kean (Dumas play), 278
Kean, Edmund, 170, 305
Kean family of Chicago, 236, 284
Kennedy, Madge, 308
Kessler, David:
  as an actor, 325, 333, 338–339, 344, 350
  and Adler, 77–79, 187, 240–241, 246, 253, 261, 264, 270–277
  and Goldfaden, 237
  and Mogulesko, 225–226
  and Schoengold, Abba, 78, 240, 277
  last illness, 350
Kessler's Second Avenue Theatre, 338–339, 355
King Solomon (Hurvitz play), 229
King Solomon's Judgment (Lateiner play), 229
"Kiss, A" (Goldfaden song), 41

"Klugt Sich" (Gradner song), 40
Kobrin, Leon, 285
  on Adler, 321
  on Gordin, 325
  on Kessler, 271
  on Liptzin, 326
  on Mogulesko, 340
Kost, Alexander, 221
Kozlova, Madame (Odessa actress), 23–25
Krantz, Philip, 260
Krantzfeld, Soore, 215–218
Kressyn, Miriam, 361
Kreutzer Sonata, The (Tolstoy play), 345
Kupfer, Israel, 45

Larrimore Francine, 316, 354
Lateiner, Joseph, 47–48, 97–100, 174, 225, 229–230, 240, 263, 326
Lebanon (progressive society), 38–40
Lebedeff, Aaron, 352
Lehrman (Elisavetgrad critic), 82–85
Lerner, Osip Michailovitch, 100–104
Lessin, A., 329
Let Us Be Gay (Behrman play), 354
Levinson, David, 300–301
Levitzky, Ellye, 283
Levitzky, Pessye, 283, 316
Levovsky, Fanya, *see* Larrimore, Francine
Levovsky, Isaac, 144
Levovsky, Soore (Adler), 9, 144, 287–288, 316
Libin, Z., 333
Libresko, Isaac, 37–39, 48, 53, 97
Lilienblum, Moishe Laib, 103–104
Linetzki, Yoel, 6, 36–38, 53–54
Liptzin, Keni (Kraindl Sacher; Keni Sonyes)
  as an actress, 256–257, 274–275, 310–311, 325, 325, 336
  in Europe, 108–110, 141–145, 161, 198
  in New York, 203, 235, 243, 325, 346
  last years of, 350
Liptzin, Volodya, 110, 161, 203
Little Pearl or Lost in New York (Marks play), 270
Living Corpse, The (Tolstoy play), 335–336
Living Orphans, The (play), 334–335
Loev, Olga Michailovna, 22–23
Lonely Inn, The (Hirschbein play), 327, 345
Lost in New York (Marks play), 270
Lost Paradise (Kobrin play), 326
Lovers of Zion (Lateiner play), 98
Love's Crooked Ways (Pinsky play), 345
Lower Depths (Gorki play), 104

Madame Sans Gene (play), 272

Madame X (play), 272, 310
Madison Square Theatre, 344
Madison Theatre, Chicago, 235
Madman for Love (Bezelinski play), 184
Madwoman, The (Barsky play), 220
Magic Melody, The (Romberg operetta), 316–317
Manhattan Opera House, 349
Manne, Annie, 167, 319
Manne, Solomon, 167, 319
Marinsky Theatre, Odessa, 15, 23, 96–105
Marks, Rudolph (Max Radkinson, 185, 252–253, 264, 270, 298
Marks, Shimen, 38, 39
Marranos, 155–156, 158
Maurice Schwartz's Yiddish Art Theatre, *see* Yiddish Art Theatre
Maynard, Meta, 307
Maytime (Romberg operetta), 316
Mechtze the Matchmaker (Geller play), 78
Medea, Keni Liptzin in, 310
Medvedyev, Mikhael, 280–282
Menasseh ben Israel, Rabbi, 157
Mendelssohn, Moses, 33–34
Merchant of Venice, The, 85, 304–307, 346, 348, 349
Michelson, Sonya, *see* Adler, Sophia Oberlander
Midsummer Night's Dream, A, 357
Miller, Louis, 258–259, 346, 351
Miloslavsky (Russian director), 25–26
Minke the Servant Girl (Thomashefsky play), 333
Mintz, Michael, 325, 350
Mirale Efros (Gordin play), 310, 326–327
Mogulesko, Siegmund (Zelig):
  as an actor, 46–50, 97, 103, 232–233, 256, 339–341
  and Adler, 261–264, 290, 320
  early years of, 45–50, 55
  and Finkel, 50, 187, 245, 295
  and Goldfaden, 46–48, 96–99
  and Kessler, 225–227
  United States debut of, 225–228
Montagu, Sir Samuel, 173, 183
Morrison, Morris, 277–278
Moscow Art Threatre, 351
Moskovitch, Masha, 61–62
Moskovitch, Morris, 308
Moscow Art Theatre, 351
Muni, Paul, 302, 357–358

Nadolsky, Leon, 78
Nadolsky, Sonya, 186
Narodnaya Volya, 119–120, 122–123
Nathan, George Jean, 308
National Theatre, 219, 225, 227, 238,

245, 250–251, 268
Nazimova, Alla, 341
Neie Zeit, Die, 349
New Varheit, 351, 353, 354
New York Times, 355
New Yorker Staat Zeitung, 224, 225
Novelty Theatre, Brooklyn, 314

Oberlander, Alexander, 15, 61, 67, 87–93, 108–110, 194, 203, 236, 316
Oberlander, Esther, 316
Oberlander, Sophia (Michelson), *see* Adler, Sonya
Odell, George C. D., 222
Opatoshu, David, 361
Oriental Theatre, 221, 222–223, 227–228, 231, 240, 245, 251
Orleneff, Alexander, 341
Othello, Adler and Kessler in, 274
Othello, Adler and Morrison in, 278
Palace Theatre, 353
Pavilion Theatre, 347
Penitent, The (Sheikevitch play), 168–169
People's Theatre, 285, 304, 333, 342
Peretz, Y. L., 100, 259
Perichole, La (Offenbach operetta), 226
Perlmutter, Sholem, 361
Picon, Molly, 352
Pillings, Frank, 238
Pinsky, David, 330
Pogrom in Russia, The (Thomashefsky play), 220
Polish Boy, The (Linetzki novel and play), 6, 53–54, 99
Poole's Theatre, 239–240, 245, 250–251, 255, 268
Porter, Stan, 361
Potash and Perlmutter (Berg play), 357
Power of Darkness, The (Tolstoy play), 289–292
Prager, Regina, 337
Proctor's Fifty-eighth Street Theatre, 307

Quo Vadis, 255

Rabinovitch (London journalist), 166, 168
Rabinovitch, Olga Mikhailovna, *see* Loev, Olga Mikhailovna
Rabinovitch, Sholem, *see* Sholem Aleichem
Rachel and Leah (Rosenfeld play), 257
Radkinson, Max, *see* Marks, Rudolph
Rafalo, Clara, 310
Ragpicker of Paris, The (Pyat play), 169–171
Rashi (Hurvitz operetta), 229
Rashi (Katzenellenbogen play), 104, 229
Rechtzeit, Seymour, 361
Recruits (Goldfaden play), 40–43, 62

Redemption (Barrymore production of Tolstoy's *Living Corpse*), 335
Resurrection (Gordin dramatization of Tolstoy novel), 310–311, 361
Robert Diable (play), 184
Rogers, Will, 349
Romberg, Sigmund, 317
Rosa Machree (play), 354
Rosenberg, Yisrol, 15, 18–21, 51–75, 87–92, 106–118, 129–150, 288–289
Rosenfeld, Morris, 207, 259
Rosenthal, Max, 185–242
Rothbluth (critic), 256
Rothschild's Biography (Pinchas Thomashefsky play), 220
Rouchel (Silverman) (Adler housekeeper), 283–284, 354, 355
Rouchel (Hurvitz operetta), 273
Roumania Opera House, 227–232, 237–238
Rumshinsky, Joseph, 302, 346
Russian Jew in America, The (Gordin play), 322, 324
Russian Pogrom, The (Gordin play), 263
Russian Solder, The or Moishele Soldat (play), 245
Russian theatre, 23–26, 75–76, 113–114

Sacher, Kraindl, *see* Liptzin, Keni
Sailor in Distress, A (Marks play), 270
Salvini, Tommaso, 37, 224, 307, 355
Samson the Great (Zolotkev play), 255
Sandler, Jacob, 273
Satz, Ludwig, 345, 352, 357, 362
Schacht, Emma, *see* Earle, Emily
Schacht, Gustave, 308–309, 358
Schildkraut, Joseph, 348
Schildkraut, Rudolph, 314, 345
Schneider, Benno, 359
Schoengold, Abba (Albert):
  in Europe, 46, 54–55, 78, 101–103, 147, 187
  in the United States, 234, 240, 245, 252–253, 270, 311–314
Schoengold, Ben, 314, 315, 346
Schoengold, Celia, 314
Schoengold, Clara (Chaya Soore), 102–103, 187, 240–241, 270
Schoengold, Frances Adler (Nunia), *see* Adler, Frances
Schoengold, Fred, 314
Schoengold, Joseph, 314–315, 319, 343, 345, 348, 359–360
Schoengold, Lulla, 319, 348, 352, 359
Schoengold, Pearl, 319, 337, 348, 349, 352, 355
Schoengold, Sadie, 314

Schoengold, Sam, 314
Schor, Moishe, 312–313
Schrage, Aaron, 319
Schreiber, Yechiel, 227, 239
Schwartz, Annetta, *see* Finkel, Annetta
Schwartz, Margaretta, 72
Schwartz, Maurice (Avrom Moishe), 277, 309–310, 344–346, 352, 358
Scooler, Zvee, 360
Seiffert, Moishe, 254, 274–275
Selling of Joseph into Egypt, The (Berman play), 33
Serkele (Ettinger play), 35–36
Shaw, George Bernard, 272
Scheikevitch, N. M., 102, 144, 333
Sherman, Anna, 312
Shigorin (Russian journalist), 52
Shloimke Charlatan (Gordin play), 271
Shmendrick (Goldfaden play), 46–47, 63–64, 88, 102, 107, 115
Sholem Aleichem, 83–84, 100, 322–323, 346
Shtettin, Dinah, *see* Adler, Dinah
Shulamith (Goldfaden opera), 97–100, 101, 178, 347
Siberia (Gordin play), 261–262
Sidney, Sylvia, 361
Siegel, Soore, *see* Karp, Sophia Goldstein
Siegel, Willie, 352
Silberman, Moishe, 46, 48, 173, 227, 229, 240, 243
Skulnick, Menashe, 359, 362
Slaves of the Public (Dymov play), 326
Smith, David, 181–187
Son of His People (Goldfaden play), 328
Sonya of East Broadway (Kobrin play), 285
Sonyes, Keni, *see* Liptzin, Keni
Spell The (Shipman play), 338
Spinner, Charlotta, 94, 108
Spivakovsky, Jacob:
 and Adler, 30, 57–58, 64, 74, 76, 81–87, 93–94, 138, 141, 347, 348
 and Goldfaden, 51, 55, 74, 84, 96–97, 236
 and Rosenberg, 57–58, 62, 74, 131, 134
 in Centrol Europe, 345
 in London, 345
 in Russia during theatre ban, 147, 347–348
 in the United States, 236, 241
Spivakovsky Troupe, 347
Standard Theatre, Chicago, 250, 277
Stanislavsky, Constantine, 354
Stranger, The (Gordin play), 195, 349

Teich, Moishe, 73–74
Terrace Garden Theatre, 225–226
Tevye the Dairyman (Sholem Aleichem play), 321–322

Thalia Theatre, 217, 245, 246, 251, 273, 277, 332, 334
Theatre Collective, 354
Theatre of Action, 354
Theatre magazine, 267, 306, 319, 334, 340
Theatre Union, 354
Thomashefsky, Bessie (Kaufman):
 as actress, 247, 256
 comment on Goldfaden, 239
 on Gordin, 263
 on Kessler, 277
 on Thomashefsky, 247–248, 275, 332
Thomashefsky, Boris (Baruch):
 and Adler, 247–250, 276–291
 character of, 209, 284–285, 286
 childhood of, 209–215
 as director, 325
 early enterprise of, 215–232
 and Finkel, 250–252
 and Goldfaden, 239, 328
 and Mogulesko, 232–233
 style of, 246, 251–253, 256, 273–275, 333, 362
Thomashefsky, Chaya Baila, 211, 295
Thomashefsky, Emma, *see* Finkel, Emma
Thomashefsky, Pinchas, 209–214, 220, 247–248, 295
Times of the Messiah (Goldfaden play), 242
Tisza Eslar (Lateiner play), 229, 231
Titus Andronicus, or the Second Destruction of the Temple (play), 260
Tobias (Tobachnikoff), Samuel (Shmuel), 203, 265
Tolstoy, Leo, 260, 289, 310–311, 335, 346
Trachtenberg, Aaron (Uncle Arke), 7, 23, 29–30, 65
Tree, Sir Beerbohm, 305
Trail at Tisza Eslar, The (Hurvitz play), 229, 231
Trotsky, Leon, 342
Turnhalle Theatre, 218, 219, 222
Twentieth Century (Zolatarevsky play), 309
Two Kuni Lemmels, The (Goldfaden play), 48, 94, 108–111
"Two Neighbors" (Goldfaden rhymed dialogue), 36
Two Schmil Schmelkes, The (Lateiner play), 47, 48
Two Worlds (Gordin play), 262

Under the Protection of Sir Moses Montefiore (play), 245
Union Theatre, 255, 263
United Hebrew Trades Council, 286
Uriel Acosta (Gutzkopf play), 101–104, 137–141, 171–172, 248

Vahheit, Die, 346, 347, 351

Index

Velvel of Zbarazh, 15
Vilna Troupe, 345
Vinyavitch, Bettye, 92, 134
Vinyavitch, Zorach, 94, 134
Virginius (James Sheridan Knowles play), 277
Vladutzul Mamei (Roumanian farce comedy), 46–47

Wandering Star (play), epigraph, 358
Warfield, David, 354
Weinblatt, Sabina, 247, 293, 303
Weinstein (folk singer), 16, 61, 63, 65
Weisenfreund, Muni, *see* Muni, Paul
Wharton, Edith, 307–308
"Wildcat and the Well, The" (Werbel story), 97–98
Wild Man, The (Gordin play), 268–270, 357, 359
Wilner, Max, 351
Windsor Theatre, 270–278, 285, 333
Witch, The (Goldfaden play), 44, 68–69, 108
Wolfe, Frank, 215–220
World We Live In (Capek play), 354

Yankele, Young Scamp (Thomashefsky play), 210, 220
"Yankev P. Adler as Artist and Man" (Rothbluth article), 256
Yente Piepernoter (Lateiner play), 97
Yiddish Art Theatre, 326, 344, 346
Yiddish Frei Folks Buehne, 324
Yiddish King Lear, The (Gordin play), 265, 267, 349, 355

Yiddish language, development of, 34–35, 100
Yiddish theatre:
  actors' life in, 286–287, 338
  atmosphere of, 313, 318–320
  beginnings of, in Europe, 32–42;
    in London, 160, 172;
    in the United States, 208–224
  cultural heritage of, 336–338, 357–362
  intelligentsia in, 260–267, 274–275, 304–308, 323–327
  "patriots" in, 183, 228, 231, 309, 338–339
  Russian ban on, 146–147, 238, 326
  strikes in, 87–92, 126–129, 237–238, 269–270, 285–287
  and vaudeville, 221–222, 332–336
Yomen, Michael, 219, 221, 222
Yoshe Kalb (Singer play), 358
Young (Jungvitz), Boaz:
  on Adler, 184, 191, 245, 264, 270, 278
  on Fanny Epstein, 187
  on Rosenthal, 185
  on Schoengold, Abba, 312
  on Yiddish theatre, 183–184, 231, 237–238
Young, Stark, 308

Zangwill, Israel, 162
Zaza (Sardou play), 272
Zetzer, Avrom, 90–91
Zhidovka, see *Juive, La*
Zuckerman, Laizer, 46, 48, 72–73, 116, 349
Zunzer, Eliakum, 15, 259